*Vivien*

# Vivien

## The Life of Vivien Leigh

*Alexander Walker*

Grove Press
New York

*For Margaret Gardner*

Grove Press
841 Broadway
New York, NY 10003

First published in Great Britain in 1987
by George Weidenfeld and Nicolson, Ltd.

**Library of Congress Cataloging-in-Publication Data**

Walker, Alexander.
  Vivien: the life of Vivien Leigh.

  Bibliography: p.
  Includes index.
  1. Leigh, Vivien, 1913–1967.    2. Actors—Great
Britain—Biography.   I. Title
PN2598.L46W35  1987     792'.028'0924[B]      87-20966
ISBN 0-8021-3259-6 (pbk.)

Manufactured in the United States of America

First American Edition 1987
First Evergreen Edition 1991

10 9 8 7 6 5 4

I am fire and air; my other elements
I give to baser life.

Shakespeare, *Antony and Cleopatra*

# Contents

# Contents

# Illustrations

With Olivier in *Lady Hamilton* (*That Hamilton Woman*) (*National Film Archive, London*)

(*Between pages 214 and 215*)
With Olivier on the set of *49th Parallel* (*BBC Hulton Picture Library*)
In *The Doctor's Dilemma*, 1942 (*courtesy of Felix Barker*)
As Sabina in *The Skin of Our Teeth* (*John Vickers*)
In the film of *Caesar and Cleopatra* (*National Film Archive, London*)
And in *Titus Andronicus*, 1955 (*Angus McBean/Mander and Mitchenson Theatre Collection*)
With Kieron Moore in *Anna Karenina* (*Tom Graves*)
Talking to Alexander Korda (*National Film Archive, London*)
In the film of *A Streetcar Named Desire* with Marlon Brando (*National Film Archive, London*)
With Bonar Colleano in *A Streetcar Named Desire*, London, 1949 (*Tom Graves*)
Peter Finch and Vivien in Ceylon, 1952
Olivier and Vivien in *Antony and Cleopatra*, 1951 (*Angus McBean/Mander & Mitchenson Theatre Collection*)
As Lady Teazle in *The School for Scandal* (*John Vickers*)
Welcoming Marilyn Monroe and Arthur Miller (*BBC Hulton Picture Library*)
Royal Variety Performance with John Mills and Olivier (*BBC Hulton Picture Library*)
Admiring her daughter Suzanne's baby (*BBC Hulton Picture Library*)
Tickerage Mill, Sussex (*BBC Hulton Picture Library*)
With Jack Merivale in *La Dame aux camélias* (*Anthony Buckley/Camera Press*)
In *Tovarich* on Broadway (*Kobal Collection*)
With Warren Beatty in *The Roman Spring of Mrs Stone* (*National Film Archive, London*)
In *Ship of Fools*, 1965, with Lee Marvin (*National Film Archive, London*)
On a 1985 postage stamp (*Angus McBean/GPO*)

# Foreword and Acknowledgments

*I*f Vivien Leigh were alive today, she would be in her seventy-fourth year; and she would probably have already written her own story with all the vitality, courage and wit that distinguished her years as an accomplished stage actress and screen star, and as one half of the most famous theatrical partnership of their day – the Oliviers.

However, Vivien died at fifty-three with tragic unexpectedness, leaving millions the sadder for the extinction of that almost royal aura and beauty which could still suggest the dazzlingly lovely girl – the 'lass unparallel'd', as one memorial puts it – who gained overnight celebrity in 1935, and never lost her power to fascinate her own generation and all subsequent ones.

She left much unachieved – and even more untold. A biographer trying to assign meaning to a life – which surely is the purpose of all biography – has to grapple with some peculiar difficulties. The first is that, where Vivien's contemporaries are concerned, she lies on the verge of living – which sometimes means dying – memory. A few of the best witnesses are simply no longer here to speak about her. A biographer needs luck as well as assistance to do justice to his story – and to Vivien. I was favoured by both. This biography benefits from information and help which in large part has not been sought out, or at least made available, until recent years. My thanks have to be offered in many quarters.

To John Gliddon, in the first instance; he was Vivien's first agent, in 1934. If anyone can be said to have 'discovered' her, it was he. He was the person best placed to observe how her remarkable blend of romanticism, ambition and tireless energy combined to secure the things she set her heart on, often without counting the cost to others or, eventually, to herself. Gliddon was in his early nineties when I met him for the purpose of this book, but his memory of events over fifty years before had remained clear, and he had also preserved his store of letters, cables and contracts. He was generous with everything. So for the first time, I believe, we are able to follow, almost month by month, the changes

*1*

in Vivien's nature and professional fortunes up to and including her great coup in winning the role of Scarlett O'Hara in *Gone With the Wind*. We come nearer to understanding how she actually got the part and at what cost to her relationship with Gliddon. The effects of her driving ambition on her early marriage to her first husband, Leigh Holman; his attitude to the celebrity which distanced his wife from him; the growing influence on Vivien of her lover, the young Laurence Olivier; and some of the early warning symptoms of the mental instability which exerted pressure on Vivien's temperament and ultimately put her sanity in jeopardy – Gliddon's account reveals all this. There is pain in it, of course, but to grasp the extent of Vivien's achievement, one has to understand the battle she had to fight with her own nature.

For helping me meet Gliddon, I am indebted to his friend of many years Helen Russell, his wife Irene Gliddon, and the author and publisher John Walter Skinner.

About the other end of Vivien's life, the last seven years of it, Jack Merivale proved an invaluable source of exceptionally detailed and sympathetic information and of human feelings which couldn't be duplicated by any other friend of Vivien's. Merivale fell in love with Vivien the first time he set eyes on her – she, however, was already in thrall to Olivier – and he became her closest companion in the years after her marriage to Olivier had ended. By then, Vivien had been cruelly marked by the effects of her manic-depressive affliction, by drugs and by her tortuous relationship with her ex-husband. It is thanks to Jack Merivale that we can understand how she became a more contented and loving woman in his company. Merivale has already spoken of these years with Vivien; but he spared himself no pains to recall new incidents and anecdotes of their greatly fulfilling, if sometimes distressingly fraught, life together. He also made available innumerable photographs and letters which round out the period in Vivien's life when she had found a companion who could offer her something that her last husband, for all his marvellous talents, could not – namely, contentment.

I thank Jack Merivale for the trust he placed in me; Sheridan Morley, his friend and relative, for helping me gain access to him; and Jack's wife, Dinah Sheridan, for making our long hours of talk so agreeable and comfortable.

As long as Laurence Olivier maintained his silence about Vivien and himself, their mutual friends remained equally discreet. But in 1982 Olivier published an autobiography containing reminiscences which spared neither himself nor his late wife. Its appearance freed many intimate friends of Olivier and Vivien from their self-imposed restraint; perhaps they now actively wished to testify to the Vivien whom *they* had known. This book has benefited from the candour and affection with which they have recalled her to a degree which I think earlier accounts of her life have had to forfeit.

For the readiness with which they agreed to be interviewed by me and talk for the record, I wish to thank (in no special order of precedence): Jean-Pierre Aumont; Elia Kazan; Katharine Hepburn; Lucinda Ballard Dietz; Sir John Gielgud CH; Rachel Kempson (Lady Redgrave); Sir Richard Attenborough CBE; Larry Adler; Sir Anthony Quayle CBE; Dorothy Hyson (Lady Quayle); Emlyn Williams CBE; Stewart Granger; Kieron Moore; Peter and Virginia Yates; Virginia Fairweather; Milton Goldman; Laurence Evans; Viscountess Lambert (Vivien's schoolfriend Patsy Quinn); Rosemary Geddes (Vivien's secretary); Angus McBean; Stanley Hall; Charles Castle; and Peter Hiley.

I am particularly grateful to Peter Hiley, who was for many years part of the Oliviers' business management, for giving me practical help and counsel which respected his former relationship without inhibiting my current enquiries – no easy task.

Likewise, I am most grateful to Suzanne Farrington (Vivien's daughter) for her willingness to speak to me frankly, but sympathetically, about her mother.

All of the above were interviewed expressly for this biography and most of our conversations were recorded for the sake of accuracy. If I have anywhere misinterpreted what was said, it is accidental and the blame is mine. Only a few interviews were not taped: when they were of a very personal or painful nature; when they took place as a result of a chance meeting (one instance) or by telephone (two); or when they were held in those London clubs which forbid tape-recorders on the premises lest they violate the privacy or somnolence of members.

I naturally approached Lord Olivier; and, unsurprisingly, he found himself unable to assist. This is less of a disappointment than it would have been before he had put his own account on public record. I am indebted to *Confessions of an Actor* for enabling me to set Vivien's story against the background of Olivier's, which helps us comprehend the pressure and penalties that both Olivier and Vivien had to accept, as well as admire their accomplishments together.

The other question many readers will ask is: did you ever meet Vivien Leigh? The answer is – yes. I met her in the best of circumstances for me and at the worst of times for her – in late 1959, when her marriage to Olivier had irretrievably broken down, and she was drawn ever closer to her intimates for sympathy. One of these was Godfrey Winn. It was in his house at Falmer, Sussex, that I recall talking with Vivien and him about many things she would probably not have discussed with a stranger like myself had he not also been a trusted house guest. Godfrey later made his 'notes' – as his mentor Somerset Maugham had taught him to do way back in the 1920s – and he used them to recall Vivien after her death, when he came to write his own memoirs. I have had to rely on memory; I hope it has served me as well.

Others who assisted my research with suggestions, information or commentary were: Beatrix Miller CBE (my Editor when I was writing for *Vogue*); Andrew Sinclair (author, publisher and filmmaker); Mary Kenny (journalist and my guide on points of Roman Catholic doctrine); Katie Stanhope-Palmer (information on Vivien's convent school); Richard Huggett (author and a source of information on Binkie Beaumont and the politics of London theatrical management); Milton Shulman and Drusilla Beyfus (information on Vivien's memorial in Eaton Square); Karol Kulik (biographer of Korda and informant on Vivien's Korda films); Phivos and Gordon Clarkin (personal information on Vivien and her mother Gertrude Hartley); Sir William and Lady Bentley (British Ambassador to Norway and his wife, for help in translating accounts of the 1937 performance of *Hamlet* at Elsinore); Dr Amadeo Limentani (advice on manic-depressive states); John Troke (information on Vivien's British films); and Sister Loveday (provincial archivist of the Society of the Sacred Heart) and Sister Cardew, both of whom took me through what remains of Vivien's old convent school at Roehampton and, with contemporary photographs and personal recall, enabled me to see and feel the place as it must have been in Vivien's formative years there. For this, too, I thank Cecilia Galizia.

A full list of books consulted appears in the Bibliography, but I am greatly indebted to three of my fellow writers: Felix Barker, whose 1953 biography *The Oliviers* remains the essential source — sometimes the only one — of information about their early and middle years; David Lewin, whose friendship encouraged Vivien to be particularly revealing in his published interviews with her; and Roland Flamini, a senior staff writer on *Time* magazine, whose account of the making of *Gone With the Wind* has (like Barker's book) become an essential secondary source.

Numerous institutions in Britain and America were endlessly helpful, sometimes calling my attention to files I did not know existed.

In London, I thank the library staff at Vogue House, particularly Alex Kroll, as well as the Condé Nast Group and Beatrix Miller; the British Museum Newspaper Library at Colindale; the *Daily Mail* cuttings library, as well as Associated Newspapers and Louis Kirby, editor of the London *Evening Standard*; the Royal Academy of Arts library, in particular Helen Valentine, for helping trace the photograph of the painting of Vivien exhibited in 1936; the British Film Institute reference library; and the National Film Archive stills collection at the BFI.

I am grateful to Brian Baxter and BBC Television for generously allowing me access to view many of Vivien's films; and to Eileen Burroughs and the National

Film Archive viewing service for screening the remainder.

In Copenhagen, I thank Erik Palsgaard, director of the Danish Tourist Board, for providing contemporary information about the Elsinore *Hamlet*.

In New York, I am indebted to the Billy Rose Collection in the Library of Performing Arts at Lincoln Center for the reviews of all Vivien's stage appearances in New York, as well as for access to related material, letters, etc., in private collections.

In California, I thank my friends at MGM Studios, Culver City, who gave me access to production files on Vivien and her MGM work, as well as files on Korda and related material, all of which places me once again in the debt of Herbert S. Nusbaum (assistant general counsel); Florence Warner (office manager legal department); and Ben Presser (head of legal files). I am also grateful to the Margaret Herrick Library at the Academy of Motion Picture Arts and Sciences, Beverly Hills, and in particular Sam Gill; to Leith Adams and the staff of the Film Department, University of Southern California, Los Angeles, for production files in the Warner Bros. Archives as well as other relevant material in the Constance McCormick Collection at USC.

The source of printed or oral quotations in the text is listed in the Notes at the end of the book; and all works consulted are listed in the Bibliography. I wish to express additional thanks to the authors, editors and publishers of works quoted at greater length than custom and practice permit: Felix Barker, *The Oliviers* (Hamish Hamilton, 1953); Alan Dent (ed.), *Vivien Leigh: A Bouquet* (Hamish Hamilton, 1969); Alec Guinness, *Blessings in Disguise* (Hamish Hamilton, 1985); Radie Harris, *Radie's World* (W. H. Allen, 1975); Laurence Olivier, *Confessions of an Actor* (Weidenfeld & Nicolson, 1982); Irene Mayer Selznick, *A Private View* (Weidenfeld & Nicolson, 1983); Godfrey Winn, *The Positive Hour* (Michael Joseph, 1970).

As few things are more irritating in a biography than undated events (especially *the year* in which they happened), I have followed my usual practice of being generous with dates; and as Vivien's relatively short life was packed with events, I have appended a Chronology.

Lastly, I thank most warmly John Curtis, editorial director of Weidenfeld & Nicolson, for encouraging me with his enthusiasm and commentary; Alex MacCormick, my editor, for her patience and practical advice; Linda Sontag, the copy-editor, for her helpful detailed suggestions; and Mark Polizzotti, my editor in America, for his unfailing generosity of comment.

Alexander Walker

# Prologue

# Notley Abbey

The Caprice had sent the usual tray over to Vivien's dressing-room at the St James's Theatre. There were little triangular-shaped sandwiches, enough for the dozen or so people who usually came round after the curtain: smoked salmon, *prosciutto* and, her own favourites, brown bread filled with thick honeycomb ('Not *runny* honey,' she'd remind Mario, the Caprice's *maître d'hôtel*). There were also four bottles of good Chablis – not for Vivien, though. She served her guests wine, but preferred a large gin and tonic to be waiting for her when she came off the stage at the end of play.

That Saturday night at the end of August 1951 the play was *Caesar and Cleopatra*. The twinning of Shaw's play with Shakespeare's *Antony and Cleopatra*, which the Oliviers were presenting in celebration of the Festival of Britain, was well into the fourth month of its triumphant London season, and Vivien Leigh and Laurence Olivier had already decided to take the plays to New York in time for Christmas.

The Oliviers had been married for eleven years. They would celebrate their anniversary at the end of the month at Notley Abbey, the country house in Buckinghamshire which Vivien and her husband had created out of the stony bones of the thirteenth-century Augustinian monastery and hospice founded by Henry II. It was for Notley that they were bound tonight, together with the weekend house-guests whom Vivien was expecting any minute in her dressing-room as the crowd of backstage visitors dwindled. There would be Orson Welles, the writer and journalist Godfrey Winn, an old friend from before the war, and Rex Harrison and his wife Lilli Palmer. In addition a number of other people from the world of theatre and films would be coming over for Sunday lunch and staying on to play tennis or croquet. After dinner there'd be charades or other party games. Perhaps they'd roll back the drawing-room carpet and have a square-dance – Vivien had had some of the latest dances and their calls sent over from America. She'd been very taken with square dancing ever since she'd seen the photos of Princess Elizabeth and her husband in jeans performing

7

the jaunty steps on a visit to Canada. Vivien loved doing things the 'proper' way, but if that involved knowing when to break with protocol, why, it was all the more fun.

The Oliviers were at the height of their power and celebrity in the early 1950s. He was the greatest actor of his generation. They were the most popular theatrical couple on the English-speaking stage. He had been knighted in 1947. They had been treated like surrogate royalty when they had led the Old Vic on an Australian tour the following year. They were screen stars too. Even in places where Vivien's name might be unknown – and they were few – the name and image of Scarlett O'Hara were surely part of cinema mythology. Olivier's *Henry V* had been both a wartime battle-cry and the most successful Shakespeare film ever. Only the year before, in 1950, Vivien was filming *A Streetcar Named Desire* with Marlon Brando in Hollywood; at the same time her husband was starring in the William Wyler film *Carrie.* They were thirty-seven and forty-four respectively, and Vivien's clear-cut, delicate beauty and Olivier's strong, dark good looks – she vivid and outgoing, he more withdrawn and self-absorbed – were hardly beginning to show any signs of the passing years.

The aura they radiated was by no means dissipated when they appeared separately, but it gained an extraordinary potency on the occasions when their public saw them together. The phrase 'The Oliviers' meant something more than the mere identification of a couple who happened to be uniquely favoured in love, talent and fame. It signified style, commitment, audacity and a sense of showmanship that was wonderfully refreshing to experience in the England of those postwar years, when the memory of grim austerity had not yet faded from day-to-day reality. Above all, the phrase had a marvellously romantic sound to it. In the public's perception of them, the Oliviers were a couple who were still deeply in love with each other, fused together in their lives, as in their careers, by the irresistible attraction which had compelled them both to break up their marriages to others in the 1930s and recklessly join their fortunes.

The throng of friends and hangers-on in Vivien's dressing-room began to leave or pass next door to Olivier's – *she* was generally their first port of call. The room was nearly empty by the time Godfrey Winn arrived at the stage door. Vivien kissed Winn and waved him towards the remnants of the sandwich tray, making small-talk about that night's play as she quickly cleansed the last of Cleopatra's heavy make-up off her face. Winn studied her, conscious of how the towel she'd wrapped turban-like round her hair emphasized the fact that her beauty was based on the proportions of a heart-shaped face he had first seen in the mid-1930s, at a house-party given by the West End star Jeanne de Casalis, and recognized as belonging to 'the most beautiful young woman who had ever come my way'. He noted again the wilfulness that melded oddly with her fragility, the hint of iron in the jaw-line which obtruded as Vivien massaged cold-cream into the muscles of a neck which was unusually long, but held so gracefully that her face gained a regal poise without trying. Her eyebrows were arched and shaped so that their apex was exactly above the pupil. Depending on the light, her iris appeared smoky blue or brilliant emerald. Without lipstick, her mouth was much smaller than one expected. But once she had applied the fuchsia-red Elizabeth Arden lipstick and extended the corners of her lips, a highly mobile and seductive smile made the extremities of her mouth turn bewitchingly up into her cheeks. The face was winsome without being coy, strikingly feminine in repose, suddenly keen and imperious when it reflected Vivien's stubbornness.

She was still faithful to the perfume Joy by Patou, which had been called 'the most expensive in the world' when she had first worn it at the end of the 1920s — a defiant scent of worldliness, at odds with the odours of sanctity wafting through her convent-school education.

She stood up and went behind a screen to change out of her towelling robe. Vivien wasn't more than a few inches over five feet, but her self-possession was so marked that she seemed taller, more commanding.

'Aren't Rex and Lilli coming?' Winn asked.

'They're next door with Larry Boy,' came Vivien's voice from behind the eighteenth-century French screen. 'Larry's going to direct Rex in *Venus Observed* in New York, when we take our plays there for Christmas. He wanted Noël first, but Noël says it's too hard a task. You must admit, all those lines aren't exactly a dish for the Coward digestion. Wasn't Rex wonderful in *The Cocktail Party*? You know, Godfrey, when he did it in London I went three or four times. It's clever — a bit *too* clever for me. But I found it very comforting, even though I didn't completely understand it. I know people have to follow their impulses — *I* should know that, if anyone! — but when things go wrong, that's when a "guardian" like the ones in *The Cocktail Party* comes in handy. I was so absorbed in the play that one night, when Rex was pouring out the wine as a libation to the woman who earns martyrdom, his finger joint cracked — you could hear it quite distinctly in the sixth row of the stalls, the audience was so quiet! — and I went round afterwards to ask him what it had *meant* — that sound. I was sure it was all part of Eliot's mystical undertones. "Just cramp," Rex snapped at me.'

As she uttered the last few words, Vivien emerged, and laughing at the memory, a laugh whose clear tones descended to a deeper, throaty, self-appreciative note.

She was wearing a charcoal-grey skirt and a blouse of heavy cream silk. She lit a cigarette; she smoked heavily, but elegantly, using the cigarette as much to emphasize her points as to inhale. Her normal make-up was applied in a minute or two, so confident was she of her looks. Then she turned her attention to the parts of her which left room for improvement: her hands (too big, she thought) and her wrists (too thick). Jewellery helped deflect attention, and Winn watched as she eased a surprising number of rings on to each hand.

First was a topaz ring which, she'd once explained, 'I gave to Larry and he broke, so I wear it because he asked me to keep it for him.' Then a ring shaped like two hands clasped in friendship, which George Cukor and Garson Kanin, the Hollywood director and screenwriter respectively, had given her during the war. Vivien had owned three wedding rings from her marriage to Olivier: the first she'd lost in a cinema, twisting it on and off as the emotions of watching *Les Enfants du paradis* had overwhelmed her; its replacement had been stolen; and now she slipped on the second replacement, a plain gold band which Olivier had had inscribed, 'The last you'll get, I hope.'

Round her wrist went a bracelet from which dangled two curious charms, small ivory tokens denoting ownership of a box in a nineteenth-century opera house. One of them was inscribed: 'The Hon. Mrs Leigh, Opera 1829, Box 2'; it had been a present from Marlene Dietrich. Rachel Kempson, the actress wife of Michael Redgrave, had given Vivien the other token. It was in the name of the Duchess of Wellington. 'As near, I suppose, as one could get to Lady Hamilton,' Vivien joked, recalling the film she and Olivier had made in 1940 as a boost to wartime morale.

Olivier suddenly stuck his head round the door, gave Winn a curt, 'Hello, Godfrey,' then said to Vivien, 'Ready, Puss?'

Vivien slipped on a bolero jacket in a dark rose-coloured silk. As they left the theatre, she said goodnight to her dresser, the night watchman, the stage-door manager, indeed every person they passed in the corridors. The Oliviers' limousine had been sent to pick up Orson Welles at the Dorchester. It arrived as they all emerged into the night air. Welles, not yet the enormous bulk he would become, but still substantial, remained seated in the back of the car, extending his hand through the window. Lilli Palmer got in with Olivier, while Rex seemed to slither his eel-like body into the back seat beside Welles. Vivien joined Godfrey Winn in his Jaguar; the Rolls-Royce, she complained, tended to sway slightly at speed, which sometimes made her feel queasy, 'though it should be stable enough tonight, with Orson in it,' she observed.

The usual autograph hunters were there, thrusting their books hopefully at the cars, delighted by the bonus that the Oliviers' weekend guests had brought them. In deference to their hosts, even Welles and Rex Harrison added a token scribble; both normally treated their admirers rather stingily in that respect. Vivien not only signed but also made small talk with all the fans until a hoot from Olivier's horn signified his impatience to be off. 'You're so pretty tonight,

Miss Leigh,' a girl called out as Winn's car followed the Rolls-Royce.

Only when they were safely away from the theatre did Vivien say, 'That's one of the two words in the English language I most detest – "pretty".'

'What's the other?' Winn asked.

' "Beautiful". That's what I got called so often at school. I think I'd hit anyone who called me that now.'

Olivier, ahead of them, drove at high speed. He seemed to have a sixth sense for knowing when the traffic lights were about to change to green and would hit the accelerator dead on cue. Winn had a hard time keeping up. They did the fifty-odd miles to Notley in just over an hour.

The grey stone structure, its monastic remains dovetailed into domestic additions of more recent eras, stood at the end of a fairly long drive just out of sight of the road. The lights were on in all the main rooms: it looked as though a ball were about to take place rather than a small weekend party. But then Vivien ran the house well, insisting on things being done properly, attending to every detail herself or confirming they'd been done by others the way she wanted. 'When I was a little girl and I was going to a party,' she used to say, 'my mother always said, "Now do what the host wants, to please him," and when I was the hostess my mother used to say, "Now do what the guests want, to please them." And I asked, "When can I do what *I* want?" Not doing what you want is good manners.'

Olivier was first into the stone-flagged hall, pouncing on a bundle of letters stacked on a side-table. 'Bills ... bills ... bills,' he chanted and then, tossing them in the air, he executed a comic soft-shoe shuffle reminiscent of a music-hall entertainer and cracked in a Cockney accent, 'It makes yer laugh, don't it?' Godfrey Winn remembered Olivier's reputed tightness with money and, conversely, Vivien's supposed extravagance.

Drinks were waiting for them in the library. By now, it was 12.45, and Winn was regretting he hadn't eaten a few more sandwiches back in the dressing-room. Dare he ask Vivien for a biscuit or two before they all went up to bed? Suddenly the library door opened and the Oliviers' manservant, 'making the most of his single line in this part of the script', as Winn was later to recall, announced, 'Dinner is served, m'lady.' It was after one o'clock in the morning, but the dining-room table was laid for a full meal, its crystal and silver gleaming in the light from red candles in three candelabra, the formality slightly relieved by vases of freshly cut sweetpeas.

They began with olives and stuffed sardines, and a good Riesling; even though Vivien rarely drank wine, she had informed herself about the right vintages. This was a favourite dish of hers, and one that on an earlier occasion had provoked an incident which she still laughed about.

She had engaged a girl to help prepare for a dinner party of two dozen. Unable to face stuffing each tiny sardine, nearly a hundred fish in all, the girl had arranged them around a mound of stuffing. Vivien ticked her off soundly later: 'I've never been so embarrassed when the first course came in – it looked like a dog's dinner.' Then, her lips curling into a tiny smile of forgiveness and perhaps self-mockery, she added, 'Mind you, it did taste delicious.'

With Orson Welles as a dinner guest, conversation never flagged. He was in London to direct and appear in *Othello*, which his host's company, Laurence Olivier Productions Ltd, begun four years earlier, would be presenting at the St James's while the Oliviers were in New York with the two *Cleopatra*s. Welles was still casting his play.

'You would make a great Iago, Larry,' he said.

Olivier, his face bowed over the *hors d'oeuvres*, flicked his eyes up under their heavy lids. 'Why not an Othello, Orson?'

'Because to play Othello you need a bass voice, Larry.'

At this, Olivier's eye-lids lowered and talk of *Othello* ended, though not before Vivien asked, 'Who do you have in mind for Iago?'

'Peter Finch,' Welles said unhesitatingly. Finch was then under contract to Olivier's company. 'At least it'll keep the part in "the family", Larry,' Welles added.

Winn wondered if this were a veiled reference to the stories he had heard of Vivien's attraction to Finch, the handsome Australian leading man whom she and Olivier had discovered on their Old Vic tour and encouraged to come to England. But, if it were, neither Vivien nor Olivier showed any disposition to follow it up.

The first course over, most of the guests had had the edge taken off their appetites and would have been happy to retire for the night. Lilli Palmer was plainly wilting. But the white wine was succeeded by a claret, and a serving dish on which reposed a dozen quail circulated round the table. Godfrey Winn was just about to plunge his knife into one of the tiny birds when Vivien restrained him, took the knife and, with an anatomist's skill, made a deep, neat incision down the breastbone. The small bird virtually collapsed into two pieces. 'That's how my father did it,' said Vivien.

Welles was regaling the table with an account of the death of the Emperor Maximilian of Mexico. He had Olivier's full attention. Olivier had a strong taste for the macabre and anything to do with the mechanics of death: it was part of a melancholy aspect which his close associates sometimes saw clouding his features, though he could be quite 'jokey' about the embarrassments of unexpected mortality. Welles's story about the Emperor insisting on going to the loo before he went to the firing squad clearly had its appeal.

The clock showed 2.15 a.m., but still the courses kept coming: a crusty *crème brûlée* in tiny porcelain pots, a gift to Vivien from Lady Diana Cooper when the Oliviers had visited her and her husband, Duff Cooper, the ambassador in Paris in 1947. The champagne had been brought in from the same source under diplomatic protection.

Coffee arrived. The port began to circulate. But Vivien didn't make a move to leave the table.

'Would you mind if I slipped away to bed, Vivien?' Lilli Palmer asked in a faint voice.

Winn noticed Vivien's look of disbelief that anyone should want to retire while they were all enjoying themselves so much.

'Johnny and Mary Mills gave a party for Rex and me last night and we got to bed late,' Lilli explained.

'Of course, darling,' said Vivien reluctantly, making it clear that she found this a lame excuse, 'if you must go....'

The remaining guests adjourned to the library and more drinks. It was well after 4 a.m., and a peach-coloured streak in the sky announced that dawn was imminent. Olivier was now visibly drooping. Rex Harrison had excused himself to 'see if Lilli's all right', and obviously wasn't coming back. Only Orson Welles seemed able to match Vivien's adrenaline flow. He was performing a bit of business with a cushion on the long sofa, then drawing a finger across his throat – perhaps showing a sleepy-eyed Olivier his idea of Desdemona's murder and Othello's suicide.

The lawns were becoming visible, pearly white in the morning dew. Winn could see the mercury-coloured River Thame at the bottom of the garden. Suddenly he was aware of a cool current of air. Vivien had opened the garden door and was calling, 'Godfrey darling, I must show you Larry's lime walk. He trims the trees himself.'

She stepped into the brightening air as if making her entry from the wings, fresh as the new day itself. Her guest wasn't so resilient. Pretending not to have heard, he slipped out of the library up the wide staircase, reached his room and collapsed on the yellow-and-white chintz bedspread, sated with food and drink, and overwhelmed with fatigue. He awoke two hours later, undressed, and got into bed. Almost immediately, it seemed, Vivien's maid appeared carrying an American-style bed-table with breakfast on it. 'Her Ladyship would like you to join her for a game of bowls, sir, as soon as it's convenient.'

The tray was immaculately arranged: a poached egg on wheat toast, fresh orange juice, crispbread, honey and a Sunday paper. There was a posy of red rosebuds and ordinary garden daisies tipped with matching red, all massed in a cut-glass finger-bowl. The coffee had been freshly ground. A napkin edged with handmade lace was embroidered with the interlinked initials 'V' and 'L'. Vivien had got a French nunnery to make them for her.

On a table beside the bed, untouched after last night's surfeit, stood a bottle of Malvern water on a silver coaster, Bath Oliver biscuits in a tin, mints in a glass dish and several books, amongst them a gardening anthology, a collection of Robert Benchley's pieces, Harold Nicolson's life of Verlaine and Bernard Shaw's essays on music — something to please almost everyone. Vivien's touch was visible everywhere.

When Winn went downstairs, Vivien was in the garden — but the game of bowls, fortunately, was over. She wore a Chinese coolie's hat and Chinese trousers which ended at the calf. Her large sun-glasses in thick white plastic frames brought a Beverly Hills touch to Buckinghamshire.

'Come along, I'll show you the garden,' she said.

Olivier and Rex Harrison were pacing up and down in the rose garden, discussing the proposed production of *Venus Observed*. Winn thought Olivier looked even more tired than when he had come off stage the night before as world-weary Caesar. Orson Welles was near by, typing away on a card-table. Winn remembered him saying that he was writing a novel about a rich and ruthless tycoon who employs a reporter to uncover his murky origins, then systematically eliminates all his associates whom the search reveals to be still alive. 'Including, I hope, the reporter,' Rex Harrison had been heard to say briskly.

Dozens of doves cooed and fluttered round a dovecot in the shape of a high, round tower with a mossy tiled roof. They passed a brook — 'Ophelia's Brook, we call that,' said Vivien — then down an alley of lime trees. 'They're a lovely green, aren't they?' remarked Vivien. 'Larry Boy and I were driving back to London from somewhere — it was at the end of the war — and I spotted this very vivid green lime tree in someone's back garden. We took a cutting and got a market gardener to identify it, and traced it to a nursery in Ireland near where Larry shot the Agincourt charge in *Henry V* and brought the trees over. Look how quickly they've grown. Larry "does" the trees and shrubs; I'm more a "garden" lady. That's called Vivien's Folly over there. Finchy named it that.' She indicated an avenue of cypress trees with a fountain in the middle of the walk. Winn remembered an interview Finch had given in a women's magazine in which he said, fancifully, that he seemed to see the cypresses at Notley turning into people in evening dress and then into Scarlett O'Hara's suitors at a Southern ball, bending towards Vivien, begging her to dance with them. Winn mentioned this.

'I never forget the waltz in *Gone With the Wind*. When I'm really run down, I'm like a *thing*, an amoeba, at the bottom of the sea. I stop everything and put on a record of the waltz. Sometimes even that doesn't work and only my friends can pull me up. I have wonderful friends, Godfrey – and a wonderful husband. If anything ever happened to Larry, I'd never remarry. I'm certain of that. Larry possesses too much of me.'

By the time they returned to the house, guests had begun arriving for lunch, each of them greeted by Vivien as if he or she was the one for whom the party was being given. The pleasure they, in turn, took in her company was plain to see. There was Roger Furse and his wife (he had designed Olivier's *Hamlet* film four years earlier); the actress Margaret Leighton; Cecil Tennant, the Oliviers' manager, an ex-Guards officer well over six feet tall and more handsome than most actors (he was sometimes mistaken for Olivier); Alan ('Jock') Dent, florid in face, his white hair in a bristly crew-cut, a theatre critic whose affection for Vivien was almost paternal and whose criticism of her nearly avuncular.

A buffet lunch was served: cold salmon, a quiche, and strawberries with cream that Vivien's first husband, Leigh Holman, with whom she remained on good terms, had sent up from his West Country estate.

Godfrey Winn crept off as soon as he could for the nap he took every afternoon – he needed it more than ever after the long night he'd just been through – but hardly had he closed his eyes than a maid was knocking at his door. 'Her Ladyship would like you to join her at deadheading the flowers, sir.'

'I'm having a rose named after me,' he told Vivien, as he plied the garden clippers she had given him.

'How lovely for you, Godfrey. But I hope it won't hang its head like the one named after me. So mortifying when I give it to my friends for Christmas.'

More and more people seemed to be turning up by the minute, including John Mills and his wife Mary Hayley Bell; Virginia Fairweather and her husband, who handled Olivier's publicity; Beatrix ('Bumble') Dawson, the costume designer and an old school chum of Vivien's; and eventually a small, agile man with a saturnine face, heavy brows and a body which bent this way and that like a rapier blade – with a tongue to match. Bobby Helpmann, the ballet dancer turned classical actor, received an especially affectionate welcome from Vivien. He was a permanent member of the Oliviers' 'court' circle, though nearer her than him. Vivien enjoyed his bitchiness; others were wary of it.

Those guests not playing croquet or tennis were recruited for 'light fatigues' – odd jobs about the garden. Jock Dent found himself in waders clearing weeds out of Ophelia's Brook, despite protesting in his nasal Scots accent that tangled vegetation gave the stream a Pre-Raphaelite look and should be left intact.

The Harrisons had retired inside. Olivier badly wanted to slip off to his study and work out some staging problem on his model theatre, but Vivien detailed him to take Virginia Fairweather and others down to the farm on the Notley estate which his brother Dickie managed. There he slipped into the role of a country squire, appraising the fat on the hogs' backs with a professional prod that could have fooled the oldest rustic. Clearly, he loved Notley. Equally clearly, he would have relished some respite from the perpetual entertainment going on around him. 'Puss, I've so much work to do. . . . Couldn't Bobby play host?'

'But, Larry, we haven't had tea.'

They had tea and still more people kept arriving. The day was developing a tempo of its own like a gramophone playing its record faster and faster.

Only Orson Welles seemed undisturbed, tapping away at his typewriter. He was wearing a large, loose garment like an artist's smock round the front of which were half-a-dozen kangaroo pouches of various sizes, at different levels, for scripts, pens and pencils, spectacles, cigars, etc.

Even though many guests had left before dinner, there were still a dozen at table. A fire had been lit in the drawing-room, when they adjourned there — for there was an autumn chill in the evening air — and soon Vivien got paper-and-pencil games going in one corner, started canasta in another, and joined in Chinese checkers in front of the fire. She never missed a moment of anyone's pleasure. She was forever freshening the drinks, sending for more coffee, keeping the score. . . . Olivier dropped out of the quiz games early, along with Rex Harrison; neither man was at his best with words that weren't lines of dialogue.

Vivien put on some jazz records. Part of the carpet was rolled back. Then she and Maggie Leighton linked arms and broke into a 1920s number, kicking their legs skittishly in the air, pouting their lips like girls spoilt by their sugar daddy, and uttering squeaks of excitement as their palms smacked together. They'd obviously done the act before; it went down well.

Vivien came out of it glowing, threw herself down on a huge velvet cushion and drained the gin and tonic which Bobby Helpmann had had waiting for her. To Godfrey Winn, she looked overexcited — her vivaciousness had turned into a highly strung restlessness. 'Let's have a square dance,' she cried.

'No,' yelled someone else, 'let's sing The Song.'

It was a song with no title, but the proposal brought such a chorus of assent that there could be no doubt which 'song' was meant.

Jock Dent sat down at the piano on whose polished top sailed a flotilla of photographs in massive silver frames, generally Vivien or Olivier or both, taken by Beaton, Angus McBean, Anthony Beauchamp, and the great Hollywood portraitists Hurrell and Clarence Bull. There was Vivien as Scarlett O'Hara enfolded in Clark Gable's embrace . . . Vivien and Olivier kissing in front of a backdrop of Vesuvius in the movie *Lady Hamilton* . . . Olivier alone, a ravaged, blinded mask in *Oedipus Rex* . . . Vivien all angular and vampish as Sabina in *The*

*Skin of Our Teeth* ... Vivien in a veil that added a tracery of mystery to her beauty in *The Doctor's Dilemma*.

Jock Dent struck a long loud note on the keyboard – 'Ready?' he called. 'Ready!' they all roared back, standing in a semicircle round the grand piano.

Then, putting on their gravest expressions, trying to preserve the utmost solemnity, with voices pitched as if for a sacred occasion – for it was an inflexible rule of The Song that you did not smile or else you had to drop out – the assembled celebrities began to chant: " 'A' stands for 'A' – 'A' ... 'A' ... 'A' ... 'A' ... 'L' stands for 'long' – 'long' ... 'long' ... 'long' ... 'A' ... 'A' ... 'A' ... 'A' ... 'long' ... 'long' ... 'long' ... 'long' ... 'S' stands for 'strong' ... 'strong' ... 'strong' ... 'strong' ... 'strong' ... 'A' ... 'A' ... 'A' ... 'A' ... 'long' ... 'long' ... 'long' ... 'long' ... 'strong' ... 'strong' ... 'strong' ... 'strong' ..." And so on and on, the women's voices rising to the beamed ceiling, the men's sinking to the oak floor, Jock Dent thumping away at the notes, with people unable to contain their smiles and dropping out, breaking up into helpless laughter as the chant progressed in length and complexity until only a few straight-faced stayers were left to round out the imperishable line: 'A long strong black pudding up my sister's arse'.

Around midnight, the party began to break up in goodbyes and yawns as those who had come down for the day decided to call it a night.

'Thank goodness we can have an early night after the show tomorrow,' Olivier said.

'Not tomorrow, Larry,' replied Vivien.

'But for heaven's sake, Pussy, why not tomorrow?'

'Because it's Bea's opening at the Café de Paris tomorrow and we *promised* to go *and* to her party afterwards.'

Olivier responded with a deep groan. He put his arm around Welles's shoulder and the two men, as if propping each other up, withdrew into his study – a Prospero's cell away (when he was lucky) from the noises that filled Notley.

But for Vivien, the night was not yet over. She rounded up those who hadn't gone or were staying the night, and bacon and eggs from the home farm, enough to feed a prairie wagon-train, were soon sizzling in the kitchen pans. Brandy and scrambled eggs were the house speciality at that hour. For one or two guests, it was too rich an end to the long day's pleasure.

Bobby Helpmann lay stretched out on one of the long sofas in the drawing-room, hands neatly folded across his chest, like the effigy of a tiny crusader stripped of armour. Vivien, on an impulse, pulled several delphinium spikes out of a huge summer arrangement she'd got up at dawn to prepare and laid them lengthwise on the sleeping Helpmann. Other guests fastened on to the rest of the blooms. Soon the vase was practically empty and Helpmann lay buried under branches of heavily perfumed stocks, stalks of gladioli, sprays of white lilies and huge swags of peonies. When he came to later, he said that for a second he thought he'd died and been laid out in a funeral parlour.

Notley Abbey once regulated its monastic tasks by rigorous application of the bells of its tower, rationing its time to accord with God's wishes and man's abilities. But time at Notley now moved to a tempo set by Vivien's will and whims. Beneath the entertainment the Oliviers offered, there was a sense of disjuncture, something unsynchronized in a marriage whose passions were at odds with the temperaments and the talents it had joined together.

It was at just such a weekend, as his memoirs later recorded, that Godfrey Winn was afforded, albeit unwillingly, an accidental glimpse of the strain inherent in living up to the image of the Oliviers. It was no more than an aside, overheard as he passed the study, where Vivien had followed Olivier, but signifying a discord in the lives and art of the couple who commanded the English stage. Passing the room, he saw Olivier with his head in his hands. He heard him 'cry beseechingly, "I have ten more years of my career, and I *must* have sleep."'

It was, Winn was later to realize, a perception of 'the death within life which was the overture to the last act'.

# PART ONE

# *Leigh*

# 1

## 'I won't sing, I'll recite'

As her pregnancy advanced, Gertrude Hartley took to getting up earlier and earlier. Around 4 a.m. her Indian maid plucked aside the muslin mosquito net in the front bedroom of the house which the Hartleys had rented earlier that year, 1913, in the hill-station of Darjeeling.

Stepping out of bed, Gertrude immediately sank on to her knees and, still in her nightgown, began her *Salve Regina*, in front of a framed oval picture of the Virgin Mary surmounted by an effigy of the crucified Redeemer.

The air was cool and sweet in Darjeeling, the pace of life leisurely and everything propitious for the birth of Gertrude's baby only a few weeks away. Her first child, a girl, had been stillborn in Calcutta just over a year before. Gertrude was a determined woman: nothing would be put at risk this time. That was why she had insisted on staying on in this peaceful place when her husband, Ernest, whom she had married two years before, had returned to his desk at the brokerage business of Piggott Chapman & Co. in Calcutta. Ernest was a junior partner with good prospects of promotion.

To Gertrude, Darjeeling felt like one of the several religious retreats she had made back home as a girl in Yorkshire. As she composed her mind by daily devotions, Gertrude Hartley concentrated her will on one thing – her coming child.

Now she washed her face in cold water, put on a few lightweight clothes and went down to have her 'little breakfast' – *chota haziri* – which preceded the more elaborate midday meal: tea, poached eggs, toast and fruit. By the time she had finished, there was a clear sky and Gertrude, her senses open to the world, felt a blessing in the light wind stirring in trees of every hue which canopied this attractive refuge for those Europeans who could get away from the summer heat of the cities.

The clouds had moved south and, to Gertrude's satisfaction, the sky to the north was without a wisp of white – purest blue. And there, as if suspended between earth and the Heaven that Gertrude commended herself to, stood the most awesome mountain range in the world: the Himalayas – an endless white wall, domed and peaked, cleft with valleys, fretted with grey rocky outcrops and frozen glaciers turning one by one into spurts of fire as the moving sun struck them.

Gertrude turned her eyes upwards towards the twin glories of Everest and triple-topped Kanchenjunga, and for the next fifteen minutes or so, in the perfect stillness of the place at that hour of day, she meditated, wishing fairness on her unborn child, willing the girl she hoped it would be to acquire the grace and beauty of the prospect in front of her.

Whether the transcendental beauty of the Himalayas passed through her thoughts and thence to her womb and the child she carried in it – for so she later claimed – her mother's belief in the efficacy of wishing for what you wanted strongly enough to get it was certainly transmitted to Vivian Mary Hartley, born on 5 November 1913, in the front bedroom of that house in Darjeeling.

It was Guy Fawkes Night and when the child was being delivered shortly after sunset, just as the gas street lights were being lit in the town below, the skies began to be illuminated by the colours of the rockets and star-shells which the English residents and their families were letting off with an enthusiasm that was all the noisier for the expatriate fervour accompanying it. On another Guy Fawkes Night a few years later, little Vivian asked her mother why people were making all that noise.

Gertrude replied: 'It's for your birthday, darling.'

'Vivian' was a name that had been used in Ernest's family, who lived in Bridlington, Yorkshire, although they were said to have French roots too. 'Mary' was Gertrude's preference for the child.

Gertrude's family origins are not quite as clear as her husband's. Indeed it is a matter of argument where the two first met, fell in love and got married. One account has it that Gertrude Robinson Yackje, of Irish descent, accepted the proposal of the handsome bachelor from the same town as herself when he returned to Bridlington in 1910–11 on his first leave from India. But her own granddaughter believes Gertrude was already in India when Ernest met her. And some of the close friends Vivian made in her schooldays felt that the child's great beauty confirmed what they'd heard about her mother being part-Indian by birth – she certainly had the striking looks, strength of mind and stoicism which often derive from this source. In later years in England Gertrude tended to dress, said the same friends, with great style, but in an ever so slightly overstated way 'as if she were the star' – which her daughter, who became the star, toned down into well-tailored understatement.

Ernest had returned to Darjeeling for the birth; thus he, his wife and the baby, accompanied by their two servants, took the train back to Calcutta ten days later and were driven by Ernest's chauffeur to the mansion they rented in the fashionable suburb of Alipore.

Little Vivian spent most of her early weeks in the large garden which her mother had planted in the herbaceous-border style of back home, though on a scale that would have been beyond their means in the mother country. Vivian took to the outdoors – then and for life. A garden, for her, had qualities of beauty and tranquillity it would not be too far fetched to call Elysian. In whichever parts of the world she later found herself, 'the garden' was present or recreated in the bouquets on first nights, in vases arranged to welcome her to strange hotel suites, in flower paintings by French Impressionists which travelled with her in her luggage and were then stood on bedside tables or hung on the walls of rented apartments to turn them into a reminder of home the minute she opened her eyes. Perhaps the particularly vivid and dramatic Indian tints impressed that first garden on the baby's vision more permanently than the blander flowerbeds would have done in England.

Her parents noticed how unusually alert the baby seemed to be. 'She was never a sleepy child,' Gertrude used to say. Vivian sat in the shade, her eyes open, following life as it moved around her, as yet uncomprehending, but evidently full of wonder. Nor was she a spoiled child. Gertrude didn't surrender her daughter to the endearments of the Indian servants – a situation which sometimes touched off maternal jealousies when the growing child turned naturally to the omnipresent Indian nurse rather than the visitor called Mama. Gertrude engaged a Catholic English nanny, but she kept the child close to herself and all Vivian's early education and spiritual instruction came from the woman who had 'willed' what she saw as the physical and moral virtues into the entity in her womb.

It was clear from an early age that Vivian was exceptionally favoured in looks. Gertrude set out to make sure there were no flaws in her nature either. Her childhood was happy. The Hartleys were good parents. But whether they were as well adapted to each other as they were to the rearing of a dearly loved only child is rather more doubtful.

Maud Diver's revealing study *The Englishwoman in India*, published in 1909, had caused quite a lot of uneasiness in married households and regimental messes. Infidelity and adultery, it argued, were an inevitable and acceptable part of expatriate life; the annual migration of wives and children to the hill-stations left a large number of grass widowers behind in the cities and set a smaller, but not negligible proportion of married women at liberty in the mountain resorts. Protocol was broken; marital bounds breached. Leave was plentiful for the military and work not too onerous for the civilians: the time was filled with flirtations, more or less serious, with and without issue.

Ernest Hartley wouldn't have been following the conventions of his sex and position if he had not had liaisons with various women. That didn't come as a surprise to Gertrude. She knew her husband's nature all too well. How far her own sexual continence contributed to Ernest's philandering is a matter of speculation. But his wife's religion held that intercourse must be enjoyed for one purpose only – to produce children. After Vivian's birth, the Hartleys had no other offspring.

Mrs Hartley was not without a sense of humour, but sometimes the way she showed it had a moral thrust: it was intended to discomfort, not divert. Thus she once arranged a formal supper party at their house in Alipore, leaving Ernest to discover that every woman whose husband escorted her through the Hartleys' front door had at one time or another been a mistress of his.

Yet their marriage endured. Gertrude found it in her heart to forgive her husband's sins. She wouldn't have countenanced a divorce; and, to her way of thinking, an annulment was almost as bad. Besides, both of them dearly loved Vivian and the child took to them as she grew older, though in ways which divided her affections between her father and mother's different natures. Gertrude signified 'order', 'security', and a 'proper' attitude to life; Ernest, on the other hand, represented 'pleasure', 'indulgence' and an instinctual savouring of what life offered or could be made to yield.

Soon after the baby was born, Ernest had slipped back into the lifestyle of his bachelor days in Calcutta. He was an amateur actor of some talent. He had presence, a fine voice and a sure ear for accents. He was good enough to be recruited for the plays and light operas which the dramatic and musical society staged at the English-language Theatre Royal. He played Chauvelin in *The Scarlet Pimpernel*; he sang in *The Mikado* and *Cavalleria Rusticana*. He had a taste for rakish roles. His good figure could turn a villain into a lively and sexually attractive character. He looked well sitting on a polo pony too. Ernest loved taking his little girl on the saddle in front of him for a Sunday morning canter and hearing her squeal with delight when a slap of her infant hand on the horse's neck, abetted by the stealthy touch of her father's riding boots, spurred it into a gallop in the Eden Gardens. A military band there played robustly under an ornamental pavilion and there was a row where riders like Ernest could exercise their horses and take note of the passing ladies.

Theatricals and clubland were Ernest's main ports of call. He liked fun and games, good sport and company, particularly female company. The Theatre Royal and the United Services Club with their dances, pantomimes and versions of the latest musical comedy brought over in sheet music from England allowed Ernest Hartley to enjoy the ladies in ways which group entertainment sanctioned — as well as in some that Gertrude wouldn't have sanctioned if she had had a jealous nature.

A Christmas visit home to England in 1914, to show off the baby, was in Gertrude's mind when the outbreak of war suddenly put a stop to it. Essential civilians and soldiery had first call on the shipping space. Ernest joined the Indian Cavalry, as was only natural with his knowledge of horseflesh. A few months after he'd arrived in India, in 1905 or thereabouts, he'd formed a syndicate with other brokerage clerks and young blades from a neighbouring bank and the racehorse they'd bought made them all a handsome profit. It was no hardship for Ernest to be assigned to training remounts for the Allied forces in Mesopotamia, a region now part of Syria and Iraq.

Gertrude decided to follow him to his posting in Uttar Pradesh, which meant a journey of 1,000 miles to the North-West Province. She rented a house for herself, Vivian and their servants in the hill-station of Mussooree. Weeks went by without them seeing Ernest. The Indian Army's campaign turned into an epic of incompetence, more than 30,000 British and Indian soldiers perishing, many with their horses. Buying, training and freighting new steeds to the army consumed Ernest's days.

Things became even more difficult when he was transferred to military barracks at Bangalore, way down in the southern peninsula of India. Vivian and Gertrude stayed 100 miles away from him at Ootacamund, a favourite hill town of the English military and their memsahibs from Madras.

There it was, in 1917, at the age of three years and four months, that Vivian gave her first performance on a stage and at the same time showed the first recorded signs of the wilfulness that was to shape so much of her later life and career.

Her mother had taught her to sing 'Little Bo Peep' and had dressed the child in nursery-tale pastoral style complete with shepherdess's crook topped with a large silk bow. Looking for all the world like a living Dresden porcelain figurine, she toddled on stage confidently enough. The parents present were ranked in order of social importance from the front row seats occupied by Lady Willing-don, wife of the Governor of Madras, and her ladies. Vivian tapped her staff for attention. Mrs Hartley was a little surprised — *this* hadn't been rehearsed.

Then she piped up. 'I won't sing,' she said very firmly, 'I'll recite.'

A photograph of Vivian taken soon after shows a bright child in full possession of her faculties. The impression is confirmed in a family snapshot taken at the Bangalore racetrack in 1918. Vivian sits by the rails, holding a slim brochure (a race card?) and looking unflinchingly into the lens. She wears a wide-brimmed, rather modish looking hat. Her dark hair falls below the collar of her dress and breaks in ringlets on her shoulders. Beneath the fragile heart-shaped face extends a pale neck somewhat longer than customary, yet which emphasizes her sense of poised alertness.

Present already in the flesh and the expression is the look of a miniature adult. She still has to grow up, but now there is no disputing it; the child would be a beauty.

She was also a quick learner. Gertrude was an industrious tutor. The English governess hadn't accompanied them to these military outposts, so Mrs Hartley took on Vivian's pre-school education. In particular she trained her daughter's powers of memory and observation. Gertrude was an early and ardent disciple of Pelmanism, the fashionable cult of systematized memory-training which tens of thousands of people, mostly women, were using to supplement the skills they had already acquired in Pitman's shorthand.

Gertrude would play Kim's Game with Vivian, the exercise used to sharpen the wits of the young recruits to the British Secret Service in Rudyard Kipling's novel *Kim*, which had appeared several years before Vivian's birth. She would lay out objects on a tray or on Vivian's bedside table before the child went to sleep, remove them and then ask her daughter to recapitulate their numbers and arrangement. In later life, returning home to her apartment or house, the grown-up pupil could detect even the smallest disarrangement of familiar objects within seconds of entering a room. Once when a few valuable items had gone missing from the flat she had rented to an actress, she fretted greatly over the gaps they left – as much as over their estimated worth. Little *objets* came to have a talismanic value for her: they stood in place of the friends, the events, the places they commemorated. By making presents of them, love and affection could be secured.

By the age of five or six, Vivian was familiar with the works of Kingsley, Kipling, Hans Christian Andersen, Lewis Carroll and the Greek myths in suitable expurgated editions. She was particularly fond of having the *Just So Stories* read to her.

Prayers, Mass and confession were insisted upon. Gertrude undertook religious instruction too, turning the Bible parables into playlets that she and Vivian acted out. The moral was drawn after the performance. 'David and Goliath' passed off sensationally well. 'Daniel in the Lion's Den' ended in tears when the 'Lion' in an excess of naturalism sank her milk teeth into Gertrude's unguarded calf.

The war ended and the Hartleys returned to Calcutta. Ernest got back to the business of making money – and he made a very great deal indeed in the post-war boom. He also became a senior partner. They lived in very comfortable style. But now Vivian's formal education had to be decided.

Putting her to school in India wasn't to their liking; nor was it the traditional thing for well-off English families, whose children were invariably sent home to the source of the Imperial experience. Gertrude was the product of a convent school and wanted the same fortifying advantage for Vivian. Ernest's money gave her the chance to choose from the best boarding schools. Her choice fell on the Convent of the Sacred Heart at Roehampton, then a rural backwater of London. The 'old' Catholic families sent their daughters to its boarding school. It was one of the best in the country and linked by the Society of the Sacred Heart to a network of similar schools on the Continent. It sent its girls into the world with the strength of conviction needed to combat temptation. It replenished its own Order from the 'old children', as past pupils were called, who elected to dedicate their lives (and any 'expectations' coming to them by inheritance) to the service of Christ. Its social standing was also immaculate.

The Hartleys set out for England with Vivian soon after the New Year, 1920. And in February or March, they kept an appointment with the Reverend Mother-General in the sturdy stone-walled convent in Roehampton Lane, about twenty minutes by motor-taxi from the West End and a world away from the bright, warm, colourful India that Vivian had known.

She was just six-and-a-half years old, and she was not to see the country of her birth again for another forty-five years.

# 2

## 'You deserve to be kissed'

*T*he Rev. Mother-General, Mother Ashton Case, thought Vivian a delicate child. She probably looked even more frail, standing in what had once been the grand ballroom of an elegant eighteenth-century mansion built by Robert Adam for a Jewish banker named Goldschmidt. Severe convent buildings had been randomly attached to it and the original house converted to its sacred purpose by relentless dismantling of its interior walls and by carving up its rooms. The surviving ballroom was now used as a sort of 'air lock' to receive visitors from the outside world before they or their children were inducted into the purity of the convent proper.

Between its two tall windows, arms outstretched in welcome, stood a statue of the Virgin. Vivian looked more tiny than ever beside the saint, and Mother Ashton Case, who was built in the perpendicular style herself, nearly bent in two to pat her head comfortingly. An *exceptionally* beautiful child was now the Reverend Mother's impression of the girl with the dark chestnut hair and blue-green eyes.

Vivian came to the convent holding a kitten, one she had adopted from a litter at her grandmother's. Because she looked so vulnerable and because the expanse of land and sea soon to separate her from her parents was so vast, the nun permitted a breach of school rules. Vivian was allowed to keep the kitten.

She kissed Gertrude; she wouldn't see her mother again for two years. Then she followed a novice nun to the room where returning pupils resumed their school uniforms and was fitted out with a winter issue of a hard-wearing dress in navy serge with braided edges and a blouse with a large white collar that chafed her neck at the back and didn't quite meet in front. All the pupils were given a number: Vivian was No. 90.

That night she took her kitten to bed with her in the Nazareth dormitory, which was below the linen rooms. She and her pet created an envious stir, but its mewing, she recalled, was soon joined by whimpers of homesickness from the other new girls. Vivian, on the contrary, appears to have entered into the complex world of a convent education without any noticeable difficulty. But then she was an orderly child to begin with, and Roehampton only made her more so. She was a 'special' child too: special in the finished delicacy of her looks, as well as in the very long way she had come to be at Roehampton; and the other girls singled her out for admiration and curiosity – there was little envy and no bullying. Roehampton had other girls from other countries – more than would probably have been found in a lay school at the time, for the Roman Catholic religion was an effective net that trawled its catch from several countries in Europe where even girls who couldn't speak English were conversant with the rituals that underpinned a Catholic education anywhere. Vivian had French, Spanish and Austrian classmates, and there were even girls from Poland, so that dance classes occasionally provided the relatively exotic experience of dancing a mazurka. Thus she entered into a cosmopolitan ethos far earlier than she might have done at a lay boarding school. If England remained her first love, she grew up to be a woman of the world too. As the novelist Antonia White, herself an 'old child' of Roehampton, wrote in her lightly fictionalized account of the place, *Frost in May*, 'Catholicism isn't a religion; it's a nationality.'

Every minute of Vivian's waking life was planned and scrupulously supervised. Outside the walls lay the snares of heresy: free thinking and loose morals. Inside, everything was done to forearm the girls against them. It was not an unkind place, still less an unjust one, but it was strict, vigilant, fastidious.

It was literally an enclosed compound. Tradesmen made their deliveries by horse and cart directly into an enclosed yard – and got no farther. Teachers of dancing and music, a doctor and a dentist made regular visits.

The convent aspired to be self-sufficient in body as well as in spirit. It grew its own vegetables and fruit, milked its own herd of cows ('the nearest ones to Marble Arch', it was said), which browsed on a meadow known, rather racily, as The South of France.

When Vivian ventured outdoors, she was delighted by what she saw. The gardens were spacious and well planted with twisted English oaks, conical Austrian ones and thick clumps of rhododendrons, which were natural coverts for the hide-and-seek that the novices played with the girls. A lawn sloped down to a lake with a fountain in it. There was an acacia walk bordering what was called Calvary Field and a pleached lime avenue abutting on to Middle Field, where she learned to play hockey in winter and in summer took her turn, albeit half-heartedly, with a cricket bat almost as big as she was.

A child in this place could not help behaving well; but then Vivian was a child who liked behaving well. Gertrude had drilled it into her and her own precocious composure commended her to the nuns. The habits she learned at that tender age were to be hers for life.

The dormitory she slept in with about twenty other girls contained a double row of well-separated beds down the length of the room. Each had a canopy and curtains that could be lowered at night. Vivian thus enjoyed a certain degree of privacy. But the open plan also facilitated surveillance in a way that plywood divisions would not. She dressed and undressed behind the curtains so that no accidental immodesty occurred within sight of the huge picture of the Virgin Mary dominating the room. Vivian probably didn't have to use the prudish 'bath shift', a cotton sack meant to cover the wet naked body to which it clung chastely but coldly till the wearer exchanged it for her night-dress. Rev. Mother Ashton Case was a reforming nun and she had abolished this practice soon after her arrival. Illumination was by gaslight and the dormitory was unheated. Everything encouraged a quick retreat under bedclothes which were starched as stiff as ice and about the same temperature.

Before retiring, Vivian had to put her blouse and used underclothes in neat layers on a stool for collection by a laundry maid who replaced them with fresh garments. Some particularly pious girls arranged their black cotton stockings on top of the pile in the shape of a cross.

Throughout her life, whether at home or travelling, Vivian observed the practice of keeping her discarded underwear under specially made lace-edged silk squares. There was an element of absolution in the old ritual, an exchanging of the day's imperfections for a clean, fresh-smelling start on the morrow. The habit wasn't without its fetishist aspect, as friends noted later on, slightly surprised at the variety of embroidered silk squares kept in the closet or packed in the travelling trunks.

Vivian rose at 6.30 a.m. to the thrice-rung Angelus bell. 'Precious blood of Our Lord Jesus Christ,' intoned a monitress; and Vivian, washing her face in cold water, would chorus, 'Wash away our sins.' Early mass was at 7.15, celebrated in front of an elaborately carved altar taking up the whole end wall of the Great Chapel and offering an earthly panorama of Christ's suffering on the road to Calvary. Breakfast followed at 8.00: bread, butter, tea. Lunch was at midday: a substantial meal of mutton or fish, convent-grown vegetables and tea.

Not a moment of the day was left unfilled. It was divided into sacred and secular duties by the regular tinkling of bells, major and minor. In the same way the movement of classes from room to room was regulated on a stop-go basis of wordless commands issued by the sharp cracking sound of wooden clickers held by the teaching nuns. Orderliness at Roehampton was next to godliness.

Vivian not only adjusted to the system very quickly, she also absorbed it lastingly. Though she was reared a Catholic, she was never a zealous worshipper.

'Pious' was the last word that could be applied to her. None of her friends in later life discerned any spiritual side to her at all. One of Vivian's school chums was an Irish girl called Patsy Quinn (today Viscountess Lambert). 'Like the rest of us, she believed what she was told,' she says. 'But she never struck me as a "believer" in the deeper sense of the word.'

It was, rather, the secular side of Roehampton which left its imprint on Vivian. She extracted a security from the well-ordered convent life. She didn't begrudge God love, but she also wanted love for herself. Vivian emerged from Roehampton more socially rounded than spiritually refined. Even the religious practices shaped her later way of life and work in a fashion which had more severely short-term ends in view than salvation and eternity.

To her, prayerful meditation was rather like the Pelmanism she had practised with her mother. It had to do in each case with getting what one wanted, hadn't it? Sometimes, of course, she didn't have her wish granted. If so, then she hadn't concentrated hard enough or had wavered in her faith. The saints were her friends, weren't they? Then they would surely intercede to help a resolute child assuage a disappointment or stiffen her resolve to gain what she wanted or recover an object she thought lost.

Vivian's day had pattern, rhythm, order and security; it also had litany, ritual, performance and drama.

Years later, when asked which she preferred, the theatre or the cinema, she would come down firmly for the theatre:

When I come into the theatre at night, I get a sense of security.... I get in early – an hour and a half before curtain-up. I say the part over to myself every night, however well I know it – not aloud, just to myself.... Sometimes I dread the truth of the lines I say. But the dread must never show. That is the wonderful discipline of the theatre. I love the theatre for that discipline, because outside I'm not disciplined at all. I'm impulsive....

Playing a preordained part, never deviating from her interpretation any more than she did from the responses in the chapel, summoned by similar bells or 'calls' to make her devotional skills manifest, her own self-doubts steadied by the discipline of the role she had been assigned: the convent walls and stage footlights demarcated areas of experience which overlapped in spite of the interval of time and space that came between them.

Not long after her seventh birthday, she was talking with a friend who was two years older than herself.

'Wouldn't it be a grand thing to be a pilot when you leave school?' asked the girl.

'When I leave school,' replied Vivian, 'I'm going to be a great actress.'

Not 'want to be', but 'going to be'. Not any kind of actress, but a 'great' one. Her ambition declared itself early and with certainty. Both girls, in fact, became actresses and even acted together in the same film seventeen years later, for Vivian's school chum was Maureen O'Sullivan and the film, *A Yank at Oxford*. Generally, she gravitated towards older girls for her friends. Her own precocious nature closed the age gap. The girls shared a taste for drama – another of them was the playwright Brigid Boland – and a quite mature attitude for their years. Vivian was the prettiest, officially judged so in a school poll. (Maureen O'Sullivan came second.)

'She had a "foreignness" that made everyone curious about her,' says Lady Lambert.

She was so small and so beautiful. Obviously delicate. Her chest was already weak – she had this little 'pigeon chest' – and used to have a hot compress put on it – one time it slipped down on to her tummy and burned the tender flesh. A 'special' child, you'd say. Even her presents from home were special, 'home' being India – silks, enamels, beads from the bazaars. I first remember her when a doll arrived for her birthday – it must have been her first at Roehampton. All the girls crowded round as she opened the big box. Alas, when she unfolded the tissue paper and lifted out the doll, its head was shattered. Every one of us felt the disappointment.

The girls kept together as they grew older and formed a clique known as 'the Exquisites', which used to sit at the feet of Rev. Mother Ashton Case.

Vivian was not a studious child, but showed a natural accomplishment in what she liked. She took violin and cello lessons from Mr Britain and Mr Gauntlet, respectively, and learned to play Debussy on the piano in one of the convent's old cells.

When she was taken with the class to see *Where the Rainbow Ends*, that curious blend of fairy-tale and patriotic endeavour, the upshot was a letter to Calcutta pleading to be allowed to take ballet lessons. A nun who had been a dance student was found to instruct her. Her grace was instinctive and good enough for a *pas seul* in the summer term's concert. She scored high marks in the 'frivolous' attainments, as Rev. Mother Ashton Case called those parts of the curriculum with a high content of pleasure. School plays were 'frivolous'. She was Fairy Mustardseed in *A Midsummer Night's Dream* and Miranda in a much truncated *Tempest*, where she seized the chance to flaunt a peacock-coloured shawl, another gift from the Calcutta bazaars, which matched her eyes.

Vivian rarely got into the nuns' bad books. If she did, it was due to impulsiveness. Once, when she and her friends were playing hide-and-seek, she took it into her head that a flat-bottomed boat, used to service the fountain in the lake, was concealing the girl they were looking for. It was moored a few suspicious yards away from the bank. Vivian immediately kicked off her shoes, peeled off her stockings and hitched up her loose white summer skirt and was stepping into the shallow water to wade out and see for herself when a great clapping of agitated palms by a novice nun summoned her back to dry land and a ladylike state. For the rest of the week she forfeited the prettily wrapped sweets that the nuns awarded the best-behaved girls.

At Easter 1921 she took her first Communion, then joined fervently in the nine days of prayer between Ascension and Whitsun. At the end of November an even more memorable event occurred.

'This day I was confirmed,' she wrote to Gertrude, enclosing a *carte de visite-* sized photograph of herself in her white gown. Gertrude wrote back that she was coming to England the following March, two years since she had last seen her child.

She found Vivian had acquired inches, an outgoing manner and a passion for the theatre. Gertrude took her to the London Hippodrome that Easter to see the bushy-browed music-hall comic George Robey in *Round in Fifty*. Reports have it that Vivian subsequently saw it sixteen times, but she laughed this off in later years: 'Only six.' Had her visits entered double figures, she certainly would have dragged her parent round to the stage door. But her first meeting with Robey — with a star in the flesh — didn't occur till the Hartleys were on holiday that summer in the Lake District and he suddenly appeared, to have breakfast at the table next to theirs in a Keswick hotel. Vivian boldly asked for his autograph, adding how many times she'd been to see him.

Such zeal couldn't be satisfied by one signed photograph. He autographed one for each visit. An epidemic of George Robey pictures hit the Roehampton dormitory, posing a dangerous, if brief, challenge to the established saints.

Thereafter Gertrude returned to England every year — Ernest every other year — and began bringing her daughter 'out' into a world wider and less vulgar than that of the English music hall. There was a trip to Stratford-upon-Avon for *Hamlet*; one even further afield to Dublin, where Vivian saw the 1922 film *Robin Hood* and fell in love with its dashing hero Douglas Fairbanks Sr. An athletic figure who acted on impulse and dared try anything, he was the sort of man who, in later years, had instant appeal for her. On the whole, though, she preferred the stage to the cinema. The stage was a world she could enter into physically, a live world, a world with rules and traditions of its own, a whole and complete world. She knew how right she'd been to say that she wanted to be 'a great actress'.

By now the Hartleys had worked out an arrangement between them. Ernest was allowed his passing infidelities, but Gertrude refused to countenance a separation. Vivian tended to be alternately indulged by her father with exotic little gifts and expensive treats when he was over in England and then purged of such distractions by her mother and put to some penitential holiday task, which she usually performed well.

She was also singled out for distinction by the nuns. One Christmas, when the waxen figure of the Infant in the chapel's Holy Crib needed some locks of hair to give it a touch of earthly verisimilitude, Vivian's was the head selected for shearing. Her parents telegraphed their approval. One effect of the 'bingle' cut — a cross between the fashionable styles of 'shingle' and 'bob' — was to make her a natural choice for the male roles in any school plays, though men's attire was frowned on and a long unisex duster coat hiding her skirt and stockinged legs preserved decorum while simulating the right gender.

Undaunted, she suddenly produced a man's pipe out of her pocket in the middle of the performance, though this disobedience was partially redeemed when she tried to light it holding it at arm's length. It was taken for comedy, not breach of convention.

Sexual awareness had, of course, no place in Roehampton's official curriculum, since it was a tenet of the teaching that a girl should repress any sexuality until it could be released in a good Catholic marriage fruitful in offspring.

At her age, the worst sin a child could commit had to do with the will, not the flesh. A rebellious girl was a dangerous source of infection. 'Break the will and set it God's way' was nowhere written up, but it was a basic rule of life at Roehampton.

To all appearances, Vivian passed for a well-behaved pupil: neat, punctual, polite, considerate and attentive. Yet she lacked one essential virtue — humility.

It wasn't that she actively resisted the system. It was just that her impulsive nature got the better of her obedient heart. At times she would bridle, toss her head and refuse to accept the admonitions of the sisters on the look out for the first shoots of adolescent pride.

One of Vivian's letters home from the middle years at Roehampton indicates a hard little knot of independence somewhere in the soul of Vivian Hartley that the Catholic sisters wished to plane smooth. Just before her twelfth birthday, in 1925, she wrote to her parents:

Mother Brace-Hall [Rev. Mother Ashton Case had died] said the other day that she hoped I had *tribulation* — she said it would do me a lot of good and she said that my best friends wished that I had it. So I said that you and Daddy jolly well didn't. So she laughed. Anyway, darling, you don't wish that I had it, do you? And you are my very very very very very very very very best friends.

And I think it was horrid of her to say so. Any-way [*sic*] I jolly well won't give myself any trouble or tribulation or whatever she calls the beastly thing.

Few of Vivian's letters then — or later — amount to more than expressions of affection. She wasn't one to dash her thoughts down on paper — more frequently, feelings came first. She retained a style of childish breathlessness characteristic of thank-you letters, which hers often were.

Very early in her life, gifts (given or received) assumed the importance they later had for their power to secure and cement friendships. Her generosity was sincere but it went well beyond the normal obligations of the well-brought-up child. Anniversaries were akin to emotional investments, like saints' days. 'Keep some of the scent I gave you for Christmas Day and my birthday and all the important days,' she wrote to her mother.

On those holidays when no parent was to hand, Vivian accompanied the lay sisters on the rounds of London museums, art galleries, concerts and suitable plays — usually Shakespeare. Her grandparents' ill health meant she seldom returned to Bridlington. Occasionally she stayed in the West Country with the Martin girls, whose father worked in the same Calcutta brokers as Ernest. Boys were sometimes part of this world — not yet of her world.

Roehampton redirected any awakening urges in its girls into the approved role-models from the brighter side of the Catholic religion. Thus there was excitement in 1925 with the announcement that a young French nun called Thérèse Martin, who had filled notebooks about her radiantly simple but exemplary life, was to be canonized as St Thérèse of Lisieux. Suddenly girls at Roehampton, Vivian included, were dedicating their lives to this attractive and accessible girl who had died in 1897 of tuberculosis.

For most of them, Vivian again included, the commitment soon wore off, but St Thérèse's *Notebooks* found their way in later life on to many a guest's bedside table in Vivian's household.

Vivian's schooling at Roehampton ended abruptly in July 1927, when she was not quite fourteen. Her knowledge of the world was suddenly enlarged. From confinement behind walls in the only country she had lived in outside of India, she now embarked on a Grand Tour of Europe that lasted for the next four years.

Her father's pleasure-loving nature was responsible for this. Ernest Hartley was now very wealthy and still relatively young. He decided to retire from business and enjoy life full-time on the continent of Europe with the same energy he had shown on the subcontinent of India. And Vivian must share the fun, he declared. Gertrude protested. Education didn't finish at thirteen. Then the world would be Vivian's finishing school, her husband said expansively.

Gertrude, too, enjoyed the style to which Ernest's fortune had accustomed her. The idea of living well, moving houses and savouring the status of moneyed travellers appealed to a socially ambitious woman. Moreover, it would be possible to plot Vivian's way through the world so as to have her reasonably close to the family, yet protected from temptations. The Society of the Sacred Heart, a French-based order, had its network of convent schools in various countries. It was arranged that Vivian should be enrolled in one of them wherever the Hartleys settled for a time.

The French resort of Dinard, on the Brittany coast, was their first stop. Before term began at the convent school, Vivian's looks were bringing the French boys to the garden gate. She was made aware of her sex appeal. Not a day too soon, in Gertrude's view, school interrupted that.

On the whole, Vivian was very flexible, following her father's ways when she was with him, adapting herself to her mother's outlook when Gertrude rejoined them. In any dispute, Vivian sided with her mother.

Vivian spent the summer of 1928 in Biarritz with her father; Gertrude was away in Paris. He took his daughter racing, bought her a flapper-style dress, and the most revealing bathing costume in the world, she thought. When Gertrude got back, there were thin-lipped silences.

Vivian was sent next to the Convent of the Sacred Heart at San Remo, on the Italian Riviera, because Gertrude wanted some workable Italian added to Vivian's reasonably fluent French. In Italy, she passed into a more sensuous zone of the Catholic religion, more sympathetic to her romantic temperament than the strait-laced ordinances of Dinard or Roehampton. She recalled scattering flower petals beneath the bare feet of monks in the Corpus Christi procession. In later years, she made sure that there were always dishes of aromatic dried flowers and seeds perfuming her rooms, and she would even put a dab of incense on a lampshade to give off its musky odours. This was a fashionable practice in the drawing-rooms of the 1930s, thanks to the influence of interior decorators like Lady Colefax, who was to become a friend, and it also helped to mask the less attractive smell of Vivian's cats; but the taste for an 'atmosphere' was one she admitted acquiring in these early days of a peripatetic education.

It was more theatrical, too, at San Remo: the chants and responses were couched in Latin, but given an Italianate sense of melodrama. This excited her. It was also stricter. Her letters home were now scrutinized before dispatch, and in one of them, a nun discovered a postscript that needed little deciphering: 'The Reverend Mother here is a —' Below was a sketch of a sour-looking cat.

At the end of the year, Vivian was 'withdrawn' from San Remo. She promptly ran wild in the West of Ireland, where Ernest had rented a shooting lodge. Lady Lambert recalls both of them wading bare-legged downstream catching minnows and picking marsh flowers, while Ernest cast for salmon in quieter waters and indulged the girls with huge high teas.

Then it was over to Paris, to be enrolled in a school in the fashionable suburb of Auteuil, from which the *grands boulevards* with their theatres were easily reached and the girls had permission to visit the capital if they went in pairs. This was indeed freedom. In fact, the theatre came to visit them. An actress from the Comédie Française was employed to teach the older girls elocution and deportment.

As Vivian later told it, her mother and father were skiing in St Moritz that January/February 1930, and ran into a friend. The friend said she had recently seen Vivian in Paris, unaccompanied. 'Isn't that out of bounds?' Gertrude enquired. 'Oh, no, the "dangerous" areas of the city are specifically identified for the girls' safety,' said the friend. It took little imagination on Gertrude's part to appreciate that such information could be useful to inquisitive girls.

Vivian was promptly removed and enrolled in a school at Bad Reichenhall, near Salzburg, to learn a smattering of German. She was also gripped by a new passion – the opera. In place of the rigorous litanies of the Catholic service, she surrendered herself to the elemental passions of Wagner. To her parents' concern, her elation didn't subside with the Wagnerian storm. She went on and on about it afterwards, as if still hearing the music in her head and trying to shout above it.

During one of these transports, Gertrude was amazed to hear her daughter saying that her mother must give her permission to get married immediately, for if she delayed she would never get married. In fact, she confided, she was already engaged to two German boys. Gertrude put this hysterical fancy down to the fulsome compliments that her seventeen-year-old daughter was receiving from any young Austrian or German who was introduced to her.

Not long afterwards, mother and daughter were lunching in a hotel in Munich. Vivian had her eyes on a young waiter who was standing attentively near their table. Suddenly she said to him in German: 'You deserve to be kissed.' She acted on the impulse. Gertrude, thoroughly alarmed, slapped her face.

# 3

## 'Had a baby – a girl'

Vivian was restless. She had no school term waiting to absorb her
energies and her wish to be an actress had been treated like a schoolgirl's passing fancy. When the Hartleys got back to London from
Ireland in the autumn of 1931, she saw *A Connecticut Yankee* at a cinema in the
Haymarket. It starred America's homespun philosopher Will Rogers and, in a
supporting role, an Irish girl with dimples placed unusually under her eyes
instead of in her cheeks. Maureen O'Sullivan, Vivian's school chum, had been
sitting the year before in a Dublin café with Patsy Quinn after roller-skating,
when she was 'discovered' by the American director Frank Borzage.

Maureen's precocious success was a boost to Vivian's own ambitions. The
Royal Academy of Dramatic Art (RADA) had just opened its doors. Wearily,
the Hartleys gave in to her nagging and agreed to enroll her. At least it would
occupy her for a few months and as yet she had almost no friends in London.
Gertrude had ambitions for 'bringing out' her daughter, doing the season of
formal balls and dinner parties. But the hotel they were living in was not a good
base for a budding debutante, and suddenly Ernest discovered he was by no
means as rich as he used to be.

Exactly what happened to the Hartleys' financial fortunes at this stage is still
obscure. 'They had a lot of money,' says Lady Lambert, 'and then they hadn't –
like that!' This suggests Ernest's stock market speculation turned out badly or
his investments were hit hard by the economic slump. Probably the latter; for
although the money wasn't there in the same quantity, they had enough to rent
a house in the West Country, which usefully scaled down their living expenses.
It was a move which changed Vivien's life.

Teignmouth, where they lived, was near her friends Clare and Hilary Martin.
One February day in 1932, the girls were watching the Dartmoor Draghounds
cantering down the high street in the village of Holcombe, when Hilary received
a brisk but friendly salute from a man on horseback.

'That's Leigh Holman,' Clare Martin said. 'What do you think of him, Vivian?
Isn't he handsome?'

'I think he looks the perfect Englishman. I'm going to marry him.'

'He's almost engaged to a girl already.'

'That doesn't matter. He hasn't seen me yet.'

He soon did. The South Devon Hunt held its ball on Torquay Pier early in 1932 and Leigh Holman was formally introduced to Vivian Hartley. After he had waltzed her round the floor, he was captivated by the grace, vivacity, self-assurance and beauty of this eighteen-year-old in a sea-green ball gown that matched her eyes. He was particularly seduced by the way her small delicate lips could expand into a crystallizing smile which plumped her cheeks into a childlike expression both innocent and inviting. Her eyes sparkled in collusion.

Herbert Leigh Holman was thirty-one. His family was old Devonshire stock. He had read Law at Cambridge. Not long before, he had entered chambers in the Middle Temple and he had a growing London practice.

'I'll be in town myself soon,' said Vivian. Some instinct told her not to mention her acting ambitions.

Like many bachelors his age, Leigh Holman was serious by nature, and he found the liveliness Vivian radiated tremendously attractive. His interest in the girl to whom he was almost engaged waned and was then extinguished by the image of Vivian.

Her beauty and intelligence flattered as well as attracted him. She would fit perfectly into his life, he thought, leavening the legal routine with her high spirits, yet willingly following his more experienced lead in matters of domestic life and happiness. He had independent means, besides what his practice was bringing in. He contemplated marrying Vivian very early on in their relation-ship.

Later he said: 'She didn't seem to me at that time to have ambition or those qualities that brought her fame. I was taken by surprise, as it happened.'

Vivian, for her part, was probably not surprised by Leigh Holman. His immediate interest in her confirmed her belief that the way to get life to resolve itself in your favour was to give it a gentle push. Concentrate on what you wanted – prayer and her mother's training had taught her that.

Leigh's greater maturity she found attractive, even comforting, quite apart from the strong resemblance he bore to the actor Leslie Howard, then making a name for himself in Hollywood. Like Howard, indeed like many young-old men of the time, Leigh smoked a pipe. She didn't like that much: the smoke lodged in her clothes and hair. But he could be cured of the habit, surely, and then wouldn't he be a perfect husband?

Vivian had little notion of what being a barrister's wife would be like or, if she had, she cared little about it. Their encounter had the romanticism she came to expect out of life: the handsome stranger on horseback, the formal ball, the evening gowns and men in white ties and hunt tails, the waltz, the promise to see each other again ... it was like the sequences of a film.

It can hardly have occurred to her that people so strongly attracted to each other in romantic circumstances might find themselves oddly incompatible when they had only ordinary life to share.

When Leigh Holman discovered that Vivian had acting ambitions, he probably put it down to the sort of amusing thing a girl of that age would conceive of doing. Domesticity would reclaim her when he and she were ready. Meantime he was an assiduous caller at the small flat which Vivian's parents had rented in Cornwall Gardens, Kensington.

Vivian was accepted at RADA in May 1932. Her audition must have been good – she did a love scene from *The Rivals* – for Kenneth Barnes, the principal, had established high standards from the day RADA started, the year before. Later he recalled she made an excellent physical impression, which compensated for a 'thin' voice. Her teacher Ethel Carrington remarked on her presence – she seemed to have a self-assurance which set her apart from the other students. In her first terms she played the tailor Starveling in *A Midsummer Night's Dream* with a couple of blacked-out front teeth, did a short scene from *As You Like It* as Rosalind, and was commended in a modern-dress playlet where she made light work of laying a breakfast table and speaking her lines at the same time – Vivian always had perfect co-ordination.

Ernest Hartley welcomed the prospect of Vivian marrying a man of good family and independent means who shared his own liking for country sports. Gertrude had reservations. She was as much in favour of a 'good match' as Ernest, but the thirteen years' difference between Vivian's and Leigh's ages disturbed her. Would it tell against them when the excitement had subsided? By now she knew her daughter's nature could occasionally be highly volatile. Perhaps marriage would stabilize her, especially if she had a family early on in life. But then again, marriage in Gertrude's eyes was for life – and Vivian was young and really very immature in some ways. Was she, as a strong-willed only child who had been alternately reined in and given her head, prepared for the adjustments and sacrifices that making a home and bringing up children would entail? Gertrude suggested Vivian receive instruction from a priest in the duties expected of a Catholic mother. Vivian turned down the idea.

The round of plays, concerts and operas claimed her attention during the summer vacation. Leigh Holman was happy to suffer such entertainments in the company of so attractive a girl and he took her down to Brede, in Sussex, to an old family friend and confidant.

Oswald Frewen was a retired Royal Navy commander and a landowner, a cousin of Winston Churchill, an antiques collector and an avid playgoer – just the man to appeal to Vivian. He had a talented sculptress sister and kept a diary, part of which was in a kind of Navy code.

Frewen was not always the most perceptive of men, especially of things going on under his nose, and his nature was trusting rather than sceptical; but it is his published account of the ensuing months that allows Vivian's courtship by Leigh Holman, her marriage and her early stage success to be seen against the changing nature of her ambitions and affections. Frewen confessed himself to be a little in love with this slim, green-eyed girl whose mouth turned up so fetchingly at the corners, wooing her listener's attention by her own implicit approval of him.

Maybe there was something a trifle too 'composed' about her, he thought at first. But when Leigh asked for his blessing, he gave it wholeheartedly.

A month later, Leigh brought Vivian down to Henley for the regatta and was gratified by the heads she turned amongst his Cambridge rowing friends in their striped blazers and straw boaters. In a cream tussore silk dress, her wide-brimmed hat trimmed with the colours of Leigh Holman's old college, Jesus, she looked a subject for the then fashionable portrait painter Glyn Philpot.

Perhaps it was because she showed such a talent for attracting other men's attention that Holman proposed a few days later. Ernest kissed his daughter and wished both of them happiness. Holman bought the ring the next day, making due allowances for the fact that Vivian's hands were disproportionately larger than the rest of her delicate scale. She gazed at the diamond engagement band with delight.

'Darling, where did you buy it?'

Holman said he had gone to Mappin & Webb's in Regent Street. Her face fell.

'But Leigh, how extraordinary you are! Imagine going to a cutlery shop.'

Tiny though it was, Vivian's reaction was symptomatic of how she wanted life to sustain her romantic vision. In her opinion, Leigh should have bought his token of love in a jeweller's and not in a shop, no matter how grand, which also sold practical things like knives and forks.

They were married on 20 December 1932 at St James's, Spanish Place, a church favoured by prominent Roman Catholic families.

Having caught a chill on a visit to Oswald Frewen's, Vivian looked pale, which made her appear even younger than her nineteen years. She wore a simple satin dress and a white crocheted Juliet cap. Patsy Quinn and another friend, Jane Glass, were bridesmaids.

For some reason she slipped her wedding ring off her finger after the ceremony, perhaps to show it around.

'Vivian!' cried Gertrude. 'That's terribly unlucky. You must never do that.'

Her going-away suit was of royal-blue wool with silver-fox trim.

When the Holmans returned to London in January, after a honeymoon spent in Germany and Austria, they moved into Leigh's flat in Eyre Court, one of the monolithic apartment blocks built between the wars on the Finchley Road boundary of St John's Wood in North London – and within a matter of days Vivian was wondering what to do with herself.

At Leigh's insistence she had left RADA at the end of the Christmas term. But there wasn't much housekeeping to do – and she wouldn't have liked doing it anyhow – in a two-roomed flat with a daily maid. She kept telephoning her fellow students at RADA, who told her she was much missed and that it was felt someone with her promise shouldn't have thrown it away so early in life. Ambition sits even less well with love than idleness does. Barely two weeks after her honeymoon, Vivian was back on the books at RADA. 'Keeping up my French,' she told her husband as she hurried off to Mme Gachet's classes.

Holman saw through the subterfuge, of course, but it would have to end when they had a family, he decided. He tried being strict with her, but her smile melted his opposition.

Vivian's progress at RADA was limited by her congenitally weak chest. Her grace and appearance projected her more forcefully than her piping voice. She was also self-conscious about her hands and the thick wrists which made them into what she called 'my paws'. But then she found out that the great Ellen Terry had shared a similar worry and used to fold *her* hands under her arms in order to hide them – which her teachers caustically described as giving her the appearance of a chicken getting ready to roost. Vivian found her dress sense came to her aid here. Gloves concealed her hands off-stage, a handbag counterbalanced them; lace cuffs hid the wrists; and she took to embellishing her fingers with rings to deflect attention from them.

Early in June 1933 she was presented at Court, sponsored by one of Leigh Holman's well-connected relations – those hands confidently covered by the regulation long white gloves.

Her next public appearance was less impeccably stage-managed. She appeared in RADA's end-of-term production of scenes from Shaw's *St Joan*, playing the warrior maid in lightweight chain mail and hinged armour that took on a life of its own, so that, when she rose from the kneeling position at prayer, the toes of her metal-shod feet remained disconcertingly turned up.

It was to be her last appearance on the RADA stage and her farewell to formal training at the college. Vivian Holman was four months into pregnancy.

The summer months of 1933 were busy ones. As well as preparing for her child, Vivian had to look for a larger place for 'the family' to live. Eventually she found the ideal house – central, fashionable, even historical, since Lynn

Fontanne had rented rooms in it when she was on the London stage. It was a narrow-fronted Queen Anne house in Little Stanhope Street, Mayfair, an address that was later blitzed out of the London street directory. With its tiers of compact square rooms, it recalled a doll's house. It looked west up Pitt's Head Mews, into what would now be the Hilton Hotel's back courtyard, and east into Shepherd Market. In those days it was — and still is — an affluent area shared by respectable families and discreetly tolerated high-class prostitutes.

Vivian and Leigh furnished the house on weekend sorties to antique shops in the Cotswold towns. A good eye for a genuinely old piece of furniture was something they discovered they had in common. Over the coming months they would discover how little else they shared.

The birth was unexpectedly early, by a full month. Under the date 12 October 1933, in her small blue diary, Vivian scribbled in pencil: 'Had a baby — a girl.' Not 'Had *my* baby' or 'So — and — so was born', as most mothers might have written. It was a painful and difficult birth. Patsy Quinn went to see Vivian in the Marylebone nursing home and didn't see much sign of exuberant motherhood.

'That was a very messy business,' said Vivian, 'I don't think I'll do it again in a hurry.'

'Suzanne' was the name given to the baby. It was Vivian's choice, but she had doubts about it later. Wasn't it a shade on the exotic side? Perhaps 'Susan' was preferable. But 'Suzanne' it stayed; and it was one of the first names that suggested themselves when she was seeking a stage name for herself in the months ahead. Its actressy sound, more French than Anglo-Saxon, appealed to her.

Mother and baby returned to a welcome from a cook, a maid and a nanny who, among them, soon relieved Vivian of the child's daily care. She did not dispute possession with them very much. Vivian's Roehampton schooldays had made her familiar with the emphasis Catholic theology placed on maternity — but, to her, maternity was placid, passive, emblematic. A real live baby simply didn't fit into the life Vivian saw for herself. A baby was a novelty, like a 'young' marriage, though she was never less than kind to Suzanne and did all the practical things necessary for her welfare.

Vivian's husband and her mother were dismayed by her relative lack of interest in bringing up her child. Her post-natal restiveness perplexed others too. Oswald Frewen noted in his diary that marriage seemed to have made her a little more 'natural' than she had been on her very first visit to him in the country, when, no doubt, she'd been on her best behaviour. Now he was struck by her 'skittishness'.

Vivian tended to regard her baby as part of the background of her elegantly furnished household; it was the world outside that stimulated her and she was impatient to join it.

Students in their last year at RADA were encouraged to take roles on stage or in the films being shot at a surprising number of tiny studios in and around London. British-made films were generally of poor quality at that time, but there were plenty of them. They were the so-called 'quota quickies', movies of negligible artistic worth churned out to provide a fixed percentage of domestic product screen time as a Government quid pro quo for allowing the major share to go to Hollywood productions.

Without telling Leigh, Vivian posed for a good society photographer in a variety of gowns and frocks. Then she used her RADA connections to circulate the portfolio of pictures around the casting agencies. With her looks, she didn't have long to wait.

A Gainsborough film entitled *Things Are Looking Up*, starring Cicely Court-neidge, the leading stage comedienne, was going into production and needed some extras who could pass for girls at a posh school – perfect casting for Mayfair debs out for pin money. Vivian was among a dozen or so hired at one guinea a day and told to hold themselves available. She was more excited by this than by having her baby.

Leigh Holman now had the full measure of his wife's determination revealed to him when she stubbornly refused to continue the holiday cruise they had already embarked on in the Baltic. Waiting for her, when they reached Copenhagen, was a telegram from the film company telling her to report 'at once'. Refusing all Holman's arguments, she caught the ferry home, leaving him to go on alone. Once back in England, she found it was only a stand-by alert – her scenes weren't ready for shooting. So with time on her hands and possibly a little guilt on her conscience, or at least conscious of her loneliness, she went down to Sussex for comfort and advice from Frewen and his sister Clare Sheridan. Asking forgiveness of Leigh wasn't on the cards, how-ever. She could best make amends by being a success. Atonement, to Vivian's way of thinking, didn't imply penitence. Achievement would be its own atonement.

As it happened, it was Leigh Holman who came back full of self-reproach. He had been alarmed by the emotional importance Vivian attached to what he regarded as earning a little bit of pocket money. He felt guilty – perhaps he had been too stern, perhaps he had precipitated her impulsive action. He began to realize how little he understood her nature.

When Vivian's shooting call finally came, Leigh Holman let himself be awakened without too much grumbling by her predawn departure for Lime Grove studios in her little two-seater. She never failed to leave behind handwritten notes for the staff, telling them how to look after her home, husband and baby while she was away.

At the studios, she and the other extras changed into short-sleeved school blouses, white socks, gym shoes and the shorts that the film-makers worked into the curriculum at every opportunity. Albert de Courville, the director, was hoping this trim attire and the eye-catching cluster of young limbs it exposed would distract filmgoers from the triteness of the story-line. Vivian hadn't much to distinguish her from the crowd when the location scenes were being shot at a country house in Kent that doubled for the school, though on the strength of the one line of dialogue that was coming to her in the dormitory scenes shot back at the studio, she squeezed herself into the little coach reserved for the speaking roles.

Playing the 'Girl Who Puts Her Tongue Out', and clad in a long nightie, she uttered the line, 'If you are not made headmistress, I shan't come back next term.'

It has to be taken on trust that she was proficient in word and deed, for no print of *Things Are Looking Up* has survived. Cicely Courtneidge played an equestrienne in a circus who shakes the sawdust off her slippers in order to masquerade as her twin sister, who teaches at a smart school for girls, and proves so popular that she wins promotion. Which shall it be: the circus or the classroom? It was at this juncture, presumably, that Vivian chimed in with her line of dialogue which raised her into the 30-shilling-a-day class of player. On its release in April 1935, the film was tolerantly described by the trade press as 'thoroughly amusing in a boisterous way'. Vivian, of course, was not mentioned.

Fired by her 'success', if two days' work could be called that, Vivian set out to follow it up. Leigh Holman began arriving home from the law courts or his chambers to find a 'Dearest Leigh' note beside his place at the dinner table as well as on his breakfast tray. Vivian was gone all hours of the day. Gertrude spent most of her afternoons tending Suzanne.

Having as yet no agent, Vivian was compelled to do her own hunting for parts. This took the agreeable form of going to all the new plays, then on to the night-clubs and generally anywhere that she was likely to hear of stage or film roles. At this time she went the rounds with girlfriends like Hazel Terry, Gillian Maud and Beryl Samson, who were already actresses and hoping to make themselves better known.

British films in those days didn't attempt to create the kind of stars that rolled off the high-volume conveyor belt of Hollywood's production machine. British 'names' were politely borrowed from among the ladies and gentlemen of Shaftesbury Avenue stage successes and they returned to the theatre after doing the cinema a favour by taking its money – easy money, but demeaningly earned by those with a stage reputation. Vivian was foolish enough to turn down the first offer of a stage role to come her way, but maybe this shows how highly she already rated herself.

Beryl Samson had taken her along to an after-the-show party where the guest of honour was Ivor Novello. He had just finished shooting the film of Dodie Smith's *Autumn Crocus* — this must have been late in the summer of 1934. He was immediately struck by the romantic looks of this exceptionally beautiful young girl who was introduced to him, and he knew she would fit perfectly into the tradition of glamorous make-believe which appealed to him more and more as he entered middle age. He offered her a role in his next stage production, told her that she would succeed on looks alone and then, with Welsh keenness, named a price.

'I wouldn't accept £4 a week,' said Vivian, adding, with slight exaggeration, 'I can earn £2 a day in films.'

'Then take the films, darling,' said Novello, not one to suffer any woman to rebuff him, especially on a matter of money. And to Vivian's annoyance, he changed the conversation to gossip.

This minor but firm put-down persuaded her she needed someone else to do the bargaining, and that autumn she met the very man.

John Gliddon had been an actor and then a show-business journalist. 'Why do stars always have to be Americans?' he had asked himself. British faces should be found for the screen and made into stars the way Hollywood did. From asking in his column, 'Why can't we do it?' he passed on to asking himself, 'Why shouldn't *I* do it?' For £100, he formed a theatrical agency, John Gliddon Ltd, of 106 Regent Street, and then began to search for his stars.

On the eve of opening for business he went to a cocktail party given by one of the actresses in *The Gay Lord Quex*, a play he had also been in. He was bewailing the lack of home-grown talent to Beryl Samson when she interrupted, 'I've got a friend you might be interested in. She hasn't done much, but she's very lovely and she's had a couple of terms at RADA.'

'I'm opening my office tomorrow morning,' said Gliddon. 'Bring her along.'

The next day Beryl and her companion arrived, and before Vivian Hartley had sat down, he knew he had his first client. Beryl Samson, seeing in whose direction the wind was blowing, excused herself and left Gliddon to Vivian.

What impressed him first were her green eyes and the way she laughed with them. Secondly, her perfume. She knew exactly how much she needed to wear in order to make the impression she wanted. This time she laughed and said, 'I call the stuff Rape.'

Gliddon asked her what she had done. 'Practically nothing — a small part in a picture.'

'Then you are never going to play anything again, except a leading role,' he assured her.

It was sheer arrogance on Gliddon's part, of course. But as she sat in the still sparsely furnished agency office, where a life-sized portrait of her would soon be hanging on the wall, Vivian felt that the absolute certainty of the man in the well-tailored suit was an echo of her own conviction whenever she spoke about the things she wanted.

'I'd like you to represent me.'

First, said Gliddon, her name had to be changed. She had no objection. She said immediately that she'd prefer a stage name like 'Suzanne Stanley'.

'Too cold ... too hard. What's your maiden name?'

'Hartley ... How about Mary Hartley?'

Gliddon turned it down on the spot. Cockney would soon make that into 'Mary 'artley'.

'Would you come along this evening and meet my husband?'

Gliddon said yes; he was as impatient to get started as she was. But the name problem still nagged at him. 'Let's all think of different names,' he suggested as they parted.

Over lunch that day he told Gordon Courtney, the general manager of the Prince of Wales Theatre, that he'd found his first star, but was stuck for a name for her. Courtney operated in the world of variety and revue. Inspiration leaped at him out of the chorus line. 'Why not "April Morn"?' he suggested.

Gliddon drily observed they would keep that in mind. That afternoon, with a list of names in his pocket, he called on Ivor Novello. He had worked in Novello's company and thought it good politics to ask his advice now he was in the agency business. At the very least, it would give him a chance to introduce his first client.

'I've already met the girl,' Novello said, compressing his thin lips still further. 'Bloody stubborn, isn't she?' He looked down at Gliddon's list of possibles and didn't like any of them.

Gliddon then claims that Novello thought for a second or two and finally said, 'Why not call her Vivian Leigh – half her own name and half her husband's. They can't fall out over that.'

John Gliddon presented himself at Little Stanhope Street that evening and sensed immediately that one of the parties to the newly minted name was far from pleased.

'I think I can make a star of your wife, Mr Holman,' Gliddon said. No gratified response to this, none at all. Gliddon shifted tack on to ground he hoped would be more familiar to the lawyer. 'But I shall have to have her sign a long-term contract with me. In our business, you must have some incentive to do your best for a client.'

Holman was blunt to the point of rudeness. 'I'm not going to have my home life more upset than it is. If Vivian wants to do some film work, all right, but any agreement she makes must be limited to a year — two at most.'

John Gliddon had to go away content with that; after all, Holman not only wanted it legal and above board, but he was a lawyer as well as the lady's husband. Gliddon recalled:

All the time we talked, Vivian sat there and smiled like the Cheshire Cat. She knew she'd get what she wanted. Later on, she told me she'd set her heart on marrying Leigh Holman that first time she laid eyes on him in the West Country and she saw her acting career in the same way.

To be quite frank, even at this early stage in our relationship, I looked at Vivian sitting there with the firelight reflected in those green eyes and then I looked at Leigh Holman and thought to myself, you'll have the devil of a hard job holding this one.

# 4

## *'I will not be ignored'*

John Gliddon got busy right away. His first step was to put his new client around – to show her off. Leigh Holman made Vivian a £200-a-year clothes allowance, a generous sum then. Vivian, though, had a wayward, impulsive attitude to money. On one occasion, her husband had given her £50 to buy a refrigerator, but on her way to the showrooms she passed an art gallery, saw a small, exquisite Boudin in the window, and put the fridge money towards its purchase – 'Far better than keeping the baby's milk cool,' she said. The dress allowance was well deployed to sell herself.

Wearing an impeccably cut new dress or cleverly varying the look of an old one with fresh accessories, Vivian allowed Gliddon to escort her to first nights and afterwards to supper at the Ivy, the Savoy Grill, the Ritz or the Colony Club. They lunched at places where West End managers could be easily importuned and introduced to the new girl. Such self-publicity didn't appeal to Vivian, though: too much display, too little decisiveness. In later years she adamantly refused to do publicity for her films or stage appearances. 'It's not proper,' she'd say.

In fact, her next part came in a much more prosaic way than through ambushing impresarios at lunchtime. John Gliddon in his newspaper days had interviewed Leslie Howard and, through him, met Howard's partner, the film director Adrian Brunel, who in turn introduced him to John Payne. Payne was one of Gliddon's backers in his new management venture and he himself ran Bramlyn's, a casting agency which supplied talent for the 'quota quickies'. For each movie he had a shoestring budget of £750. 'The great thing for landing a role was to be cheap and quick,' says Gliddon. 'Vivian was both.'

She was offered the leading female role in *The Village Squire*: four days' work at five guineas a day. *Kinematograph Weekly* later described it as 'a simple comedy of village life . . . safe for youngsters, but not their meat'.

Vivian was the daughter of a peppery village squire who grudgingly lets the Little Theatre put on a charity production of *Macbeth* to save the cottage hospital. It is a fiasco, until Vivian shoots a bewitching look at a visiting Hollywood star and persuades him to play the lead. 'Too heavily steeped in Shakespearian quotations', was the trade verdict, though Vivian received a mention for the first time – or almost did. 'Moyra Lind, Vivian Leight [*sic*] and Margaret Watson are quite good as support.'

A month later, Vivian made another quickie, *Gentlemen's Agreement*, shot in a 'back-to-back' arrangement for the same company, British and Dominion Films, the local subsidiary of Paramount Pictures, in which she played an out-of-work typist living in an East End doss house – not an auspicious background. This dip into low life possibly explains a trade paper's description of the film as 'a sociological romantic comedy'. Otherwise, the anonymous reviewer was heartless: 'hopelessly novelettish ... acting with few exceptions is amateurish'. However, she was one of the exceptions: 'Vivian Leigh shows promise.' Neither film was reviewed in the national press and Leigh Holman began to feel that his wife's infatuation would die a natural death like that of other disappointed hopefuls.

As so often happens, however, simply being in the right place at the right time was far more valuable than giving a notable performance in a disregarded part.

The veteran actor David Horne had starred in both these films and at the beginning of 1935 he was rehearsing for *The Green Sash*, a stage romance set in Florence, when the actress cast as his flirtatious young wife fell ill. Horne remembered Vivian. Could Gliddon rush her down for an audition? He recalls:

'There were the usual questions – "What have you done?" etc., etc. Stage work, they meant. Of course she hadn't done any. But she started to say, "The Comédie Française ... " and I cut her off abruptly. She'd been going to add, " ... used to send a teacher to instruct us at my finishing school in Paris." But Leon M. Lion, who ran the theatre, believed she'd been at the Comédie Française and was duly impressed. "Let her rehearse for the day on approval," I said, "and if she's no good, say so." Well, of course, with her beauty and willpower, Vivian got her way.'

The role of Giusta was still beyond her experience and by all accounts not very well written, but her self-confidence was such that her shortcomings tended to be blamed on the writing. 'The dramatists have given so vague a sketch of Giusta,' said the novelist Charles Morgan, then *The Times* dramatic critic, 'that Miss Vivian Leigh has little opportunity for portraiture, but her acting has a precision and lightness which should serve her well when her material is of more substance.'

Now, a word of praise from Morgan carried more weight than a paragraph from another critic. Although *The Green Sash* didn't last long, Gliddon used the critic's opinion as a calling card to gain the attention of the formidable stage and film director Basil Dean, who had opened the Associated Talking Pictures Studios at Ealing a few years earlier. Dean and Gliddon had been at school together.

However, Dean was no soft touch. If this girl had potential, he wanted to make sure no one else developed it after he had tapped it. He asked Gliddon for an option on her services. Give him an option on her services, then he'd see about casting her in *Look Up and Laugh*, a 'Grade A' social comedy starring Gracie Fields with a J. B. Priestley script. If all went well, she'd be making £300 a picture. Vivian was excited. At this stage the money was inducement enough. So Dean secured his option.

Otherwise it was an inauspicious debut, even an unpleasant one. Dean belonged to the sarcastic, whip-cracking school of producer-directors. He made her feel ill at ease, and his own feeling was that she was not yet a competent actress. He recalled that she was 'uncontrollably nervous so that for quite a while she seemed unable to take direction'. She was badly photographed. Her low-cut costume emphasized her long neck and just before he shot the first set-up, Bob Martin, the cameraman, turned to Basil Dean with a hoarse whisper of concern: 'Jeez! It's a swan!' A few years later she returned to the same studio, by then a star, and the same cameraman said, 'Well, she must 'ave done something to it.'

The part didn't amount to much. Naturally enough, it was Gracie Fields's film and Priestley's radical sentiments were thrown behind her as a militant working-class girl who musters the marketplace stall-holders and provokes a cheerfully slapstick showdown with the capitalist store-owner. All Vivian had to do as the boss's daughter was provide the collateral sentiment by falling in love with Gracie's brother – played by Tommy Fields, her real-life brother. Otherwise her contribution to the workers' revolution (and the film's success) was minimal. No review mentioned her.

But comfort came from the shrewd Gracie Fields. 'That girl of yours', she told Gliddon, 'is going to make a name for herself. But she'll need very careful handling.'

Aubrey Blackburn, the studio casting director, felt so too. 'I am delighted to have another pretty face down at the studios,' he wrote to Gliddon on 12 March 1935. 'If you have photographs of her, they would be very valuable at the moment. Later I will see that she is really well photographed at the studios. Do let me have as soon as possible not only the photographs, but the details of her life.'

Basil Dean, however, wavered. Pretty faces were commonplace: a lot more than two could be bought for a penny at that time. For the moment he let the option for Vivian's services lie on his desk. Had he, in fact, picked it up, the course of her life and career would very likely have been totally different.

She fretted. She became difficult at home. Far from taking a compensating interest in her husband and child, she devoted more and more time to telling Gliddon to bestir himself. Holman saw the important role he had visualized her playing in a rising barrister's career dwindling as the weeks went by and Vivian's erratic engagements at casting agencies took her away from him. Without losing her love for him, she had relegated him and much of what another woman would have made the centre of her life to the background of her existence. It was as if they were part of a jigsaw she was doing in her mind: once she had pressed them into place, her eye was already roving round for the contiguous piece, her fingers pressing any shapely possibilities into the larger pattern of which they were part.

Leigh Holman was not a demonstrative man. He kept his concern to himself. He was aware of seeming slightly ridiculous at having a much younger wife whom he couldn't control.

If he ever thought of telling her that she was behaving like her father, following her bent for self-expression in exciting and pleasurable ways, rather than adopting her mother's orthodox sense of family responsibility, Leigh Holman apparently held back and played a waiting game. When they went down to Oswald Frewen's in March 1935, soon after *The Green Sash* had ended its fortnight's run, Vivian and her host passed the cold day shrieking with laughter over word-games. Leigh Holman put in an hour or two in the kitchen garden, silently digging a trench for the root vegetables.

Some time prior to May 1935, Gliddon drove Vivian down to Isleworth Film Studios, where John Myers, the publicity director, had arranged a meeting with Alexander Korda. Korda was then England's best known and most successful producer, riding high internationally on the success of *The Private Life of Henry VIII* and *The Scarlet Pimpernel*. With the financial backing of the Prudential Assurance Co. he was preparing to expand his reputation and output by building a new film studio at Denham. It would have facilities for colour, for independent producers and for his own outfit, London Films. John Gliddon had decided Korda would need new faces too. It was time to show him Vivian.

Things did not go well for them. Korda was famous for his disregard of other people's time, which he used to flatter them or reduce their importance, and he kept the agent and his client waiting in his anteroom while minions came and went with clear priority over them.

'I thought we had an appointment,' Vivian snapped. 'I will not be ignored.' The force behind her words surprised even Gliddon, who had found out by now that she had a sharp tongue.

What particularly annoyed her was one superior-looking young man who every so often passed in and out of Korda's sanctum and took not the slightest notice of the beautiful girl cooling her heels outside. It was Anthony Asquith.

Finally they got through the door themselves, and Vivian switched on her most attractive smile, as if they had only that minute arrived. But Korda was clearly not interested in her.

'All right, Gliddon, we'll make a test of Miss Leigh ... Goodbye.'

Vivian went down to Isleworth by herself for the test. Nothing more was heard of it or from Korda. Gliddon guessed what had happened. Korda believed as fervently in the star system as did the Hollywood he was intent upon challenging. But the system had its own strict rule. A star depended on uniqueness of personality and looks and repeated exposure in a string of similar roles. This was the way a star was made, and only after several films would the producer discover whether his choice had caught the fancy of the filmgoers enough to build up their interest and preserve their loyalty. Korda already had a quartet of leading actresses under contract, each chosen for a special quality that made her suited to a particular kind of role.

Wendy Barrie and Joan Gardner were 'English rose' types; Diana Napier was, in Korda's thickly accented Hungarian drawl, 'a high-class beetch'; Merle Oberon was an 'exotic' with whom he was even then beginning an affair that eventually led to her becoming his second wife. To him, Vivian was just another 'English rose' — and he had two of them already.

Meanwhile, Aubrey Blackburn was still urging his production chief, Basil Dean, to take up Vivian's option. As it was in his own interest to demonstrate the demand for the girl, he reacted promptly to a telephone call from a West End impresario, Sydney Carroll.

'I'm putting on a play for Jeanne de Casalis ... *The Mask of Virtue*. I need a girl for the *ingénue* role. Anyone you can send me? Doesn't have to act ... must be pretty.'

The casting director said at once, 'Vivian Leigh.'

Gliddon, in due course, presented the opportunity of 'an important role' to his client, tactfully suppressing the news of how few demands it would make on her.

In Sydney Carroll's office there were already four other girls waiting, all dressed in black to show off their youthful looks. The part was that of a young eighteenth-century prostitute who is presented as a girl of unblemished reputation and rank in order to compromise a French aristocrat. The dramatist Ashley Dukes had adapted it from the German of Carl Sternheim, who in turn had lifted it from a *conte* by Diderot (and much later, in 1945, it would form the basis of the Robert Bresson–Jean Cocteau film *Les Dames du Bois de Boulogne*).

Though the girl's was not the leading role, it was one that would grip the audience and to say that the actress 'didn't have to act' was a considerable misstatement. She had to suggest how her real love for the victim of the cruel joke chastened and redeemed her. Perhaps Sydney Carroll's opinion of what was needed revealed more about his own limitations than it did about the part he was casting. Carroll was a man of conceit and power, something of a Svengali in London theatrical management since he liked to assume total influence over those he put under contract.

He did several jobs, which nowadays would constitute a clear conflict of interest. For some years he had been the *Sunday Times* theatre critic and he still wrote a column for the *Daily Telegraph and Morning Post* while running his own theatre management. He had a talent for 'discovering' actresses to whom he could be a theatrical godfather – and sometimes something closer. As he was not a well-favoured man, this too was a test of a protégée's ambitions.

His producer on *The Mask of Virtue* was Maxwell Wray, a former dialogue director for Korda – in those days, London theatre and cinema was a very small world. He was a pliable man, which is how Carroll liked things; but the latter was surprised when Wray, who had strolled out to inspect Gliddon's candidate, returned and said, 'If Vivian Leigh's the girl at the end, then as far as I'm concerned the part's cast.'

Gliddon saw Carroll's face show surprise at being preempted. Hastily he said, 'You met her yourself, Sydney, at *The Green Sash*. You gave her your card. You must remember what Charles Morgan said about her.' Carroll, mollified by the feeling that he had already passed a good opinion on Vivian, said, 'Bring her in.'

'I remember him sitting back in his office chair, just looking at this beautiful girl,' Gliddon says. 'He was smitten – and Vivian knew it. She did her usual spell-binding act and in what seemed an amazingly short time Sydney Carroll had hired her at £10 a week, subject to a satisfactory audition. She got more than the job – she got Sydney Carroll round her little finger.'

Carroll made only one immediate demand on her, a small one, but it signified the proprietorial interest he was already taking in her. He didn't like her first name. ' "Vivian" – it's neither one thing nor the other. It'll confuse people. They won't know if you're a man or a woman. Will you agree to spelling it "Vivien"?'

'I changed my name again today,' she told her husband that evening. To Holman 'Vivien Leigh ' seemed an even more distant being, a different woman from the one he had married. A world he did not understand or have much use for had been gradually separating his wife from him and now, as if to register their apartness, it had changed her name for life.

Vivien looked so young and inexperienced at the audition that even Sydney

Carroll began to doubt whether this virtual child understood that the part she was to play was, in the euphemism then employed, 'a woman of easy virtue'. Not wishing to embarrass her, he prevailed on the actress Liliian Braithwaite, fortuitously encountered at lunch, to plumb the extent of Vivien's knowledge of life. 'Sydney,' said this emissary, after a discreet tête-à-tête on the Ambassadors' empty stage, 'put your mind at rest. Miss Leigh is married and already has a child.'

As Vivien read for Sydney Carroll and Maxwell Wray, their anxiety shifted from moral to technical grounds. Her voice was clear and crisp enough, but small in volume and thin in tone. When she raised it, she tended to go shrill. But there was a month's rehearsal – time to work on her voice. And with the right lighting and positioning, she was certain to *look* dazzling: her movements, her grace, the period costumes and her youth ensured that. Sydney Carroll knew the extra sensation that the 'discovery' of a virtually unknown actress would impart to his production. As he told her that she had the part, he invited her out to dinner to tell him more about herself.

She acquired one characteristic habit on the rounds of West End restaurants and supper-clubs while Sydney Carroll was presenting her as 'his' discovery. He had a fondness for asking for something special, something not on the menu, something perhaps coming into season. Invariably, he ordered that dish – it was a way of making it recognized that he was knowledgeable and exacting. John Gliddon noticed how Vivien soon began quizzing the *maître d'hôtel* instead of going straight to the bill of fare. 'What she couldn't have, she wanted,' was Lady Lambert's comment in later years, referring to Vivien's attraction to the 'all but engaged' Leigh Holman. What was within the gift of others, she wanted even sooner. Young Vivien had a ruthlessness that drove straight to the point in things large and small.

She also had a realistic view of her own limitations and this, as well as Sydney Carroll's obvious fondness for her company, probably reprieved her in those first few weeks of rehearsals for *The Mask of Virtue*. It was a small cast: Lady Tree, Jeanne de Casalis and Frank Cellier (as the Marquis) were all accomplished players. Vivien was a tremulous beginner. They took pity on her. The play's construction as a chamber drama fostered a working intimacy between them all. They generously guided Vivien through the passages where her inexperience was shown up painfully. For two-thirds of the way, her role was relatively straightforward, personifying the putative chastity and purity that are used as bait for the nobleman; but the last third, when her duplicity is exposed, was much more taxing. Prostrating herself before the angry man, who is threatening to shoot her, she has both to beg forgiveness and declare that her love for him is genuine.

The intelligence with which she read her lines might well have seen her through, but the muted appeal of her naturally small voice caused the audience to come to her, to lean towards her, so to speak, so as not to miss a word. Almost without trying, she invited them into her confidence, thus concentrating their attention, while those virginal looks which had perturbed the play's producers excited their sympathy.

In later years, however, Vivien was the first to admit that she had been very lucky in the direction she received from Maxwell Wray and her fellow players.

'Every day during the three-week rehearsal they nearly fired me because I was so awful. I remember someone saying at the Ivy restaurant: "She'll have to go — she is terrible." I was lucky enough to wear a lovely pink dress, a lovely black dress and a wonderful nightdress ... but I didn't know what to do. ...

'One of the women in the play had to say to me, "I shall not make many demands on you," and I said, "Not more than the gentlemen, I'm sure," and it brought the house down and I never knew why. I was that much of an ass. I suppose, though, I must have had some sort of timing to get the laugh.'

That was the naïve side of Vivien, which some of her school friends had noticed: oddly, although she had a notable sense of often randy humour, she kept her professional innocence for quite a time — as one of her later films was to show.

Those who knew Vivien best have given accounts which suggest that her part in the play was a triumph of personality over performance — allied to the expectancy that Sydney Carroll had created over the preceding weeks. John Gliddon was present. 'The play itself wasn't of much interest. But Vivien charmed everyone. The second act curtain went up and there she sat as the prostitute charming the old man. She charmed the whole audience. You could feel her charm come over the footlights.' Oswald Frewen agreed, though he waited for a week or so before going to see 'the Vivling' as he affectionately nicknamed the 'dear little creature'. He found her deficient in exposing her own frailties — 'She had to cry two times and she could not do so convincingly, looking merely bored — or even asleep! — when she laid her head on the table to weep.' But he found her 'natural sweetness and loveliness' coming across strongly — and so, apparently, did everyone else.

By the end of the evening, the promise that Sydney Carroll had hyped, to use a modern idiom, had been converted into what Harold Conway, the *Daily Mail's* theatre critic, called the next morning, 'one of the biggest personal ovations a newcomer has had on the London stage for quite a long time'.

The following forty-eight hours gave shape to Vivien's fortunes and ambitions for years to come. Her parents and her husband had been in the first-night audience on 15 May 1935, and all of them, accompanied by friends, made up a table at the Florida, a fashionable night-club, until the first editions came off the Fleet Street presses. Vivien didn't need to strain her eyes in the dim lights of the night-club in order to discern her triumph — it was writ in headlines. The critics praised her without exception and the reporters succeeded in extracting a news angle from her 'discovery', so that it ran both in the review columns and on the news pages. A very powerful combination.

'New 19-years-old Star', cried the *Daily Mail*. Harold Conway hadn't waited for his enthusiasm to cool. He had gone straight to Vivien's dressing-room to report (and create) the phenomenon. 'A new young British star ... arose on the British stage last night with a spectacular suddenness which set playgoers cheering with surprised delight.... In a difficult leading costume role, her exceptional beauty and assured acting set the experienced first-night audience excitedly asking each other who this unknown actress was.' The praise in the other papers was pervasive and unanimous. A sense of exhilaration was created by headlines and sub-heads like 'New Star to Win All London' ... 'Young Actress's Triumph' ... 'Actress Is a Discovery'.

The interviews with Vivien which began appearing in the papers show the manner in which the Press then, as now, could wish celebrity on someone, irrespective of whether the facts justified the extravagant myths that are manufactured. Indeed a sudden discovery such as hers engenders a carefree attitude towards the facts by reporters pressed for time or misled by their own myth-making. Thus Vivien, just six months short of her twenty-second birthday, discovered that the newspapers preferred her to be nineteen; that, although she had attended RADA for a few months only, she had apparently won 'the gold medal' there; that she had a father in the Indian Cavalry (true in a limited sense); and that she had appeared at the Comédie Française. All this, given the years subtracted from her real age, added an element of precocious achievement to what was certainly a 'discovery', but as yet no more.

By breakfast time, the reporters from London's three evening newspapers had converged on the house in Little Stanhope Street, knocking on the door and ringing the bell. Again, the competitiveness of their respective newsrooms urged the reporters on to new angles.

Vivien very willingly consented to be interviewed and photographed, and, judging from the published results, she spent a very busy morning in quick changes of clothes and equally breathless opinions.

According to the paper's sophistication and readership, she was arranged to conform to the required view of her: curled up in the corner of a sofa in homely comfort; sitting on a pile of cushions vaguely suggestive of a harem; clad in a light white summer frock with her bare legs well to the fore; playing a ukulele, that favourite instrument for the outdoor girl of the times; and with hat, purse, unseasonable fur cape and dark town suit — probably the paper borrowed the photograph — holding little Suzanne in her arms, every inch the sophisticated matron at her Mayfair residence.

Under creative pressure from deadlines, other aspects of Vivien were now given a glaze of plausibility instead of strictly reflecting the truth.

Leigh Holman must have winced on reading that 'My husband does not object to me being on the stage.... In fact his belief in my ability has always been an inspiration.' She was asked about her ambitions: not just the ones she had for herself, but also the ones she was cherishing for Suzanne, who was only nineteen months old at this time. Vivien's reply makes it sound as if she were recapitulating her own life in terms of the hopes she held out for her child. 'I believe that Suzanne is going to be an actress too. I hope she will go on the stage when she gets older and I am going to see that she is taught languages.'

The question of Vivien's motherhood understandably came up again and again — despite the fact that, if the papers' first estimate of her age had been correct, she would have had to have given birth to Suzanne at the age of seventeen and a half and been married to Leigh Holman at sixteen and a half at the very least! But achieving fame *and* motherhood at an undeniably early age gave an allure of unconventional feminism in keeping with the ideal of the 1930s woman who excelled in independent enterprises — flying, golfing, car-racing and so on — which didn't necessarily challenge their menfolk's hegemony too sharply. Acting was another such 'safe' area. 'Married and Has Daughter' (or some such variant) was often the second deck of the headlines announcing Vivien's triumph.

Margaret Lane had her report in the *Daily Mail* headlined 'Combining Marriage with a Career ... YOU CAN BE HAPPY'. It wasn't simply 'fame in a night' that Vivien had acquired, she wrote. She had 'other things to manage', such as 'a husband; house in Mayfair; small staff of servants; an eighteen-month-old daughter'. Winding up a clockwork pig to keep Suzanne absorbed, Vivien found herself quoted as saying, 'It was a very arduous regime. I had to leave the house by six or seven every morning when I was filming and part of the time I was rehearsing and playing at the theatre as well. I had to run the house by a sort of correspondence course with my housekeeper — I'd leave her a note last thing at night about the baby and the next day's meals, but I'd be gone before she got up in the morning. Then she'd leave me notes before she went to bed which I'd get when I got home late at night. There simply wasn't any leisure, and my husband and I hardly saw each other at all. That was rather awful, of course, but he was as much interested in my acting as I was, and was very nice to put up with it.'

One of the editorial writers even used these views as a text for a sermon on what would today be called women's rights. It is doubtful whether an increasingly resentful Leigh Holman would have symphathized with it. As one curtain rose publicly and dramatically on Vivien, another seemed to be dropping between him and his wife.

Sydney Carroll had sent Alexander Korda two tickets for *The Mask of Virtue*, following it up with a telephone call to alert him to Vivien's West End debut. But if Paul Tabori, an early biographer of Korda, is to be believed, the appearance of the film magnate in Vivien's dressing-room after the curtain was a fluke – the last and perhaps greatest stroke of luck for her. Tabori's anecdote has doubtful aspects to it – he says 'one of the film critics' sent Korda the tickets and he writes as if Korda had not yet met her. But there are plenty of ironic parallels in the film world to the spectacle of Korda lazily working his way through supper at the Savoy Grill, along with Joseph M. Schenck, head of United Artists, and only remembering his theatre appointment when the play was half over. He and his American companion got there, says Tabori (who had the story from Korda's financial adviser Monty Marks), in time for only the last few scenes. But Vivien's looks so stunned them – the story continues – that Korda and Schenck held an impromptu conference as to which of them should go backstage and try to sign her up. Korda got first try – and won. However, the neatness of this tale is its own undoing. Korda had indeed said to John Gliddon, 'Come and see me tomorrow.' (He pointedly excluded Vivien; he was not going to let her charm him.) But it was far from cut and dried. Besides Vivien, Gliddon alone knew that 'The only film contract in England she would sign was with Korda – she had told me so.' But he certainly wasn't telling this to Korda.

Her ultimatum was influenced by her annoyance over Basil Dean's delay in taking up her Associated British Pictures option. She felt his lack of interest to be 'demeaning'. Gliddon did not see it this way.

'Actually, this decision saved her career,' says the agent. If Dean *had* taken up the option, she would have been bound to a company which was provincial minded and had no links with America – United Artists was then distributing Korda's films in the States. 'In all likelihood, Vivien would have been offered a run of cheap little parts in cheap little films. She'd have rebelled pretty soon and got herself a bad reputation in the business.'

Gliddon had just 'happened' to pitch his asking price for an option rather high; so on the date when Dean had to pick it up or pass on it, it had quietly expired. As there seemed to be no one else bidding for Vivien's services, thought Dean, why hurry to pay more now when one might pay less later?

'They did in fact ring back before *The Mask of Virtue* opened to say they'd meet our terms – maybe they'd heard something. "You're too late," I told them.'

This left Gliddon completely free to do a deal with Korda. Even so, he did not bestir himself the following day. Though he had a letter to Basil Bleck, Korda's solicitor, signed by Vivien and authorizing Gliddon to negotiate for her, he sat in his Regent Street offices, biding his time, taking the in-coming calls of congratulation, noting the eager enquiries about Vivien, but not committing himself and not making any calls of his own. Eventually the one he was waiting for arrived at midday. 'Aren't you coming to Isleworth?' asked John Myers. 'Korda's waiting for you – he's all on edge.'

But Gliddon made an appointment for the *next* day, a Friday, he remembers.

That night he considered what terms he might negotiate. He knew Vivien wanted money; this he felt sure he could get. But she also wanted independence: she wanted to be able to do a play, if she liked. This was more problematical. However, if both advantages could be combined in a contract, then 'she'd be a West End actress *and* a Korda film star'. That would really get her somewhere.

Korda looked at him coldly the next day. 'You know, I don't bargain, Gliddon.' He then offered £10 a week for a year's option on Vivien's services. 'It's what I gave Merle Oberon.' Gliddon turned him down flat.

An hour's very hard bargaining followed. At the end of it, a deal had been made on a five-year contract with annual options. It ran as follows: first year, £700 for the first film, £800 for the second; second year: £1,200 and £1,500 respectively; third year: £2,000 and £2,500; fourth year: £4,000 and £5,000; fifth year: £8,000 and £10,000. (This agreement, with London Film Productions, was signed on 15 August 1935.) 'For the time, it was a very great deal of money and Korda also agreed, with reluctance, to Vivien's being free to do a play during a six-month period in each year. Though I say so myself, it was quite a coup,' says Gliddon.

'Now,' said Korda, 'what shall we tell the Press?'

They totted up the worth of the contract over five years and came up with a figure of £35,700. 'Let's say £50,000,' said Korda, 'it looks better.' By the time Gliddon arrived back at his office – stopping *en route* to telephone the news to Vivien – the evening papers, alerted by Korda's publicity department, had their bills on the streets: '£50,000 CONTRACT FOR VIVIEN LEIGH'. It was an enormous sum – the equivalent in today's purchasing power of well over £1 million. Following hot on the heels of Vivien's 'discovery' only three days earlier, the deluge of stories about her life, marriage, family and ambitions and the photographs of her that had appeared even in some of the Continental papers, such a figure added the final glitter to what had been presented as a real-life fairy-story. Newspapers being rather hazy on the intricate series of interlocking 'ifs' and 'whens' in film contracts, it was made to appear that Vivien had already earned £50,000. No one disabused them, least of all Vivien. 'Isn't it Amazing?' the sub-head to the *Daily Mail*'s story on Saturday morning had her exclaiming. 'Think of it,' Vivien, still an uncorrected 'nineteen years old' to the *Mail*'s man Seton Margrave, was quoted as saying, 'all this has happened in two days!'

Then, in a reference which perhaps put her home life into rather sharper focus than the early interviews had managed, she added: 'So many actresses tell people they just love washing dishes. I just don't believe it. I hate sloppy things. ... But you will say, won't you, that I haven't got swelled headed?' On the subject of her benefactor, she said, 'I think it is the dream of every young actress in London to work for Mr Korda in films.'

Korda, as he was fond of putting it, 'sent the lift back' with a compliment that, although prophetic in the standard manner of such forecasts about the future of someone under exclusive contract to him, assumed an ironic ring in view of what the future actually brought. 'I am absolutely certain Miss Leigh has a brilliant future and is far too talented to be cast in just one type of character. She will be a great star, and I am so sure of this that I had to take action to keep her in London. In time I may exchange her with United Artists in Hollywood for one of their stars, but she will go to Hollywood for never more than three months at a time.'

Between the matinée and the evening performances of *The Mask of Virtue* that day, Vivien paid a call on John Gliddon. With him she left an Asprey's silver cigarette case inscribed in manuscript: 'With love, Vivien Leigh'.

The following Monday brought another unexpected call and this time it didn't yield any gifts.

'Mr Leigh Holman,' announced Gliddon's secretary, and a stern-faced Holman entered with a stranger in tow.

'This', said the barrister, 'is my solicitor.'

# 5

## 'What a virile performance!'

From the expression on Leigh Holman's face, one would have thought that Vivien was being publicly reviled instead of immoderately praised. He came straight to the point. 'Mr Gliddon, do you realize that my wife's £50,000 will make you richer by £5,000? That seems quite unsatisfactory to us.'

It was obvious to Gliddon that the barrister had little worldly wisdom when it came to show business. He had been misled by the publicity ruse that traded on Vivien's aggregate remuneration over five years – *if all went well with her career*. But Gliddon also suspected that Holman feared five years of acting would give Vivien's career a drive and continuity that would harm their marriage. Maybe this visit was intended to rein in the agent's participation in her success, so restoring Leigh Holman's rights as a husband. Holman and his legal adviser proposed a scaled down contract – the more Vivien earned, the less of it would come to Gliddon. Just the opposite of the customary agreement between agent and client. They also demanded the right to terminate his services if Korda failed to come up with a suitable film.

Gliddon took legal advice of his own. 'Stay as you are,' he was told. He held the strongest card – Vivien's written authorization to represent her. Eventually they compromised. Gliddon would represent Vivien for three years or for the period that London Film Productions chose to exercise their option for her services – whichever was longer. Leigh Holman reluctantly agreed to this.

By now an inevitable reaction had set in. The more considered reviews of *The Mask of Virtue* acknowledged Vivien's beauty and grace of movement, no argument there. It was her technical weakness that came in for comment. 'Miss Leigh has incisiveness, *retenue* and obvious intelligence,' James Agate wrote in the *Sunday Times*. 'She gives to this part all that it asks, except in the matter of speech. If this young lady wants to become an actress, as distinct from a film star, she should at once seek means to improve her overtone, which is displeasing to the fastidious ear.' Agate was the most trenchant critic of the day. Vivien took his admonition to heart and immediately enrolled for voice production lessons.

Sydney Carroll saw a chance to pluck controversy out of stricture. He jumped into print in his own *Daily Telegraph* column to boost the stock of an actress whom he had under contract and in his own production. What qualities should an 'absolute beginner' have, he asked, and implicitly taking Vivien as his pattern, he then shamelessly enumerated them. 'Nerve, power of attack, power of retention, control of the body and mind, imagination, sensibility, judgment, clear diction, a sense of timing, a regard for variety and a love of repose.' Clearly Carroll himself was not deficient in nerve or power of attack. Agate, badly stung, riposted. He attacked Carroll in *John O' London's Weekly*, one of the other papers he wrote for under the pseudonym of Richard Prentiss. To speak of an actress in the same breath as Bernhardt or Ellen Terry, he decreed, one should wait until she had accomplishment behind her, not merely promise for the future – by which time she wouldn't see forty again.

Now it was Carroll's turn. And he launched a cutting personal attack on Agate, using the latter's homosexual habits to score a left-handed hit: 'Mr Prentiss – I hope I am right in my assumption of his sex....' Supported by a photo of Vivien, hands cupped beneath her chin, eyes gazing into the future, he berated Prentiss/Agate for an underhand attempt to 'discourage a young performer on the threshold of her life' – and still he made no mention of his vested interest in her talents.

Seeing eminent critics jousting publicly over her appealed to Vivien, but it did nothing for the play. Her discovery had been the oxygen allowing *The Mask of Virtue* a brief breathing-space at the Ambassadors. But Carroll, anxious to maximize his box-office, moved it to the larger St James's Theatre, and there Vivien's voice was lost in the void. The play faltered and closed after twelve weeks, but it had served its purpose. It had launched Vivien Leigh.

The boost to her ambitions couldn't be calculated in financial gain, but for the record she made £293 on the run, even allowing for a salary cut.

She and Gliddon tried to keep her before the public by means of her celebrity rather than her talents; and to Holman's additional irritation she began sponsoring commercial products and making paid personal appearances. She earned £21 for opening the dance floor at Chiltern Court, according to her agent's accounts book, fifteen guineas for advertising 'Matita', probably a skin food, ten guineas for a billboard portrait promoting the magazine *Everywoman* and two guineas for rendering the same service to *Britannia and Eve*.

Vivien also showed her ingenuity in stretching her £200 dress allowance by making an agreement to model for Victor Stiebel, a couturier from South Africa who had lately opened his London house and was to become her lifelong friend.

Those outfits of his she particularly liked, she bought at discount prices. She discovered she could put on the personality that matched the gown – though sometimes the gowns she chose had personalities that the later Vivien Leigh would not care to assume.

'If you want a label for her type,' said a caption in *Vogue* under one of Cecil Beaton's earliest gallery portraits of her wearing Stiebel's blue and green plaid velveteen jacket over a dark skirt, 'call it "exotic". She is slim and luminous. And she can get away with her taste in clothes – which runs to heavy, almost barbaric jewellery, leopardskin and queer colours ... she is like a Persian gazelle in the dark studio forest.' One fears this was written by Beaton too.

One peculiarity regarding what she wore became fixed early on. When she came to pick a gown or a suit from the Stiebel collection (or any other couturier's), she nearly always had some alteration made to its design – a button, a hem, a detail of the cuff or reverse – often after lengthy, sometimes spirited discussion. Again, what was *not* on the menu was preferred to what the atelier had created.

Vivien was desperate to get back on stage; home life held no excitement like it. She was out almost every night now, her very inactivity giving her more time for socializing and being seen. Her daughter Suzanne was to grow up with next to no memories of her mother during infancy; she knew her grandmother better than her mother, and she could recall her father's visits to the nursery and his clowning with a tricycle which he pretended to try and ride. Vivien, however, did not neglect the child's creature comforts.

It must have been around this time that the companionship of her escorts developed into her first extra-marital affairs. In comparison with her amusing and lively escorts, her husband assumed the faded character of a distant relative, someone 'in the family', held in affectionate memory but never really much in her thoughts.

One of her earliest companions was an actor called John Buckmaster. He was Gladys Cooper's son by Herbert Buckmaster, best remembered as the founder of Buck's, the St James's men's club. Buckmaster had a look to him that Vivien found immediately appealing. He had a rakish physique and a swashbuckling manner to go with it. He spoke his mind without much caring about conventional opinion. Some of the roles he played caught the caddish manner he affected to great advantage, like the spoilt-rich brat who steals the cigarette box in Galsworthy's *The Silver Box* and lets the poor servant take the blame for it. He was mercurial, unpredictable and fun. Buckmaster had developed an entertainment that appealed very much to Vivien's fondness for witty, slightly cynical *jeux d'esprit*: a one-man supper-club cabaret in which he would perform sketches he'd written. Some of these anticipated the kind of satire associated in the late

1950s and early 1960s with the *Beyond the Fringe* college satirists. One of them was a Shakespeare pastiche made up of place names from the history plays, but the hit of the evening was usually a 'lecture' he gave on what you could do with a piece of string – he ended up hanging himself with it.

His highly strung, uneven temperament obviously found difficulty containing itself in traditional parts in long runs, and he was often at liberty to accompany Vivien to a play and supper afterwards. They became very close and probably had a physical relationship. Vivien's sexual needs were probably not being satisfied inside marriage – and along with a reaction against the religious side of her education had come a need to liberate herself from the sexual constraints she'd been under. She didn't appear to have any guilt about it. She wasn't ignorant of the fact that she was committing adultery: it was merely something that was done, and then didn't need to be thought about. She wasn't promiscuous in terms of numbers, but by temperament she was impetuous and this could make for sudden attachments.

Her impetuosity had displayed itself on a visit she had made the year before to the first night of a new comedy which had arrived at the Lyric Theatre fresh from success on Broadway. There it had been called *The Royal Family*. For obvious reasons the title of this Edna Ferber and George Kaufman play had been changed when it transferred and it was now known as *Theatre Royal*. A flamboyant satire on theatrical folk and their outsize egos, it starred a twenty-seven-year-old actor, Laurence Olivier, portraying a thinly disguised John Barrymore at his most self-consciously romantic.

Every actor longs to play another actor, particularly an outstanding one. Olivier in white silk shirt open to the navel and black duelling tights satirized the American matinée idol's vanities of looks and figure, at the same time demonstrating his own energetic virtues as he fought a mock duel, vaulted on to a balcony and swaggered around like a dog emerging from water and drenching everyone in the drops it shook off. 'What a virile performance!' Vivien remarked.

It was generally accounted Olivier's best to date. Though dashed off on broad lines, as if by a relaxed caricaturist, it was a powerhouse of fire and romance. Vivien sensed how he relished the role, how he exulted in what he could do with his body, how flamboyantly he could project his romantic appeal.

In Hollywood the previous year, 1933, Olivier had suffered a humiliating rebuff from none other than Greta Garbo, whom he was cast to star opposite in *Queen Christina*. Garbo deliberately went cold on him at their first rehearsal, so that he had to be replaced by her old flame John Gilbert. In *Theatre Royal*, playing Tony Cavendish, Olivier found a cathartic opportunity for revenge by satirizing the Great Lover that Gilbert had been in his heyday. Hence perhaps the exceptional relish of his playing. He went after what he wanted and, having got it, proceeded to ring the changes on it. Vivien's temperament was patterned this way too, except that once she had achieved her goal, she did not often strive to transcend it. *Theatre Royal* was an uncomplicated play, and a good vehicle for a star turn. Olivier's performance spoke to her with an exciting directness – he was witty, handsome, manly and seductive looking as the whites of his eyes flashed mischievously against his mascara. She went backstage. What they said to each other has gone unrecorded – but Vivien recalled stooping impulsively over him, as he sat perspiring from his display of prowess, and she planted a light kiss on his shoulder.

Olivier was also to recall the sense of instant enslavement he had felt at his first view of Vivien on the stage. He went to see her in *The Mask of Virtue* when it was a few days into its run. The publicity surrounding her discovery attracted him: her beauty turned curiosity into adoration. 'Apart from her looks, which were magical, she possessed beautiful poise; her neck looked almost too fragile to support her head and bore it with a sense of surprise, and something of the pride of the master juggler who can make a brilliant manoeuvre appear almost accidental.' Just as she had been excited by the thrust of the sexuality behind his own theatrically tempestuous playing in *Theatre Royal*, Olivier now perceived in the woman who was soon to become his mistress 'an attraction of the most perturbing nature I have ever encountered'.

In many ways, Laurence Olivier's character was more shadowy and complex than Vivien's; hers was often unnervingly clear-cut. In an interview with a Manchester newspaper during the tour of *Private Lives* in 1930, just a few weeks after his marriage to Jill Esmond, Olivier confessed that 'only fools are happy ... I always examine things so very closely that immediate pleasures are dwarfed by my insistence on ultimate benefits.' There is a fair hint here of the guilt he was born with and used so creatively to unburden himself in some of the greatest moments in acting. Acting is a form of public confession; both words came together in the title Olivier used for his 1982 autobiography, *Confessions of an Actor*. It is a book permeated, to an uncomfortable extent, by the pleasures of self-abasement. He came from a post-World War I generation that didn't rebel against its parents, but, on the contrary, thought itself guilty of having survived Armageddon – he did what he was told for a good many years. In this, he was like Vivien, though obedience to her connoted order and security. To him, it was akin to obtaining a state of grace and only the independence that reared its romantic-looking tousled head in early manhood mitigated what he called his 'reflex action' to obey others, especially his father.

Olivier's father brought into their home an atmosphere not unlike the one in which Vivien spent her formative childhood years. He was a High Anglican priest – so high as to be suspected of Romish sympathies. Indeed he liked being called 'Father Olivier'.

For some years, he had been a stern schoolmaster and had a reputation for laying on the rod, before he took Holy Orders. Then he lost his vocation and recovered it only with the birth of Olivier, his second child and first son, for whose appearance in the world he 'couldn't see the slightest purpose'. Olivier's mother was so lovely that no photo could do her justice, according to her son; she died early in his infancy. Beauty in a woman had a power of recall that was as disturbing to him as it was seductive.

If Vivien was one on whom intensive religious training left little mark, Olivier was the opposite. When he had failed to secure a role he dearly wanted at Birmingham Repertory Company in 1928, in a play about a saint, the disappointment was almost unbearably sharpened when he was told it was because he couldn't convey spiritual exaltation. He disputed this hotly: 'I was deeply and devotedly religious.' He went to a good choir school, where the 'high dramatic tirades' of the priest castigating the sinners in the congregation were equated by him with histrionics. As a choirboy he had botched his own swansong anthem – more public humiliation requiring penitential writhing. The compliment paid his father for young Olivier's performance as a schoolboy Brutus by the actor-manager Sir Johnston Forbes-Robertson likewise had to be paid for with abasement – it was surely 'a palpable exaggeration'. His first professional job was suitably humble – second assistant stage manager. His first stage entrance typically involved prostration – he tripped up. Taking a holiday even gave him strong guilt feelings. Work was the way he assuaged his guilt: 'Work is life for me' ought to be carved on his memorial slab.

Vivien's sexuality had burst forth early, spasmodically and erratically. With Olivier, there had been no problem at all: he remained a virgin until he was twenty-four.

Both he and Vivien, however, had rushed into marriage. Or rather, Olivier had proposed within three weeks of meeting Jill Esmond, though she did not give in to his entreaties for another couple of years. His haste was in some measure due to his need for relief from self-imposed chastity. Adventures without marriage would be, in his religion-steeped upbringing, a mortal sin. He has confessed he was dying to enjoy sex, but 'only with the blessing of God'.

In this, he was very much the opposite of Vivien. Though she rushed into marriage, she did so for reasons both romantic and severely practical – that duality which was to characterize her nature throughout life. She wanted what she set eyes on, whether or not anyone else had prior claims; and she probably wanted independence from her family with its unresolved conflict between her father's hedonism and her mother's severity. She was already a very worldly girl when she married Leigh Holman – too worldly for him.

Olivier was a very unworldly boy when Jill Esmond finally said yes – and he married into one of the great theatrical families of England, a clan which guarded its connections with some jealousy and must have viewed this new-comer from a lofty height at that year's most fashionable wedding. In fact, Olivier gravitated to women who possessed sharp wits as well as strong wills. Later Greer Garson, who became his protégée in a short-lived fling as an actor-manager, made a third such woman with her beauty and her London University degree.

We have only his word for it that a few weeks before his wedding Jill Esmond had told him 'she was in love elsewhere and could not love me as completely as I could wish'. 'How soon the day o'ercast,' he has recorded. Typically, he compared his predicament to a scene in a play latent with dramatic promise. Off-stage, so to speak, he let it rip and, like Vivien, didn't pursue his religious practices any more. Unlike her, his guilt never left him.

This, then, was the state of preparedness Olivier was in whenever he encountered Vivien's 'disturbing' presence. Each was ready for the other. Both had marriages which were becoming such in name only. Both had spouses who, for similar reasons, would seek to avoid the indignities inflicted by the infidelities of their respective partners: Leigh Holman because he dearly loved Vivien and knew too well the cruel hypocrisies that the law inflicted in such cases, and Jill Esmond because she probably had very little love left for Olivier by the time his adultery became public and had preserved a lot of her own dignity within the clan of her acting family.

She had certainly helped Olivier acquire a social confidence he was the first to admit he lacked – 'rough but not ready', was how he described himself. They had both built reputations on the West End stage; Jill Esmond's in these early years of the 1930s was rather more secure than her husband's. His great torrent of talent was building up, but so far he had only enjoyed popular success in chic, well-made matinée plays. He had not yet had the opportunity, nor had he gained enough insight into himself to act the great cathartic roles of Shakespeare.

'I want events to go my way,' his lament ran in these years, 'I don't want to be driven by events.' But they hadn't gone his way – and didn't do so until he forged an independence that took him farther from his wife's side in every sense. At one time, he and Jill Esmond may have hoped to become the Alfred Lunt and Lynn Fontanne of England, but talent and temperament pulled them in opposite directions. Plays kept them apart rather than in partnership.

It has been argued that Jill's maturer, harder intelligence taught him a lot about acting. She was certainly a good counsellor in the social graces and put a smart coat of society varnish on him. What she began Vivien carried on, though where acting was concerned, it was to be Olivier who tutored Vivien. By then he was a ready mentor and she a willing learner.

Coward's inclusion of him in *Private Lives* reversed his rather wilting stage fortunes in 1930, and he and his wife appeared with Coward and Gertrude Lawrence in the Broadway run in 1931. But a speculative trip to Hollywood – 'Hahlleewood', as Coward derisively called it – proved their undoing. Though Olivier looked the Ronald Colman type to his profit at home, it was death in Hollywood, where there was only one Ronald Colman; and Jill Esmond, who looked about to be cast by David Selznick in *A Bill of Divorcement*, lost the role to Katharine Hepburn. Both returned to England with great distaste for the movies – rubbed in painfully again when Olivier unwisely let himself be enticed back to Hollywood by the Garbo film. He signed a contract with Korda in 1934 only to get money for his stage work.

Olivier began work on *Moscow Nights* under his Korda contract in the summer of 1935 and Vivien urged Gliddon to take her down to Denham, where it was being shot. They went by rented limousine, as a film actress was expected to do. 'She was wearing a superbly cut Stiebel suit,' the agent remembers, 'along with an Aage Thaarup hat, and looked exquisite.' She was oddly nervous or excited. Gliddon thought her confidence needed bolstering and said, 'Vivien, you're going to be a great star – as great as Garbo.' Then for no reason he knew of except that she was *so* attractive, sitting beside him and at that exciting point in her career when recognition has been gained and even greater achievement awaits, he added, 'But I should like to feel we would always work together, however big you become.'

Vivien put her hand on Gliddon's. 'Of course we shall, dear John.' He must have shown a bit of sentiment at this, for she looked at him sharply. 'You're very emotional, aren't you?' she said.

They arrived at Denham, which hadn't been open for production more than a few months, and to Vivien's obvious disappointment Olivier wasn't there; they were doing retakes on *Moscow Nights*, which had been directed by Anthony Asquith, the young man who had so pointedly ignored Vivien the year before. Korda himself was supervising them.

He looked their way, didn't at first seem to recognize Vivien, then with an 'Oh, yes, Vivien Leigh,' strolled across and shook hands. 'Sorry we haven't had a film for you. But we'll have one soon, I hope.'

It was a dispiriting end to the visit and Vivien was much more wrapped up in her thoughts on the drive back to town. She felt she was becoming a victim of Korda's practice of signing up proven or promising talents so as not to have to borrow them expensively from other producers, but then having no films of his own ready to employ them. As a result, actresses like her were lent out to other producers or left to languish. Vivien's euphoria was evaporating as impatience took over.

The next news from Denham really irritated her. Korda called one day in the early autumn of 1935: Vivien's first picture for him would be *Cyrano de Bergerac*, which he and Charles Laughton had been planning for over a year. But her anticipation of playing Roxanne dwindled when told her hair must be dyed blonde. 'Dyed! Why not a wig?' Because, she was told, Laughton was a perfectionist (as well as a chronic worrier whose anxiety complex was beginning to infect Korda) and anything he sensed to be 'not right' grated on his sensibilities. Before Vivien could object further, Gliddon received a cable from Leslie Howard, who was producing and starring in *Hamlet* on Broadway, 'CAN VIVIEN LEIGH COME OVER IMMEDIATELY?' He wanted her for Ophelia. It was up to Korda to say yes or no, but while she wavered over having her hair dipped in the dye-bowl, Howard cabled he could wait no longer. And then Laughton and Korda failed to agree on major matters like the length of Cyrano's nose, as well as minor things like making the film in colour, or shooting simultaneous French and English versions, and the project was postponed, never to be made. So Vivien lost both opportunities.

'I don't think much of your £50,000 contract,' she said to Gliddon. He sensed a hardening of her will. It recalled to him the glimpse of that temper he had had on the morning after her discovery. She had seen a photograph of herself in the evening papers and didn't like it, so she ordered him to have it 'stopped'. He had thrust it out of his mind in the exhilaration of the deal with Korda; now he realized how stubborn Vivien could be. He began to wonder if some of her new friends were telling her to get tough.

The news that Laurence Olivier and John Gielgud were to star in a production of *Romeo and Juliet*, alternating the roles of Romeo and Mercutio, was the theatrical sensation of the 1935 autumn season. Gielgud, who was also to direct the play, saw it as his farewell to Romeo, a part he had already played twice and each time stamped with his romantic sensibility. Olivier's admirers saw him as the challenger, both to Gielgud's stardom and the tradition of poetry and refined feeling that a Shakespearian production then represented. Olivier's concept of Romeo was shocking, even to fellow professionals in rehearsal with him. He saw him as a rude boy in the raw meaning of the word, boisterous, bursting with sexuality, probably capable of the rude gesture too. For most of the first-night critics, the shock of such naturalism was too much; to a few, though, it was a liberating break with tradition, comparable in the impact made on London's theatre world with the arrival of 'The Method' on Broadway in the 1950s (and later in Hollywood).

To Vivien, it was a romantic experience. She was at the first night and returned again and again to see Olivier whenever he played Romeo, wishing she could be in Peggy Ashcroft's slippers as Juliet. Now that he was in a passionate love-story and not playing a parody Great Lover, the charge of Olivier's sensuality — what Ralph Richardson called, with reference to Romeo, his 'animal exactness' — was far purer and more potent. 'A passionate sixteen-year-old boy in love with love', is how Peggy Ashcroft described his Romeo in later years. Vivien saw Olivier throw himself into the role body and soul; it did not matter to her if his physical attractiveness got in the way of soulfulness.

This experience intensified Vivien's wish to be a classical actress and, with her way of breaking down huge leaps into small steps, she worked on this desire over the coming months. She was part of Olivier's world of theatre; not yet at the centre of it, but determination would help her find the way that led to him.

Her impatience to get her career going again now knew no bounds. In December 1935 she received an offer, through Gliddon, from the man who had so lately told her to 'take the films, darling'. Ivor Novello asked her to play Jenny Mere opposite him in Clemence Dane's adaptation of *The Happy Hypocrite*.

Max Beerbohm's novella was about the transfiguring power of love. Well, she was in the mood for that — but there was an additional twist to the tale which appealed to her even more. Beerbohm's conceit was that if you live up to the mask of saintliness — like the real mask which the cynical rake Lord George Hell uses to conceal his own ravaged features and lecherous nature — you will find that assumed virtue becomes a permanent part of your being. Your countenance obligingly alters, too, in this spiritual face-lift. All this was very attractive to a girl who already believed in wish-fulfilment.

It was on her mind all through Christmas 1935, which she and Leigh spent in the Cotswold village of Broadway. On New Year's Day she sat down in the Lygon Arms and with the vigour of a good resolution — tempered by a hint of desperation at her inactivity — she wrote to Gliddon: 'I can't help feeling that this play is of tremendous importance, firstly because it's essential I should *work* again and quickly, and that it will be a wonderful experience which is just what I want.' Even if it coincided with Korda's casting her in a film, she would work by day in the studios and at night in the theatre just to do it, since '... working with Ivor can't fail to be a big and very good thing. Do, do try and arrange this. If you'd read *The Happy Hypocrite* you'd understand more how anxious I am to do it.'

Gliddon had told her that Sydney Carroll, as well as Korda, had the right to decide whether she should be in the play, since Korda could decree that a film had priority and Carroll had an option on her next play, whatever that was.

'There's only one solution,' Gliddon told her. 'Buy yourself out of Sydney's option.'

'Do it,' she said with a decisiveness that pleased her agent, since he rather resented the way Carroll was playing theatrical godfather to a baby that Gliddon had found on the doorstep of opportunity. His accounts book for 1936 includes the laconic entry: 'Payment by Miss Leigh to Sydney Carroll for release from contract: £65.'

Korda required more delicate negotiation. True, he had no film ready for Vivien, but he might *just* use any infraction of her contract as cause for terminating it and saving himself the financial obligation of its 'pay or play' conditions. But Korda agreed – and then, when Vivien's excitement was again engaged by the prospect of work, her hopes were dashed: Novello had to postpone his production until April 1936.

Meantime Vivien did all she could to keep herself or, at least, her face in the public eye. Thomas Dugdale ARA asked her to sit for him and in due course the portrait was hung in the Royal Academy's spring exhibition in 1936. It showed Vivien in a diaphanous blue nightgown. 'I painted her as I found her,' the artist said somewhat ambiguously. 'It is nice to be in oils,' declared Vivien, 'but greasepaint would be nicer still.'

The painting of her portrait had, however, taken second place to an equally prestigious but altogether more exciting offer. Oxford University Dramatic Society (OUDS) was staging *Richard II*, with John Gielgud and Glen Byam Shaw as joint directors. It was OUDS's custom to recruit West End actresses for the female roles in plays that were otherwise cast from talented undergraduates. In this case Richard II was played by Michael Rennie, who was soon to become a client of John Gliddon's too.

Who put Vivien up for the OUDS production is a question that's never been answered, but the likelihood is that Olivier pressed her case. There was now an awareness on both their parts that they were falling in love – with each other *and* with the classical theatre. The latter was coming to mean more, far more to Olivier than the matinée plays in which he had set himself to shine. He had flexed his muscles in the power politics of the West End by turning actor-manager at the absurdly early age of twenty-seven and presenting *The Ring-master* and *The Golden Arrow*, which had both foundered. He had co-starred Greer Garson in the latter, hopeful of finding malleable material which would make them into a team like the Lunts and provide compensation for the feeling that his own marriage was not going to yield any theatrical partnership, and indeed would be lucky to survive. But Greer Garson had accepted a contract from MGM, the company that had allowed Garbo to humiliate him, and departed for Hollywood. He was ripe to test himself on the larger stage of Shakespeare –

he had found he liked the shock value of his Romeo and was impatient to drive a pioneering trail across the other Shakespeare plays and upset conventions here too.

Vivien appeared at exactly the right moment to catch his enthusiasm and be infected by his ambition – and, as it turned out, his love. There was a meeting of minds as well as bodies.

Others sensed it too, well before either of them declared it. The story has been told of Vivien and John Buckmaster dining in the Savoy Grill one night early in the New Year and seeing Olivier and Jill Esmond across the room. Olivier had shaved off his matinée idol moustache in order to simulate a beardless adolescent in *Romeo and Juliet*. Buckmaster said, 'What a silly little thing Larry looks without his lip covering.' Vivien snapped back, 'I think he looks adorable – he's the sort of man I'd like to marry.'

But there were other, more objective, observers than someone who was already Vivien's lover. That same year Jean-Pierre Aumont was having dinner in a Soho restaurant when he saw Vivien and Leigh Holman at a table. At another table near by was a young man with darkly romantic looks accompanied by a blonde woman. The man was Olivier, though Aumont had no means of knowing that at the time, but what some sensor of his own did detect was a strong amorous undercurrent flowing between the two tables.

Vivien appeared at the New Theatre one January afternoon to audition for her role as the Queen in *Richard II*. It was the same theatre where she'd so often been to sigh her heart out at Olivier's Romeo; now she was facing the stalls and, sitting where she had sat, was Glen Byam Shaw. 'Begin with Act v, Scene 1, please Miss Leigh.'

'This way the king will come,' she began, 'this is the way ...'

Some accounts have Olivier sitting out front, giving her confidence in a text for which he most likely had rehearsed her. He probably did coach her, but he was too prudent to urge her candidacy on his peers by even his mute presence.

The play opened at Oxford on 17 February 1936 and ran for its allotted week; no one received any pay. It was all like a party to Vivien. Her role was brief and untaxing, and anyhow she'd always been ready for the fun afterwards. There seemed far more of that than usual in Oxford this month. Edward viii's accession in January had already spread its promise of youth and change among undergraduates who possessed the one and were eager for the other. Vivien had motored up to Oxford in her little wire-wheeled two-seater and, as she reported on her return to London, 'drove it into just about every ditch around after the parties'. She encountered what she considered a good omen. Max Beerbohm accepted an invitation to respond to the toast of 'The Guests' after the last performance of *Richard II*. Vivien tried to lure him into hearing her

Jenny Mere role in *The Happy Hypocrite* – she had already made herself word perfect. Max declined in his usual courtly way. Maybe Vivien in that university setting reminded him of his own *femme fatale* Zuleika Dobson and the havoc she had wrought in undergraduate hearts. Max was spell-proof.

Even when rehearsals began in London in March he sat courteously but unresponsively through them, and, in fact, did not betray what he thought of Vivien until many years later. Then from his villa at Rapallo he wrote, rather equivocally perhaps: 'Miss Vivien Leigh's performance was of exquisite sensibility – a foreshadowing of how much to come in later years!'

Clemence Dane told Vivien's fortune during a spare moment in the rehearsals. 'Oh,' she exclaimed, 'there's a Devil in my Jenny's cards!'

*The Happy Hypocrite* opened on 8 April 1936 and, in spite of good notices, wilted quickly. Novello's fans were disappointed at seeing a profile which was handsome by the standards then, though rather too sharply bevelled for later tastes, being submerged under the coarse features and leering looks of the morally unreconstructed Lord George Hell. Vivien was as sweet and innocent as one of the buttercups which the rake boasted he hadn't laid eyes on for twenty years. But sweetness was not enough.... The play's failure left her with some flattering mentions and earnings that amounted to £332.10s.0d.

She probably remembered it best for an incident which happened backstage. Amongst the first-nighters were Laurence Olivier and his wife. Jill Esmond was six months pregnant, or thereabouts. 'I think I'll have a son and call him Tarquin,' Olivier had said to his wife when an attempt was being made to keep their marriage together. After the curtain, Olivier suggested to Jill Esmond that they go backstage and see Vivien Leigh.

Vivien was holding court, elated by her personal success, and somewhat off her guard. Olivier introduced his wife. It was the first time they had met. Vivien looked at the swelling form of her lover's wife and the words were out of her mouth before she could stop them. 'And how's little Tarquin coming along?' she asked. For many a long year Olivier was to remember the embarrassment that moment had held for him. It was as good as a public announcement that he had taken a mistress.

# 6

## 'We're in love'

*I*t had been nearly eighteen months since Vivien had signed her Korda contract and she had still not made a film. Apologies were called for. Basil Bleck, Korda's lawyer, sat down on 9 April 1936 and wrote to Gliddon:

I would not like this opportunity to pass without telling you how Mr Korda and I, for my part, regret that no opportunity has yet arisen for availing ourselves of Miss Leigh's services. Please assure her of Mr Korda's interest in her and his belief in her services and chances as a film actress are not a bit diminished. . . . All through the winter we have been struggling not only with studio circumstances, but with the difficulty of finding a suitable subject for Mr Laughton.

Vivien sniffed when she heard that. Then Bleck came to the point: 'Mr Korda has immediate plans for Miss Leigh, the first being that she should play opposite Mr Conrad Veidt in a film of *Under the Red Robe* and he also wants her to play an important part in Mr Pommer's picture based on Mr A. E. W. Mason's story in which I understand both Larry Olivier and Ralph Richardson are playing.' Vivien began to perk up.

It has been a topic of speculation among some biographers – and asserted as a fact by at least one – that Vivien was having a sensual affair with Alexander Korda in the months preceding *Fire Over England*. Evidence for this remains speculative, but it is on the whole improbable. Korda lacked the romantic allure of Olivier and Buckmaster or some of the other young men who now squired her round the town. However, he substituted the seductive aura of power.

He and Vivien already had certain things in common which established a social, if not a sexual, intimacy between them. Neither had been born in England: both, in a sense, had adopted the country and subsequently became more English than the natives. Vivien knew Europe through her education there; Korda by working in Berlin and Paris before trying his luck in Hollywood and subsequently settling in London. Both liked living well and enjoyed a busy social life. Both found real fulfilment only in work. Korda had taste, though he wasn't quite the connoisseur he pretended to be. His brother Vincent, the art director, made good Alex's deficiencies. Korda had assembled his art collection largely on Vincent's advice. But Vivien learned through him what to buy and, more important, what to pay. Nevertheless Vivien began making subtle alterations in her looks and appearance around this time, contriving the more exotic appearance to which reference has been made, dressing in brighter colours and using darker make-up in 'gypsy' tones – as one magazine called them.

It was fairly common knowledge that Korda was having an affair with Merle Oberon. Like Vivien, she had been born and raised in India. What wasn't known – perhaps not even to Korda – was that she was of Anglo-Indian parentage, a fact she strenuously concealed in her lifetime to the extent of employing her mother, who was of Indian appearance, as her servant. But if it did cross Vivien's mind to emulate Korda's 'type' of woman so that he would pay her more attention, she was almost surely disappointed. According to John Gliddon, 'Korda was far too deeply involved with courting Merle and fending off Maria [still his wife by his first and most acrimonious marriage] to start an affair with Vivien. She was the type of woman he found intellectually stimulating, but not sexually appealing.' Vincent Korda was more emphatic still: 'Where Vivien was concerned, Alex was a paternal figure.'

There was an even better reason for Korda not to embroil himself romantically with Vivien, had he been tempted to do so. It would have been bad business. The strength of the passion she was now displaying for Olivier, and his infatuation with her, would have been enough to dissuade any employer who had them both under contract from intruding on his own account. Besides, Korda saw potential for exploiting the attraction between his two stars.

Business came first with him, as Vivien learned when, despite his lawyer's encouraging letter, Korda cast the French actress Annabella in what was to have been her part in Victor Seastrom's *Under the Red Robe*. He coolly explained that, as there was French money in the film, he wanted a name that meant something in France.

In a pique, Vivien rushed to Gliddon with a proposal to tide her over: he should get her a part in the Regent's Park open-air production of *Henry VIII*. She needed all the experience she could gain in classical theatre, even if it was 'park acting'. It meant they had to go back again to Sydney Carroll, who had helped found the *al fresco* theatre seasons in 1934, but she was quickly accommodated in the role of Anne Boleyn. She squelched her way through an exceptionally wet summer, which enforced hasty retreats to a canvas-covered pavilion, where the drumming of the rain on the roof smothered her small voice even more than the open air did on fine days. She had begun taking voice lessons from Olivier's ruthless old teacher Elsie Fogerty of the Central School of Speech Training and Dramatic Art, whose first act was to compel her to kick off her smart Bond Street pumps and stand in her stockinged feet until she felt her voice-box vibrate through her delicate physique. Even so, the critics who exercised their own mercy on plays afflicted by far from gentle rain judged Vivien's voice to be 'on the slight side'.

No matter, for she was spending her days at Olivier's side. Her engagement in the play had coincided with Korda's decision to rush *Fire Over England* into production, so for a time she was acting in Regent's Park in the evenings and at Denham Studios by day. It was to take a serious toll on her health. But at the moment, if her temperature ran high, the cause was love-sickness.

*Fire Over England* had been cobbled together quickly – but the scenes that Vivien and Olivier shared were improved from the first script through the two re-writes. She plays a young lady-in-waiting in the court of Elizabeth I; he is a secret agent deployed to penetrate the court of King Philip of Spain (Raymond Massey) and bring back a list of English traitors. The original script opened with a sea battle and boarding parties. The shooting script opened on Vivien and immediately emphasized her beauty and grace as she ran around searching for a pearl which had fallen off the Queen's gown. Though Flora Robson's regal presence is what people rightly remember, the romantic interest depended wholly on Vivien and Olivier, and their love scenes were given full value. Too much value for Graham Greene, who remarked acidulously in the *Spectator* that Elizabeth Tudor would never have allowed 'so much cuddling and kissing in her presence'. What the screen showed, however, was a reflection of what was going on between the real lovers off the set.

Like many in their lovestruck state, they were totally unaware of the existence of other people. Both of them held the film they were making in fairly low esteem – and this was another bond between them. Olivier felt that A. E. W. Mason's novel had been distorted and diminished in its adaptation for the screen – a view Mason subsequently shared. Olivier thought the enterprise a waste of their talents and Vivien deferred to his judgment in this matter too. In things artistic, he had the upper hand; in love, there was nothing to choose between them. Both were still at the skittish, giggling stage. One day a Denham employee stumbled on them cuddling puppyishly in Vivien's dressing-room – they were not the slightest bit embarrassed by his intrusion.

According to Paul Tabori, they suddenly appeared in Korda's office. 'Alex, we must tell you our great secret,' said Vivien. 'We're in love and we're going to get married.' Korda smiled and said, 'Don't be silly – everybody knows that. I've known it for weeks and weeks.'

Someone who obviously didn't know was Oswald Frewen, who was making a call at Little Stanhope Street one day when Vivien and Olivier walked in together; it was Frewen's first encounter with Olivier. Leigh Holman was absent at the time. Vivien was suffering from a viral cough, and Olivier suggested rum; whereupon the good-hearted Frewen left them and popped into the pub in Pitt's Head Mews to get a tumblerful of hot toddy, which he then 'pumped into the Vivling'. A comedy of frustration then seems to have ensued, with Frewen suggesting Larry should go and he would sit on with Vivien and 'talk her to sleep', and Olivier saying somewhat irritably that both of them should be on their way and let her get her rest. The fifty-year-old Frewen appears to have had a very unsuspecting side to him — as well as a very good-natured one — and his diary offers no evidence that he was aware of a love affair being barely suppressed in his presence. Twenty years later, he was to recall it ruefully. He said in an interview in 1955 that Olivier would work on Vivien's voice and line delivery, 'then they'd often go out to lunch. Leigh Holman knew about it, but he didn't pay it any attention. He assumed it was just another of those theatrical relationships. Jill Esmond knew about it too ... but I don't think that [she] ever had the whisper of an idea that Larry had more on his mind than helping out a young actress friend of both of them.'

Mid-way through August 1936, Jill Esmond gave birth to a son. Even this event didn't break up a pair of lovers whose indifference to opinion made it appear as if they were living on the same plane as the one on which they acted.

In due course, a christening party was held at the Cheyne Walk house where Olivier and Jill Esmond were living. It had once belonged to the painter Whistler and the reception was held in his old studio, where, one of the guests recalls, the crib holding the infant Tarquin was placed on a low plinth the artist had used for his models. A large number of guests, mostly from the theatrical establishment, milled around it, exchanging the usual gossip of the 'stock market' in success, failure and reputations. 'It turned into a kind of cocktail party,' said one of the actresses present. 'Larry had been away filming — but suddenly he appeared and he had this girl in slacks and a red jumper with him. It was Vivien. They didn't quite come in, but stood near the door and everyone was soon saying to themselves, Hello ... Oh that's it, is it? They were together — one couldn't mistake it. After a few minutes, they vanished. Vivien didn't come back, but Larry did — with what looked like lipstick on his cheek. I suppose it would have been considered scandalous in any ordinary group. But we were all theatricals — it was just something that happened.'

Almost as soon as she had completed her role in *Fire Over England*, Vivien was put into *Dark Journey*, an improbable and confused fiction about spies in Stockholm during the First World War. She played a couturière in the secrets-stealing business. Korda had recently signed Conrad Veidt on a long-term contract and was anxious to find English-speaking roles to fit this accomplished actor, who was an early refugee from the Nazi dictatorship. He played a German agent and had the advantage over Vivien of a flashing monocle, with which he could divert attention from what Graham Greene called the 'wicked cosmopolitan dialogue'.

Vivien as a 'pretty, innocent little spyess whose acting, like that of the rest of the company, is good without being brilliant', as the *Spectator* film critic put it, did possess one advantage. She looked lovelier than ever, thanks to the luminous quality of Georges Perinal's photography. Moreover, her close-ups benefited from the attention of Harry Stradling, who had been photographing Marlene Dietrich in *Knight Without Armour* on the stage next door and was hired to give Vivien the same ravishing treatment on *Dark Journey*.

Nevertheless, Vivien's opinion of film-making was now infected by Olivier's feeling that he was prostituting his stage talent; and during the première of *Dark Journey*, to which she was escorted by Noël Coward, Vivien's dissatisfaction was audible in the continual stream of sarcastic queries addressed to him, or indeed to anyone in her vicinity, as to what on earth was happening on the screen. 'Goodness, why did I say that? . . . What am I doing now?'

Friends of Vivien's and Olivier's noticed, around this time, how she began assuming quite a number of his characteristic attitudes and even his habits – a fondness for expletives, for example. 'Olivier', says Anthony Quayle, 'was the very first person I ever heard use the word "fucking" as a sort of free-and-easy embellishment in everyday speech – remember, it wasn't as commonplace then as it has become now. He looked in on my dressing-room, saw this little dog I had with me and said to it, "Oh, look at you, aren't you fucking beautiful?" Well, Vivien caught this trick off him, I believe.'

She grew noticeably relaxed about swear words and, though the ladylike way she used them, coupled with her looks, actually enhanced her appeal to many men, it was a habit which later made some women uncomfortable in Vivien's formidable presence.

Olivier told her he was taking a holiday in Capri with Jill Esmond once *Fire Over England* was finished. While he had been duelling his way out of Philip of Spain's fortress-palace, Vivien was coping on an adjoining set with such stiff-necked lines from Conrad Veidt as, 'You love me. Why are you trying to resist?' Now they both needed a break. Vivien proposed to Leigh that they snatch time off somewhere in the Mediterranean before her next stint for Korda. As it was the beginning of the Michaelmas law term, he could not free himself to accompany her. Instead, the job of chaperon fell to Oswald Frewen. It would be like an elder brother escorting his schoolgirl sister on her first holiday. They had separate sleeping compartments on the train to Rome – Sicily was their ultimate destination – but the connecting door was kept open, as Vivien didn't like being alone – a relic, perhaps, of her days in the tented line of dormitory beds. 'She was so natural that sex didn't obtrude and I was never conscious of a defensive action on her part,' wrote Frewen, which suggests that there was at least enough sexuality in the atmosphere to warrant a denial.

They registered at the monastic-looking San Domenico Hotel in Taormina on 27 October. Frewen proposed a visit to the Graeco-Roman amphitheatre, but Vivien was captivated by their view of Etna, then in a disturbed state and trailing smoke from its crater like a long chiffon scarf. It reminded her of Leigh Holman and his pipe – she'd not been able to break him of that smelly habit – and a letter she sent home on 29 October perhaps offers a tiny gloss on what their domestic relationship had become. Describing Mount Etna she wrote: 'Apparently he often smokes for want of anything better to do, and it never comes to anything really big.'

After driving up Etna in a rented car – a 3,000-foot ascent requiring red wine to warm them in the cold, misty region at the top of the volcano – Vivien's plans for the remainder of their holiday took a decisive turn. She had always wanted, she said, to see Naples. There was a sea-plane from Syracuse and, since Capri was so close, why not stay there? She'd heard the Grand Hotel Quisisana well spoken of. In a letter to Leigh Holman, she wrote: 'One night in Naples and Rome AND BACK TO YOU MY DARLING. I would hate coming back if I didn't think you were lonely.'

She didn't mention her intention to go on to Capri, nor the fact that Olivier and his wife were at the Quisisana.

The trip began with an alarming, but appropriate, intimation of the trouble they were flying into when the sea-plane botched its take-off and kept bouncing up off the sea, then pancaking on to it again, while the pilot tried to hoist his load of passengers and freight into the air. Frewen heard Vivien beside him muttering Catholic invocations in which he caught the words 'St Thérèse' – presumably St Thérèse of Lisieux, one of the patron saints of hopeless cases. Fear of flying was to remain with her for the rest of her life. She stayed pale and subdued until they reached Capri. It was only there that Frewen became aware of the Oliviers' presence.

'Larry, the other side of the hall, cried in a loud voice "Vivien!" and Viv, my side of the hall, cried loudly "Darling!" and Jill uttered further love-cries as all three met in the middle of what I could only describe as a joint passionate embrace, the while I smiled agedly and with benignity!' It was a scene as false in its greetings as in its contrived unexpectedness. But then three of the parties were accomplished performers skilled at dissimulation. One wonders whether Olivier and Jill Esmond had a nostalgic twinge of *Private Lives*, in which they had played together on Broadway. Life aped Coward's brittle artifice – and seems to have been played the same way.

By now Jill Esmond must have been aware of her husband's romantic involvement with Vivien, yet she doesn't appear to have betrayed any public resentment of it. The 'performances' probably deserved a larger audience than a bystander like Frewen. The Oliviers escorted the newcomers to the rooms assigned them – Frewen on one side of them, Vivien on the other, though there was a constant coming-and-going through the connecting doors for the duration of their stay.

The 'surprise' arrival generated a momentum which carried everyone through that evening and the next day in a non-stop rush of high spirits, and thus allowed Vivien and Olivier to bask in each other's glances under the guise of conviviality. Frewen realized things were not all they seemed, but he appears to have quieted his conscience fairly easily. He loved the company of 'the Young' and felt distanced by age from passing moral judgment on their impulsive ways. He also enjoyed seeing Vivien made happy. She took the blame for the trick she'd played, owning up so impishly that he couldn't find it in his heart to be angry with her.

Playing out their amorous feelings for each other in public, yet inside what appeared to be the theatrical conventions of a triangular affair, intensified Vivien's and Olivier's attachment. Capri's sensuous atmosphere no doubt played its part too.

They took all their meals except breakfast on the terrace. What they talked about can easily be conjectured. Olivier had come abroad with a suitcase packed with critical commentaries on *Hamlet*, in which he was to appear directed by Tyrone Guthrie. Guthrie had consulted Dr Ernest Jones, the leading British Freudian, as to Hamlet's motives. The main theme of the play would still be revenge, but Hamlet's hesitations were to be interpreted as guilt at his incestuous feelings for his mother, which were thwarted so long as Claudius remained alive and married to her. A forbidden love, a guilty conscience, an affair frustrated yet heightened by the presence of a partner in marriage; the echoes of the play can hardly have escaped at least three of the party at the Quisisana.

But a current love affair provided Vivien with a far more appropriate parallel to her own situation. The King and Mrs Simpson had just completed a most irregular holiday cruise together in the eastern Mediterranean aboard the yacht *Narwhal*. Fashionable spots like Capri had been rife with reported sightings. Vivien considered the liaison as romantic – and as illicit – as her own with Olivier. Wallis Simpson was charming, cultured, accomplished, impeccably dressed, strong-willed and not averse to speaking her mind, guileful and, so Vivien believed, determined to get what she wanted by defying both convention and the British Constitution. Vivien identified closely with Wallis Simpson, even to the point of saying, 'I could be a king's mistress very easily.' Her own liaison with Olivier seemed to her, in a way, to be licensed by this other example of love, devotion and sacrifice.

As might be expected, given his nature, Olivier suffered far more pangs of conscience at the consequences of his feelings than did Vivien. His love affair placed him in a deep emotional quandary while he was preparing *Hamlet*, which he saw and continued to see fifteen years later when he came to film it as the story of 'a man who could not make up his mind'. Dr Ernest Jones, one feels, would have had much to interest him had he made the fifth guest on the Quisisana terrace.

The disturbing nature of the couple's involvement barely filters through Frewen's published record; his obliqueness suggests a reluctance to be more involved than he already had been by Vivien's duplicity. They left the Oliviers and returned to Rome on either 1 or 2 November and had hardly arrived at their hotel when a telephone call from Olivier sent Vivien into a state of great agitation – a veritable *crise de nerfs*, her companion described it. It has been assumed that Olivier had there and then intended to make the break with Jill Esmond, which would have abruptly propelled Vivien to the edge of her own break with Leigh Holman. But it is equally probable that he had had a fit of conscience and told her they mustn't see each other again for some time. (Conscience would become a Hamlet in training.) Whatever the phone call was about, Vivien and Frewen continued the trip home, and she had recovered by the time they reached London on 5 November, her twenty-third birthday. The next month, Vivien began shooting her third film for Korda, *Storm in a Teacup*.

Adapted and anglicized from a German play called *Sturm im Wasserglas* by Bruno Frank, this was surprisingly enough one of the first 'entertainment' films to attack the European dictators. Though it was relocated in a Scottish town, the laird (Cecil Parker) was comporting himself like a petty Hitler, with self-aggrandizing cohorts of yes-men and a town hall built on Reischstag lines and proportions. 'Where are we?' Rex Harrison's newsman asks pointedly, 'In Berlin, Moscow or where?'

It was also Vivien's first major comedy role and her pairing with Harrison followed the usual Hollywood style of the Depression era in which a rich and snooty lady is first humiliated and then humanized by a plainspoken and personable man of the people – though Harrison substituted personal abrasiveness for populist sentiment in the character he was playing. The chemistry works very well. His flippant sarcasms ('Finished being "finished"?') are deflected by her deb-like disdain. Even the Kensington accent which some, like Athene Seyler, felt marred her *Mask of Virtue* attempt at a prostitute, was useful for emphasizing the ludicrousness of a high-class dame stooping to enter the family Rolls-Royce with a child's lollipop sticking to the tight seat of her immaculately cut skirt. But this was about as far as Vivien would go. She obstinately refused to fall on her backside, even though the director, Victor Saville, told her that Hollywood heroines like Katharine Hepburn, Joan Crawford and Rosalind Russell were doing it all the time in their screwball comedies. 'I am an English actress,' she told him frostily.

Repartee of the kind in this film between her and Harrison appealed to the critics: it was suggested they become a screen team, like William Powell and Myrna Loy of *Thin Man* fame. And Vivien redeemed her initial hauteur in the film when love finally broke through the class barrier. Her face dimples into a sparkling smile, bewitching in its unexpected and impish warmth. In that shot one sees in Vivien what other men were seeing in her off-screen at that time.

Her talk off the set, however, had one topic and one only. She reminded Harrison of the hopeless crush he had had on his first childhood sweetheart: 'All she wanted to do was to talk about Larry, and so I went along with that, gazing on that beautiful face with unhopeful ardour.' Anthony Quayle, who did *not* fall in love with her, being not only more wary of her nature but already in love with Dorothy Hyson, recalls that 'To mention Larry was like talking to the Virgin Mary about God.'

Sometimes she went direct from the studios to catch his *Hamlet* without bothering to call at Little Stanhope Street to bathe and change or see her husband. Olivier's Hamlet combined psychology and physicality to a degree rare in the English theatre. The Dane's traditional gloominess was transformed by Ernest Jones's counsel into a perverse fixation on prohibited love, while Olivier's body exuded zest and muscular attack.

Vivien was bitterly vexed that all the theatre could offer her at this time was a little modern play called *Because We Must.* There was exciting talk of taking *Hamlet* to Denmark in the summer and playing it in the courtyard of Elsinore Castle. She yearned to be in it and, according to Harrison, broke down when her efforts to be included in the expedition looked like failing, and wept with 'wild hysteria, anger and anguish'.

Her lobbying continued through the first months of 1937; but a new kind of obsession was developing simultaneously.

Margaret Mitchell's novel *Gone With the Wind* had been published in America in May 1936 and in England at the end of the year. Vivien took a copy of it with her when she and Leigh went to Kitzbühel for Christmas. When her always tenuous sense of balance betrayed her on the ski slopes and she broke an ankle, she rested up reading the book which was to change her life.

# 7

## 'I shall play Scarlett O'Hara'

*L*ater on, when Margaret Mitchell met Vivien Leigh for the first time, she felt the strong affinity between Vivien and her own Scarlett O'Hara. But Vivien had been even more forcibly impressed on first reading the novel – to her it was as though she were meeting her double in the heroine of *Gone With the Wind*. It was difficult not to believe the novelist had had Vivien in mind when drawing the character of a woman who had 'high spirits, vivacity and charm'; whose 'vanity leaped to the aid of her desire to believe, making belief a certainty'; for whom 'no pang of conscience at loving another woman's husband disturbed her pleasure in her youth'; and who believed that 'the only time crying ever did any good was when there was a man around from whom you wanted favors'. All these are phrases that Margaret Mitchell used to characterize her impulsive Southern heroine; they, and many more in the book, were equally applicable to Vivien.

Like Vivien, Scarlett had been brought up a Roman Catholic; they were similar, too, in their attitudes to religion. 'Religion had always been a bargaining point with Scarlett. She promised God good behavior in return for favors. God had broken the bargain time and again, to her way of thinking, and she felt she owed him nothing at all in return.' Like Scarlett, Vivien knew that her religious-minded mother must find this attitude 'hideous' – though the knowledge hadn't yet begun to afflict Vivien's conscience, as it would later. Both women, real and fictional, had 'a hard self-honesty' to them; yet both, on critical occasions, behaved 'like a child who still feels that to state a desire is to gain that desire'. This was particularly true when they were in love with men they couldn't have, a factor which did not stop them trying. 'Scarlett's mind ticked on steadily,' Margaret Mitchell wrote. 'Coldly and logically an idea grew in her brain. I'll marry him, she thought. . . .' In the novel, of course, Scarlett never marries Ashley Wilkes, yet keeps on desiring him despite her discovery that this sensitive man is also a very dull one, perhaps just because he is out of reach. Vivien had married Leigh Holman, made much the same discovery, yet her affection for him was to endure and even grow throughout her second marriage, since she recognized the same sort of steadying integrity that made Ashley so attractive.

The central love affair in *Gone With the Wind* is, of course, a love-hate one between Scarlett and Rhett Butler – the outsider with a will to match her own, who doesn't mix with the crowd, who admires 'the way she knows what she wants', the way 'she doesn't mind speaking her mind – or throwing vases'.

Though Olivier's looks were striking, his social poise at this period was insecure; it was Vivien who was to bring him out and make him, for a time, a worldly man. Rhett needed no polishing; but art and life were again to be matched in the fates of Scarlett and Vivien when the former discovered her real desire for Rhett – and Vivien fulfilled her dream by marrying Olivier.

There was, however, one thing about Scarlett which did not fit Vivien; the first five words of the book made this plain. 'Scarlett O'Hara was not beautiful . . .', yet the likeness is restored only a few lines later: 'The green eyes in the carefully sweet face were turbulent, wilful, lusty with life, distinctly at variance with her decorous demeanor. Her manners had been imposed on her ... her eyes were her own.'

Vivien immersed herself so thoroughly in the character that, when she played her on the screen and was asked about the similarities between them, she itemized them with ease and candour. Though this interview anticipates events that were only a gleam in her eye in the year she read the book, it is worth quoting at this point to confirm which of Scarlett's characteristics she admitted to sharing and which she denied.

'While Scarlett wasn't the most easy-going type, neither am I,' she told Robert Carroll in *Motion Picture*, in February 1940:

I cannot let well enough alone. I get restless. I have to be doing different things. I am a very impatient person and headstrong. If I've made up my mind to do something, I can't be persuaded out of it. . . . When Scarlett wanted something from life, she schemed about how to get it. That was her trouble. I just plunge ahead without thinking. That's my trouble. Every so often I bump into stone walls and have to pick myself up and climb over them.

Scarlett had a strong sense of property. I have not a little. . . . She could take care of herself when she had to. I think I could, too. . . . I went to school for a time in Germany. That meant that being a girl I had to learn what every *Hausfrau* should know, and hated it. That was one of the things that helped me make up my mind to become an actress. . . . I hope I've one thing that Scarlett never had. A sense of humor. I want some joy out of life. . . . And she had one thing I hope I never have. Selfish egotism. . . . Scarlett was a fascinating person whatever she did, but she was never a good person. She was too petty, too self-centred.... But one thing about her was admirable. Her courage. She had more than I'll ever have.

Vivien was so mesmerised by the novel that she wished to make others share her fixation, and so she presented a copy of it to every member of the cast of *Because We Must* as an opening-night present. Then she lobbied John Gliddon. How could she bring herself to the notice of David O. Selznick, who had just begun a well-publicized search throughout America for a girl to play Scarlett?

'You're under contract to Korda', Gliddon reminded her. (Contracts, he found, seemed to matter less to Vivien than a first-night notice.) To her chagrin, she found Korda unsympathetic. He couldn't see her as an American Jezebel, but he agreed to call Selznick's attention to her role in *Fire Over England*, which was to open first in London at the end of February 1937 and then in New York on 4 March.

Katharine (Kay) Brown, Selznick's office manager in New York, must have felt Vivien had 'something' when she saw the film for she cabled her boss. Selznick's reply on 3 February was discouraging: 'I have no enthusiasm for Vivien Leigh. Maybe I will have, but as yet have never even seen photographs of her.'

Meanwhile, Vivien's play opened and closed in a few weeks and she began rehearsals for *Bats in the Belfry*, which Sydney Carroll was presenting at the Ambassadors. That couldn't have pleased her: it was a dismal return to the very theatre where she had enjoyed her dazzling debut nearly two years earlier. In addition her envy was aroused by the spectacle of Olivier playing opposite his wife in *Twelfth Night*, which succeeded *Hamlet* at the Old Vic. Going along to admire his bulging Toby Belch meant seeing Jill Esmond as Viola, a role Vivien now considered herself ready to play.

Her impatience seems to have boiled over, for around March 1937 she made a move to replace Jill Esmond in the only role that really mattered to her by begging Olivier to leave his wife and go off with her. Olivier still hesitated.

So another of those curious four-hander scenes was played out, this time at the Moulin d'Or restaurant, where Olivier and his wife came on after the theatre to join Vivien and Oswald Frewen. Jill Esmond may have been enjoying her husband's discomfort or she may not have believed that Vivien would succeed in prising him away from her. She has kept silence now for fifty years. Vivien, according to Frewen, made this the occasion for a romantic ultimatum – she may have been acting under the influence of the ruthless Scarlett, who believed that by putting on the right dress and pouring her love out to Ashley on the eve of his engagement, she could shake his fidelity to Melanie. Frewen talked earnestly to her until two in the morning, by which time he had extracted a

Vivian Mary Hartley, aged about three, carrying a rose, always her favourite flower.

'I won't sing, I'll recite'. As a Dresden shepherdess for a children's concert at Ootacamund, India, 1917.

Vivien was acclaimed an overnight discovery in *The Mask of Virtue*, 1935. She generously attributed her success to the dressers.

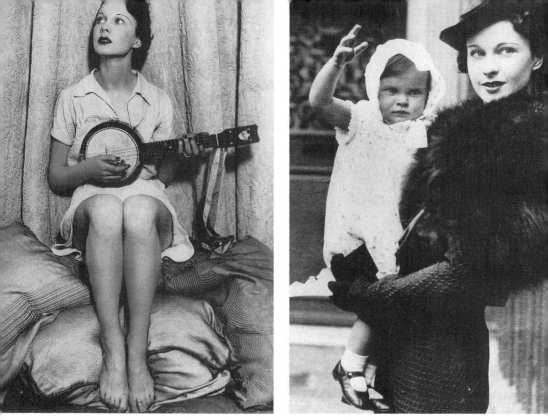

Morning-after pictures: she tried to suppress the shot with the ukelele; (*above right*) with her daughter.

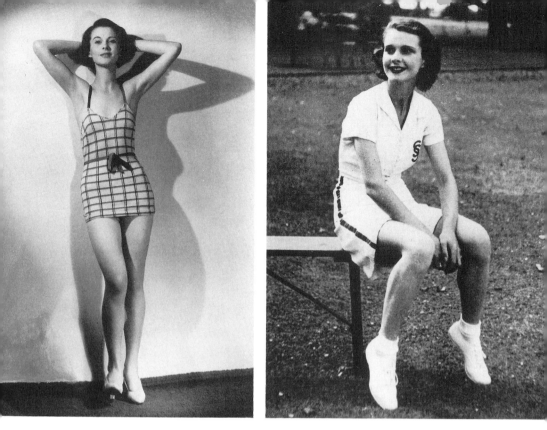

(*Above left*) An early publicity shot. (*Above right*) In her first film role as a schoolgirl in *Things Are Looking Up*, 1935, and (*below*) in the dorm, Vivien is third from left in the back row.

On the walls of the Royal Academy of Arts, 1936, courtesy of Thomas Dugdale ARA; and (*right*) in *Hamlet* at Elsinore with Olivier, courtesy of the Old Vic.

In *Fire Over England*: already lovers in real life too.

With Helpmann in *A Midsummer Night's Dream*, 1937; he remained an influence on her all her life.

With Rex Harrison in *St Martin's Lane* (*Sidewalks of London*).

Location shooting actually on the 'sidewalks'. Tyrone Guthrie is the busker in the middle and Charles Laughton left.

Predatory woman (as the leopard skin signifies) with designs on Robert Taylor in *A Yank at Oxford*.

With Olivier, as lovers on the run in *Twenty-One Days*; it was during filming, in 1937, that their respective marriages broke up.

(*Below right*) Scarlett and Rhett: one of the most famous embraces in movie history.

'iddle-de-dee!' Vivien Leigh *was* Scarlett O'Hara to millions who saw *Gone With the Wind*. Here carlett goes her own sweet way despite Hattie McDaniel, just as Vivien did.

t the Oscars: Olivier took this picture of Douglas Fairbanks Jr, Vivien, Olivia de Havilland and ock Whitney, 1940.

(*Above left*) She wished it were Olivier at her side, but at least she took precedence over Robert Taylor on the posters for *Waterloo Bridge*. It was widely screened in Russia, where it remains *the* Vivien Leigh classic. (*Above right*) With Olivier in their ill-fated *Romeo and Juliet*, 1940.

(*Below*) They had better luck together in *Lady Hamilton* (*That Hamilton Woman*).

promise to let things cool for a year. But she gave her word reluctantly and irresolutely.

Olivier plunged into another play – work was his best refuge. He at first detested *Henry V*, with its 'scoutmaster king', whom he thought narrow-minded and priggish. Only gradually did love of the poetry overwhelm his dislike of this super-patriot. Sudden enlightenment came when Charles Laughton visited him backstage with an admiring cry of, 'You're England!' That May, as they stood among Korda's contract stars watching the Coronation procession of George VI, Vivien squeezed his arm and whispered in an echo of Laughton: 'That's England!'

Her spirits had improved. Korda had cast them both in a film version of a Galsworthy play, *The First and the Last*, finally entitled *Twenty-One Days*. But vastly more exciting was the project of staging *Hamlet* at Elsinore. Vivien had been invited to join the Old Vic Company as Ophelia.

With only two small Shakespearian roles behind her, how did she land this major one in such a prestigious company? The Old Vic's chatelaine, Lilian Baylis, guarded her family jealously against intruders and upstarts.

It has been assumed that Olivier asked for Vivien. He has always denied this and, up to a point, with justification. The idea of setting *Hamlet* in Kronborg Castle came from the Danish State Tourist Board. Their press attaché in London, Robert Jorgensen, persuaded the Old Vic to perform without a fee. But Jorgensen had another job, too: he handled publicity for some of Sydney Carroll's presentations, including *The Mask of Virtue*. Here, surely, is the connection. This ambitious impresario would have thought it useful, to say the least, to have both Olivier and Vivien beholden to him. Miss Baylis's letter to Vivien inviting her to join the company at Elsinore hints that she has been put under a certain obligation by her Danish sponsors. 'The Danish authorities would very much like it if you could play Ophelia and we, too, would be delighted.'

Whilst she and Olivier were filming *Twenty-One Days* at Denham, he gave Vivien a crash-course in Ophelia in the back of the car on the way to the studios. Then they would report after filming to a Lambeth drill-hall, where Tyrone Guthrie took over. Vivien at first feared Guthrie would resent her as an intruder. He didn't show it, but he did express concern over the castle's huge courtyard swallowing up her still underdeveloped voice.

Another imagined adversary awaited her each day at Denham: Basil Dean, who had lost her to Korda, was directing the film. But, if he harboured any animosity towards her, Dean was also too professional to let it show. Moreover, he had discovered his match in Korda, whose ambitions for Vivien at this date are made clear in Dean's memoirs. 'I had my doubts about [casting Vivien] because of her obvious lack of experience,' he writes, 'but Alex was adamant....

His ultimate purpose ... was to build Vivien into an international film star. Both Galsworthy's story and myself had been pawns in this larger game.'

Korda realized that Dean would have reservations about Vivien, but he was worried about the censorship problems presented by the dubious morality of this potboiler and he wanted Vivien to play opposite Olivier to distract the film's critics with the intimate relationship he hoped they would get going on the screen. The story concerns a man who accidentally kills his mistress's husband, then lets someone else take the blame for it while he alternately enjoys himself with her and wrestles with his conscience.

The two stars obviously had other things on their minds than what they made clear were very silly roles. Olivier took Dean to one side. Should he and Vivien run off together? he asked. Dean snorted, 'Please yourself.' He knew Olivier usually did. It had already become his habit to ask lots of people for advice, then end up doing things his own way.

Korda showed his sympathy more practically and expensively. Dean was just starting to shoot one of the most elaborate sequences in the film, a courtroom scene involving scores of extras, when he was summoned by Korda and told to have the set struck overnight. 'I have some retakes to make for another picture. I need the stage.' Dean spluttered that he had four days' work to do – postponing it and rehiring everyone would be costly. 'Take some exteriors,' Korda drawled. Four days and a weekend was all his lovers needed to slip over to Denmark and consummate their theatrical passions as Hamlet and Ophelia at Elsinore.

The bill for giving the lovesick pair time off was no doubt met by Korda's backer, the Prudential Assurance Co., whose executives had entered into the film business imagining it was simply an extension of the business of calculating risks. To Korda, it was also about indulging lovers' whims.

Anthony Quayle, cast as Laertes in the *Hamlet* company that set sail for Denmark, recalls that for the two days and nights of rehearsals in the courtyard of Kronborg Castle, Vivien wore a long raincoat and rubber overshoes, and tried simultaneously to ward off heavy squalls of rain and make her piping voice audible over the intermittent rumble of thunder. Olivier was wrapped in towels and did his soliloquies under an umbrella. The nearby shipyards resounded with the measured beat of steam hammers. When Olivier filmed *Hamlet* thirteen years later, he used the noise of an amplified heartbeat to signal the Ghost's appearance. He acknowledged borrowing it from Jean-Louis Barrault's stage production in Paris, but the beat of those hammers may well have lingered in his memory.

It was Denmark's wettest summer for twenty-three years. At times it looked as though a relief operation were under way instead of a rehearsal. Bleak, too, was the face of Leigh Holman, who was remembered by Quayle as wandering mournfully, almost spectrally, through the corridors of the Marienlyst Hotel, where the company was quartered. Jill Esmond was also there, but uninvolved, standing under a canvas shelter watching Vivien and her husband play their scenes, wet through, but as indifferent to the rain as they were to their respective spouses.

On the opening day, the rain descended with redoubled force causing every sad and sodden player to decamp gratefully indoors. The play was given on the cabaret stage of the hotel ballroom, now doing duty as Elsinore's ramparts, with the company taking care not to trip over the long legs of the Crown Prince of Denmark, who occupied a front-row chair near the actors' chalked 'marks'. The shift of venue was lucky for Vivien. Her voice wasn't blown away by the wind. Those English critics who had hazarded the sea crossing judged her 'effective' or 'promising'. When the storm abated on the second day, *Hamlet* was given its true and proper setting under the dark (but thankfully dry) sky, with ships' lights winking as they sailed through the straits and nearly 2,000 people watching by the light of flaming braziers supplemented by searchlights. Vivien was thrilled. She was playing Shakespeare with the man she loved. 'I feel part of a great theatrical tradition,' she said. She was determined not to be separated from it — or from Olivier.

A few days after her return to London, she told Leigh Holman that she was leaving him and gave the same news to Oswald Frewen on a postcard dated 28 June 1937.

Holman behaved like a perfect gentleman, thus confirming his nature and settling his fate. There may even have been relief in his resignation. His own temperament was calmer by far than his wife's and well ballasted, too, by his law practice. He was a man anchored in the sort of social conventions that Vivien regarded as dull and Olivier as 'contemptible'. He viewed Vivien's defection as a temporary measure. He put her volatility down to 'artistic temperament', and thought a separation might be the best thing in the long run, to let her calm down and come to her senses. He had every hope of getting her back eventually, he told Oswald Frewen.

Holman was not a jealous man. Since he didn't share Vivien's infatuation with the theatre — indeed he didn't much care for playgoing — he saw Olivier without the glamour, as a rather conventional fellow in his own way, a good chap, though limited in his line of talk, who was transfigured into Vivien's 'genius' only when he climbed into a costume and put make-up on his face. Olivier, for his part, regarded Holman as a dull stick, though quite likeable. He had his good side, but he was fatally lacking in those qualities that he and Vivien set so much store by — he was 'not exciting or outwardly romantic'. In

Vivien's eyes, of course, Olivier could not help but be both.

During the last few days' shooting on the Korda film, a strange incident occurred to indicate how Vivien's mind embraced the next desire almost as soon as she had gained the last.

One sequence of *Twenty-One Days* involving her and Olivier had to be shot in a single evening aboard a pleasure cruiser going down the Thames. Korda profited from his practice of keeping in with the London press, which generally meant entertaining them lavishly and pouring out with the wine a stream of communiqués about his plans, which might be as short-lived as the bottle but could likewise be appreciated by his guests. So a contingent of film critics was invited to join the party aboard the boat. Drinks and a buffet were laid on.

The Thames weather was almost as bad as the Danish and the stars had more time than normal to talk to the critics. Olivier, as usual, wasn't very responsive, but Vivien was a model of courtesy and bright witty talk between takes and games of gin rummy. Caroline Lejeune, the *Observer's* film critic, remembered the strangely prescient turn the conversation took:

> The talk inevitably came round to the film that MGM was planning to make of *Gone With the Wind*. No casting had yet been announced, but there were hot tips that Paulette Goddard, Bette Davis, Barbara Stanwyck, Miriam Hopkins and other celebrated stars were certainties for the Scarlett O'Hara role.
>
> Somebody turned to Olivier and said, 'Larry, you'd be marvellous as Rhett Butler.' He laughed it off, but the suggestion was not too preposterous; by this time he had an international reputation as an actor.
>
> Someone else ventured that *she* saw Rhett Butler as Robert Taylor. Others saw him as Gary Cooper, Errol Flynn and Cary Grant. Discussion of the casting went on in a desultory fashion, until the new girl, Vivien Leigh, brought it to a sudden stop.
>
> She drew herself up on the rainswept deck, all five foot nothing of her, pulled a coat snug round her shoulders and stunned us with the sybilline utterance: 'Larry won't play Rhett Butler, but *I* shall play Scarlett O'Hara. Wait and see.'

At last they were free of *Twenty-One Days*. To Vivien, it seemed to have lasted twenty-one years. Korda thought so poorly of it that he put it in the Denham vaults and labelled it as one of his 'assets' – his preferred way of fattening the company's balance sheet; it would cease to be an 'asset' when released and become someone else's liability. Its London première didn't take place until January 1940, and its American debut came in May the same year under the cosier title *Twenty-One Days Together*. It flopped in the States despite reviews that were surprisingly indulgent and were possibly a sympathetic reaction to the many shots it contained of London, a city then bracing itself for the blitz. Vivien and Olivier saw it for the first time during its American opening; both left before the end.

Neither had overcome his or her condescending attitude to films. Yet now that they were about to move from under their respective spouses' roofs and establish a home of their own, they were more than ever in need of money – and film fees were far beyond what even the most successful stage shows could bring in. So Olivier reluctantly went into another Korda film, *The Divorce of Lady X*, which co-starred him with Merle Oberon. He suspected (rightly) that his role would involve little more than being twisted round her finger; he also thought – again rightly – that Ralph Richardson would steal the notices. The very title depressed him further: 'divorce' seemed too close to home at that moment, and playing a barrister reminded him uncomfortably of the man he was cuckolding and who might well name him as co-respondent in a court action. The pressure from an old theatrical family like the Esmonds must have been a considerable burden to bear at this time. All such families were oligarchies in the London theatre; it did not do to fall out with them and, by walking out on the daughter of the famous actor-manager H. V. Esmond and the distinguished actress Eva Moore, who knew what pitfalls and prejudices his career might encounter?

At moments like this, Vivien's spirits buoyed him up. 'I won't think about it now; I'll think about it tomorrow' – Scarlett's reflex to any trouble served Vivien well in these weeks as she hurried round the estate agents seeking a house for her and Olivier. She found Durham Cottage at 4 Christchurch Street, Chelsea, and Olivier took a lease on it.

Jill Esmond, like Leigh Holman, seemed reconciled to biding her time. Her solicitors rebuffed Olivier's tentative approaches about a divorce and told him to consider his position – in legal language that meant 'think again'. Such intransigence fell harder on Vivien, who was impatient to become Mrs Laurence Olivier. This was not for the sake of appearances; Olivier worried far more about appearances than Vivien. In his memoirs he records the concern he felt at this time lest he should be booed from the gallery, and he was vastly reassured when the Queen honoured his *Macbeth* with her presence, showing that the news of his infidelity had not alienated the Palace.

But Vivien felt that marriage would consummate their talent as well as their love. 'I believe she was prodigiously ambitious for them both from the very beginning,' says Anthony Quayle. 'In that respect, she was the more determined by far. As well as expressing her love for Larry at every possible moment, she sensed that they were to be yoked together in their careers. Larry was doing

*Macbeth* at that time. I think Vivien saw things with the clarity of a Lady Macbeth, though she resolved it would be a romantic destiny for them both, not a tragic one.'

Seeking a way to induce as friendly a divorce as possible, Vivien turned for help to John Gliddon – and once again Gliddon came up with the right connection.

A friend of his, Harry Nathan, with whom he had seen service in the trenches in World War I, when both men had been gassed, was now a partner in the law firm of Oppenheimer, Nathan & Vandyk – he was also Lloyd George's solicitor. He might be helpful and would at least be discreet. Vivien and Olivier were reluctant to pay a formal call on solicitors, so Gliddon asked Nathan to see them at the lawyer's own home, where only his teenage daughter was there to witness, with the thrill of a fan, two of her matinée idols under her father's roof at the same time.

Harry (later Lord) Nathan listened with the abstracted look of a man who has seen this particular play too many times and merely wonders how the dialogue is being varied by the change of cast.

'You, Mr Olivier, can do nothing for the moment,' he began. 'You will probably have to wait until a settlement is agreed to before your wife will divorce you. As for you, Miss Leigh, your husband is a Catholic and probably doesn't think he can reconcile divorce with the tenets of his Church. Well, I advise you to be patient. He seems to me to be a man who sets great store by family life. Having been deserted, he may well feel the need to start another family or, if he is a charitable man, will not wish to stop you doing the same. Let human nature take its course.'

Plainly, such advice was an anticlimax to the two romantic petitioners. As soon as the front door had closed, Vivien's impatience showed itself. 'What a ridiculous little man,' she snapped. But as it happened, the little man was talking sense.

Now that they were living together, Olivier began to influence Vivien's career more and more – or so John Gliddon thought. He found she had far less patience; her demands turned intemperate. 'John, you're not tough enough!' became a repeated reproach in which the agent thought he detected Olivier's tones. Vivien's discontent over her next film, he put down to the way Olivier denigrated the roles they were both assigned by Korda.

*A Yank at Oxford* was not at all to Vivien's liking. It would take her away from Denham, where she had hoped her shooting would overlap with Olivier's appearance in *The Divorce of Lady X*. Korda had done a 'loan-out' deal with MGM, whose new British studios at Borehamwood *A Yank at Oxford* was to inaugurate. It would be shot there with Robert Taylor as the pushy young American who is taught a lesson in love, manners and sportsmanship while up at Oxford. Possibly because she was out of sorts, Vivien did not hit it off from the start with Michael Balcon, head of MGM's British production. Balcon, in her eyes, lacked Alex Korda's charm and indulgent ways. He was first and foremost a businessman-producer and had no patience with young ladies who were in love with leading men.

Vivien specifically took against – of all things! – 'Mickey' Balcon's business suits. Korda wore his custom-tailored clothes with style, she said; Balcon merely wore his to the office – he was 'bourgeois'. Gliddon, who received the full force of Vivien's dislike of Balcon, was not alone in failing to realize that Vivien's irrational behaviour was the start of something more serious, though he was soon to learn this.

She told Gliddon that the part was all wrong for her. She was to play the town vamp, the wife of a fusty bookseller, who bicycled around Oxford seducing any young man who put a spoke in her wheels – notably Robert Taylor. But the agent felt it was a question of status rather than role. She was to be the second female lead; the girl who co-starred with Taylor and won him in the end was that dimpled Irish girl from Vivien's old convent school, Maureen O'Sullivan. By now she was a much bigger star than Vivien, thanks to playing Jane to Johnny Weissmuller's Tarzan and appearing as a well-characterized *ingénue* in such films as *The Thin Man, David Copperfield* and *The Barretts of Wimpole Street.*

Outwardly the two young women were convivial companions; privately, for Vivien, the relationship was an edgy one. The previous year Maureen O'Sullivan had married the screenwriter John Farrow, who was a devout Roman Catholic and would write a biography of the Papist martyr Sir Thomas More. The Farrows' marriage was successful and blessed with numerous children. The breach Vivien had just made in her own marriage, and the fact that she had abandoned her child, weighed on her conscience whenever she was in Maureen's presence. Rightly or wrongly, she felt she was being judged.

As often happens, the secondary role, though obviously smaller, was far more fun to play than the female lead. It also carried undertones that were to emerge in later, far more famous parts: a spark of Scarlett O'Hara's headstrong nature, a hint of Blanche DuBois' nymphomania. When Vivien literally runs into Taylor on her bike and says half apologetically, half seductively, 'I'm drawn like this to strangers,' there is an eerie anticipation of those other strangers on whose kindness Blanche depends.

Vivien had a good, no-nonsense American director, George B. Seitz, and her performance shows something of the Hollywood energy he brought with him from MGM. She is 'obvious' but entertaining, a duplicitously tearful seductress, shrill with coy temptation, breathy with reproach, watchfully beady-eyed for the next man to cycle across her path. Vivien wanted to play it for subtlety, but was wisely overruled. For this reason, she detested the leopardskin collar on her predatory town outfit — it was 'common', she said. Yet she injected a note of mania into the part which succeeded in colouring her acting more realistically than another actress playing it simply for comedy might have done. It is the first of her screen performances to exhibit that duality which was to become more and more a part of her nature, and which Gavin Lambert, a screenwriter on one of her much later films, was to call 'a mixture of exquisite control and passionate excess'. Behind the comic sense one detects, for the first time on screen, something desperate.

Elsa Craddock, her character, looks like a lady, yet behaves with unladylike directness, tempered only by beauty and sex appeal. She also uses marriage as a stalking-horse, usually mentioning it in her first breath on encountering a likely young man, disparaging her husband for not giving her the attentions that she needs. All this Vivien brings off effectively and amusingly. And she shows a surprisingly touching penitence on meeting Lionel Barrymore, Taylor's down-to-earth father from small-town America, at the very moment his boy has been expelled because of her flirtatiousness.

Vivien also had the most memorable line in the film. It occurs in the scene where, having got Taylor's expulsion rescinded, she is warned by the shrewd old University tutor that she is an unfortunate influence on the students. Oh, there'll be no problem in future, she brightly reassures him, her husband is already making plans for them both to leave town. 'We're moving to Aldershot. He thinks there'll be a good opening there near the officers' club.' It is rather like Zuleika Dobson, at the end of Beerbohm's novel, looking up the train timetable to Cambridge, having driven Oxford's lovestruck young to suicide. The place name of an Army garrison town was chosen by scriptwriter Sydney Gilliat with a precision worthy of Coward.

Vivien was impatient to get the film over and done with. Olivier was rehearsing his Macbeth at the Old Vic and she desperately wanted to be there with him. Her conduct began to bewilder people. With hindsight it is possible to diagnose an early stage of incipient mania, but at the time it was attributed to 'acting up'. She suddenly developed a severe pain in her foot, which caused her to limp. 'I have to go up to London to see my chiropractor, I just can't stand the pain in my toe.' Just as she was preparing to leave, she was recalled on Balcon's orders. 'We can cut a hole in your shoe,' the wardrobe department told her — unfeelingly, she thought — 'and that way you can stand up without it hurting you.'

'Vivien was sunk,' says Gliddon, 'but didn't she make a fuss about the cost of a ruined pair of shoes! She demanded MGM reimburse her.'

Vivien initiated a lengthy correspondence about her footwear.

'I am enclosing copies of two letters from MGM regarding some shoes ordered by you for the picture,' Gliddon wrote to her on 8 October 1937. 'They are quite correct in pointing out that under the terms of your contract you will supply any modern shoes that may be required.' He added that this obligation included her stockings and underwear 'unless of a period nature'. But Vivien wasn't having this. So off went another letter, this time to Korda's lawyer, Basil Bleck. 'I have already explained the position to Miss Leigh,' Gliddon wrote, hoping the note of weariness he tactfully sounded would show where his sympathies lay, 'but I understand it was necessary for her to order five pairs of shoes to go with five changes of dress. Miss Leigh thinks that MGM might, under the circumstances, be agreeable to paying half the cost.' It was all typical of movie companies, which authorize the expenditure of huge sums for vague ends, but cavil over invoiced minutiae. But MGM didn't see it Vivien's way at all.

'My Dear Vivien,' wrote Gliddon to her on 4 November 1937, 'Further to our conversation yesterday morning regarding the payment for your shoes, I enclose a copy of the letter received this morning from Mr Bleck, and if these facts are true, it will make it rather difficult for us to claim for half the amount of the shoes ordered by you. Regarding the shoes that have been damaged, I will do my utmost to get them to pay for these. To make matters more complicated still, Mr Bleck told me yesterday over the telephone that you were not asked to buy any shoes at all.'

At Vivien's insistence, Gliddon eventually took up the matter with Balcon, who finally and wearily initialled a payment docket. 'Well done, John,' said Vivien, as if he had pulled off a major film deal.

A few days later, however, Gliddon was summoned to Denham. It wasn't, he discovered, to pick up a cheque, but an ultimatum. He was read a stern lesson by one of Korda's senior staff: 'Miss Leigh's behaviour is incomprehensible and inexcusable. It is making things very difficult for us. Please tell her she must behave herself in future. If not, we shall have to reconsider taking up her option when it next falls due.'

This was serious. Having telephoned Vivien in advance to expect him, Gliddon drove straight to Durham Cottage. Vivien was alone.

'Who told you they might not take up my option? Who, John? Tell me? Who? Who? Who?'

Gliddon had never seen her so angry. He was deeply discomfited. 'I can't tell you, Vivien. It was simply left to me to relay that message. But they mean it.'

That precipitated an attack of fury. 'She flew at me,' he recalls. 'She wasn't shouting now. But it was far more frightening than if she had bawled me out.

Her voice turned suddenly hard ... rasping ... contemptuous. But the worst thing was her eyes – the look in them. They had completely changed from the smiling eyes I was accustomed to seeing. They were the eyes of a stranger.'

'Unless you tell me this minute, you must leave the house.'

'I'm not telling you.'

'Then get out!'

Confused and shaken, Gliddon took his leave. This wasn't a side of Vivien he had even suspected existed. Yet soon afterwards she telephoned him and he knew at once she was 'the old Vivien' again, chastened, embarrassed. He passed it off as lightly as he could – 'Overwork ... nerves ... frustration.'

'No, John,' said Vivien, 'I'm liable to have an outburst like this now and then. It frightens me sometimes – and I'm always deeply sorry for it, as I am now. What I really need is a clause in my contract giving me two or three days off when I'm filming and I feel one of these "states" coming on me. Please do forgive me, John.'

And, of course, he did. He was always to forgive Vivien, even for what happened later.

Actually, *A Yank at Oxford* had done her more good than she could ever have suspected in her pursuit of the Scarlett O'Hara role, for she had made an unofficial canvasser out of Robert Taylor. He returned to Hollywood, to MGM, the studio that was to partner Selznick in his epic venture, and put it about that he had worked with a wonderfully high-spirited English girl, who was beautiful, too, and a lot of fun to be with. She even acted a bit like Scarlett O'Hara, he said, defying Oxford conventions and going straight for her man. Maybe they should take a look at her.

PART TWO

# Larry

# 8

# 'I'll only be gone a few days'

etting up house with Laurence Olivier in 1937 meant that for a time
Vivien lived a divided life. To begin with, she had two homes. Leaving
Leigh and Little Stanhope Street had caused her sadness, but no remorse.
She did not love him any the less; the trouble was, she hadn't been able to find
it in her heart to love him more after they had got married. Leigh Holman, for
his part, didn't manifest bitterness or behave obstructively when she came to
see little Suzanne, who was now aged three.

She paid frequent visits to the child. Vivien was honest enough to admit to
herself that she did not miss her to the degree where grief entered into it — it
was only much, much later, when mother and daughter were both at an age to
understand what had happened, that Vivien would reproach herself in the
presence of other people and call herself a bitch for doing what she had done.
But at this date, a visit from mother was the 'done thing' rather than the heartfelt
one: it was expected of her. As with so much of her life, even the intimate joys
of motherhood were arranged in an orderly fashion: playtime in the nursery,
an outing with the pram in the park, a session with a picture book or a present,
a good-night kiss ... and then nanny took over.

In later years Suzanne remembered an outing to the West Country —
presumably a holiday at her father's manor house at Zeals in Devon — when
Vivien and she had had to take quick evasive action on discovering half-way
across a field that what looked like a sleepy cow was in fact a deceptively
wakeful bull. Such an incident was out of place somehow, and therefore it had
snagged a thread in the child's memory. Otherwise, it was a life lived largely
without mother, but with Gertrude Hartley compensating for her own child's
dereliction of duty. Gertrude was, of course, shocked by the break-up of Vivien's
marriage and for a long time she hoped her daughter would return to her
husband, if not her Church. Her upbringing in the Catholic faith, she could see,
was a vaccine that hadn't taken with Vivien. She hadn't exactly rebelled: she

had lapsed into her father's enjoyment of life, while retaining her mother's self-will and the concern for security created by an ordered life that her religious schooling had drilled into her.

Vivien rejected her mother's influence, but was often in need of Gertrude's company and support. In the period ahead her mother's help was to be invaluable, when she nursed Vivien through her periodic disturbances. But the nature of these disturbances was not well understood by Gertrude, Leigh Holman or indeed Olivier himself. Vivien was temperamental, but wasn't that a commonplace with actresses? She lived on her nerves, but wasn't that because of the pressure of her work and the celebrity it thrust upon her? Vivien was drinking a lot. It was not that she was an alcoholic or coming even near it; it was just one of the 'normal' excesses that came with a life in the theatre – and it would have been hard for any untrained person to spot where high spirits left off and a more serious emotional disturbance was beginning.

Above all else, there was the excitement of having Olivier as a lover. He found her irresistible too, though he, unlike her, suffered the torment of at least his conscience, if not his flesh. To have abstained was unthinkable, except when thinking on it gave him what he was to call 'rapturous torment'.

If Olivier was disgusted with himself – and evidence shows he sometimes was – he probably turned that emotion to good theatrical use: after all, wasn't it one of the best ways to know oneself and weren't the parts he played on stage the greatest possible way of adding to his sum of self-knowledge? It is no coincidence that Laurence Olivier made his lengthiest strides into greatness at precisely those periods when his private life and conscience were under most strain. If it was the nature of drama to exhaust an actor's emotions, as he believed, then it was the function of life to top them up again. Life co-operated with an intensity he could not resist when he and Vivien were caught up in their infatuation – especially as they weren't able to reward themselves with what Olivier called 'the selfish relief of confession' to their respective spouses for more than a year after their liaison had begun.

Vivien's proximity to Olivier now meant no more sneaky meetings in film studios, dressing-rooms or in Little Stanhope Street when Leigh was out. It meant she shared his excitement as preparing for his Shakespeare roles taxed and stretched him. Now she saw at first hand, in the private laboratory of his special effects and experiments, what she had previously witnessed only from a distance and on a stage where the completed illusion concealed the construction.

With Olivier right there beside her, night and day, she could be a rapt pupil. Olivier found her a promising actress; in the years ahead, he was to help make her a considerable one. For the moment, craft and passion coursed along the same channel – they took both at the flood.

While Olivier prepared his next roles for the Old Vic, Iago and Coriolanus, Vivien busied herself making Durham Cottage into their home. It was a compact seventeenth-century house with a walled garden and a conservatory. Her friend Lady Colefax lived near by in King's Road; she was then entering her Regency phase – good furniture, but not much of it, stripes on walls and curtains, cool colours, but a sudden plethora of *objets* here and there on table-tops, florists' cornucopiae in the corners, the scent of dried rosemary in saucers. It was 'good taste', not yet characterized by Betjeman as 'ghastly'. Nor did it have the slightly florid theatricality that later crept into Vivien's home décor – it was a cosy house, the Oliviers' 'court' hadn't yet assembled.

Korda still resisted her pleas to make a test of her as Scarlett O'Hara and send it to Selznick as her calling card. So Vivien asked Angus McBean, the noted society and theatrical photographer, to use the tail end of a photo session to make a few portraits of her got up as she imagined a Southern belle would look – low neckline and pendulous curls. As he was finishing, Olivier walked in. 'Why are you got up like a tart?' he demanded.

'To see how I'd look as Scarlett,' she shot back, adding for the nth time, 'I *am* going to play her.'

'You're not. Norma Shearer is. It's in today's *Times*.'

So it was; but by next week's *Times*, Selznick had changed his mind; the candidacy was wide open again.

On 27 December 1937, the Old Vic staged the most bewitching version of *A Midsummer Night's Dream* that London had ever seen. Oliver Messel designed it as a Victorian period fantasy, all muslin fairy-wings, chaplets of coral roses, painted gauze drop-curtains giving a magical perspective to the Athenian woods, moonlight effects trembling with bright and dark sequins, a flying *corps de ballet* and a pit orchestra playing Mendelssohn. Vivien appeared as Titania. 'She's just the right weight,' Tyrone Guthrie pronounced, rather equivocally.

Robert Helpmann had successfully auditioned for Oberon. This was Vivien's first pairing with a man whose influence on her was to grow with the years – not always with happy results. Helpmann resembled her in some ways – in others, not at all. He was a homosexual with a sting, a mimic, a gossip, a wit, a man of transfiguring ambitiousness who had trained himself up to leading roles on the ballet stage, but, being unsuited by temperament and looks for *jeune premier* roles, had made the rare transition to the theatre and was ultimately to turn director. Vivien found his bitchiness amusing, Olivier less so. Helpmann became her court favourite. As he was as sure-footed in the international set as he was on the ballet stage, he knew everyone Vivien knew or wanted to know. Through Bobby Helpmann, she soon vastly enlarged the number of her acquaintances. The coded looks and phrases they would exchange to relieve the tedium of a dull occasion as well as the paper-and-pencil games they excelled at on jollier ones helped unite them temperamentally, though never sexually. A stranger seeing them might have taken them for an exceptionally beautiful girl and her eye-catching but not quite so well favoured brother. It is a pity Laclos's epistolary novel *Les Liaisons dangereuses* hadn't then been adapted for the English stage. Vivien and Bobby Helpmann would have found parts to shine in.

Their closeness to each other assumed embarrassing reality, however, when both were presented to Royalty after the performance. The two little Princesses, Elizabeth and Margaret Rose, then eleven and seven years old, received Titania and Oberon in the royal retiring-room. Vivien curtsied; Helpmann bowed very low. Then, on attempting to straighten up, they discovered their sylvan headdresses of gilded twigs and ferns (hers) and silver antlers (his) had become interlocked. They were obliged to do a sort of slow-motion *pas de deux* backwards until out of sight of Royalty, when they collapsed amidst laughter and much rending of Oliver Messel's fantasies.

The spring of 1938 saw Olivier as Iago and Coriolanus at the Old Vic. They were his graduation pieces: it was as if he was trying to break out from the pressure-chamber passions of his private life and, as Melvyn Bragg was to put it many years later, in so doing 'reached out for air and grasped greedily at Shakespeare to give him new lives'.

His desire to leave an audience astonished seemed to have fed on his break with social conventions. As Iago, he daringly – *very* daringly indeed, for that time – substituted homosexual-based jealousy for conventional heterosexual envy; and as Coriolanus he devised a head-over-heels triple tumble down the staircase to a death at the footlights. Vivien felt the power of these interpretations which took him well beyond the bounds of the text, and, in turn, she yearned to emulate it.

For Olivier's thirty-first birthday on 22 May, she threw a party at Durham Cottage for nearly fifty guests with a tiny jazz combo tucked into the conservatory. Somehow the celebrations turned into an announcement of her own intent to follow Olivier into the great testing-ground of Shakespearian tragedy with a four-play season – *Hamlet*, *Macbeth*, *Othello* and *King Lear* – 'which Vivien and I will do after the summer hols', he announced.

Some of the more sober guests took this to be a lover's boast rather than a serious commitment. Vivien, at her present stage of development, couldn't have scaled such peaks, even roped to a mountaineer like Olivier. But the occasion may also have been used to make the first public announcement of their ambition to become a great acting team. The idea of the Oliviers as a couple was beginning, even though not yet sealed by marriage vows.

Vivien's own spring of 1938 was spent in a film studio and on location in the West End of London outside some of the very theatres she and Olivier aspired to play in, though for the moment she was playing a street busker.

Her fifth film for Korda — another loan-out, this time to Erich Pommer's production company — was *St Martin's Lane* (American title: *Sidewalks of London*). Produced by Pommer, it starred his business partner Charles Laughton, who had, with characteristic selfishness, expelled his own wife Elsa Lanchester from the cast when Korda offered to finance it if Vivien was his co-star. Vivien's reluctance to be cast in the film was almost as great as Elsa Lanchester's annoyance at being dropped from it. She hadn't forgotten Laughton's pernickety demand that she dye her hair blonde for *Cyrano*. She disliked his gross body; she said she felt she could never get near enough to him. Also she disliked her role as a (not very convincing) Cockney street entertainer and sneak-thief, accepting board (but refusing bed) from the music-hall 'ham', played by Laughton, who stays on the streets while Vivien, by a combination of luck, ruthlessness and her own good looks, climbs the show-business ladder to stardom in Novello-type musicals.

The script offered her some compensation in an on-screen affair with Rex Harrison, partnering her again as a man-about-town who finances the shows. But their scripted romance was severely cut before shooting, lest it distract from Laughton's gluttonous enjoyment of his humiliation in love and by life generally.

Tim Wheelan was a Hollywood director, but it was Pommer's Teutonic attachment to the detailed realism of German films like *Variety*, as well as Laughton's appetite for wolfing down heaped helpings of humiliation like Jannings in *The Blue Angel*, which gave the film its sense of a pitiless destiny. It was all the more interesting against the usual bright, upbeat look of all-British show-business stories. Not until Chaplin made *Limelight* in 1952 was the same kind of *milieu* presented quite so picaresquely.

Vivien in a beret and slacks, which she switches for top hat, bow tie, striped trousers and a cane to do a tap dance, is an attractive street urchin — but her 'East End' accent is all over the metropolis. In a heavily shadowed scene typical of German cinema, she does a quite magical ballet-like dance in the moonlight of an abandoned house, watched only by a hidden Laughton. She is interesting because of the way the character is drawn, for ambition forces a rasping hardness on her: 'You'd better look in the frying pan, 'adn't you?' she positively snarls, thrusting the pan at him like a mirror when Laughton proposes marriage and is rebuffed.

The harmonica player and composer Larry Adler had a small role. (He'd been asked to be musical director for the whole picture, but Val Parnell, the impresario, wouldn't release him from his touring engagements.) Adler found Vivien difficult to work with. 'She didn't like Charles and he didn't like her. But he was much more professional. One weekend there were a few close-ups of Vivien to be done outside a theatre and Charles, who invariably went down to the country with Elsa at weekends, stayed up in town to "feed" Vivien lines from behind the camera. I doubt if she'd have done as much for him. Olivier would show up on the set and they'd disappear into her dressing-room and it was quite a business to get her back to work.' Olivier, Adler noticed, turned up to oversee Vivien's scenes with Rex Harrison.

Both of them were tired by late spring and threw themselves into the luxury of a holiday in France, travelling down by road in a second-hand Ford V8 belonging to Vivien – the Rolls-Royce, for which Gliddon had helped her find a chauffeur, had stayed behind with Leigh Holman.

John Gielgud and Hugh ('Binkie') Beaumont were staying near by in Vence. Just over a year before, Beaumont had moved from the Howard & Wyndham theatrical agency to H. M. Tennent, which he was in the process of building into the most powerful management and production company in London. It may have been his idea to present Olivier and Vivien in the Shakespeare season they had announced earlier that summer; empire-building Beaumont-style traded heavily on the power of names. But, if so, he was shrewd enough to let it be quietly forgotten as an idea whose time had not yet come.

As they lunched, with Vivien cuddling a kitten she had adopted out of the hotel cat's litter, Beaumont gave Vivien the kind of advice that was to make him one of the most influential figures in her career and one of the few who could persuade her to do something she was set against.

'You want to play Scarlett O'Hara, Vivien – then you need an American agent. I'm surprised you haven't got one already.'

Back in London, Vivien spoke to John Gliddon. She was surprised she had no American agent, she said. Olivier backed her up. Now that he was supporting two households, money was more useful than ever – and Hollywood was where money, *real* money was. If pushed, they could forget the lack of art. Olivier was already represented by Myron Selznick, brother of David O. Selznick, whose London office was managed by a tall, handsome ex-Guards officer called Cecil Tennant.

So Gliddon found himself going to Tennant and asking if the Selznick agency would represent him (Gliddon) in Hollywood on a fifty-fifty basis. Yes, said Tennant.

Gliddon recognized the fatal consequences of his move too late. 'Cecil Tennant represented Myron Selznick; he represented Larry Olivier; now he was going to represent Vivien. But as it turned out, he had absolutely no interest in representing me.'

In fact, Hollywood had shown an interest in Olivier even while they were on holiday. A telegram from Cecil Tennant interrupted their stay at the Calanque d'Or. 'ARE YOU INTERESTED GOLDWYN IDEA FOR SEPTEMBER FIRST FOR VIVIEN YOURSELF AND MERLE OBERON IN WUTHERING HEIGHTS STOP ANSWER AS SOON AS POSSIBLE STOP.'

No, they weren't interested, if it meant that Vivien would have to take the thankless secondary role of Isabella while Merle Oberon played the lead opposite Olivier. But then the script arrived; to their surprise, it read very attractively. William Wyler was to direct it, and Olivier knew that Wyler was a very hot property himself at that moment with Bette Davis's new film *Jezebel*. *Jezebel* was the film rushed into production to be Warner Bros.' answer to *Gone With the Wind* even before Selznick had shot a foot of it. Vivien suggested that they should at least meet Wyler.

Wyler came to supper at Durham Cottage. Vivien showed her scrupulous attention to detail: as well as cold salmon, there was wine from the director's native Alsace. Before he could bring persuasion to bear on them for *Wuthering Heights*, she pumped him for news of how the casting of Scarlett O'Hara was going. Wyler felt the conversation being taken over by Selznick's project, rather than Goldwyn's. Then Olivier took him off to see *St Martin's Lane* in a private screening-room and strenuously urged Vivien's claim to play Cathy opposite his Heathcliff. Wyler telephoned Goldwyn after the film, but the American producer was inflexible. 'Then I don't want any part in the film,' Vivien decided firmly.

'Look, Vivien,' Wyler said, 'you're not yet known in the States. You *may* become a big star. But for a first role in an American film you'll never do better than Isabella in *Wuthering Heights*.' (It was a verdict he was to laugh about ruefully later.)

What broke the *impasse* was Vivien's fear of a falling out between Olivier and herself. She could see he was weakening: he was falling in love with the notion of playing Heathcliff. Maybe if she continued to make his acceptance conditional on her co-starring with him in the film, he would begin to fall out of love with her! Then, too, there was the money ... $50,000. Far more than he could earn in a whole season at the Old Vic.

The deciding factor was the advice of a man whom Olivier treated as a rival to be wary of on stage or screen, but turned to frequently in private for guidance as if he were a tribal elder – Ralph Richardson. 'Bit of fame! Good!' Richardson snorted with oracular brevity. Olivier cabled his acceptance. But then the question arose: what would Vivien do with herself while he was away in Hollywood? They both tried not to think of that.

A play she was going into helped concentrate their minds on each other and postpone thoughts of the day of separation. It was a case of 'I won't think of it today, I'll think of it tomorrow' on Vivien's part.

The play was *Serena Blandish*, adapted by S.N. Behrman from the Enid Bagnold novel *A Lady of Quality*. It was to be put on at the little Gate Theatre; though very much an 'art' production, it was a good launching platform for the commercial theatre to take stock of new talent. Some of that talent was now under John Gliddon's management, for his agency had been expanding quickly due to his quick eye for spotting promise. By the early years of the war he was representing, amongst others, Michael Rennie, Alexander Knox, Deborah Kerr, James McKechnie, James Donald, Cyril Fletcher, Yvonne Mitchell – and an actor called James Stewart, who had assumed the professional name of Stewart Granger to avoid confusion with the Hollywood star.

Granger secured the role of Lord Ivor Cream in *Serena Blandish*, playing opposite Vivien. Both of them were on £3 a week, a token fee accepted 'for art's sake'. The director was to be Esme Percy.

Late in the day, however, Olivier appeared and took rehearsals of those scenes in which Vivien appeared, giving her every emphasis, putting her over and over her lines until her version corresponded precisely with his conception. 'And she was appalling,' Granger recalls, 'because when Vivien spoke, you could hear Larry.' Their passion for one another was fatally closing the gap that professional judgment should have created when one blocked in the other's performance. 'I also got the impression that Larry would have liked to play Lord Ivor Cream instead of me,' says Granger – Olivier wasn't to leave for Hollywood until November. He would have had plenty of time, for *Serena Blandish* barely ran eight weeks after it opened on 13 September 1938.

But on that very day, an extraordinary offer was made for Vivien's services by none other than Cecil B. DeMille. Gliddon received the cable and with triumph in his heart rushed round to Durham Cottage. Olivier and Vivien were putting in a quiet few hours before the curtain went up at the Gate – and the agent believed his news would galvanize Vivien's spirits, which were low at the thought of losing Olivier to the Goldwyn picture.

DeMille was proposing to cast her in *Union Pacific*, co-starring with Joel McCrea, at $2,000 (£500) a week with a seven-week guarantee, $160 (£40) a week expenses and yearly options for four more films at $20,800 (£5,200), $28,000 (£7,000), $40,000 (£10,000) and finally $56,000 (£14,000), with pro rata living expenses. It was a terrific coup for a girl with little reputation in America. She was to report between 15 and 25 October 1938, for a week's wardrobe and make-up tests, salary to begin one week after arrival, first-class transportation all the way. It would need working out with Korda, but *this*, said the elated agent, was the career offer they'd been waiting for – *and* she could be in Hollywood at the same time as Larry!

But instead of the anticipated cry of, 'Oh, John, you're wonderful!' she merely picked up the cable and read it over to herself, as if trying to pick holes in the promises. Olivier said only one thing: 'That's a better offer than Greer Garson got from MGM.'

Finally, Vivien said, 'Let's show it to Cecil Tennant over at Myron Selznick's office – to see if the picture's an important one.'

Gliddon couldn't believe his ears. Later, when he pieced together the bits of the puzzle, he began to see why Vivien had treated the offer as an ultimatum rather than an opportunity. If she accepted it, she would have to surrender for good all chance of obtaining the role of Scarlett O'Hara, which she had set her heart on, as Olivier said, 'with an almost demonic determination'.

She was prepared to turn down present riches and the prospect of future stardom in order to keep the door open on her ambition to play a role for which, at that date, she was not even a contender.

Finally, she laid down her terms. Gliddon was speechless. If Cecil B. DeMille would pay her £5,000 for six weeks' work, she would consent to grant him – one of Hollywood's most powerful producers! – the favour of a further option, at £8,000 for six weeks' work, to be used within one year of the first film at a time to suit her convenience.

'That's as good as a refusal, Vivien,' Gliddon snapped, 'and you know it. You're throwing all this away ... the film, the money, stardom maybe. You're not making sense.'

Vivien glared at him. 'I'd rather earn £3 a week and do *Serena Blandish* on the stage than make a film in Hollywood. I'd rather be a Marie Tempest than a Greta Garbo.'

There was nothing more to be said. She could not be moved. Olivier remained silent. None of it rang true to Gliddon, but other alarm bells began to go off in his mind, growing louder and louder over the subsequent months. 'It became obvious to me', he says, 'that if ever I was fortunate enough to bring an offer to Vivien that would prove acceptable to her *and* meet with Olivier's approval, then it would be a miracle. It was from that moment on that I knew my usefulness to Vivien was running out. She had found another adviser and he was one with whom I simply couldn't compete.'

DeMille had ended his cable with the words: 'Other important leading women, including [Claudette] Colbert being considered. Answer immediately as consider big studio interest in Leigh.' In reply, Gliddon cabled Vivien's 'terms'. As he had predicted, nothing more was heard from DeMille.

On 1 November 1938, the agent received a letter from Vivien. This was unusual. She always preferred to telephone him. As he read it, he recognized the unmistakable flavour of a 'letter for the record', not at all in Vivien's style:

Dear John,

According to the contract made with you on November 29, 1934, your option for being my sole manager and agent (for plays) ended on June 30, 1938. Naturally, I consider that with regard to films I remain under contract to you until the expiry of my contract with London Film Productions. As far as the theatre is concerned, however, I do not feel that I need a manager and therefore, under the terms of our agreement will not be accountable to you for my engagements, except of course for any theatrical engagements which you find and arrange for me.'

Four days later, on her twenty-fifth birthday, Vivien drove Olivier down to Southampton in her old Ford to board the ss *Normandie* bound for New York. Into his hands she pressed a small silhouette portrait of Emily Brontë cut out of black paper, which, with characteristic patience and luck, she had found among the junk in a Wiltshire antique shop.

She couldn't wait to wave Olivier goodbye from the quay, for she had to be back in time for the *Serena Blandish* curtain. But they opened a bottle of champagne in his stateroom, though it wasn't either's favourite drink, and both of them felt burdened by the thought of months of separation ahead. Even Olivier couldn't call up much joy at the prospect of Goldwyn's film.

'To Heathcliff,' he said a bit glumly, for form's sake.

Vivien clinked glasses. Then she said with a sweet tantalizing smile, 'To Scarlett' – and, draining her glass in one go, she dashed it impetuously to the floor.

Olivier's depression increased once he reached Hollywood. Now that he had him under contract, Wyler turned from a tempter into a tormentor. The early rushes showed an Olivier who still approached screen acting like stage acting, without adjustment to the screen's more detailed naturalism, and with a disdain that too often showed through his performance, such as it was. Every whiplash of scorn Wyler could lay on Olivier's stiff neck was applied publicly – and Goldwyn chipped in with his *ex cathedra* judgment that, 'This is the ugliest actor in pictures.' Olivier admitted later – and kept on admitting at every hint of a prompt in a multitude of interviews throughout his life – that his conceit and maladroitness earned him all he had to take, except perhaps Merle Oberon's snappy reproach for spitting at her as he declaimed his lines.

He wrote Vivien piteous tales of his suffering and humiliation. To her, it all seemed like some saint wrestling with demons in the desert. He needed a good angel to sustain him, help him emerge from purgatory with a sharper vision, a stronger faith.

The first news John Gliddon had of her intention to fly to Hollywood came when she telephoned him at the end of November. 'But you're due to start rehearsals for the *Dream* on 10 December,' he protested – the Old Vic Victorian production was being revived for Christmas.

'Oh, John, don't worry so! There'll be plenty of time. After all, I'll only be gone a few days.'

Gliddon wondered to himself if travelling 6,000 miles – five or six days on the *Queen Mary* to New York, then a fifteen-hour flight (with stop-overs) to Los Angeles – wasn't an early warning symptom of a fresh attack of 'temperament'. But he put it down to love and prudently warned Tyrone Guthrie that she might be a little late reporting for rehearsals. It was a considerable understatement. Nearly a year went by before Vivien saw England again.

'Pure, driving, uncontainable, passionate love,' as Olivier put it, carried Vivien in an almost trance-like state across the wintry Atlantic, keeping herself to herself, but always, whether on deck or in her cabin, reading and re-reading *Gone With the Wind*.

Even as she was travelling to him, Olivier was coming through the trials and tribulations that Wyler had used to test him with a make-or-break ruthlessness. He wore Olivier down to the state where he was almost indifferent to his fate, even guiltily welcoming it at times, much as Vivien's teachers at convent school broke the will of their charges and then reset it in God's way. But it worked, and Olivier suddenly found a new faith in film acting. It happened very quickly, inside a few days, if we are to believe him. 'It was for me a new medium, a new vernacular,' he affirmed later, like a convert to a new religion. And the penitent not only began to practise his 'religion' with a startling improvement to his Heathcliff performance, but he became a proselytizer for it when Vivien arrived in Hollywood.

'It was Wyler who gave me the simple thought – if you do it right, you can do anything,' he was to recall. 'And if he hadn't said that, I think I wouldn't have done [the film] *Henry V* five years later.'

The timing of his conversion was crucial. But for this experience, he might not have found the zeal – or even the continuing employment on his own film – which helped him nurse Vivien's ambition when she landed at Los Angeles's Clover Field airport.

# 9

## 'Please do not tell anybody about this'

Olivier was waiting for Vivien, 'crouched in the back of a car a few feet beyond the airport entrance' – a detail of their reunion he recalled over forty years later. What apparently escaped his memory was the reason for keeping such a low profile. It was Vivien herself who alerted the media, which in those days almost exclusively meant the newspapers. When the *Queen Mary* was in New York harbour, a tender of the usual port officials and press reporters boarded the liner to start processing passengers. 'Why are you coming to America, Miss Leigh?' a newsman asked Vivien, as there had been no news of her appearing in a film or play. 'To see Laurence Olivier,' she ingenuously replied.

One or two papers pounced on this unusually precise response. Sam Goldwyn's New York representative, detailed to meet Vivien and get her on to a Los Angeles-bound plane, was alarmed by the risk that her candour posed to Goldwyn's investment in his picture by drawing attention to Olivier's broken marriage and abandoned child. Vivien was politely but firmly told to keep her mouth shut – and Olivier to keep a low profile.

Feeling they were being made part of a conspiracy only gratified the lovers all the more – taking risks made their love that much sweeter.

Olivier had Vivien driven to the Beverly Hills Hotel – in those days an easy-going compound, where tongues were loosened by alcohol rather than gossip. A few hours later, she was being introduced to Myron Selznick, who had been alerted by Olivier that 'someone who might possibly be of extraordinary interest' was on her way. He looked at her, then at Olivier and it was easy to read what his thoughts held. 'I think we ought to take her along to meet David, don't you, Myron?' Olivier said.

What happened next has remained a matter of conjecture for many years, and will remain so until the few people left alive who were privy to it consent to fit the last few pieces of the puzzle into place. Irene Mayer Selznick's own memoirs throw out a tantalizing hint that Binkie Beaumont had a hand in preparing Vivien's way to the Scarlett O'Hara role. Beaumont, unfortunately, died without committing his memories to print; and Mrs Selznick will not elaborate. But it is unlikely that the full story was as accidental as the public record makes it sound or as coy as Olivier's partial recall manages to suggest. A lot turned on the different characters of the two Selznick brothers.

Myron was in many ways the opposite of David. David assiduously cultivated the image of an impetuous genius, sanctifying an impromptu decision by issuing a definitive memorandum. He was, like every gambler, fortified by a belief in his own instinct – the risk increased the thrill of the game and singled him out for Jehovah's approbation or, sometimes, rebuke. In several ways, *mutatis mutandis*, his temperament resembled Vivien's. In each there was a strong drive to control every detail of a situation; neither had any sense of time passing or of other people growing exhausted; both were highly gregarious social animals, giving parties, writing letters (memos in David's case), preserving the whole international network of favours done and debts incurred.

Myron Selznick, on the other hand, didn't view movie-making as art – he left *that* to his brother – or even principally as business, though his agency was then the most high-powered in Hollywood. He saw it as a means of retribution, getting even with the studio moguls who had conspired to ruin old Lewis J. Selznick, his imperious father, who had been forced into obscurity and bankruptcy by his more ruthless competitors and even partners. Myron used the bargaining power acquired through his roster of star names to humble the studio bosses by making them pay through the nose for the services of his clients. He was a progenitor of the modern deal, which Pauline Kael once called Hollywood's only true art form: a deal could be both reward and punishment, depending on whose side it was viewed from. David was the creative force; Myron, the power-broker. To both men, a newcomer like Vivien was worth assaying for the value, if any, she might hold for them.

It is Myron's tracks that one scents leading to David's casting office, but through the back door. Instead of taking her along to meet David, he took Vivien to the Santa Anita racetrack – an odd place to go, surely, on her second day in town, though a location Myron Selznick was familiar with on almost every day. There he introduced her to Nat Deverich, an ex-jockey and one of his most valued informants – not on the horses, though, but on the bettors – the studio executives in particular. Such knowledge about who the losers were and how much they lost could be used to fortify Selznick's subsequent bargaining with the front office over the pay and status of his clients. Racetrack favours would not be recognized as such when they were returned as favours to people in the film community.

Nat Deverich in turn introduced Vivien to Daniel O'Shea, a David Selznick staffman who shared a love of the racetrack, poker table and poolroom. O'Shea arranged to set up a Scarlett O'Hara screen test for Vivien.

Thus, within three days of arriving in Hollywood, she had been entered in the race. All of this suggests that her 'form' had been studied by people who were natural gamblers on stars *and* horses.

Myron Selznick's next move shows how well he read his brother's nature, for Vivien didn't knock on any door and then spend time cooling her heels in the anteroom: she literally walked into the filming of *Gone With the Wind*. The movie itself was her introduction; it set the scene, an advantage that no other Hollywood star had enjoyed when David O. Selznick tested them.

Shooting was not due to start until the following January, though Selznick's backer, the millionaire John Hay Whitney, and Louis B. Mayer, his father-in-law and production chief at MGM, who was loaning him Clark Gable, were both fretting at the delay in getting the project rolling. Selznick decided to shoot the burning of Atlanta sequence before principal photography got under way; by doing so, he would light a beacon in the Hollywood night sky that told everyone he was making good his boast to produce the greatest epic in film history. More practically, it would allow him to burn up some old outdoor stock sets on the back lot of his studios and thus clear the ground for the construction of his *Gone With the Wind* exteriors.

Before the fire had died down that night, 10 December 1938, Vivien had stepped, phoenix-like, out of the embers and presented herself to David O. Selznick.

Myron had arranged for a late supper that Saturday night at the Brown Derby restaurant. He knew his brother's notorious reputation for unpunctuality. He guessed the producer wouldn't apply the match to the tinder on time; and he didn't want Vivien walking into the middle of the conflagration – this lady wasn't for burning. It is more than likely that an informant at the studios kept him in touch by phone with the progress of Atlanta's destruction – when the oil-sprinklers that would regulate the inferno were turned on; how often the horse and buggy driven by stand-ins for Rhett and Scarlett (unrecognizable in long-shot) had plunged through the flames with an unseen Melanie and her newly-born baby in the back; what David and George Cukor, the director, were up to on their thirty-foot observation tower that required them to use megaphones to direct the operators of the seven Technicolor cameras.

Myron appears to have allowed a good two hours for starting, stopping and retakes. At about 11 p.m., he set off accompanied by Olivier and Vivien.

Vivien was wearing a full-length mink, her Christmas present from Olivier, as well as a dark halo hat that set off her face and allowed her long hair to fall on to her shoulders. Her make-up had been carefully applied by a professional studio make-up man. He had been instructed to use his imagination and 'do a Scarlett O'Hara face'.

Arriving at the Selznick lot, they waited until David and Cukor had climbed down from their tower. It is untrue that Vivien climbed up to them. For one thing, she would have been a distraction; for another, her vertigo would have dissuaded her.

As soon as his brother was within earshot, Myron called out, 'Hey, genius, meet your Scarlett O'Hara.' 'Genius' was a sarcasm he used to his sibling, especially when he had been drinking.

Vivien was standing so that David Selznick saw her face illuminated by the fire that was still raging. She stepped forward, letting her mink coat fall open, revealing a beige silk dress that emphasized her tiny nipped-in waist. 'Good evening, Mr Selznick,' she said, liltingly with a hint of laughter, as if half-apologizing for Myron's presumption.

Cukor, who was observing this, said many years later that he recognized a Myron Selznick 'plant' — an 'inspired bit of agentry'. David peered at Vivien and Olivier, gave a perfunctory, 'Hello, Larry', then began to chat to Vivien. He was obviously intrigued by the suddenness and circumstances of her appearance. In England a year or so earlier, Cukor had been asked by Max Breen of *Picturegoer* magazine whether he thought Vivien Leigh's performance in *St Martin's Lane* might make her a contender for Scarlett O'Hara. 'I saw her in *A Yank at Oxford*,' he had replied, 'and she seems to be a little static, not quite sufficiently fiery for the role.' Now he reflected, as if to rebuff him, Vivien had lit a fire around herself.

She was also taking advantage of Selznick's fondness for fateful encounters. For one thing, she had caught him when he was on an emotional high, during 'one of the biggest thrills I have had out of making pictures', as he wrote to his wife Irene two days later about the burning of Atlanta, 'first, because of the scene itself, and second, because of the frightening but exciting knowledge that *Gone With the Wind* was finally in work'. Later still, he was to turn his memory of meeting Vivien into the same kind of fateful myth that had been enshrined in *A Star Is Born*, a film he had produced only the year before. In a magazine article, he wrote: 'I took one look and knew that she was right.'

As the flames were almost out and a December chill was regaining its hold on the Hollywood night, the party adjourned to Selznick's office and broke out the whisky. Now the red glow of the flames was no longer adding highlights to her hair and green eyes, but Selznick could see that her beauty wasn't one whit dimmed by unromantic electric lighting. Would she be willing to test for the part? The answer was never in doubt. Daniel O'Shea, standing close by his boss, did not remind him that arrangements for a screen test had already been made by his brother. After all, why break the romantic spell that Selznick's own 'discovery' of her had cast over him?

In that same letter to his wife, David Selznick added: 'Shhh! She's the Scarlett dark horse and looks damned good. (Not for anybody's ears, but your own: it's narrowed down to Paulette [Goddard], Jean Arthur, Joan Bennett and Vivien Leigh.)'

Despite the late hour – it was 1 a.m. – Selznick asked Vivien if she'd like there and then to run through the dialogue of the test scenes with Cukor, provided she wasn't too tired. 'I'm *never* tired,' Vivien said. Selznick, who was taking Benzedrine to give him the stamina required for eighteen-hour days, and as yet suffering no side-effects, was impressed by that too.

Vivien liked Cukor the minute she saw him: he 'smelled' of theatre, which she felt at ease with and admired more than movies. Indeed, before he was engaged as a dialogue director in the era of the new talkies, Cukor had directed repertory companies in New England. Vivien understood such a man and could get on with him easily; they were to remain friends for life.

In an adjoining office she read the scenes, without of course being required to act them, though she could have done that too, as she had read the novel so many times, and Selznick rigidly refused to let his writers depart from Margaret Mitchell's dialogue. Cukor was impressed. Her rapid British tones somehow deputized for the high-tempered Southern accent that would no doubt come easily to her once she had had the proper coaching.

Asked years later what he remembered best about her from that meeting, he was to reply by opening the novel at the first page and reading out the second paragraph about Scarlett's 'green eyes . . . distinctly at variance with her decorous demeanor'. Vivien to him suggested a lady – but a lady who enjoyed being 'at variance' with ladylike good form: the good-bad girl of the class. Involuntarily echoing Margaret Mitchell's description, he added, 'She was Rabelaisian, this exquisite creature, and told outrageous jokes in that sweet little voice.'

Myron Selznick had already gone off to join his cronies at the poker table and when, at long last, Vivien and Olivier left, Cukor told David Selznick, 'I don't think she'll find the Southern accent any trouble.'

'The accent doesn't worry me,' said Selznick. 'Better that it's not *too* Southern, or else we'll have all the Yankees' hackles up.'

All the following week was spent by Vivien rehearsing the three test scenes with Olivier after his day's shooting on *Wuthering Heights*. He became first Mammy, the O'Haras' kindly but bossy black housekeeper, lacing Scarlett into her stays and inflicting a reprimand for every uppity breach of good behaviour by tightening the draw-strings so that her proud flesh was nipped; then Ashley Wilkes, the dreamer and idealist, whom all of Scarlett's seductive wiles will not wrench away from Melanie – there were two scenes with Ashley. Olivier's newly discovered joy in film-acting made his reading of the scenes an asset that none of the other contenders for the role could possibly have enjoyed – which is not to diminish Vivien's skill, only to illuminate it.

She still made time to shop for Christmas presents for Suzanne and Leigh: children's picture books for one, sweaters for the other. (Too late she discovered a 'Made in Scotland' tag on the latter; she sent them off anyhow, hoping Leigh would not have to pay customs duty on reimported goods.)

Vivien's letter accompanying these gifts to Leigh has an ambiguity of tone that reflects how deeply equivocal her relationship with him was becoming. No doubt, if Leigh Holman had consented to an annulment, Vivien would have married Olivier without delaying a day over the stipulated period. But he had not done so thus far. Yet her letter to him reads as if it were from someone who, without actually saying so, regards herself still as an affectionate wife, an absent one maybe, but one still close to him in sympathy. It was doubtless this contradictory note which deceived Holman into continuing to think that, given time, Vivien might return to him – and so he postponed actions that would have made a free woman of her. 'I am afraid it will mean my staying here (if I get the part) for a long time and *that* I know I don't want to do ... Darling Leigh, I do hope you are well. I shall write and let you know what is happening. With dearest love, Vivien.'

A degree of deception is detectable here, at least in retrospect. The implication in this letter, strengthened in later ones, that she hated Hollywood was just the thing to reassure her husband that she might be happier at home – and with him.

She was certainly not deceiving herself: she did hate the place. Yet how much more would she have hated it had she gone there and been obliged to return without the prize she went to claim?

Before the screen tests, scheduled for the following Wednesday, 21 December 1938, Vivien took care of one important and highly confidential matter. The previous day, at Myron Selznick's offices on the corner of Wilshire and Roxbury, she put her name to an agreement authorizing him to be her agent and manage her career. No announcement of this appeared in the film trade press, an odd omission. News of it was not conveyed, then or afterwards, to John Gliddon, which was not so odd.

The reasoning appears to have been that, if Vivien won the Scarlett O'Hara role, the advantage of managing her for that film and all subsequent ones under the Selznick contract would go to Myron Selznick's agency – which also represented Olivier – not to Gliddon's.

Came the day of the test, Vivien was highly nervous. She muttered a few words of prayer; then Cukor made a bawdy remark that broke her up – and from then one, she was totally in control. It didn't matter that she had not quite mastered a Southern accent. When she came to be encased in her period corset by Mammy, her vigorous protests as the laces nipped displayed her fiery 'Missee' temperament so fiercely that a few stray English vowels hardly mattered at this stage. Her second test played even more strikingly because of the neurotic desperation that charged her emotions. The intensity of the rivalry between Vivien and the other three candidates was brought home to her when she slipped into the crinoline costume, which felt as if it were still warm from the actress who had been Scarlett a short time before. The others had played the scene for its straightforward passionate content, begging Ashley to marry them with many a yearning look. But Vivien didn't plead: she demanded. Ashley *must* marry her. She introduced a note of near panic, like someone teetering on the edge of imperious hysteria. She managed to touch the precariousness of her own stability and it heightened her sexuality. She ended the scene with an unnerving laugh of desire combined with despair of such passionate authority that this test was used as a model when it came to shooting the actual scene in the film. Vivien never thought she quite recaptured that first rapture of ardour and desperation.

For some reason the third test was shot a day later, with Douglass Montgomery standing in for Leslie Howard as Scarlett tried to seduce Ashley in the *post bellum* days when pride fights hunger at Tara.

The tests of all the four actresses were freighted by air to New York so that Selznick's partner, John Whitney, could vet them. Selznick himself often made decisions like the one now impending in a spirit of opposition to other people's opinion. This time there was no need. He'd told Whitney his choice and, when it went unchallenged, his preference turned into a resolute decision.

Vivien and Olivier found themselves at Cukor's house for brunch on Christmas Day. 'The part's been cast,' he said, taking her to one side.

'My heart sank to the bottom of George's swimming-pool,' she recalled. She was sure it had gone to one of her rivals.

The search for Scarlett had taken two years, cost $92,000 and included 1,400 candidates, of whom ninety had been tested. It ended that day on the terrace of Cukor's house in half-a-dozen unromantically phrased words: 'I guess we're stuck with you.' Vivien had won the most coveted role in films within three weeks of arriving in Hollywood – and she had paid her own fare over for the privilege.

Myron Selznick had already taken every precaution to safeguard her. Maybe his brother had tipped him the wink, but the very day he secretly signed up Vivien as a client, a cable was dispatched in her name to John Gliddon: 'DEAR

JOHN, VERY IMPORTANT YOU AIRMAIL KORDA CONTRACT AT ONCE. GREAT CHANCE DEPENDS ON ITS IMMEDIATE DESPATCH TO MYRON SELZNICK . . . VERY HAPPY CHRISTMAS AND FONDEST WISHES NEW YEAR. LOVE. VIVIEN.'

'I knew what that meant,' Gliddon says. 'Even in London I'd heard rumours that she was testing for Scarlett. That really shook me.'

Vivien's need to have her contract rushed over to her shows both the speed at which things were progressing and the *ad hoc* nature of her campaign to land the role. David Selznick now had to persuade Korda to adjust the terms of his agreement with Vivien. Korda was celebrating Christmas in Hollywood with Merle Oberon, whom he was shortly to make his second wife. To Vivien's alarm, he showed himself no more enthusiastic when told of her success than he had been a year earlier when he'd told her she was all wrong to play a spoilt Southern brat and would be rejected by the American public. Whether he really believed this or, more likely, was stiffening his resistance in order to put up the price of his agreement, the result was to send Vivien rushing to David Selznick with entreaties and promises if he could win over Korda.

Selznick calmed her. He knew the way that sellers did business. In a memo to Jock Whitney he put it ruefully: 'The lucky Hungarian has fallen into something and we're going to make a fortune for him.' However, he added, 'If [Vivien] is really as good as we hope, I suppose we're lucky, too, and shouldn't be greedy [*sic*] that someone else gets something out of it.'

While talks with Korda continued at high pressure, Vivien had to bide her time and hold her tongue, both of which she found frustrating, especially since New Year's Eve was celebrated in the company of some of the stars who had been her rivals for the role (and still thought they might be in the running) at Myron Selznick's lodge at Lake Arrowhead. The agent invited her and Olivier along with Paulette Goddard, Miriam Hopkins, Joan Bennett, David Niven and a raffish Errol Flynn, who jitterbugged in the aisle of their rented coach to the music of a small jazz combo and downed one cocktail after another mixed by Selznick's barman.

Agreement appears to have been reached in the first few days of January, for on the fifth of the month John Gliddon had a cable from Vivien forwarded to him by Cecil Tennant at Myron Selznick's London office (a fact that should have aroused his suspicion, but didn't). 'DEAR JOHN PROBABILITY WILL SIGN WITH SELZNICK INTERNATIONAL FOR IMPORTANT PICTURE' — secrecy still had to be kept, even in cabling — 'PRESENT LONDON FILMS CONTRACT WILL BE CANCELLED AND NEW AND BETTER CONTRACT WILL BE MADE.'

She then detailed the arrangements worked out for sharing her services between Korda and Selznick, Selznick getting the next picture after *Gone With the Wind*, then one to Korda and Selznick alternately. Then came the shock for

Gliddon. 'YOU WILL PARTICIPATE IN THE KORDA SET-UP ONLY. PLEASE DO NOT TELL ANYBODY ABOUT THIS. WOULD APPRECIATE YOUR REACTION.'

Gliddon's reaction was sharp and brutal: it appeared to him that he was being cut out of a lucrative deal.

When he had approached the Myron Selznick office in October 1938, asking them to represent *him* in any American interest in Vivien, he had meant on a picture-by-picture basis, entitling him to receive a share of the commission. Yet here was Vivien signing herself up for years hence and for films from which he would derive no percentage. He replied by cable on 6 January 1939: 'DEAR VIVIEN MANY THANKS FOR CABLE. YOUR NEW PROPOSALS MEAN SERIOUS LOSS TO ME. BUT IN ORDER TO ASSIST YOU WOULD BE WILLING TO CANCEL YOUR PRESENT OBLIGATIONS TO ME ON CONDITION THAT YOU AND MYRON SELZNICK JOINTLY PAY ME £2,700 BY THREE EQUAL YEARLY INSTALMENTS, THIS FIGURE BEING MINIMUM AMOUNT OF MY LOSS. LOVE, JOHN GLIDDON.' In deciding not to hinder the deal, Gliddon was motivated by the consideration that it wouldn't exactly harm his agency if the star he managed was to become the world-famous Scarlett O'Hara. The figure he specified was the percentage he calculated he would have received for pictures due under the old Korda contract.

On 11 January 1939, he had Vivien's reply, passed on to him again by Cecil Tennant: 'DEAR JOHN I DO NOT FEEL YOUR PROPOSAL A FAIR ONE BECAUSE IT INVOLVES MY PAYING COMMISSIONS ON FUTURE EARNINGS WHICH I MAY OR MAY NOT RECEIVE. CONSIDER MY ORIGINAL SUGGESTION EXTREMELY FAIR BOTH TO YOU AND MYSELF, NAMELY TO PAY YOU YOUR COMMISSIONS ON MONIES RECEIVED UNDER MY NEW KORDA CONTRACT AS AND WHEN I GET PAID. IF I LIVE, YOU ARE WAY AHEAD. LOVE, VIVIEN.'

What Gliddon didn't know was that Vivien had begun to play one side against the other. She did so not for money, but for her freedom, something that Hollywood was (and remains) traditionally more reluctant to concede than money.

The contract David Selznick was offering her was the standard seven-year Hollywood one, with renewable options at the end of each year and an escalating scale of fees. For *Gone With the Wind*, she was to be paid $25,000 (around £6,000 then). It was not a large sum: indeed it was beggarly considering it was the rate for a part that had engaged the wiles and wishes of established stars for two years and more. She was already receiving as much under her old Korda contract. But if the movie were a success, Myron reminded her, the contract could always be renegotiated.

It was the thought of spending further time in Hollywood, committing herself to make more pictures there, that caused her intense anxiety − and this was connected directly with her love for Olivier. It was very unlikely that his ambitions could be tied in with the seven-year lien that Selznick wanted on her services. Despite his newly discovered love for the detailed realism of movie-acting, Olivier's ambitions were still directed towards becoming the greatest actor of his generation in the theatre. Vivien's ambitions for herself were determined by his. If she gave in to Selznick and agreed to make Hollywood the centre of her career – a place she already disliked for being a cultural desert with no theatrical traditions at all – she would have to forfeit her chance to become a great stage actress. She might even have to forfeit her love for Larry.

'I will never make a fuss about the financial side,' she wrote to Leigh Holman at this date, 'but I am determined to ask for more time in the theatre, etc. I know perfectly well I could not stay here half the year.'

Now she used Gliddon's objections to the financial aspects of the contract to persuade Selznick to change it from a long-term one into a short-term arrangement. 'I don't want to sign a long-term deal,' she told Selznick. 'My agent in London always kept me free for the theatre.'

The impatient Selznick barked, 'Get *him* out here then, if it's going to make you happy.' Selznick couldn't believe the 'ingratitude' Vivien was displaying. Even before she had signed, she wanted to break the deal.

Needless to say, no invitation ever went out to John Gliddon from 520 Crescent Drive, where Vivien and Olivier were sharing a rented house. In any case, as Gliddon admitted later, he would have been out of his depth. He still hadn't been told of Vivien's defection to another agency.

Vivien eventually settled for a contract which said that time off for work in the theatre would not be unreasonably withheld; it was not as much as she'd wanted and, indeed, was more a matter of intent than law, but Selznick was adamant. 'All their standards are financial ones,' Vivien groaned in a letter to Leigh. As things were to turn out in years to come, the contract had a self-destruct element built into it which accomplished what Vivien was seeking.

So on 16 January 1939, a mere ten days before shooting had to begin, all was settled and the signing only was awaited. This was performed at a ceremony in the presence of Cukor, Olivia de Havilland, a pensive, pipe-sucking Leslie Howard and a toothily beaming David Selznick. Clark Cable had already been signed up when MGM made its deal with Selznick to trade him in return for distribution rights in the film.

For the signing, Vivien wore a black outfit, a large-brimmed, off-the-brow hat secured with a long cream silk scarf which looped round its crown and usefully concealed her long neck on the way back. She did not remove her gloves when she picked up the pen: she was still sensitive about her outsize hands.

The press release described her as 'Mrs Leigh Holman, wife of a London barrister'. It carefully avoided saying she was English and made reference only to 'recent screen work in England'. By mentioning Irish, French and even Anglo-Indian origins for her family, it usefully obscured precisely what nationality she was. All this reflected Selznick's nervousness about getting an English girl accepted as an American heroine. He need not have worried.

Gallup rode to the rescue with a poll indicating that thirty-five per cent approved Vivien, sixteen per cent were against her being cast, and twenty per cent didn't care much either way. Despite Selznick's huge publicity campaign, the remaining twenty-nine per cent hadn't heard about the Scarlett O'Hara contest at all. The Daughters of the Confederacy, a powerful posse of Southern matrons who still opposed the verdict of history, astounded Selznick by passing an immediate resolution approving of Vivien. Then he heard that one of them had said, 'Better an English girl than a Yankee.'

# 10

## *'I shall never be happy here'*

The morning after she signed her contract, Vivien's limousine drove her through the portico of the Selznick studios, a structure the producer used as his company logo on the screen. With its purple bougainvilleas and white magnolias, it added a deceptive touch of Southern aristocracy to what was itself a board-and-stucco deception. Behind it lay drab, work-a-day offices and stages. For almost the next nine months, every day, virtually without a break, this was where Vivien reported – *and worked*. It was a gruelling routine from the start, however romantic the end product looked.

Her day began at 9 a.m. sharp with elocution lessons to get her Georgia accent right; then came wardrobe fittings for some of the thirty-one changes of costume; then lunch; then an intense three-hour rehearsal with Cukor (the best bit of the day, since she grew more and more to respect this 'imaginative and intelligent' man of the theatre); then photographic tests in costume and make-up; then another two hours on her accent.

Selznick's notorious concern for detail pushed even the perfectionist Vivien to the limits. He ordered her hair and eyebrows to be made more natural, more period-looking, but, thankfully, not dyed or cut. Vivien's small breasts worried him disproportionately. What there was of them spread sideways, which was not in the Hollywood tradition. 'Tape them up,' he ordered; and she had to undergo this indignity, as well as having wads of cotton wool pushed into her corsage to make her 'breastwork' even more outstanding. Correspondence then ensued with Joseph Breen, the man responsible for seeing the self-censoring Motion Picture Production Code was enforced, over how many buttons of her bodice could be left undone. Two, he ordered, conceding that in the scenes where Vivien went about her mission of mercy among the Atlanta wounded, a third button might be popped – missionary zeal apparently pardoning mammary exposure.

She was alternately amused by such details and contemptuous of the time spent trying to resolve the problems they caused. How different it was from the way the theatre did things.

However, none of this showed on 26 January 1939, when, clad in a white crinoline patterned with green sprigs of leaves and flowers (later changed to an all-white one in the retakes at the end of filming), Vivien stood on the steps of Tara and declared to the Tarleton twins: 'If you boys say "war" just once again, I'll walk into the house and slam the door.... All this war talk's just ruining every party I go to. There isn't going to be any war!' She was perfection. Two more complicated scenes were shot that first day. The American crew were surprised at how Vivien turned her emotions on and off like a light switch, saving her current until Cukor's soft command of, 'Action'. Very shortly they were even more surprised at the expletives uttered by this English lady – bits of Scarlett that Margaret Mitchell had left out of the book. In those days, a woman using 'men's talk' in public was as exceptional as Katharine Hepburn wearing men's trousers in public had once been. In both cases, the undoubtedly ladylike demeanour of the swearer and the wearer could carry it off, but it was still a shock.

It shocked even Clark Gable, when he first made Vivien's acquaintance, which admittedly wasn't in the happiest circumstances. Clarence Bull, one of MGM's great staff stills photographers, had an appointment to shoot pre-production stills of Vivien and Gable on an old Southern staircase that was a standing prop and had been used in so many MGM costume pictures that its carpet was threadbare. Gable showed up and they waited; an hour and a half later, Vivien still hadn't arrived. Gable was 'madder than a hornet'.

'Is this the way they do things over there?' he rasped, meaning England. 'If it is, I don't want to make this picture with her.' Bull discovered the appointment had been set up by Selznick's man for two hours later. Gable took a walk, came back and, still in a sour mood, said, 'I still think I'll walk out of this picture with a dame like that!'

'I quite agree, Mr Gable,' came a clear voice from the side of the set, where the missing person had been standing, regarding Bull and the star who was to be her Rhett Butler. 'If I were a man, I'd tell that Vivien Leigh to go straight back to England and fuck herself.'

The anger immediately left Gable. 'Five minutes after they'd met,' Bull recalled, 'she wrapped him round her little finger.' Gable later said to him, 'Damn it – you're right!' and Bull concluded, 'She really had charm.'

Charm, but not as far as Gable was concerned the sexiness that might have fired their on-screen romance. He was more curious about this woman than amorous towards her. Above all, he was wary of her.

Gable was due to marry Carole Lombard in March 1939. He had already sacrificed half his assets as well as the trust fund set up for him by MGM in order to buy his way out of his marriage to his second wife, Rhea Langham. He was not about to complicate matters by having an affair with an English actress who was still a married woman.

Vivien, for her part, was not sexually attracted to Gable. Just as she could not see Olivier as Rhett Butler, now she could not visualize Gable as a substitute for Olivier. Both men were dedicated to different art forms and belonged to different romantic traditions.

Though Gable's stardom far exceeded Vivien's at this point, her confidence outstripped his where the film was concerned. She found it easy to become Scarlett in front of the camera: she had an affinity with the role that Gable didn't have with his part. Despite an overwhelming popular vote for him to play Rhett Butler, he simply could not see himself living up to the heroic image of the book. Vivien's theatrical tradition allowed her to steep herself in Scarlett's role. Though Gable had begun as a stage actor and owed his Hollywood contract to the impact he had made on Broadway, he was now a star personality – identified with the movies and committed to appearing on the screen and nowhere else. Vivien's scorn for Hollywood gave her the self-confidence to tackle her semi-mythical role: after all, if she failed, she could always go back to the stage. Gable, in contrast, already knew what he was being asked to measure up to and feared he would fall short.

Two weeks into filming, on 13 February 1939, George Cukor suddenly withdrew from the job. Why he did so has puzzled many commentators; it was said to have puzzled even Cukor himself in later years. He has been accused of being a 'woman's director', of tipping the film's bias of interest in favour of Vivien Leigh and Olivia de Havilland. Gable has been identified as the villain who insisted on Cukor's replacement by the more he-manish Victor Fleming. But Gable scarcely appeared in the first fortnight's shooting. Cukor would have been too honest a craftsman, anyhow, to attempt to subvert the film's distribution of interest.

One reason for Cukor's departure was probably David Selznick's apprehension that *his* vision of the film, which he carried in his mind's eye, was not likely to emerge on the screen. This was to be a producer's, not a director's film. Selznick uses the word 'author' of himself in one of his memos to Cukor. 'Authorship', in the sense of attributing the creative shaping of a film to the director, was not to be admitted into the Hollywood lexicon for another thirty years, until directors had become producers or gained so much other muscle that their contractual rights, inflated by their agents, enshrined their artistic vision, or at least their egos. This was going to be DAVID O. SELZNICK'S production of Margaret Mitchell's GONE WITH THE WIND – as the credits had it in large capitals.

Vivien and Olivia de Havilland were playing a scene dressed in mourning (for Scarlett's first husband, an early war casualty) when the news of Cukor's departure reached them. Appropriately garbed to express their grief, they left the set and flew down the corridor like flapping and squawking blackbirds into Selznick's office, driving him backwards into the bow window, where he put his hands before his face and almost had to beat them off physically. They got nowhere.

Vivien then changed, left the studios and had her chauffeur take her straight to Myron Selznick's. He looked at her standing there, bristling with indignation. Then he said, very coldly indeed: 'If you quit this film, you will be in court till your last day on earth. You will never work again on stage or screen. You will never be free. David will see to that. And so, too, Miss Leigh, will I.'

This was Vivien's first taste of Hollywood ruthlessness. She had met her match. There was no appeal. It was back to work. To Leigh Holman, whom she seemed to write to regularly now whenever she needed comfort and sympathy, she confessed, George Cukor 'was my last hope of ever enjoying the film'. The part of a lifetime had already turned into a burdensome penance.

In fact, Cukor continued to direct Vivien for many weeks after his departure. After finishing her day's work at the studios, she would secretly steal over to his home, where he would rehearse her in the scenes for the following day. He rendered Olivia de Havilland the same service. For a long time neither knew that the other was being tutored by him. This work-extension course took its toll on Vivien's health. Once she fell asleep by the pool where she'd been unwinding after 'lessons' and, as she was unrousable, the director's manservant had to wrap her in blankets and carry her to the spare bedroom, where she passed the night.

She had other worries too, though these were farther afield. Not until well into March 1939 did John Gliddon discover, and then only by accident, that she had signed up with Myron Selznick.

He had written to Myron's London office asking for a copy of Vivien's contract — by which he meant her new *film* contract with David Selznick and Korda. Instead, he was sent a copy of the 20 December 1938 agreement appointing Myron her manager. Gliddon was 'devastated'. He had known Vivien was becoming difficult, but duplicity he had not suspected — and this from the exquisite girl he had discovered. Immediate action was called for.

'You and your American organization have known for some time that Miss Leigh was under contract to me,' he wrote on 27 March 1939 to Myron Selznick. 'Her agreement of December 20 with you must have surely been entered into with the full knowledge that in signing [it] she was acting in breach of her contract with me. I have never received any notification that I am not acting as

Miss Leigh's manager. I must reserve all my rights in the matter....' The next day he wrote to Vivien proposing 'a satisfactory way out of the problem' – a new contract between her, him and Myron Selznick allowing him to be her agent everywhere except in America and requiring Selznick to pay him half of any commission received on her work inside America. Meanwhile, he added, he would like early payment of his share of the *Gone With the Wind* commission. No reply to this or to a second similarly worded letter sent on 24 May 1939 was ever received.

Gliddon thought back bitterly to a letter he had received from Vivien in early February, in response to his complaint about the terms of her new film contract cutting him out of any American deals. It now seemed to have been written by her – or dictated to her – against the day when he would discover he was no longer managing her:

My Dear John,

Please forgive me for not having written before to explain this situation to you. It is awfully rude of me. I was very distressed to get your wire saying you would be willing to sell your contract to Selznick, as I had been insisting that all the English side of my contract would still be with you. I cannot see how you would lose by this, excepting for this year. But in the long run, surely, there would be no question of your losing. As you said yourself, Korda would certainly not have taken up his option after this year [a reference to the warning Gliddon had passed on to Vivien after her behaviour on *A Yank at Oxford*] and by this agreement it is practically impossible for him not to do so, as he will have had a 'name' made for him and I will be found more useful than before. I would never have signed this contract, as you know, except for this particular picture, but it seemed impossible to refuse it, and, besides, they would not consider it without a contract. I do hope you will remember this, John, as I do not want to leave you at all.... Please believe me, John, that I have thought of you throughout this thing and I have your interest at heart. I hate Hollywood as much as I thought I would and I know I shall never be happy here. I can't think what will happen when I am alone.... So please write me as soon as you can. I do want to know what you think of this.

With much love,

Vivien.

ps. I've really been working terrifically hard or I would have written sooner. I'm so sorry for the delay.

Gliddon's solicitor said, in effect, 'Forget all that. She has let you down.' Korda at a much later date remarked, 'They treated Gliddon very badly.' But when Korda was appealed to at the time, his famous Hungarian charm was not exercised on Gliddon's behalf. 'It's not my practice to intervene in disputes between artist and agent,' Korda said coldly.

Vivien didn't meet Gliddon again until 1941. It was obvious the matter was on her mind, if not her conscience, for almost as soon as they met she said, 'You're not thinking of suing me, are you, John?' And of course, he wasn't. How could he have battled with a major Hollywood company far away and in the middle of a world war? John Gliddon preserved a residual affection for Vivien Leigh all his life, mingled with bitterness at the politics of the movie business which, he alleged, had stolen her away from him.

Ironically, when she *was* brought to court for breaching her contract, it was David O. Selznick who brought the charge, not John Gliddon.

Eventually, a Myron Selznick executive proposed a compromise. Korda had received £7,500 in compensation for letting Vivien go to America to make *Gone With the Wind*: Gliddon was eventually paid £2,220 in settlement of the balance of the old Korda contract – 'And even then I had a job actually to get the money.' Over the years to come he received percentages in the films made under her agreement with the Myron Selznick agency, though these, too, trickled in slowly.

Looking back, what disturbed him even more than the way his relationship with the first star he had discovered was reduced to a matter of dribs and drabs on a balance sheet was the message that a Selznick executive brought over to England at the end of the war. 'You know,' he said, 'David would have paid Vivien a percentage on the net receipts of *Gone With the Wind* if she hadn't behaved so badly while they were making it. That dame is screwy.'

Victor Fleming was just finishing *The Wizard of Oz* at MGM when he was pulled off the set and sent to replace Cukor as director of *Gone With the Wind*. He didn't even have time to read the script, never mind the book. This immediately earned him low marks with Vivien. Now that her beloved George was gone, she had appointed herself the authority on Margaret Mitchell. A copy of the novel was always to hand: she referred to it in any argument and seemed to treat it as a sort of talisman. Fleming's forceful temper had no time for what he regarded as her fussy disposition. 'Miss Leigh,' he barked one day, 'you can take this script and stick it up your royal British ass.'

But before many weeks had passed, Fleming too fell victim to Selznick's creative interference on all levels, and a third director, the journeyman Sam Wood, was brought in. Vivien's complaints increased in volume.

There was not enough time for rehearsal, she said; this scene was not as good as that one in the book; her character lacked logic – when she asked Fleming, 'What do I do here?' he just answered curtly, 'Ham it up.' Was *that* helpful?

Even allowing for Vivien's engrossing perfectionism, some of this may have been a way of showing her sublimated resentment at Selznick for separating her from Olivier during the shooting. As his film began to develop its epic stretch in the daily rushes, Selznick became commensurately apprehensive that some forgotten factor, some act of God or human folly, would yet frustrate his grand design. High on the list was the damage that scandal might do. One source of potential scandal, of course, was the marital status and living arrangements of his star and her paramour.

It is unrealistic to believe that the Hollywood press corps was not aware that Vivien and Olivier had broken marriages – each involving a very young child – in their recent pasts, were still undivorced and were living together like a married couple. All of this was highly inflammatory material. If no gossip columnists exploited it, that was due to the power of the studios in those days to blacklist awkward journalists and to an unwritten agreement among the columnists that they only dished the dirt when the studios had finished extracting the paying element from it.

It is no coincidence that Ruth Waterbury's well-researched article on the couple's affair appeared in *Photoplay*, the leading mass-circulation fan magazine, in December 1939, the very month of *Gone With the Wind*'s première. Far from stigmatizing them, it presented the couple as embattled but bold-hearted romantics. 'A Love Worth Fighting For' ran the headline on the piece: '... the high tumultuous romance that laughs at careers, hurdles the conventions, loses its head along with its heart, and laughs for the exhilarating joy of such wildness.' Ruth Waterbury's article, certainly read by millions, has the feeling about it of a neat compromise made by a journalist who wants to 'tell all' and a studio which believes it safer to have 'all' told in a complimentary style.

The frankness of its revelations was tempered by the writer's Tennysonian passion for the rewards and sacrifices of a Great Love. Even when the divorce court cast its shadow across the affair, Miss Waterbury screwed honesty out of dishonour:

> They each have a child which perhaps they will never be permitted to see again. They may have to listen to some pretty severe things said about them, the English not being inclined to mince [their words about] such matters. Larry and Vivien care terribly about all that. There is a passion and a vitality that touches both of them, that makes them care terribly about all things. But they care more for each other. They care more for each other than they do for money or careers or friends or harsh words or even life itself.

Despite its gushing tone, this is an important piece; it is one of the earliest public couplings in print of Larry and Vivien, just at the moment *her* film *Gone*

*With the Wind* was about to provide the romantic follow-up to *his* film, *Wuthering Heights*, which had been released eight months earlier. It helped give the phenomenon of 'the Oliviers' its popular warranty as a great romance, though Ruth Waterbury should also be given the credit for asking in a snide last paragraph: 'As for what will happen to them after they wed – well, we were talking of romance – and matrimony is quite a different story.'

But none of what was to happen could have been foreseen by Selznick during the first month or two's shooting on his own great romance with Margaret Mitchell's novel. He had cause for concern, though, when some of Vivien's remarks were reported to him. She and Olivier, naturally enough, resented any intrusion into their private lives, but they responded in a peculiarly British way. They sardonically exaggerated their interviewer's interest in them, treating it as the unsophisticated prurience of a typical Hollywood hack. '*Of course* we're living in sin,' Vivien was heard to say, going off into a peal of laughter. Selznick probably had a bad night imagining the headline ' "Living in Sin No Big Deal" – Scarlett O'Hara'.

It is assumed that his fear of scandal led him to prevail on his brother Myron to get Olivier out of town as soon as possible, so that he and Vivien would not be sheltered by the same compromising roof. Hence, as *Wuthering Heights* opened in April 1939 to great personal acclaim for him, Olivier departed for a role opposite Katharine Cornell in S. N. Behrman's *No Time for Comedy*, which was having a month's out-of-town tour before opening on Broadway.

The separation made sense in other ways too. If the play were a success, it would consolidate the reputation Olivier had made on Broadway in *The Green Bay Tree* in 1933. He hated Hollywood and to be idle there while Vivien completed her film would be unbearable. Vivien recognized the danger in this too; she had already seen how losing an opportunity made her beloved despondent and unresponsive. But with him away from April onwards, she was the one who grew fretful and bored. Soon things became worse.

Her schedule was a gruelling one. She appeared in far more scenes than any other player, yet she took it into her head that, if she worked a longer day, the picture would take a shorter time to shoot and so she could get to Olivier earlier.

As shooting continued, Selznick developed an affection for filming on location and this subjected Vivien to even longer hours and more arduous working conditions. (Hollywood unions had not yet developed the muscle they later used to curb their employers' exploitation of them.) The scene at war-ravaged Tara, when Scarlett grasps a fistful of radishes from the red soil, cramming them greedily into her mouth with the declamation, 'As God is my witness, I'll never be hungry again,' was photographed in the San Fernando Valley. To get the sense of a moment of epic commitment, when a new, mature Scarlett will arise out of the rags of the old self-indulgent one, it had to be a dawn shot without a hint of cloud. This required Vivien to be costumed, made up and on the spot by 5.30 a.m., which meant she had to be out of bed three hours earlier. It had to be repeated half-a-dozen times on almost as many days, since the sun failed to rise when bidden by Selznick or else clouds would form disrespectfully and drift into the camera range.

Frustrated and exhausted, Vivien drew the line at 'getting ill to her stomach', as the screenplay puts it, so Olivia de Havilland volunteered to dub in the unladylike retching sounds in her place.

A platoon of aides and technicians danced constant attendance on Vivien. Their very number became oppressive. In addition, the countless costumes and the detailed attention they required severely tested her temper. She had to cope with no less than twenty-seven copies of the same cheap calico dress, each in a different stage of disintegration, which Scarlett wore in the months of penury and penitent resolve. When a continuity girl fussed over the baubles of a frock she had run up out of Tara's once resplendent green velvet curtains, Vivien snapped, 'For God's sake, leave me alone.'

She had two days off each month, corresponding with her menstrual cycle, the tally of her own periods and those of the other female principals being kept by a studio aide specially detailed for this delicate task. But Selznick saw a deeper malaise in Vivien, one which no biological reason could easily explain. She clashed with him now with a hysterical fierceness. She took to shouting on the set, then just as suddenly switching to tears. A running cause of conflict was a passage that Vivien claimed to be the truest one in the script, but which Selznick kept eliminating from each new revision of the screenplay. It came right after the funeral of Scarlett's second husband – the one she married for his money after stealing him away from her sister. Drowning her guilt in the bottle, Scarlett tells Rhett how glad she is her mother has not lived to see what she has done: 'She brought me up to be kind and thoughtful and ladylike, just like her, and I've been such a disappointment.' Selznick kept cutting the dialogue, lest it weaken audience sympathy for his heroine. In the final shooting script, all Scarlett is left with is: 'Oh, Rhett, for the first time I'm finding out what it is to be sorry for something I've done! For the first time I'm glad that Mother died! (*She dissolves into tears again*).' Vivien kept insisting on the original, quite irrationally in Selznick's opinion. He was not to know that the lines expressed a self-chastising sentiment she probably felt with regard to her own mother.

An even darker symptom of guilt surfaced in a curiously unpleasant game that Vivien proposed her guests play at her parties. It was called 'Ways to Kill Babies'. The players took it in turn to mime some out-of-the-ordinary means of disposing of an unwanted infant. They weren't used to this sort of diversion in the Hollywood community; unwanted babies *were* got rid of there, but in rather unimaginative ways which were seldom discussed, much less mimed.

Even allowing for English eccentricity, this game gave rise to so much gossip that Selznick decided Vivien was in need of the very man he had pulled strings to have sent out of the way. So, just before *No Time for Comedy*'s Broadway opening, Olivier made a dash by air to be with Vivien for twenty-four hours in Los Angeles. She threw her arms around his neck and, between kisses and embraces, lamented the hardship she was suffering: movies *were* unworthy of artists like themselves. But Olivier was a reformed fellow on that point of doctrine following his purgatorial experience with *Wuthering Heights*. He was being lauded across the nation for the sex appeal he had, up to this point, been unable to project in movies. It was *stage* acting which now seemed to him to be unnatural and unsatisfying. 'I simply didn't notice it before,' he told Vivien, 'but now it seems to me that audiences in the theatre swallow dialogue and acting conventions that on the screen would draw howls of derisive laughter.'

Since he returned late to New York and missed his curtain, the next time Selznick gave permission for the two lovers to meet they used Kansas City as a half-way house. 'Oh, David, I'm so grateful,' Vivien said on her return. 'Larry met me in the hotel lobby and we went upstairs and we fucked and we fucked and we fucked the whole weekend.'

However, with Olivier opening on Broadway, work alone was not enough to assuage Vivien's loneliness in Hollywood. All her really close friends were in the English colony – Ronald Colman, David Niven, C. Aubrey Smith and Robert Coote (who had been in *A Yank at Oxford* with her) – but many of them had been dispersed by the war. She had two German servants to look after her at home, and was glad of it – their meals at least preserved the taste of Europe.

On Sunday mornings she would drive over to Santa Monica and spend the day with Anatole Litvak and his wife, Miriam Hopkins. Litvak was a Jewish refugee from Hitler's Germany who had come to Hollywood a few years earlier and was now trying to open the reluctant movie colony's eyes to the threat that the Nazis posed to European and possibly world peace. As the studios had huge investments in the German box-office, he was making little headway. Vivien was disgusted at this: it confirmed her even more in her hatred of this privileged place whose comfortable isolationism affronted her.

Vivien was already a royalist by romantic persuasion. Earlier that year she had taken part in an all-British tribute on the NBC radio network to the King and Queen, who were visiting President and Mrs Roosevelt in Washington. It was organized by the columnist Radie Harris and she suggested Vivien's contribution should be Elizabeth Barrett Browning's love poem to her husband, 'A Woman's Last Word'.

She said to Radie Harris:

'When I say the final couplet – "Must a little weep, Love.... And so fall asleep, Love, Loved by thee," I shall be saying them to Larry.' Olivier, in New York, recited John of Gaunt's speech from *Richard II*. Unfortunately, it could not be turned into a covert declaration of undying passion for Vivien, but as she listened, according to Radie Harris, 'The expression on her face was one of enraptured pride.'

Both of them very easily associated their love for each other with their love for England. Exile in Hollywood had reinforced their longing for home, where 'true art' was to be found. Very shortly, they were to make a second film together to express the English spirit in their country's hour of need.

By April 1939, Vivien had the satisfaction of seeing American public opinion rather chastened by Hitler's war moves. 'They're a little cowed now, thank God,' she wrote to Leigh Holman.

When she was feeling in such a mood, expressing some of her own probably well-justified discontent with the rigours of filming by working up a passion for American involvement in her country's struggle to preserve the peace, Vivien found the Litvaks' house a refuge as well as a home from home. Her mind was also very much on the other home she had left. She wrote to Leigh Holman asking to be sent snapshots of Suzanne. And she prayed nightly for the end of the film she had once prayed to be in.

Then, as soon as she heard that Olivier was likely to star in *Rebecca*, which Alfred Hitchcock was preparing for Selznick, she prayed to be cast in that film too. After all, *her* next picture was to be one for Selznick also; Korda didn't get his turn for some time yet. So she could cancel one debt she owed Selznick, a man who thought he had prescriptive rights over what she did and where and with whom, and be back at her beloved's side. Why shouldn't such a plan work out? Hadn't she captured Scarlett O'Hara by the power of positive thinking? She could do it again. And she began concentrating all her thoughts on the second Mrs de Winter.

On 27 June 1939, five months after her first scene was shot, Vivien completed the last take on *Gone With the Wind*, ate a salad and sandwich lunch alone in her dressing-room, cast an unregretful look at her dog-eared copy of Margaret Mitchell's novel and walked over to make-up and thence to a rehearsal stage on the Selznick lot to test for *Rebecca*. Things did not go well.

Vivien made a discovery around this time – possibly during these tests – that was to stalk her ambitions and eventually upset her emotional balance for the rest of her life. She found that the role she had just played was coming between her and the next one she had to assume. Whenever she had committed herself to a part over a lengthy period, one that caused her stress and drained her physically, even precipitating intemperate outbursts at work or after hours, then she found it hard to shake off the experience, put it out of her mind, even erase the dialogue from her memory. In later years – so some of her closest friends believed – she overlaid the roles she played so that they accumulated like different identities, stacked out of sight and mind while times were benign, but suddenly and uncontrollably repossessing her in some cycle of crisis.

*Rebecca* was more than a matter of miscasting: though it would certainly have taxed *anyone* to switch from a woman like Scarlett O'Hara to play Daphne du Maurier's timid heroine. Vivien simply couldn't make the transition, however confident she professed to be. 'It would solve a lot of problems if she *were* right,' Selznick confided to Jock Whitney, not least the one of how to keep Olivier happy when he reported back to Hollywood to begin the film in August/ September. Better to have Vivien in the film with him than idling round the set. Yet Selznick's unwillingness to settle for less than the perfection he sought dissuaded him from compromise. Moreover, Vivien hadn't shown the slightest interest in the role until she heard of Olivier's casting.

She was leaving for New York within the week. At last, in order to appease her, Selznick agreed to let her and Olivier make a test together; he was genuinely curious to see if the chemistry between them would work for this modern romantic melodrama.

The tests have not survived, but they must indeed have been disappointing. Selznick, in his usual agony of exhausting all the options, showed them to Cukor without giving him the least hint of his dissatisfaction. 'Cukor viewed them very seriously and quietly and conscientiously and with no comment at all during the running, except for some loud guffaws at Vivien's attempt to play it,' he wrote later to Irene Selznick. Soon afterwards he cast Joan Fontaine in the role. Selznick's famous reliance on his hunch was the decisive factor. He had found himself seated next to Joan Fontaine at a dinner party and had overheard her arguing that Margaret Sullavan should play the lead in *Rebecca*. It struck him that an actress who could thus deprecate her own suitability for a much sought after part had exactly the right kind of humility for the role of the second Mrs de Winter. The way in which Vivien had been chosen to play Scarlett O'Hara was not dissimilar: in both cases the actress was 'found' almost as if she had stepped from the film for which she was eventually cast.

Vivien arrived in New York in time to catch Olivier's last performance in *No Time for Comedy*, for he had given in his notice as soon as she had an end-date for *Gone With the Wind* and now they planned a brief return trip to England. But before they left New York on the liner *Majestic* on 11 July 1939, Vivien had witnessed the enormous change in Olivier's public image. He had become a star in the fully-fledged Hollywood sense of the word. His Heathcliff had hit a responsive chord in younger audiences, who were entranced by 'his broad lowering brow, his scowl, the churlishness, the wild tenderness, the bearing, speech and manner of the demon-possessed', to quote Frank Nugent in the *New York Times*.

'I am torn by DESIRE ... tortured by HATE' ran the slogan on the movie posters, where Olivier's dark face, half obscured by Merle Oberon's pale profile, glared with one highlighted Cyclopean eye at the filmgoers waiting in line.

Those anxious to be themselves torn and tortured made a detour from the Rivoli cinema to the stage door of *No Time for Comedy*. There they besieged Olivier as he entered or left, running alongside the limousine with him and Vivien in it, even trying to enter their hotel suite by false pretences. It was a mini-mania predating the bobbysoxers' hysteria for Frank Sinatra and turning Olivier into a sex symbol, albeit a reluctant one. Very soon Vivien's film would make her as recognizable to the man in the street, and, more important, the man's wife or girlfriend. Both of them were cast in the romantic mould of the movies at around the same time, so that, when they married, it seemed predestined by the very roles they had played. What Olivier later called 'that beautiful fifteen years of my life when I dominated everything' was beginning; and, more than ever, Vivien wanted to be a part of it.

Radie Harris had gone with her to the matinée of *No Time for Comedy* — Vivien was so impatient to see Olivier that she couldn't wait for the evening performance. They went together to Olivier's dressing-room at the interval. 'They clung to each other as if they were never going to see each other again,' Radie recalled. Olivier kept on his make-up table miniatures of Vivien to match the ones of him she had on her dressing-table in Hollywood. 'When we were back in our seats, Vivien's eyes were shining. "Isn't he marvellous? Isn't he wonderful?" This professional worship of Larry never changed. Long before he was acclaimed the greatest actor in the world, Vivien was confident that this was his destiny and it was her own ambition to develop as an actress so that she could share this pinnacle with him.'

# 11

## 'Send back the wine!'

They returned to find England preparing for war: trenches being dug in the royal parks, gas masks being distributed, air-raid wardens being appointed to police the streets during the blackout.

They snatched a brief holiday in France, then Vivien went to see Leigh Holman. He was still as considerate for her well-being as he was for five-year-old Suzanne's. But he wasn't yet prepared to grant Vivien's plea for a divorce and he refused to let her take the child back to America with her. Maybe, Vivien thought, he'd reconsider his decision if war came and London were attacked. Gertrude accompanied Vivien and Olivier on the *Majestic*'s return crossing. Vivien's recent state of mind had persuaded her that she needed her mother near her. It was the beginning of a pattern, the daughter calling in the mother when her emotional problems got out of control, but at other times going her own independent way and sometimes considering Gertrude's well-meant intervention an irritation.

In mid-Atlantic, Vivien and Olivier received a cable from Selznick finally rejecting her for *Rebecca* on the grounds that her career would be 'materially damaged' if she attempted such an unsuitable role. Olivier took it philosophically; Vivien less so. It was her first rebuff: the first time in her professional life that she hadn't got what she'd set her heart and mind on. She was to remain 'resentful', as Irene Selznick put it, for a very long time.

Vivien and Olivier heard Prime Minister Neville Chamberlain's declaration of war between Britain and Germany on the 8 a.m. news bulletin aboard a yacht anchored in Catalina Island's Emerald Bay, just off the California coast. The yacht was rented by Douglas Fairbanks Jr and he and his guests were up early, considering they were supposed to be on holiday. They included Mary Lee Fairbanks, Nigel Bruce and the Ronald Colmans. David Niven and Robert Coote arrived in their own small sloop not long afterwards and felt the sombre mood even before they scrambled aboard. 'I know it's early, but I think we should drink a toast to victory,' said Fairbanks gamely.

Vivien and Olivier had drawn apart and were talking in low tones, he gripping the gunwale, she plucking his sleeve to get his attention. Unusually for him at this early hour, he had one or two 'toasts' already inside him. Then he vanished, presumably to his cabin; but the next thing Vivien heard from him was a shout from the water. Had he fallen overboard? Suddenly Olivier came whizzing by in the yacht's small motorboat, making a tour of the other vessels still at anchor and waking up their occupants with a doom-laden announcement: 'You are finished, all of you. You are relics ... that's what you are, relics!' Vivien's gloom was dispelled; throwing back her head, she tossed off peal after peal of ringing laughter. Olivier's cavortings seemed to her like a scene from one of the screwball comedies Hollywood was then turning out.

Her seriousness soon returned, however. What should she and Olivier do? Go back to England? Send for the children to join them in the safety of neutral America? Gertrude, who was with them aboard the yacht, wanted to go ashore and telephone London immediately.

As soon as they were able, Vivien and Olivier got in touch with their friend Duff Cooper at the Ministry of Information in London, only to be told that prominent Britons like themselves had a duty to stay put and help the war effort by backing charities and behaving patriotically. 'No one will believe that,' Olivier grumbled, envious of David Niven, a reserve officer in a Highland regiment, who would presumably soon know what was expected of him. *Rebecca* now seemed to him a trivial diversion; the one consolation it promised was being at the studios while Vivien was shooting retakes for *Gone With the Wind*. Selznick was determined not to let her slip back to England. She owed him another film. At first she hoped it would be *Pride and Prejudice*, which MGM was producing and George Cukor directing.

To her disappointment and annoyance, Olivier was cast for it and; his co-star was Greer Garson, whom he had directed five years earlier on the London stage. Vivien went into *Waterloo Bridge* with Robert Taylor, who had been her Yank at Oxford. Fate, it seemed to her, had got its directions confused. Old resolutions had wilted in the heat of the new-found fame now beating on them. As he was setting off for Hollywood in 1938, Olivier had written to Vivien's mother: 'It is difficult to make a decision to work apart, but I do believe we were wise to make it, and it will bid more for our ultimate happiness together to work (even if we don't like it very much) at the expense of our temporary personal happiness.' Now a war was on, how much time they would have for 'personal happiness' was hard to guess, and suddenly they were desperate to work together. To have studio policy force them apart seemed to them intolerable.

Actually, what they were experiencing was the economics of stardom.

Selznick considered it extravagant to put them both in the same picture. Olivier's huge post-Heathcliff appeal would, he hoped, bring the crowds to see Joan Fontaine in *Rebecca*. Having no immediate film of his own for Vivien, he could send her to MGM on loan-out at a fee that was enhanced by the as yet unreleased *Gone With the Wind* — unreleased, but not unseen. In October, Vivien heard it had been sneak previewed to tremendous acclaim at one of the most emotionally charged events of its kind in Hollywood history. The audience attending a perfectly ordinary evening film show was first alerted to what was coming when the show was stopped and a slide announced the immediate preview of 'a very long film'. Anyone who wished to leave should do so now, for the doors would then be locked. Irene Selznick's memoirs recapture the emotional impact of the first time *Gone With the Wind* was seen by people who had been kept in suspense for years:

> The lights darkened and the studio trademark appeared on the screen. The audience's hopes soared. When the main title came on, the house went mad. I fell apart and sobbed as though my heart would break. I couldn't bear to see the first scenes. I was crouched down in my seat, protesting wildly. David [Selznick] and Jock [Whitney] took off their jackets and tried to bury me as though they were putting out a fire.... The film took over and the hours sped by. The applause was enormous and, when the lights came on, everyone stood up, but most of them didn't move. It was as though something wonderful or terrible had happened. Half an hour later there were still people standing around.

The word was out. The news could not be contained: it spread through Hollywood and then throughout America via the cable services, radio networks and newspaper columns. From that moment, Vivien Leigh became a star of the first magnitude. One film had done it. It was the biggest success in history for an English actress. She had come from virtually nowhere; suddenly she was everywhere. Vivien and Scarlett were personalities who overlapped so potently in people's imaginations that one seemed the embodiment of the other. Even the fact that almost nothing was known about Vivien Leigh proved a huge point in her favour. She came as a stranger to a film whose leading character became an instant folk heroine and thus reversed the process by which stars were made. With most players who become stars, their personality and the well-publicized facts (or invented fictions) of their lives fuse together with the character — and it is at this point of fusion that the audience identifies a new sort of personality whose celebrity is enhanced by the transfer. But Vivien had the attributes of Scarlett projected on to her by millions who had been waiting for her — for *Scarlett* — and the extraordinary resemblance between her and

Margaret Mitchell's heroine reinforced their gratification. There were no earlier star roles to detract from the impact, and not enough known about Vivien to get in the way of people's identification of her with the role. As far as the public was concerned, Vivien Leigh *was* Scarlett O'Hara.

When Vivien heard Olivier might not be allowed to accompany her to the world première in Atlanta, Georgia, in December because of Selznick's persistent fear of scandal, she put her foot down with all Scarlett's firmness: 'Then I won't be going either.' Selznick sighed — and gave way. 'She's not going to be exactly Pollyanna about what we put her through,' he resignedly told Kay Brown. Eventually it was agreed Olivier could go, but the reason for his being there had to be explained as a sort of trailer for *Rebecca*, which had finished shooting during the time *Gone With the Wind* took to edit. The mayor of Atlanta was asked to make sure the names of Vivien and Olivier were not linked in any intimate context. The poor man took this so much to heart that he announced Olivier's presence with overcautious formality: 'And now I am going to intro-duce a gentleman who is here in Atlanta strictly on his own business.'

As it turned out, Vivien was the only one who nearly caused an incident when, on landing, she heard the band of military cadets striking up *Dixie* and cried in delight, 'They're playing the tune from our picture.' Howard Dietz, the MGM publicist who stood in fear of no one, not even Selznick, saved the day and possibly the visit by passing off this unintended snub to the South's unofficial anthem as a jest uttered in response to the overwhelming warmth of the welcome.

Flanked by platoons of Georgia state police, Vivien and Olivier, the Selznicks, Leslie Howard and Olivia de Havilland — Gable and Carole Lombard were arriving later in a private plane — drove through Atlanta in an open-topped motorcade. Many of the crowd had rooted out their grandparents' period finery and wore it as witness to their own sense of pride in the events which the film commemorated. 'Reminds you of the Coronation,' Vivien yelled to Olivier, finding, like every tourist, some part of home in foreign places.

In the smart department store windows she saw her image replicated a hundredfold: not just in photo blow-ups, but on full-size period mannequins. She was on candy boxes, banners and badges, and occasionally her heart leaped a trifle higher as a Union Jack was waved from the six-deep ranks on the sidewalks. She stood in the floodlights bathing the steps of the historic Terrace Hotel, arms linked with Olivia de Havilland, her dark hair spotted with confetti, blinking in the electric storm of flashbulbs. Then she went upstairs to bathe and rest before at last meeting the woman who had made all of this dream possible.

Margaret Mitchell, an intensely private person, had deliberately steered clear of all the controversy surrounding the casting, scripting and direction of the film of her book. But after a few minutes' talk with Vivien, she was conceding 'this Scarlett' knew a lot about Southern history. Vivien knew how to woo a writer; not many years later, she would turn the same flattering power on George Bernard Shaw by mirroring his preferences.

The next night, amidst 6,000 people in the Atlanta Municipal Auditorium, many dressed in costumes worn by the extras which Howard Dietz had freighted into town in box-cars, watched Vivien and the mayor open the ball with the *Gone With the Wind* waltz. (She later carried this piece of music, on record, around on her travels, though it wasn't always when her spirits were high that she played it. Sometimes, her friends thought, she played it to make herself sad.)

Many thousands more gathered outside Loew's Grand Theater on Peachtree Street for the première the next night, 15 December 1939. Again *Dixie* was played everywhere they went; Vivien whispered to Olivier that she was sorry for the King of England having to hear 'his tune' played ceremoniously over and over again. Before the night ended, though, her sympathy for Royalty had shifted elsewhere. The movie, she remarked privately, was 'hard on one's ass'. The ovation rolled them back to the banquet like overlapping sea breakers, and Margaret Mitchell finally pronounced on Vivien's performance. 'She is *my* Scarlett,' was all she said. It was sufficient.

For the rest of her days, Vivien Leigh was always someone's Scarlett. The legend reached out that night and enfolded her.

Vivien went before the cameras again at the start of the new year, 1940, playing the role of the ballet dancer in *Waterloo Bridge* who loses her lover in World War I and, deprived of her faith in humanity, becomes a streetwalker. It was a clever tearjerker, given topicality by opening during a World War II air raid. This afforded Vivien at least proxy participation in the European crisis from which she and Olivier felt themselves so shamefully detached.

Just how big a star she had become can be gathered from two interesting documents in the archives at MGM studios. One is a reprimand delivered to a New York advertising agency which had failed to put Vivien's name before Robert Taylor's, resulting in a breach of contract. This may seem a small matter, but in reality only the scale of a star's fees was fought more bitterly than the prominence and position of a star's name on the credits and advertising of films in that era. Apart from the egotism involved, it signified the box-office ranking the studios themselves attached to their highly priced contract artists. For Vivien, after one film, to have leap-frogged over an MGM leading man, a co-star of Irene Dunne, Joan Crawford and Greta Garbo amongst others, confirms the power that came with Scarlett.

The other documentation is an even more revealing set of requests issued by Selznick himself to Bennie Thau, the man who personally negotiated all MGM's star contracts and was Louis B. Mayer's most trusted confidant after the death of Irving Thalberg. *Waterloo Bridge* was an MGM film and Selznick wanted to make sure his star got the best possible treatment. Accordingly, he wrote on 17 November 1939:

> Miss Leigh is not one of those girls (are there any?) who can be photographed by any cameraman. I have seen old pictures in which she did not look well at all. In *Gone With the Wind* we tested with several cameramen before we got one who really caught her very strange beauty. I would greatly appreciate your assurances on the following:
>
> 1) That you will check with me on the cameraman. 2) That [he] will make tests well ahead of time, so that if he doesn't seem to have 'caught' her there will be ample time to change. 3) That you will show me these tests. 4) That you will thoroughly protect her on the camerawork and that any bad close-ups or anything of the kind will be re-taken, just as though she were your star, under contract, instead of ours.

Not surprisingly, then, the film has some of the choicest romantic close-ups ever taken of Vivien – such shots were an MGM trademark. It was a studio that had a greater appreciation of womanly beauty – on the screen, that is – than any other in Hollywood. Following the strong Technicolor tones which had dramatized Scarlett's wilful looks and temperament in *Gone With the Wind*, the photography of *Waterloo Bridge* imparted to Vivien the phantom unreality of a dream-image.

It was the perfect follow-up film. Begun, completed and on the screen in a little over four months, it proved that her sensational American début in *Gone With the Wind* was no fluke. Bosley Crowther in the *New York Times* wrote: 'Miss Leigh shapes the role of the girl with such superb comprehension, progresses from the innocent, frail dancer to an empty bedizened streetwalker with such surety of characterization and creates a performance of such appealing naturalism that the picture gains considerable substance ... ' Vivien, he added, was 'as fine an actress as we have on the screen today. Maybe even the finest.'

Hate Hollywood though she did, it was the 'company town' that taught Vivien her screen craft. Compared to the films she made there, her early British ones look amateurish. Hollywood and its tough corps of no-nonsense directors – Victor Fleming, Mervyn LeRoy, who made *Waterloo Bridge*, and especially her beloved George Cukor – knocked technical craftsmanship into Vivien without bruising her beauty. The experience annealed her: the porcelain emerged finished.

Perhaps the fact that she was shortly going to be a free woman, able to marry the man she loved, added a lustre to Vivien's looks. Leigh Holman and

Jill Esmond had decided their marriages wouldn't be mended by waiting any longer. No doubt a financial settlement had been agreed to by Olivier; but the vast uncertainty of war played its curiously healing part, as well as the distance that now physically separated people who had anyhow long been living apart. On 5 January 1940, Sub-Lt Leigh Holman, RNVR, Ramsgate, petitioned for divorce from his wife, Vivian Mary Holman, naming Olivier as co-respondent; it was granted the following month. Two weeks after his petition, Jill Esmond was also granted a divorce. She had cited Vivien. The Danish expedition to play *Hamlet* in Elsinore was named as the occasion for the break-up. Both petitioners obtained custody of their children.

Vivien thanked Leigh for being 'so kind and wonderful', admitting that such perfunctory thanks must seem 'bald and cold'. The odd thing was that the letters she continued to write him would seem to anyone ignorant of the affair to be model missives of a loving wife. Just twelve days after his divorce petition, Vivien was asking him if he and Suzanne had any use for tinned butter, bacon or a Balaclava helmet – she was knitting comforters for the troops. He said he needed a Balaclava, and she sent him one. Her enquiries were mundane, but they were like those of tens of thousands of servicemen's wives. The part of Vivien that couldn't associate marriage with domesticity and child-bearing was nevertheless perfectly happy supplying the comforts and performing the many acts of kindness which held wartime homes together. Her correspondence remains affectionate, yet curiously detached. By not mentioning any unpleasant reality, she forgot it – it ceased to exist.

In both divorces there was the customary six months' wait before the decree *nisi* became final. This term of abstinence was filled by Vivien and Olivier with a project which would permit them all the indulgences of love without incurring any of the penalties of the law. They decided to appear in their own stage production of *Romeo and Juliet*.

Their motive for mounting this most romantic of all Shakespearian plays at that particular time was not, however, entirely due to a desire to carry on their affair by other means. Being their own producers would also give them a welcome degree of independence. Film studios lavished many gifts on contract artists, but not that dangerous indulgence. Secondly, they both needed money: for living expenses, for alimony, for wartime exigencies when Olivier's hoped for induction into the Fleet Air Arm would reduce his film and stage fees to the paypacket of a serving officer. *Romeo and Juliet* had been suggested by George Cukor, but really, in their mood, was there any other choice? They could capitalize on their screen celebrity as romantic lovers. Much to their irritation, the gossipy tabloids had started to call them 'the love-birds'. The tag might be vulgar, but it could be turned to their advantage. The publicity was bound to heighten interest in a production where their affair could be verified in the flesh, so to speak, yet purged of offence by the context.

Only one small dissenting voice was raised. It was a murmured warning from Ralph Richardson, when Olivier referred the project to him for his opinion or his blessing. 'A bit too luxurious for wartime,' he thought. But it is the nature of lovers to turn a deaf ear to all but their own rapture.

So Vivien and Olivier, as sure as Cukor had been that they 'could make a fortune in no time at all', invested their savings, some $60,000, in the project. Warner Bros. put up the same, hoping perhaps that the stars might later wish to repeat their success in a Warner film of the play. In the long term, too, a success on Broadway would be a useful calling card when peace came and brought them back to act together on the American stage.

Vivien's delight was stretched by Olivier's absorption in every pre-production detail. He sat in his star's canvas chair on the set of *Pride and Prejudice*, wearing Darcy's anachronistic but figure-flattering Regency dress, awaiting his call by Cukor and meanwhile, no doubt with Cukor's licence, working out the moves, the lighting, the total look of *Romeo and Juliet*. He wanted the stage to assume the naturalism of the cinema – his performance and Vivien's to have the detail that the camera loved. A *believable* production at all costs. A convert to naturalism, Olivier became the master builder of a production that would look real, yet must feel romantic.

To speed the play on its way, he used the equivalent of cinematic cutting. He settled on a circular stage. As it revolved, each of the twenty-one scenes was brought to the fore in rapid succession setting the action free to flow with the continuity and logic of a film sequence. Thus the Capulets' hallway showed a staircase leading upstairs – *revolve* – Juliet's bedroom came into view with a balcony in the background – *revolve again* – the balcony was being scaled by just the sort of impetuous youth who would bark his shins in his haste to get to his beloved. Olivier loved strenuous action. If he could fit physical acrobatics into a performance, it enhanced the vocal bravura he brought to it and earned audible gasps, and even applause, from the astounded audience. Showing off, yes, but the sweat involved was honest sweat.

Despite the great pressure on wartime shipping space, he brought over from London two of the three women comprising the Motley stage design company and the play was literally carpentered together at the Old Vitagraph studios in New York before being freighted to California for the cross-country tour ending on Broadway.

While in Hollywood, Olivier took lessons in musical composition and devised flourishes for his own stage entrances and exits. 'Nothing will stir him from the piano,' Vivien wrote to Gertrude, who had left for England to look after Suzanne.

She hoped to do her own music too; if not, Olivier would oblige. She had taken up the unlikely hobby of accordion-playing in order to stretch her chest and improve her vocal projection.

Actors were recruited from the British players still in Hollywood, supplemented by proficient Americans, and Dame May Whitty was prevailed upon to coach Vivien in verse-speaking four times a week, as well as to play the Nurse.

In short, it was to be a production of unusual ambition and passion. It would set the seal on their artistic partnership and be a prelude to their legal union – or so they hoped.

Among the players whom Olivier had assembled was a strikingly handsome twenty-three-year-old actor named John ('Jack') Merivale. Born in Toronto in 1917, he was a stepson of Gladys Cooper by her second marriage to the actor Philip Merivale. Oxford-educated and RADA-trained, Merivale had been a student-player at the Old Vic a few years earlier when Olivier had played Macbeth. Merivale had been cast as Monteith and as Malcolm's understudy – and he had got his chance in the latter role at the first Saturday matinée of a troubled production. He had been nervous, and with good reason: Lilian Baylis's secretary had rooted him out of his digs and told him he was on with a few hours to spare. He had been forced to finish learning his speeches – amongst them, one of the longest in Shakespeare – in the taxi rushing him to the theatre.

As he had panted up the stairs to his dressing-room, he had caught up with a young woman heading for Olivier's door. 'She was moving like a dream. She turned round – she had a beautiful face. "Good luck," she said, and gave me a bewitching smile.'

The next time Jack Merivale had seen Vivien was as Titania.

And now he met her in Hollywood, when he and his stepmother, who had been in *Rebecca* with Olivier, went to a Saturday night party in the mansion that Olivier and Vivien were renting on San Ysidro Drive, next door to Danny Kaye.

'Jackie,' said Olivier, 'I'd like you to come up here tomorrow and read for *Romeo and Juliet* – I think you'd be good as Paris.'

Merivale's heart sank a little. 'I knew I wasn't right for it. But I went – and I wasn't. I couldn't do it at all, not the way Larry wanted, anyhow. "If you want it played your way," I told him, "the man you should get is my half-brother, John Buckmaster."' At this, Olivier's mouth tightened. Merivale didn't know that Buckmaster and Vivien had had an affair in the early days of her marriage to Leigh Holman. 'Oh, yes?' said Olivier, 'Vivien has said that, too ... but I don't know anything about his acting.'

In the end, they settled on Merivale playing Balthazar and understudying Olivier's Romeo.

From the minute rehearsals began in Los Angeles, Vivien and Olivier endeared themselves to the whole company. In the very best tradition of actor-managers, they were endlessly considerate towards everyone who worked for them. It was to be the pattern of their entire theatrical career. The players were like an extended family. Vivien lavished gifts on them like a young aunt to her nephews and nieces.

Olivier's Romeo, Jack Merivale observed, wasn't so different from the 'roaring boy' with which he had stormed the Old Vic a few years earlier. He tidied up his looks, breathed music more easily into his colloquial way with verse, but still marked the shift from virginal adolescence to sexually experienced manhood by leaping exultantly on top of the wall and disappearing in a swallow dive off it. In helping Vivien interpret Juliet, something of Olivier's love for her was apparent. He envisaged a Juliet barely out of childhood, seductively playful, bouncing a ball against the garden wall and virtually chanting her soliloquy to the rhythm of the ball until she flings it away when the Nurse approaches, as if ashamed of being caught with childish things. Olivier's main concern was to bring Juliet up to sexual pitch at the very moment his own wave of amorous impatience breaks against her. This asked a lot of Vivien. Despite intensive training, she lacked variety in the great lyrical passages. Her natural advantage lay in the area of psychology, for, as Olivier saw it, this 'child' actually came to dominate Romeo. In everything to do with love, she was to prove the stronger partner.

They interrupted rehearsals on 29 February 1940 to attend the Academy Awards ceremony. Olivier's Heathcliff lost to Robert Donat's Mr Chips, but then Rhett Butler was an also-ran too. Spencer Tracy slowly tore open the envelope containing the name of the 'Best Actress'. He scanned the room. It was so deathly silent he hardly needed to do more than whisper the name: 'Miss Vivien Leigh'.

Vivien said later it was like going through the fire of Atlanta again, only instead of flames, it was people reaching out to touch her. Could there have been a better omen for the tour?

But things went wrong from the very start. Olivier's manifold responsibilities took their toll on him on the opening night when, like a man who has overtrained himself, his tired muscles refused to pull him up on to the wall and he hung dangling by his fingertips. 'After a century', he recalled later, 'the curtain came down.' A bad augury. He tired himself further by scheduling more rehearsals for Vivien and himself. 'She was totally subservient to him,' Jack Merivale recalls. ' "Shall I do this? Shall I do that?" It was for Larry to decide. Such a labour of love distracted him from imperfections in other actors, who grew worse by neglect. A particularly weak case was Dame May Whitty's husband,

Ben Webster, cast as Montagu. Both players were there on sufferance. Vivien and Olivier would have preferred Edith Evans – in which case Vivien would have had an inspired tutor for those domestic sessions on San Ysidro Drive when Dame May rehearsed the balcony speech with Vivien standing on the kitchen table. But wartime restrictions on travel ruled out Edith Evans. Dame May didn't want to leave Ben, so he was given the Montagu part. His memory was far from good and in his first entrance on the opening night he confronted Olivier's young whippersnapper Romeo with parental dignity which suddenly crumbled as he mumbled, 'Give me m' lines.' After that, Dame May was told to learn Ben's part as well; soon great chunks of Montagu's lines were being spoken by the Nurse.

With more than a little relief, they left San Francisco (and lukewarm notices) for Chicago, a sixty-hour train journey in those days. Early on, Merivale went in search of bridge partners. No use trying to rope in 'the guv'nor and his lady' – 'They were totally wrapped up in each other. Her eyes very nearly changed colour when Larry spoke to her.' Dame May begged off, but suggested Ben. 'Where are you going, Jackie?' Olivier asked as he passed their drawing-room compartment. In search of Ben, he told them. Olivier exploded: 'If Ben can remember where thirteen cards are, he can bloody well remember his lines!'

This was the first time that Vivien's delicate constitution had been put to the test of touring and she was not standing up to it well. She soon discovered she was running a high temperature.

Olivier, on the other hand, was full of energy again. The sap of repertory was starting to flow through his system after a year or more of Hollywood drought. In Chicago, he even forgot the war long enough to talk of future stage plans, showing how much Vivien was going to be a part of them. 'I have wanted more than anything else to take half-a-dozen Shakespeare plays and rotate them constantly. If I'm alive, we'll do them in 1941 [*sic*], giving at least *As You Like It, Romeo and Juliet, Hamlet* ... and maybe *Antony and Cleopatra*. We're not old enough for *Macbeth*.'

Olivier left interviewers with the feeling that he and Vivien were 'consumed' with each other – 'I have never seen an actress quicker to divine a director's meaning,' he told them. 'I have an idea. I start to explain it, none too articulately perhaps, but she has it and by the next rehearsal has enriched it.'

For all that, the Chicago notices didn't quite reflect their expectations. Well, Olivier and Vivien thought, if they didn't appreciate it, too bad. New York would; that's where the intelligentsia were. 'We still thought we could get away with it,' says Merivale. 'It would be all right on Broadway.'

The New York notices devastated them. It is safe to say that never again did

Laurence Olivier and Vivien Leigh receive such a roasting. Fault was found with almost every element in the three-hour, twenty-minute production, beginning with the playing time. Brooks Atkinson, in the *New York Times*, headed his notice 'Much Scenery: No Play'. Undermining all the realism Olivier had prided himself on – the doors that banged, the hardware that rattled, the clocks that followed the advancing day and the waning of the light – was the simple fact that the audience was physically too far away from the action to be involved in the play. In order to enable the sets to revolve, they had had to be mounted so far up stage that the players could not easily be seen or heard. Distance bred disenchantment with the view. Amongst other things, Atkinson found Olivier 'mannered and affected. . . . In costumes that flare extravagantly at the shoulders, he looks like a belligerent sparrow.' Other critics were even harsher. John Mason Brown, in the *Post*, had him 'gulping down his lines as if they were so many bad oysters'. 'His legs ... often give the impression that they are trying to surround him or trip him up,' said the *Eagle*'s Andrew Pollock, while to John Anderson in the *Journal American* he suggested 'the general romantic attitude of a window cleaner'.

Vivien wasn't attacked in such gale-force terms, but she had to face the subtler humiliation of condescension. 'Her slender girlish beauty is perfect for Juliet,' wrote Brooks Atkinson, then added: 'She makes an earnest attempt to act the part as it is written. But she is not yet accomplished enough as an actress to go deep into the heart of an imaginative character wrought out of sensuous poetry.' In similar vein, John Anderson conceded, 'She is bright, lithe and energetic. . . . Unfortunately, none of these qualities is of much use to her when she has to play the Potion Scene, where she managed to recite the terrifying lines with a series of screeches that seemed not only meaningless, but a little silly.'

Indisputably the performance had shortcomings, but the tone of the notices betrayed an animosity which had more to do with celebrity than the lack of proficiency. For the moment, Vivien and Olivier were being seen by the theatre critics as uppity movie idols expecting an easy ride into town on the waves of fan worship and advance publicity. 'Scarlett O'Hara returned in person last night ... ' was Walter Winchell's opening in the *Mirror*. 'Scarlett Capulet' was the heading on Richard Watts Jr's review in the *Herald Tribune*, which began: 'Being celebrated visitors from another medium, if not another planet, Miss Vivien Leigh and Mr Laurence Olivier must expect to have their local sojourn in *Romeo and Juliet* taken as a spectacular personal appearance of Heathcliff and Scarlett O'Hara rather than as an earnest impersonation of the star-crossed lovers in the Shakespeare tragedy.'

They were, in short, suffering from one of the characteristics of too sudden and too lavish an amount of fame – the backlash. And they had only themselves to blame. Love had truly blinded them to their best interests. Their appearance in the play had been trumpeted in advance by trailers in the cinemas – a most unusual (and expensive) way of letting Broadway hear what was going to hit its theatres. 'See the Great Lovers in person,' blared the captions and (worse still), 'See real lovers make love in public.' Even the 51st Street Theater, which housed the production, was at other times the Warner Bros.' flagship cinema. Disappointment gave way to resentment. John Anderson, with a final turn of the knife, said : 'In view of Shakespeare's general absence ... just call what they are doing *Laurence and Vivien*, and let it go at that.'

Vivien's first thought was that all their savings had been invested in the play – now they were irrecoverably lost. Hundreds of people were already demanding their money back on advance bookings and the production was to lose $5,000 a week in cancellations until Olivier swallowed his pride and put a stop to the refunds. Vivien's second thought was of the immediate economies they needed to make. 'Send back the wine!' she cried at her secretary – and back to the store went the crates of expensive vintage wines they had ordered for the running relays of parties they'd intended to hold. At this point, a stranger was announced whose name meant nothing to them, until he showed up in their suite. He turned out to be their Beverly Hills chauffeur, delivering the Cadillac that in their former expansive mood they had ordered driven across the continent so that they could be swept in and out of the theatre in style.

After the curtain on the second night, they went to the Red Cross Relief Ball that Noël Coward was hosting at Radio City Music Hall. They would have preferred not to show their faces in public again, but patriotic feelings were stronger than personal pride. 'Darlings,' said Coward admiringly, 'how *brave* of you to come!'

# 12

## *'Perhaps I saw you as a danger'*

Vivien put it bluntly to Jack Merivale: 'Larry and I were too greedy.'
Throughout the doomed tour, they had deliberately chosen to play in
theatres that were designed for concerts and therefore far too large for
a play like *Romeo and Juliet*. Olivier and Vivien had thought that the bigger the
house, the bigger the box-office since they couldn't fail to draw capacity
audiences; but the box-office shrank ... and the theatre remained the same
cavernous size, only emptier.

Shortly after the New York opening, they moved out of their expensive
hotel and into Katharine Cornell's guest house at Sneden's Landing in up-state
New York. It was a pretty place with a garden sloping down to the Hudson
River. They commuted in and out for the dispiriting run of the play which
should have solemnized their artistic union, but was now dissipating their
combined savings. Yet they tried unselfishly to dispel other people's gloom.
'On the second night we were all down in the dumps,' says Merivale, 'and Larry
cheered us up with a pep talk reminding us how much better off we were than
the chaps at Dunkirk.' More than ever, their thoughts turned to home; their
impatience to be there and 'do something about it' resulted in calls to their friends
who were now either in uniform or, like Duff Cooper, holding government office.
Vivien did what she could in New York and was featured in *Look* assembling
'bundles for Britain'. Olivier took flying lessons in a beaten-up old river plane
with natation floats, using the Hudson as a splash-down strip, hoping it would
make up the number of flying hours he had to log in order to ease his way into
the Fleet Air Arm and an active commission.

Although the Sneden's Landing house was cramped, they had members of
the cast to stay for weekends. The talk inevitably centred on the war. 'One
night we were speculating what might happen if the Germans won,' says
Merivale. 'One of the actresses said, "I hear all the pretty girls will be drafted
into brothels and the rest will be made to do road work. I'm sure I'll be put on
hard labour." "Oh, no," Vivien burst in brightly, "don't be silly, darling, *of course*
you'll be in a brothel!" '

The play's disaster generated a form of hysterical togetherness. 'What fun we had!' Merivale recalls. 'Piling into cars after the show, Larry driving the Cadillac, Vivien egging him on to crash the red lights, screaming along the Hudson – it took just over an hour to get to Kit Cornell's house at that time of night and at that speed. On some afternoons Jock Whitney would send his speedboat over, a thing the length of a cricket pitch, and Larry would stick a captain's cap on and Vivien would say "We'll have a drink" – which seemed a good order to give the crew – and we'd descend on our friends' river frontages. I remember Helen Hayes had a tea party going and didn't take kindly to a troupe of inebriated actors, some of them wet through, tramping in on her.'

One suspects there were times of acute depression, too, when their guests had gone and Vivien and Olivier were left alone to ponder on the war, their children back in England and their own futures. Sneden's Landing was an odd place to be stranded, a kind of limbo neither could adapt to. Years later Anthony Quayle found himself driving past the place with Olivier, both of them weekend guests at someone's estate near by. Olivier gave it a glance of recognition. 'That terrible house,' he growled.

Vivien was the more restless of the two; at least Olivier had his flying instruction. So when Jack Merivale telephoned she said, 'Come over – right now.' After the play's closure, Jack had done two weeks in summer repertory in Connecticut. He'd found himself thinking often of Vivien. For the opening night in New York, she'd given each player a specially chosen gift. His had been a copy of Richard Llewellyn's *How Green Was My Valley* – the book of the moment – with a warm and, he thought, affectionate inscription in her large, hurried handwriting.

Vivien liked dry martinis. That evening at Sneden's Landing, they sank a pitcherful. After supper Olivier took to a wing chair, immersed in his flying manual.

'Oh, if you're going to do homework,' said Vivien, 'Jack and I'll amuse ourselves with Chinkers Chess' – her pet name for the board game Chinese checkers, at which she considered herself a champion. But not this time.

Jack bottled up one of her marbles on his side of the board. 'If you don't take this lad out, I'll hold it here and you'll never get free,' he said.

He felt Vivien's hackles begin to rise. 'Don't be silly. You'll have to get your marble into your triangle and then I'll escape.'

'Yes, but you'll have to take it all the way across the board. There won't be anything to hop over and by then I'll be home and dry.'

'Stuff and nonsense! Play on!'

Vivien soon realized that Jack's tactic was working out just as he had said.

To his surprise, she became furious, as if some hidden accelerator pedal had been depressed. 'How dare you cheat!' she cried.

'That's not cheating – I won.' But he was shaken by her reproachful tone and the way her eyes filled with anger over a game.

'You invite yourself here and then *you cheat!*' she snapped – like Scarlett in a temper.

Jack appealed to Olivier. 'Larry, stop her! She doesn't mean that.' But Olivier sat as if deaf to the sudden melodrama a few feet away. Apparently he was hoping the storm would blow itself out as quickly as it had arisen.

'Don't you try to come between us,' Vivien cried at Merivale. 'We've been together for years. Nobody's coming between us. Don't you try!' There was a weary movement from Olivier, like someone making a gesture without the will behind it. Merivale's pride was hurt, but he was more alarmed than anything else by this sudden breach of an affectionate relationship. He retired to bed before further harm was done. 'I'd better be on my way tomorrow,' he said stiffly as he left the room.

'Yes, you had,' said Vivien. 'Tom will have the car ready to take you to the station.'

'And so', says Merivale, 'we parted like "brass rags".' He passed a mostly sleepless night, haunted by the quarrelling he imagined taking place downstairs.

He didn't know then – nor was he to find out for many years to come – that Vivien's instability led to these sudden fugues, taking her and her embarrassed victims by surprise. He later wondered if this had been one such flare-up, but he wasn't totally convinced. It occurred to him that, consciously or not, Vivien might have precipitated their falling out in order to put him out of temptation's way. He was very attracted to her. In later years, when he reminded her of the incident, she swore she had put it out of her mind entirely. But the only explanation she offered tended, if anything, to confirm Jack's surmise. 'Well,' she said, 'perhaps I saw you as a danger.'

The doldrums of life at Sneden's Landing were at last ended by a telephone call from Alexander Korda. He was coming to America on a secret mission for Winston Churchill – to make a propaganda film.

Korda wanted Olivier and Vivien for the roles of Horatio Nelson and Emma Hamilton in a film to be called *The Enchantress*. With two such romantic stars it would be a great love story and – of more immediate moment to His Majesty's Government – a film to rouse American sentiment for the beleaguered British by playing on the historical parallel to their present crisis. To be blunt, Korda went on, it would be an incitement to Americans to enter the war, and it had Roosevelt's own strong, if tacit, approval. In case patriotism were not enough, he promised generous fees, expenses, even an unofficial bonus to the stars. It would allow them to return to Hollywood with their heads high and work at hand.

A love story on this scale, said the Hungarian tempter, might fulfil their passions rather better than the self-indulgence of *Romeo and Juliet*. In any case, Vivien's next film *had* to be for him.

Their spirits restored, they spent ten days at Kit Cornell's estate on Martha's Vineyard, then pushed on to the lake-island home of the critic Alexander Woollcott. Vivien sparkled in the stimulating company of vacationing East-siders, endless quiz games, cribbage, bathing parties and the house speciality, a brand of rogue croquet, the rules of which were writ in the natural hazards of the lawn and inattentiveness of the opponents. After dinner, their host read Dickens out loud to them. Vivien resolved to read all his works.

By August, they were back in Hollywood, in a modest home with an oval swimming-pool on Cedarbrook Drive. Between working on the script with Korda and his writers, Walter Reisch and R. C. Sherriff, Olivier pressed on with his flying instruction under a particularly hard-bitten veteran at nearby Clover Field. He succeeded in incapacitating several aircraft, but fortunately not himself, before the film's insurers grounded him.

On 28 August 1940, the date on which Jill Esmond's decree *nisi* became final, Olivier and Vivien finally became free to marry. Ronald and Benita Colman were the only ones taken into their confidence. Benita bought Vivien's ring by pretending it was for her own finger, though the fact that it did not fit her far more petite hand must have aroused suspicions. To elude the Press, the marriage ceremony was to be performed at a guest cottage on the Colmans' ranch at Santa Barbara with a local judge officiating. The Colmans would be waiting for the Oliviers on their yacht at San Pedro.

So determined were Vivien and Olivier to keep it a 'state secret' that they refused to tell Garson Kanin over the telephone the vital news that he was to be their best man. He had to leave a script conference he was holding with Katharine Hepburn to answer what sounded to him like a life-or-death summons to their home. They then all decided that the only way to make amends to Hepburn was to cut her in on the secret. Why not invite her to be matron of honour? Kanin says that she sportingly agreed to get out of bed – she always retired early – and join the wedding party.

'At that time', says Katharine Hepburn, 'I really didn't know Vivien or Larry well. Vivien led the social whirl kind of life that was anathema to me. But Gar Kanin and I sat in the back seat of Larry's Packard' – the Cadillac had been sold in a fit of economy and humility – 'and Larry drove and, of course, Vivien sat close to him in the front seat. I remember feeling the conversation she and Larry were having as we drove along was, well, rather racy. But this was probably the prudish reaction of a girl like myself who had been sheltered from the great world.'

At one minute past midnight, on 31 August 1940, the earliest moment after the three days' notice required under California marriage law, Olivier and Vivien became husband and wife. The marriage ceremony was concluded in five minutes. Various accounts of it say that, as the newlyweds kissed each other, Judge Fred Harsh called out 'Bingo!' A not entirely inappropriate blessing for a pair who had been kept in enforced suspense for so long. But this cry of triumph may well be a later embellishment. 'I've certainly no recollection of anyone calling out Bingo!' says Katharine Hepburn. 'It would seem to me a very odd thing to do.'

The Colmans' yacht weighed anchor the minute Vivien and Olivier were aboard and made for honeymoon waters off Catalina Island. As the day wore on without the radio announcing the news of their marriage, the newlyweds began to feel disenchanted. Their ruse might have been too successful: they felt they were being denied the full satisfaction of their stealthy manoeuvring to become Mr and Mrs Laurence Olivier. 'At ten o'clock, thank goodness, the story broke,' Colman commented, 'and thinly disguised relief was plain on every face. "Too bad," said Larry heartily. "Too good to last," said Vivien with an incandescent smile. "Well, that's the way it goes," contributed Benita. After that we had a very happy evening.'

Despite stringent newsprint rationing, the British papers put the story on the front pages, and elsewhere the event was given even more urgent attention. As the new term began at the Convent of the Sacred Heart school, the pupils at early morning Mass were beseeched to pray 'for the soul of our old child Vivian Mary Hartley', who had married outside the faith.

Korda's film started shooting in October 1940, under the new title of *Lady Hamilton*. When released in America, it would be called *That Hamilton Woman*, a title which still invites the charge of Hollywood vulgarity, even though Nelson's son, a naval officer, vented his frustration and anger in that very phrase when writing home about his father's mistress. The schedule was extremely short – a little over five weeks. It had to be. If time was short for getting the patriotic message to the Americans while Britain was still holding out, money was in even shorter supply. In a letter to Leigh Holman at the start of November, Vivien spoke of the film having to be rushed through 'because apparently after Thursday there is no more money'. Economies became so savage that only the half of Lady Hamilton's face exposed to the camera was made up.

Korda's brother Vincent, the art director, reduced overheads by designing a functional and brilliant composite set, a half-rotunda incorporating Sir William

Hamilton's reception hall in his lavish Ambassador's residence overlooking the Bay of Naples, as well as the dining-room, terrace — and bedroom. Vincent had earlier built an impressive library. Alex Korda eyed it coldly. 'This is a love story, Vincent. You cannot make love in a library. Rebuild it as a bedroom.'

As sometimes happens with such high-pressure undertakings, when no one has any time for other people's egos, all went sweetly. Korda, as director, felt comfortable with the subject. Though by no means the key-hole view of great historical personages given in *The Private Life of Henry VIII*, it allied Korda's ironic humour with the daily lives of the famous, whom he delighted in humanizing and, ultimately, rendering tragic on an epic scale. Moreover, as a Hungarian, he was not inhibited by any great deference to English history.

Vivien had the more rewarding role as the prostitute sent over by his nephew to Sir William Hamilton, British Ambassador to the Court of Naples, who stays on to become Her Excellency and then the mistress of the sailor on whom England's salvation depends. Olivier would have liked to delve deeper into Nelson's vanity and ambition, to say nothing of his lustfulness, but felt inhibited by patriotic need to appear a symbol: as Nelson, he must be *England* again. Handicapped by an eye-patch and an empty sleeve, he had to rely on his voice more than ever. One can hear how he was fashioning it into a marvellous instrument capable of being tuned to every moment and shade of emotion — even though he had to infuse it with a gallantry that sometimes makes Nelson seem as if he has already been placed on top of his column in Trafalgar Square.

Vivien's performance showed how splendidly she had graduated into permanent stardom. She relates her story in flashback between a prologue and an epilogue which depicts Lady Hamilton as a fallen woman spurned by the nation to whom Nelson had 'bequeathed' her. She ends as an alcoholic, a thief and an *habituée* of the Calais taverns, out of one of which she is thrown into the actual and figurative gutter. It was necessary to show Emma's moral downfall before and after her 'immoral' rise in order to allay the hostility of the Hollywood censors, who were still opposed to the notion of happy adultresses. With the help of Rudolph Mate's photography, Vivien creates a credible outcast, her face ominously shadowed, rather than ravaged, by time and drink. She took her voice a couple of notes lower, as if accompanying her downward path. The visible and audible result is a curiously mature Vivien, prefiguring her later roles in the 1960s of once beautiful women slipping into indignity or worse.

Her sly smile of satisfaction as the tipsy Emma manages to pronounce the word 'phenomena' to the streetgirls sharing her cell is a particular joy. Because much of the film had of necessity to be shot in sequence, she builds such details convincingly into the conversion of a beautiful, charming but empty-headed girl reacting to the outbreak of the European war like a spoilt society hostess coping with a suddenly depleted supper table ('Bang goes the French ambassador!') into an altogether more serious woman prepared to do her duty by her country even if it means sacrificing her lover. At Olivier's line, 'Lady Hamilton is one of the best women in the world and an honour to her sex,' Vivien's face assumes a sobriety all the more touching because so unexpected, as if Nelson were a mirror for her inward nature.

When he has to reject her for reasons of state, her passionate, desperate, swooping run along the terrace, backed by the lights of Naples on the dark-varnished waters, only to arrive too late at the jetty steps, describes the romantic-pathetic aspect of their love-affair better than pages of dialogue.

Thanks to her American training on *Gone With the Wind*, she had mastered the trick of reaction shots. Olivier's presence made her close-ups more than usually revealing: it is one of the few films of any date in which the stars actually do look as if they are in love.

Korda had only one criticism of Vivien's performance. 'My dear Vivien,' he said, 'Emma was vulgar.' Vivien snapped back, 'My dear Alex, you wouldn't have given me a contract if I'd been vulgar.'

'And then what? What happened after?' Emma's fellow harlots clamour to be told at the end, as the story returns from the cold shock of Nelson's death to Emma's utter loneliness in her prison cell. In a low, husky voice drained of all life and emotion, she answers: 'There is no "then" ... there is no "after".' Not even Garbo could have spoken it more eloquently.

To Korda's alarm, however, the censor wasn't moved by the pity of the syllables. Nor by his grafting on to Lady Hamilton's love affair a rather unhistorical *crise de conscience*. 'What we are doing is most dreadfully wrong, and because it is wrong it cannot bring happiness,' Vivien had to say – and, not surprisingly, because she herself had followed precisely the same 'bad example', she said it most unconvincingly. So Korda had an extra scene written between Nelson and his clergyman father. As Olivier's own father had been just such a clergyman, an austere priest shocked by his married son's relationship with another woman, Korda mischievously contributed a few lines of dialogue to Olivier's discomfiture. In the scene, Nelson's father, a man of the cloth, shines with virtue in the firelight while he counsels his son, standing in the shadows, to give up Emma, 'even if it forces all three of us to live in misery for the rest of our lives'.

Once the film had been passed by the censors and was on release, these scenes were either shortened or cut completely; they had served their purpose.

After the completion of *Lady Hamilton*, the Oliviers dallied briefly with the idea of doing Shaw's *Caesar and Cleopatra* as a Theater Guild production on

Broadway. John Gliddon had proposed the play to them two years earlier. They were still smarting over the drubbing they'd received in *Romeo and Juliet*. A second shot at a love story, this one prudently tempered by a distancing wit, was tempting, but the pull of home proved stronger.

Only one detour was made. Vivien flew to Vancouver early in November 1940, to see her seven-year-old daughter, who had been brought there by Gertrude in mid-July. By chance, four-year-old Tarquin Olivier had been on the same evacuee ship with his mother Jill Esmond. Having both their children far from the bombardment London was suffering somewhat eased the Oliviers' consciences over their own desertion of them. Unfortunately, Vivien's visit to Suzanne had most unwelcome consequences.

She had used the name 'Mrs Leigh Holman', hoping to avoid detection by the Press – in vain. Her now famous looks brought a sibilant whisper of 'Scarlett' in her wake wherever she travelled and reporters easily traced her to Suzanne. Her hosts' son, hoping to persuade the Press to go away, hinted that publicity might put the child of so celebrated a mother at risk from kidnapping. Inevitably, this heightened the human interest of the story and it was on the front pages and wire services within the day. As the Reverend Mother of the convent school where they had enrolled Suzanne now feared for the other children's safety if their famous pupil were among her boarders, a day school had to be quickly found, and this decided Gertrude to remain in Canada to look after her. She was now separated by thousands of miles from Ernest back in England, though a gap of another kind had already opened in their marriage. Vivien returned to Hollywood with the guilt over the unintentional extra burden she'd put on her mother offsetting the pleasure of seeing Suzanne again.

They packed up the house on Cedarwood Drive, tearfully arranging foster homes for the 'nice stray cat' that had shown a cunning self-interest by attaching herself to Vivien, and the Old English sheepdog named Jupiter that had come with the house. Passing through New York, they went to a farewell party thrown for them by two of the Motley girls, Peggy Harris and Elizabeth Montgomery, and there ran into Jack Merivale.

'Vivien was all sweetness and light to me again,' he says. Merivale's father, though, had made a shrewd comment in a letter to his son from Hollywood. 'He felt that Vivien was far more on the ball than Larry, but was being wonderfully feminine in letting him seem to make the decisions.'

Another man who had noted Vivien's managerial qualities early on in their relationship was Garson Kanin. Even before he was best man at their wedding, he was close enough to witness a spat which blew up between them at a George Cukor party, where Vivien was upstaged for once in such a group by Greta

Garbo's presence — and angered by the attentions Olivier was paying the star who, she said, had once spurned him — a reference to *Queen Christina*.

As Garbo and Olivier returned from a walk they'd taken together in Cukor's garden, Vivien's displeased features 'suddenly changed expression. A beautiful smile illuminated her face as she said, "Ah, *there* you are! *Bonne promenade?*"'

'Less than five minutes later,' Kanin recounts,

we were in my car, Vivien, Larry, and I, and I was driving them home. Our departure had been so swiftly and gracefully engineered by Vivien that I could remember none of the details. Had I said goodbye to everyone? To Garbo? Had I thanked George, our host? I could not remember.

At my side, the most romantic couple in the world were having a spat.

' — the last time I go to lunch with *you!*' said Vivien. 'Do you hear? The last. I'd rather *starve.*'

'Now be reasonable, Puss.'

And so the bickering continued.

Vivien was by nature the more demanding partner in love — it was no coincidence that Olivier had made her Juliet take the lead in his conception of the love story.

They had no trouble securing a passage from New York to Lisbon on an American liner, the ss *Excambion*, two days after Christmas 1940. She had been packed with 400 refugees from Europe on the westward voyage. Now, barely twenty passengers occupied the same accommodation on the return journey to Europe. Years later Vivien's film *Ship of Fools* added to the emotional crisis she was undergoing by bringing back to mind that lonely and nervous voyage aboard a vessel with a large number of German-American officers, whose loyalties were suspect in the Oliviers' eyes. As they were now world-famous nationals of a country at war with the Axis, they felt they had a high hostage value and their constant nightmare was of hearing, as Olivier later put it, 'an ominous scraping sound against the side of the ship, followed by a sharp rap on our cabin door, through which we could be unceremoniously pulled on to the outside deck, thrust down a rope ladder, to disappear as prisoners-of-war into the waiting U-boat.'

With relief, they disembarked at Lisbon to find that *Wuthering Heights* was the hit film there. This helped Olivier pull a few diplomatic strings and they secured seats on a Portuguese Dakota for the five-hour flight to Bristol. The only excitement *en route* was the navigator's decision to fire a rocket recognition signal in mid-flight without remembering to open the cabin window.

The Oliviers landed in Bristol to the sound of anti-aircraft guns ineffectually answering an air raid and were lucky enough to find a room in a blitzed hotel, which had one wall open to the freezing night except for a flapping tarpaulin. They heaped their outside clothes over the flimsy bedsheets and fell asleep exhausted.

# 13

# 'Time is very precious to us all'

Their first weeks back in London were unhappy ones. They so badly wanted to 'do their bit', but all they experienced was a feeling of being out of place.

Even the devotion they showed to the rules and regulations that bureaucracy heaped on civilians in wartime tended to be lightly ridiculed by those who'd already developed a self-protective mockery of Government red tape. Vivien recalled getting on a bus after a long wait for a taxi and finding the girls going off to night shift giggling at her.

'Why are you laughing?' she asked. They pointed at the patent leather gasmask case she'd slung rather stylishly on her shoulder before leaving home.

Durham Cottage had been blitzed by a nearby bomb and the dining-room ceiling was cracked. Fortunately Gertrude had shrouded Vivien's antiques in decorators' sheets before she left for Canada; and neighbours had boarded up the little conservatory's windows. But worse than the dilapidation was the cold and the damp, yet Vivien wouldn't have exchanged any of it for California: *there* she had felt embalmed, *here* at least she knew she existed.

Leigh Holman was serving at a naval base, whereabouts officially unknown for security reasons; the house in Little Stanhope Street had been flattened in the bombing of Mayfair.

Friends fortunately proved more solid landmarks: Ralph Richardson (in his Fleet Air Arm uniform, much to Olivier's chagrin), John Mills (in the Royal Engineers), Olivier's brother Dickie (an RNVR officer), Roger Furse, the stage designer (in sailor's rig). Everyone had a uniformed role but himself, Olivier said gloomily. He had failed his medical for active service because of a ruptured nerve in his eardrum and now depended on getting a nonoperational posting as a flying instructor. Not a very glamorous war after all; others had nabbed the better parts.

As the strangeness of being home wore off, Vivien fell prey to inactivity. She was like a pet denied exercise. Olivier made a striking cameo appearance

as a French-Canadian trapper in the Michael Powell/Emerič Pressburger production of *49th Parallel*; but Glynis Johns (succeeding an actress who had
defected to America when the film unit went on location there) had already
been cast in the sole leading female role among twenty men.

Vivien hadn't left America with Selznick's blessing: anything but.... After
*Lady Hamilton*, she owed Selznick her next picture under contract, but every
project he proposed she rapidly turned down. He called her ungrateful; she
treated him, according to Irene Selznick, as if he were imposing on her. What
did a contract matter if her country needed her? 'In the early years I was frankly
on her side,' Mrs Selznick wrote. 'I felt she was being courageous and romantic,
and that after the war she would make amends. It turned out that I was the
romantic one.'

Vivien and Olivier toured the air bases with a concert troupe composed of
stage friends, among them John Clements and Constance Cummings. They
played the scene from *Henry V* in which the King woos the French Princess.
The Old Vic's wartime headquarters was in Burnley, so up they went, hoping
Tyrone Guthrie had a job to offer Vivien. But the prickly Guthrie was never
her friend, she felt, and he for his part sensed trouble in a fractious Vivien who
might soon be separated from Olivier for long stretches. Her fame, he told her,
had outgrown the Hobson's choice of rotating roles in a repertory company.
Vivien arched her back at this. But *Gone With the Wind* had opened in April
and *Waterloo Bridge* in November 1940, both to great acclaim. Put Vivien Leigh's
name on an Old Vic poster and the public would be right to resent seeing a
star in a bit part.

Now the euphoria of being back home was succeeded by a sense of dis-
placement. Then, in mid-April 1941, Olivier was ordered to report to Lee-on-
Solent for several weeks of flying instruction. Vivien refused point blank to be
left behind. Then Ralph and Mu Richardson placed a nearby cottage at their
disposal and they piled Vivien's little open car with personal belongings, adding
to the heap her favourite paintings by Boudin and Sickert, an Aubusson carpet,
and Dickens's complete works. As Vivien's car wouldn't start – it had lain idle
for months – it became a luggage van to be towed by a second-hand Invicta
that Olivier had bought off Richardson. Vivien steered and kept a stray cat
(named Tissy) on her lap. Progress to Plymouth was slow, but jolly.

Soon they moved out of the cottage into a rented house at Worthy Down,
near Winchester, called 'Forakers' – a name they elided into a more ribald word –
and sent to London for a cook.

Thus did Vivien become a wartime wife, waving Olivier goodbye after
breakfast as he set out on his motorbike for lessons at the sea-plane base, then
trying to fill the day with shopping, reading, gardening, living very much a

fixed life since transport was a problem. Olivier could occasionally pull rank as an instructor to wangle a few extra gallons for the Invicta, but Vivien was stranded when he was at the base. Because of her poor sense of balance, she couldn't ride a bicycle. She'd thought of buying a tricycle. Olivier was against it. It would look rather odd, he said.

Nevertheless, he soon grew worried by Vivien's increasing dejection. She had to get back to work. Binkie Beaumont was appealed to at H. M. Tennent. Well, he asked, had *they* any plays to suggest? Why not George Bernard Shaw's *The Doctor's Dilemma*, with Vivien as Jennifer Dubedat? It was the only major role for a woman in a play with eleven men, undoubtedly a star part. But Vivien didn't much care for Shaw's sermon on the artist's place in society – such a singularly unpleasant artist too. And then the accent of the drama was placed so firmly on Louis Dubedat that the actress who played his wife and widow would have a hard job to be interesting. Shaw had warned Lillah McCarthy in 1906 that it was a thankless part.

Binkie Beaumont, however, saw the production with the eye of an entrepreneur in terms of wartime escapism. Its Edwardian setting and costumes would not only exploit Vivien's flair for wearing elegant formal clothes: it would also be an antidote to the austerity, rationing and drabness of a nation in uniform; and then again, there was hope of a film version.

Returning to Hollywood after their last brief prewar holiday in France in the summer of 1939, Vivien and Olivier had made the Atlantic crossing on the *Normandie* in the company of the film producer Gabriel Pascal. Like Korda, Pascal was Hungarian, but brasher and coarser and unashamedly boastful where his compatriot was discreet and worldly. Yet Pascal, too, could play against the phlegmatic English grain and turn on the charm with a persistence that made it hard for the victims to tell if they were being captivated or conned; probably both, they realized later.

Pascal's successful 1938 film version of Shaw's *Pygmalion* had brought Shaw firmly under his influence. The author was magnetized by the sort of charmer who could succeed where more sober men had failed, and was greedy for the experience that a new medium like the cinema offered him, as well as the profits which went with it. Pascal had shown Vivien and Olivier a letter from Shaw appointing him 'sole director' of a planned film version of *The Doctor's Dilemma*. He had intended it for Greer Garson, with whom he was greatly infatuated, calling her 'my red-haired Circe'. He had told them during the voyage that Shaw saw him not only as the production arm of his own genius, but also as a surrogate son. Pascal had much amused them. They assured him he'd be in his element in Hollywood.

But unfortunately for Pascal, Shaw wouldn't countenance his 'son' settling in

Hollywood, where there was money, as well as Circe, simply to produce Americanized versions of his plays. So Pascal returned to wartime Britain, endured some paternal scolding, became a naturalized British subject, and sought help from David Selznick and Jock Whitney, amongst others, in filming *Major Barbara*. Thus the interests of Pascal, Vivien and Selznick – to whom she owed her next film – all coincided.

So Vivien agreed to do *The Doctor's Dilemma*. Even if it weren't filmed, it might lead her to the Shaw play she really wanted to do on the stage or screen, *Caesar and Cleopatra*. One feels other people marking out the stepping stones for her, assured that her willpower would keep her going if they gave her a gentle push. Once more Binkie Beaumont was there as guide-companion.

In the summer of 1941, *Lady Hamilton* opened in London and Vivien was left perplexed and distressed by some of the critics' notices, which she thought very hurtful. In later years the film and the performances of its two stars were to be regarded with a respect and affection the reviewers didn't feel at the time.

'It is my impression that [the film] would have been better if it had stuck to this man Nelson and bothered less about that woman Hamilton,' wrote C. A. Lejeune in the *Observer*. 'These are not days when we have much patience for looking at history through the eyes of a trollop.' The reason for this and other cool notices is suggested by Caroline Lejeune's feline last paragraph: 'I am not at all sure that English people, who have been fighting for two years for something they like to call an ideal, will care very much for the implication that the future died with Nelson. So there's no "then" is there?' she wrote, recalling Emma Hamilton's last words in the film. 'So there's no "after"? Come over here, Mr Korda, and watch the future being made.' In short the film became the focus of the considerable resentment felt in Britain at what was seen as Korda's desertion of his beleaguered country for the easy life of a moviemaker in California.

We know now how false an accusation this was. All the evidence – not least Korda's receipt of a knighthood the next year, 1942 – supports the producer's story that he went to America on a patriotic mission for Winston Churchill and made the Oliviers a part of it.

Despite the critics' notices, the film was an enormous popular success. Churchill soon gave it his personal blessing by having it screened aboard the *Prince of Wales* on the occasion of his mid-Atlantic meeting with Roosevelt, and showing it repeatedly to guests and VIPs at his country house, Chartwell Manor. It became his favourite film and was to lead to his meeting Olivier and Vivien.

Vivien herself received flattering notices for the film. Though the *Daily Telegraph*'s film critic Campbell Dixon felt her a bit on the petite side for the

Lady Hamilton immortalized by the painter Romney, he thought it 'easily the finest performance Miss Leigh has given us, and it confirms her position among the first actresses of the screen'.

Buoyed by this, she began to rehearse *The Doctor's Dilemma* in August 1941 with renewed vigour and dedication. This meant being separated from Olivier for quite long periods. Opening in Manchester in September 1941, the production toured England and Scotland for six months during one of the coldest winters on record. Vivien spent hours making long journeys in unheated trains, packed with troops on leave or returning to camp, hardly able to read the works of Dickens by the dim lightbulbs conforming to wartime blackout orders. She lugged the books everywhere, as well as a copy of the greatest Victorian writer's letters which Alexander Woollcott had sent her as a wedding present.

Few recognized Scarlett O'Hara or Lady Hamilton in this pale young woman with her nose in a book, occasionally trying to swab a piece of steam-age grit out of her eye as the train trundled through the iron-hard English countryside, stopping for long unannounced halts to let priority goods trains rush past them.

On one occasion she heard two RAF boys joking together and caught the word 'Larry'. One said: 'He's a duck out of water.' Instinctively, she knew it was her Larry they meant. The heroic role he had imagined for himself never materialized; instead he was put to training air cadets.

Vivien would see his face tired with tedium rather than from more heroic exploits whenever he picked her up at Winchester station in the old Invicta with its leaking canvas top and flapping side windows. Sometimes he would roar up unexpectedly on his service motorbike to some seedy provincial hotel where the company was billeted, but he confessed to feeling a shirker if he stayed more than a night away from his duties, such as they were.

Vivien had settled comfortably into the play and, as Binkie Beaumont had predicted, it was proving just the tonic for wartime audiences. She looked exquisite. The photograph of her in a close-fitting Edwardian hat with a chin-length veil and a lace fichu secured at the neck with a Victorian pin she had found in a Winchester antique shop became Olivier's favourite picture of her.

But sometimes, he thought, she looked disturbingly frail and she went through a spell of constant colds – all of which she dismissed as not worth talking about. As for going to the doctor, that suggestion elicited a blunt refusal.

Leigh Holman occasionally sent her a cheque to defray the cost of Suzanne's upkeep and education in Canada. He doubted if *The Doctor's Dilemma* was really the best play for her. Vivien still worried about Louis Dubedat getting any sympathy going – 'That is where Cyril [Cusack] fails a bit,' she wrote to Leigh, 'but he is such a good actor he will probably improve all the time.' To make herself look more mature as Jennifer Dubedat, she took to speaking and moving in a more measured way. One day in Blackpool she went horse-riding on the beach; that evening, she noted ruefully, her performance was much stiffer.

The play opened in London in March 1942, receiving excellent notices and running for thirteen months – then a record for a play by Shaw. Vivien might have found such a long run boring; but, instead, she welcomed the regularity it restored to her life. Variety was provided by the number of her leading men who fell victim to one kind of misfortune or another: Cyril Cusack was taken ill in the first week and was replaced by Peter Glenville, who contracted jaundice and then, to Vivien's great delight, John Gielgud learned the Louis Dubedat part in a weekend and so gained one of the two Shavian roles he had coveted – the other being the poet Marchbanks in *Candida*.

Replacements were commonplace in wartime shows and one of the recasting auditions Vivien attended was for the role of the Newspaper Man. One boy among the hopefuls who auditioned looked hardly out of his teens. Richard Attenborough was trying for the understudy's role, but was so word-perfect in just about the whole play that 'I could have understudied anyone's part in it,' he recalled.

'When the audition ended,' Attenborough continues, 'a voice I recognized as Binkie Beaumont's called out from the dark, "Thank you ... we'll be in touch." Then a woman's voice added, "We'll *certainly* see you again." A day or so later, I got a message to come to Vivien Leigh's dressing-room before the show.'

Behind the door with the gilt star edged in red sat Vivien, making herself up. She came to the point there and then. 'There's no doubt about it. You're perfect for the part. But it's an understudy's role. Would you be happy with that?'

Attenborough mumbled the usual thing about the privilege of joining the company, watching others' craftsmanship, etc. But Vivien suddenly became very practical. 'You're waiting to be called up, aren't you? How long have you got?'

'Oh, long enough to understudy ... '

'That's not the point. You will probably be in uniform for a few years at the rate this war's going. In all that time, you probably won't ever get a chance to act – and if you hang around here, waiting for someone to fall ill, you won't ever know the thrill of actually playing in a London theatre. Go away – and look for a part you can play *now*. Time is very precious to us all.'

He took her advice and before he joined the RAF a year later, Attenborough had appeared in *The Little Foxes*, then in the stage adaptation of Graham Greene's *Brighton Rock* as well as making a screen appearance in *In Which We Serve*.

'Vivien was a very shrewd career-plotter,' he says. 'She could see the way ahead with enormous clarity and certainty – for others as well as for herself.'

Despite the success of *The Doctor's Dilemma*, Bernard Shaw didn't come to see it. He had a horror of seeing his own works on the stage. He was therefore unfamiliar with Vivien, though not uninformed about her. Perhaps Pascal had pricked his curiosity even more by telling him Vivien was determined to play Cleopatra. He could see the value of an actress who was English enough to please Shaw, yet international enough to sell the film in America. Shaw asked what age she was. 'In her twenties.' This was just about true: in fact, Vivien was set to celebrate her thirtieth birthday in 1943. Was she fat or tall? 'No, she's slim and petite.'

'It's a curious fact', said Shaw, 'that ladies who set their hearts on that particular part are invariably giantesses or over fifty. Miss Leigh must be exceptional.'

Shaw had already suffered a setback trying to cast a leading lady for *St Joan* – which he and Pascal hoped would be the first of a three-picture deal with J. Arthur Rank. Elisabeth Bergner he found 'too tear-y'; Deborah Kerr, 'not thick enough'; Garbo, a mere 'sex appealer'; Wendy Hiller had 'not enough feel for religious parts'; and Ingrid Bergman, to his annoyance, opted for Maxwell Anderson's *Joan the Maid*. So *St Joan* was temporarily discarded; *Caesar and Cleopatra* replaced it on the roster, and the one candidate Shaw hadn't seen was summoned to his flat at Whitehall Court.

Binkie Beaumont accompanied Vivien and watched her give an impeccable performance. It was the Scarlett O'Hara technique over again: as near as possible, and without speaking any of the lines of the play she assumed the role she wanted. Her eyes had slightly heavier mascara, bringing that exotic quality of early *Vogue* fashion photographs into prominence, yet she behaved with a maidenly demureness which immediately appealed to the eighty-seven-year-old Shaw's fondness for tutorial relationships with young women, especially clever young women. For Vivien signalled early on what a game all this was really – she charmed the old pretender with her childish wiles.

After they'd been making small talk for some minutes, Beaumont realized what Vivien was about – she was transposing the seductive power-play of the opening scene between Cleopatra and the tired old gentleman conqueror of Egypt into the sitting-room of Whitehall Court. She and Shaw discussed anything *but* the play, though their conversation had a captivating parallel with it. Vivien was never renowned for shyness, yet Shaw assured Pascal soon after meeting her that, 'Vivien's shyness does not matter. I can knock all that out of her and get going in half a jiffy' – a remark that shows how well she assumed the right complexion to get the part. The unspoken collusion between the two of them continued, neither of them referring to what both knew to be the visit's real purpose, until Shaw said mischievously, 'You know, what you ought to do is play Cleopatra.'

'Do you think so?' Vivien asked. 'Would I be good enough?'

Shaw, now completely hooked, assured her she would look wonderful. 'You don't need to be an actress,' he added. 'The part's foolproof.' (Coincidentally, that was near enough Sydney Carroll's evaluation of Vivien's breakthrough role in *The Mask of Virtue*, though in this case the comment probably referred to Shaw's estimation of himself as a playwright rather than Vivien as an actress.)

Shaw shook hands with Vivien at the door, then holding her hand as if to make sure she concentrated on the remark, he said, 'You are the Mrs Pat Campbell of the age.' Felix Barker suggests what may have been behind this ambiguous parting shot: 'Many of Mrs Campbell's early letters are concerned with subtle stratagems and long battles of wits with Shaw for getting her own way as an actress.' But if Vivien herself ever saw it this way, she dissembled well and always alluded to Shaw's utterance as 'the compliment I most relished in my life'. She maintained he was referring to her performance in the play of his she was appearing in – not to the strategy employed to secure the leading role in the next film she was to make.

It was almost *not* the next film, however. *That* could have been *Henry V*, but for David O. Selznick.

The Oliviers had moved from Worthy Down into a pleasant country cottage at Fulmer, Buckinghamshire, to be nearer Denham studios. Olivier had been granted leave from the Fleet Air Arm to make yet another patriotic film aimed at enhancing the Allies' mutual trust and understanding. *This Demi-Paradise* (US title: *Adventure for Two*), directed by Anthony Asquith, cast him as a Russian marine engineer in England on a wartime mission grappling with the British way of life. Olivier regarded it, wisely, as a purely technical exercise and accumulated a lot of amusing Russian details. But on returning to duty, he found his last hope of seeing active service had vanished with the withdrawal of the Walrus-type flying-boats. Lacking a contemporary battle to fight, he turned the more readily to an historical battlepiece in which he could be assured the leading role – and began planning his film of *Henry V*.

Vivien could have expected to play Katherine, the French princess, a role she had already done when they had toured the air bases in 1941. But to her intense frustration, David Selznick refused to let her.

His contract with Vivien had been suspended by mutual agreement on 19 November 1941 and a further extension granted up to 15 September 1943. Attempts had been made to get Vivien back to Hollywood. All had proved fruitless. Selznick's aide, Dan O'Shea, wrote a memorandum on 27 September 1943, to F. L. Hendrickson, head of the Legal Department at MGM studios, in which he said: 'Inasmuch as [Vivien] has been absent from the screen for some time, they [Selznick's company] feel it is necessary that she come back in an important picture, as her value has decreased in America, although in England she is still very popular as they are still releasing *Gone With the Wind*.' Vivien had been offered other roles by Selznick, including *Jane Eyre*, but she had chosen to ignore them. Now Selznick felt that for her to play a role as small as that of Katherine would be inappropriate casting for someone of her star status. He was anxious to protect his investment; he saw himself as a star-builder; he was not going to let Vivien dissipate her stardom by playing bit parts, however illustrious the subject.

On the other hand, wrote O'Shea, 'Pascal is going to produce *Caesar and Cleopatra* for Rank, this being an excellent vehicle for her.' After that, O'Shea added, Korda was proposing to use Vivien in a love story with Robert Donat – O'Shea couldn't remember the title, but it was undoubtedly *Perfect Strangers* – in which she would replace Merle Oberon, who was ill. This, too, would be 'excellent'. But Katherine – that was out of the question.

Renee Asherson got the part instead; and Vivien hardened her heart even more against David Selznick – by keeping her out of *Henry V*, he had come between her and the man she loved.

Meanwhile, Pascal was having trouble casting Caesar's role and had left for America to see who was available there. Shooting wouldn't get under way until 1944. So, when *The Doctor's Dilemma* closed in April 1943, Vivien accepted Binkie Beaumont's proposal to fill in time by entertaining the troops in North Africa.

She did so even more cheerfully on discovering that her fellow entertainers included Bea Lillie, and the music-hall artists Dorothy Dickson and Leslie Henson. But what would she actually do? The question was put by John Gielgud, who was co-ordinating the show. Her mind went back to *Romeo and Juliet* and she suggested the Potion Scene. There was a second's intake of breath, then Gielgud remarked unwittingly, 'Oh, no, Vivien! Only a great actress can do that sort of thing.' She let that pass. Eventually, she decided on two dramatic recitations, Newbolt's 'Drake's Drum' and Lewis Carroll's 'You Are Old, Father William'.

'I think it was I who suggested that Vivien do the Carroll poem,' Sir John Gielgud recalls, 'and Vivien's contribution was to do it in a copy of one of the dresses she had worn as Scarlett O'Hara. It was most peculiar, but very effective.'

The pseudonymous versifier Sagittarius wrote some material for Vivien allowing her to claim she was 'not so scarlet as Scarlett O'Hara' – and with Bea Lillie coaching her, she was soon delivering it like a veteran trouper.

For three months they toured the North African theatre of war from Gibraltar to Cairo. They endured gruelling heat to play to a few beds in a makeshift hospital for the badly wounded, or to audiences of up to 8,000 men. Their stages were often set amidst the sand dunes and once they played in the great Roman amphitheatre at Leptis Magna, near Tripoli.

Felix Barker, himself a Desert Rat, witnessed this last occasion. 'There was a remarkable moment when Vivien Leigh stood all alone on the vast stage, picked out in the darkness by a spotlight, and hardened soldiers who had fought through a gruelling campaign sat spellbound as she recited Lewis Carroll's poem.'

The tour attracted a full house of wartime commanders-in-chief including Generals Eisenhower, Montgomery and Doolittle, as well as a Royal Command Performance on the seaward-facing terrace of a villa at Tunis, where King George VI was quartered on a tour of the war fronts. The King suggested she extend her repertoire to include his favourite poem. Vivien enquired what this was. Alice Durer Miller's 'The White Cliffs of Dover', replied His Majesty. 'How very inspiring,' said Vivien, who then wrote to tell Olivier of the request. Perhaps he had Noël Coward with him when he replied to Vivien, who was by this time in Cairo, over the official Forces Signals Network: 'How peculiar! Be careful of the donkeys! I hear they're very forward.'

News of the troupe's arrival would invariably bring West End stars who were now in uniform rushing round to the 'stage door' tent flap, and the air was pierced with 'Darlings!' to the consternation of the old sweats. On one occasion, Vivien and Bea Lillie heard that Alec Guinness and Peter Bull, both naval commanders now, were on ships lying at anchor off the Algerian coast. They sent them a signal, inviting them to catch the afternoon show at a garrison theatre some sixty miles inshore. The two actors arrived to find Binkie Beaumont conducting business with London by phone, as if peace reigned again and he was in his West End office. They had strict orders to be back in time to take their ships out of harbour that night, and they began fretting, as Vivien thought, unnecessarily early. Guinness later related how she fixed it so that they'd make the deadline.

> She buttonholed, with all her wheedling charm, a starry-eyed Admiral. Caressing the lapels of his uniform, admiring his campaign ribbons, she suddenly asked him what he was doing for the next few hours. His eyes danced with excitement and he blushingly replied, 'Nothing!' – 'Then,' Vivien went on, 'you won't be needing your car.' – 'It's at your disposal, fair lady.' – 'You are *too* sweet,' she said. 'You see, I have two darling friends here, and they've simply got to be driven back to a little place, just around the corner. . . . So you're going to be the dear thing you are and send them home in your

car.' — The Admiral's face fell: but he bowed acceptance and defeat — 'To show you how grateful I am,' Vivien went on, 'I'm going to give you a little kiss and then, perhaps, a nice big drink.'

Vivien conquered her homesickness long enough to extend her North African tour by three weeks, so as to visit out-of-the-way hospitals and field units. She arrived back in England early in September 1943.

As there was still no starting date for *Caesar and Cleopatra*, she busied herself with the cat and the garden, noting how both had proliferated in her absence, while Olivier began editing *Henry V* at nearby Denham studios. Friends called — John and Mary Mills, David Niven and his wife Primula — and weekend parties sometimes took a ribald turn urged on by Vivien. Thus Brendan Bracken, a crony of Churchill's (and Korda's) and a wartime Cabinet Minister, dropped by for a late drink and was startled by the Hallowe'en Night scene confronting him when he entered the house. There was Olivier, swathed in an Egyptian djellaba which Vivien had brought back with her, attempting to sing the 'Hallelujah Chorus', Vivien in a veil performing as if she were in *The Miracle*, and Bobby Helpmann listing towards *Salome* in nothing more than a jock-strap.

The practical side of Vivien's character is well illustrated by a story later told about her at this date by the American actress Lynn Fontanne.

'At a party she went to one Easter, Vivien was presented with a beautifully painted Easter egg. She was fluent in her thanks to the giver, going on and on enthusiastically about the beauty of the gift — "Didn't the Chinese keep eggs for a hundred years?" and this egg would certainly be kept *at least* a hundred years — and then, having said a great deal more than enough, she went home, clasping the egg happily to her bosom.

'We were staying with her and Larry at the time, as were Bobby Helpmann and Gar Kanin. The next day we had a particularly delicious lunch — scrambled eggs and bacon from America. Bobby said, "By the way, Vivien, what have you done with that lovely Easter egg that was given you last night?" Vivien replied coldly, "You're eating it now." '

Taxed with insincerity some time afterwards, Vivien dodged the charge: 'Well, it *was* during the war when there were no eggs available.'

When *Caesar and Cleopatra* at last went before the cameras at Denham in June 1944, the long wait since she had first committed herself to make the film had sapped much of Vivien's initial enthusiasm. Yet this alone cannot account for the pallid impression she made in most of the film. Her energy seems to have drained away, too, to an alarming extent. The dehydrating effect of the lengthy desert tour had given her face a strained look and lent her voice a thinness which it was no use her trying to deepen since her Cleopatra was supposed to be a sixteen-year-old girl.

Then again Pascal was an uninspiring director. Pedantic and static, the film belies all the promise of its title: it is an argument, not a love affair; grandiose without ever being epic; populated with Shavian mouthpieces, not independently minded human beings. Its extravagance depressed even Shaw. 'I pity poor Rank. It will cost him a million,' he said after a visit to the sets. It was an underestimate. Its final cost was £1.3 million, compared to Olivier's £475,000 budget for *Henry V*, which became very profitable wherever it was shown, whereas the Shaw film was a failure everywhere – deservedly so. Shaw's insistence that not a line, not a single word should be altered without his permission turned Vivien and the cast into the pupils of a slavish grammarian. But, when he saw Claude Rains, who was playing Caesar, even Shaw had to amend the sacred text. By no stretch of the imagination could he be called 'thin and stringy'. Shaw wrote to Vivien: 'Will you say instead, "You are hundreds of years old, but you have a nice voice, etc., etc." I think this is the only personal remark that needs altering; but if there is anything else let me know.'

Vivien didn't need teacher's encouragement to speak up. But she promptly had her knuckles rapped for impertinence when she told Shaw she thought she could make the original lines believable by saying them a certain way. Shaw wrote back: 'Rains is not stringy, and would resent any deliberate attempt to make him appear so ... I never change a line except for the better. Don't be an idiot.' (In fact, the line Vivien spoke in the film was, 'You are old and rather wrinkly ...' emphasizing the childishness of her character, and, perhaps, echoing the poem 'You Are Old, Father William'.)

Relations between Shaw and Vivien deteriorated further when the playwright came down to Denham to see the meeting of Caesar and Cleopatra at the Little Sphinx.

She was word-perfect; that was fine. At least she wasn't the cause of the endless retakes that the finicky Pascal demanded at Rank's expense. It was her pronunciation which drew Shaw's disapproval. He was every bit as stern as Professor Higgins was with Eliza Doolittle. When Vivien had been to see Shaw at his country home, they got on well: he even started tweaking her bottom if she turned her back on him for an unguarded instant. But now he was impossible to please. In one of his famous postcards to Pascal, he complained: 'With Vivien Leigh gabbling tonelessly such sounds as *cuminecho* and *oaljentlemin*! Does she always go on like that or should I have had her here to drill her in the diction of the part?'

Vivien's temper started fraying. *Gone With the Wind* had been a test of endurance, too, but Pascal was no Selznick. The latter interfered creatively; the former only created interference. She was also extremely displeased by her appearance. 'There was more of Cleopatra in her Scarlett O'Hara than in this pale elf,' C. A. Lejeune was to write in her review.

But more than any troublesome feature of the filming, what distracted her from her performance was her pregnancy.

She had gone into the film knowing she was carrying Olivier's child. At long last, she hoped, their union would be blessed with a family. But she felt unwell and recalled with foreboding the heartbreak she had suffered less than two years earlier, in September 1942, when she had had a miscarriage. The English summer of 1944 was cold and she was forced to imagine Alexandria's heat standing in Oliver Messel's Egyptian chiffons in the rawness of the outdoor sets. Worse still, Pascal's agonizingly slow progress, further inhibited by the new V1 flying bombs that landed near the studios, caused her to worry that her pregnancy would show before filming ended, which might mean that she would have to be replaced.

Some six weeks after shooting began, in mid-July 1944, she was playing one of the few scenes in the film that had anything like action in it. 'I've had a fine time this morning,' she wrote to the avuncular theatre critic Alan Dent, 'running up and down Memphis Palace beating the slave.' But Pascal viewed the rushes and, as the lighting displeased him, ordered retakes for the next day. So again Vivien seized the whip and beat the one rather tubby Nubian left in Cleopatra's palace after all her other retainers had fled before the Romans. She was to chase the man off the set in long-shot, throw away her whip, skim along the polished floor of the throne room and leap on to the dais, throwing up her arms with a cry of exultation: 'I am a Queen at last − a real, real Queen! Cleopatra the Queen!' But just as she swivelled round to begin running, she slipped on the highly polished floor and crashed to the ground. She was carried to her dressing-room and a doctor was called. No bones appeared broken; but he ordered an X-ray and a few days' rest. Shortly afterwards, she had her second miscarriage.

Vivien put on as brave a face as she could. 'There'll be plenty more where that one came from,' she told friends. But she had lost the link she needed to tie herself even more fondly to Olivier and to achieve the motherhood she hadn't appreciated the first time round.

She was soon back at work, but something besides the baby seemed to have expired within her. She simply found no part of her being involved in the filming. Her spirits began to droop visibly. In front of the camera she would fail to respond to the call of 'Action'. And then, with startling suddenness, her depression turned into manifest hysteria.

Towards the end of September they were filming one of the most lavish and important sequences − Cleopatra's banquet in Caesar's honour held on the roof terrace of the palace. Earlier, Cleopatra has commanded her body-servant Ftatateeta to murder her bitter enemy Pothinus. Caesar is to hear the man's dying cry off screen – and realize for the first time the total amorality of this innocent-looking child-queen. Vivien advanced and began leading Caesar, his henchman Rufio and the tanned Sicilian dilettante Apollodorus (played by Stewart Granger), towards the eating area – and then she stopped dead. As the other players faltered, they saw her features transfigured. Her face sharpened. She broke away from Shaw's dialogue and began berating her dresser for some small sin of omission she discerned in her costuming. Her voice was now high and harsh. Her brows had hardened into an angry line. Bystanders saw her eyes take on a piercing glare, possibly the same look that had so disconcerted John Gliddon a few years earlier.

A break was called and Vivien, protesting vigorously that nothing was wrong with her, was led to her dressing-room. There she suffered a hysterical fit, but it was short-lived and ceased as suddenly as it had come on her. She immediately sat down to write letters of apology to the director and her co-stars.

Though she appeared rational again, she was put in her limousine and driven home, all the time insisting on studying the scenes scheduled for the next day. She did not return for five or six weeks.

Olivier at first attributed her collapse to delayed depression following the miscarriage. But then Vivien began going in and out of a manic-depressive state for several weeks. However, she appeared to make a good recovery and he found it unthinkable that the gentle, loving woman he was with had been the person with the glowering looks and abusive temper. She seemed not to believe it herself, or to remember how she had behaved. She asked what she had done and to whom she owed apologies. She refused to go into hospital, assuring Olivier that she had recovered. The disturbance seemed so localized, almost a social *faux pas*, that the idea of mental impairment didn't seriously suggest itself to Olivier. His pity and relief at her return to apparent normality were immense – and dissuaded him from insisting that she be examined further against her will.

When Vivien returned to the film, her very calmness lent a strength to her performance that it had previously lacked – and Pascal had one of his few inspirations.

He proceeded directly to the sequences where Cleopatra, hardened by Caesar's reproaches for her callousness, gains the dignity of a queen who is a woman to be dreaded and no longer a playful child. Thus Vivien's final scenes in *Caesar and Cleopatra* are the film's best ones: her features look refined, sharp-edged and, now that she can lower her voice to suit the sombre mood, she grows in sudden effectiveness.

The last scenes were good, but not good enough to save the film. Shaw insisted on being shown it privately, with only Pascal and an unnamed friend present. What he saw of Vivien displeased him. 'She's not right at all: that should be a delicious piece of comedy,' he kept on repeating. Afterwards, Vivien telephoned to know what Shaw had thought of her. 'There was nothing for it but to lie,' the friend later recalled, 'but I didn't make it sound very convincing and I'm surprised that she forgave me.'

She certainly was not taken in. She was to let six years go by before she could bear to see the film – and then it was only because she was playing the role again, but this time with Olivier as her Caesar.

# 14

## 'I have everything at Notley, including Larry'

*V*ivien recovered her health and spirits soon after finishing her role in *Caesar and Cleopatra*. The main reason for this was the prospect of returning to work in her first love – the theatre. It offered her the sanctuary of a relatively rational existence after the frustrations of the film studios, regular hours and a set performance. And then Olivier was directing her.

The play was Thornton Wilder's *The Skin of Our Teeth*, a serio-comic masque describing mankind's obstinate insistence on surviving its Creator's apocalyptic second thoughts and its own perennial folly.

The play had come to the Oliviers from New York, where Tallulah Bankhead was starring in the role which Vivien adored the instant Binkie Beaumont presented her with the script – that of Sabina, a siren, soul sister of the Cleopatra she had just played, but mercifully without the historical constraints of what she now called 'Shaw's newt of the Nile'. Sabina portrayed the Eternal Feminine through all the ages of the world, herself unageing, assuming the carnality of a beauty queen or the flighty posturing of a flirtatious housemaid. A marvellous chameleon role in cut and texture, it perfectly suited Vivien's quick-change talents.

She toured the wartime cabarets and revues at London's little theatres to brush up on the techniques of burlesque and parody; and Felix Barker thinks that some of the tricks of Bea Lillie, who had more secrets to transmit than the Sphinx, had rubbed off on Vivien during her North African concert tour.

Rehearsals began in February 1945 without a break from playing Cleopatra. The Oliviers wanted it on stage as soon as possible. For one thing, they needed the money. Vivien had been paid £25,000 for *Caesar and Cleopatra*, but the film had taken twice the allotted schedule to shoot. Olivier had taken a cut in his own fees over the eighteen months it took him to make *Henry V*, simply to get the film under way. Wartime taxes were high. Furthermore, sensing the European conflict to be near its end, they hankered for permanence and had already spent months surveying a Buckinghamshire property called Notley Abbey. Its purchase and restoration would take up all their savings.

Then came an unexpected setback – all the way from Hollywood. David Selznick refused to let Vivien appear in the Wilder play.

Just as John Gliddon had done, it was now Selznick's turn to suspect Olivier of being behind much of Vivien's wilful refusal to return to Hollywood and honour her contract with him. He appeared to be feeling the pull of a rival producer – one who was married to the star. Some interesting facts emerged in an exasperated memo which Selznick sent Dan O'Shea on 19 February 1945, ominously marked with an intimidating 'Immediate Action'. He'd agreed, he said, to Vivien's appearance in *Romeo and Juliet* only because of her and Olivier's urgings. But the terrible reviews had seriously damaged her career. 'This is one reason', he added, 'why we are fearful of another theatrical engagement *prompted and participated in by Olivier* [emphasis added], with possibility of damage to our property.' She had been granted only a twelve-week leave of absence to follow Olivier back to England for patriotic reasons, and this she'd stretched into a fifth year. It was intolerable: she should be made to return to America.

Selznick wasn't the only film-maker who found Vivien's wilfulness costly and frustrating at this time. Korda was another. As head of MGM production in Britain he had bought the film rights to Enid Bagnold's novel *Lottie Dundass* from Myron Selznick for $40,000 expressly to star Vivien in the film. He was intending to shoot it in May 1945. Now she had cooled on it. He proposed alternative pictures, among them *The Old Wives' Tale* and *Far from the Madding Crowd*. He'd already arranged to borrow the French director Julien Duvivier from MGM in America. He'd spent a small fortune. It would mean throwing away a year's work. But Vivien was deaf to Korda's pleas. She wanted to do a play – and a play she would do. She defied him to go to court to enforce his side of the bargain. Of course he didn't. In England, one didn't behave that way.

But he did something more in character and far more astute. Korda saw which way the wind was blowing and therefore opened negotiations to dispose of what remained of Vivien's contract with him. Before he retired from MGM British in December 1945, he had made it part of his settlement to exchange her services to MGM for two pictures from Deborah Kerr, who was a much more reasonable lady.

David Selznick was not so clever. On 23 February 1945, he brought suit in the Chancery Division of the English High Court to restrain Vivien from playing in *The Skin of Our Teeth*. 'We are aware', his lawyer had cabled her, 'that you do not care whether you ever make another film, but obviously this cannot be our viewpoint.'

Selznick lost ignominiously. Vivien's counsel, Valentine Holmes KC, argued that, if she didn't do the play, she might be put to work in something more onerous than the Hollywood dream factory — namely, a British munitions factory. She was still subject to National Service regulations. 'Whether there is actual affirmative evidence that she would get a job as a charwoman, temporary cook, or anything like that, I cannot say,' her counsel stated, adding with the merest hint of a legal blush, 'I don't suppose there is.' But it was enough for the next day's *Daily Mail* headline: 'Vivien Leigh Might Be a Char — Counsel'.

Actually, Vivien did not win her case on these grounds, as some biographers have it, but simply because the judge couldn't see Selznick suffering 'any appreciable damage' if she appeared in this particular play. The injunction was refused on a point of law.

She never made another film for Selznick; and the files in the MGM archives testify to the difficulties the studio had in attempting to make its contract with Vivien stick. They never succeeded for a brutally simple reason: Korda and Selznick, true to their natures, had acted so independently of each other's interest that the whole process of aligning the options on her services under the *Gone With the Wind* contract of 1939 had been thrown into disarray. Korda had made an especially grave mistake in failing to insist that Vivien should pull out of *The Skin of Our Teeth* in 1945 to make *Lottie Dundass*. The contract, counsel said, was now virtually unenforceable. Like Sabina, Vivien seemed able to slip through the great catastrophes of life and emerge unharmed in a new and shining skin.

Edinburgh audiences were politely bemused when *The Skin of Our Teeth* opened there in April 1945. The British stage had seen few plays like it: American vaudeville crossed with the Marx Brothers, a situation comedy obeying the logic of the theatre of the absurd. The free-form humour of the 1941 comedy *Hellzapoppin*, which had arrived in England not long before, may well have been in Olivier's mind when he directed it. The cast behaved with vaudeville aplomb, insulting the audience, the stage manager and each other, veering into a crazy logic that was later to find its English parallel in the lunacy of Peter Sellers and *The Goon Show*. The play was too extravagant for the tastes and comprehension of most provincial audiences attracted by Vivien's name on the bill.

When the production arrived in Blackpool, one of the stage-door callers who forced his way to her dressing-room against the tidal flow of disgruntled playgoers was Jack Merivale. Jack had married the actress Jan Sterling in 1941; but it was not to be a lasting match. He was now in the Royal Canadian Air Force and stationed just down the road. He had loved the play; Vivien was delighted to see him. 'What are you going to do now the war's almost over?' she asked.

'Go back on stage, if it'll have me.' The Merivales' stage connections had recently been enlarged by Jack's step-sister's marriage to the actor-playwright Robert Morley. Vivien made him promise to keep in touch. 'I didn't need to promise,' he recalled. He said goodbye reluctantly. Vivien still seemed to him the most exquisite creature he'd ever seen, although he thought her thinner than she should be.

The play opened in London on 15 May 1945 and was an immediate sensation. On that one night, in the immediate aftermath of the VE Day celebrations for the defeat of the Axis powers in Europe, all the glamour returned to the post-war English theatre. The London opening announced the beginning of the reign of two stars who would dominate the West End stage for the next sixteen years as much because of their marriage as their talents. The production balanced the virtuosity of Olivier's direction with the versatility of Vivien's performance. As well as carrying the show by the vivacity of a quick-change act counted by millennia rather than minutes, her many-faceted character was like a glitterball that dazzled and delighted the first-night audience as Thornton Wilder's wit struck off her in every direction.

The play represented the shock of the new, even to Shaftesbury Avenue sophisticates. The less discriminating and the downright hostile flocked to it too, deliberately hoping for an affront to their sensibilities. But the partnership between Vivien and Olivier was more than a union of celebrities. In the years ahead 'the Oliviers' would be synonymous with wit, beauty, taste, audaciousness, power and even semi-royal status. They set the seal on a style of life with the same romantic richness as the Duke and Duchess of Windsor, except that their marriage gained in glamour from its public exposure, while the Windsors were forced into exile. What they lacked in family ancestry, they made up for in the aristocratic nature of their talents. Their timing was perfect: the Oliviers could not have arrived at a more benign moment.

The British edition of *Vogue* had declared in January that the year 1945 would be the '*Annus Mirabilis* ... [when] hope dares to raise her voice.' At the start of the year, *Vogue*'s gaze was focused on the continent of Europe, where those who had survived by the skin of *their* teeth were struggling back into focus for the intrepid photographers to record. Here were the refugees leaving their overloaded hand-carts in Lee Miller's pictures to recite a prayer of gratitude at wayside shrines. ... Imperceptibly, they gave way, as one turned the pages in each month's issue, to the Jeeps of the GIs parked outside the Crillon ... the frieze-figures of Picasso, Aragon and Eluard at a thanksgiving ceremony in Père Lachaise cemetery ... the Grand Hotel being restored to life as the rowdy Allies Club ... the short dresses that were 'inevitable for dining out with non-existent transport except a *bicyclette*', their austerity softened, here and there, by a hint of the New Look – all worn by Schiaparelli models posed by Cecil Beaton against barrows laden with vegetables, the garden marrows of 'Dig for Victory' days wittily juxtaposed with chartreuse velvet drum-muffs and even toques ... on the next page Vivien had been photographed (also by Beaton) as Cleopatra beside her Denham Sphinx, 'a kittenish, vixenish *élégante*'.

Before the *annus mirabilis* was half over, here was another Vivien, bursting out of Olivier's *Skin of Our Teeth* production like a dancing girl out of a birthday cake in shoulder-length wig dyed carmine, a skirt like a cake decoration and fishnet nylon tights that were replenished throughout the run by weekly replacements sent air-mail from America. Vivien seemed like the totem figure of everything resilient and free-spirited that it was hoped peace would bring.

The turn-out for the first night presaged the way in which the theatre's establishment would group itself around the Oliviers. On this occasion, they were presented by H. M. Tennent (and Binkie Beaumont); soon it would be by the Old Vic; and then Laurence Olivier Productions would become the centre of power.

Wardrobes and trunks were rummaged through for pre-war dinner jackets and evening dresses of outmoded cut, but authentic label; the glamour-starved audiences of the war years could at last dress up again. The Oliviers had given everyone an occasion to celebrate.

'Ten days after London had cheered itself hoarse with excitement at the end of the war in Europe, the play opened', wrote Felix Barker, 'to just the sort of audience that might have decorated just such an occasion in the Thirties.... From the applause at the end [Vivien] knew she had made a great personal success, and the Press was to confirm that Sabina was the most outstanding performance she had given so far.' 'Entrancing mischief' ... 'as sparkling as a diamond' ... 'as volatile as quicksilver', raved the reviews.

It was her first major role in a comedy. Her friends were used to hearing her débutante's trill modulated into a gutsy chuckle as some *risqué* joke was cracked in her company. But a witty, bitchy and sometimes downright randy Vivien was a revelation to the wider public. Her highly-strung temperament, sometimes pushed to extremes of instability, helped to bring her like an express lift up to comic pitch. Many of the notices commented on her 'volatility.'

The part had brought out a different Vivien, and Olivier desperately wanted the critics to recognize this and acclaim her. In his own state of nerves, he even cuffed James Agate roughly for returning late to his seat after the interval. Agate's notice, however, could not have been better: 'Through it all, lovely to look at, flitted and fluttered Miss Leigh's hired girl, Sabina, an enchanting piece of nonsense-cum-allure, half dabchick and half dragonfly.'

By the time the production opened, the Oliviers had moved into a new home that reflected the way they now regarded themselves as well as their status in society and the theatre.

Notley Abbey was an historic residence. A thirteenth-century building of grey stone with mullion windows, set in an estate of nearly seventy acres in Buckinghamshire countryside some fifty miles north of London, it had been founded in Henry II's reign as a church, dwelling-place and hospice for the Augustinian order. On Henry VIII's dissolution of the monasteries, it passed into the private ownership of a Protestant family. Over the centuries, the estate had shrunk as packets of it were sold off, and the building had grown as extensions were added and outhouses expanded.

When the Oliviers first lit on it in 1943, it had over twenty rooms, a refectory barn, a farm manager's cottage, a piggery, chicken houses and dilapidated greenhouses long deprived of winter warmth by fuel rationing. With the property came any fishing rights that were still worth exercising in the weed-choked stretch of the River Thame that ran through the grounds.

Vivien was distinctly put off by the first sight of it. She said it reminded her of Tara after David Selznick's Civil War plunderers had pillaged it. Olivier was of another mind entirely. One look and he said decisively, 'That's it.' When he heard later that Henry V had endowed the place, he was confirmed in his choice. What better omen could there be when he had just played that same English sovereign in his new film?

Over the years, Olivier lavished an excessive amount of love on Notley. He felt it almost sinful to love a *thing* more than people – but there it was. Notley had the advantage of sparing him the intrusions of his fellow men. He could relax there, he hoped, and recharge himself. Much of his love for the place derived from his own strongly religious family upbringing. Moreover, he had been born in a beautiful Queen Anne rectory, which stood 'in lovely serenity' next to the twelfth-century St Mary's Old Church. His father had selfishly (in Olivier's view) surrendered that serenity for a jerry-built minister's house in Letchworth Garden City. Notley meant that his son could return to a religious setting, but above all, it meant 'England' to him at a time when military victory had vindicated his patriotic zeal – alas, in his own case, so often frustrated. Melvyn Bragg has shrewdly noted that Olivier's Englishness or, as he called it, his 'birthright' had been diffused through his work in the theatre, with Shakespeare as its 'pivot', and now it would be concentrated in the English earth of Notley.

In vain did Vivien harp on the cost of refurbishment – as well as the tedious task of unpicking the wartime bundle of red tape just to obtain the building permits. Notley had no modern bathrooms; waterpipes were blocked and some had burst; ceilings were ready to fall at any moment; a few rooms were simply too dangerous to enter because of dry rot in the floorboards and the Oliviers had to look at parts of their desirable residence through the windows. Vivien could see the grounds had 'potential' – but what effort would have to go into realizing it! The huge thicket of the old rose garden would have to be thinned and replanted; the overgrown river frontage cleared; the untidy cypresses clipped and shaped. But Olivier was already viewing it with that inner eye with which he could pull together all the disparate elements of a film or play. Vivien realized she was up against a love as strong as her own, a deep and irrepressible yearning in Olivier to possess and create. She surrendered to it, and Notley became their country home before 1945 was half over.

It is a sad irony that Vivien herself came to love Notley only when infirmity compelled her to live there. Soon after *The Skin of Our Teeth* had opened, people noticed her growing exhaustion. She would exit into the wings with a sprightly enough step; but once back in her dressing-room she collapsed in a sweat and her dresser had to wrap a bath towel round her bare shoulders to staunch the perspiration before the short interval bell called her back on stage. A cough that had first appeared in Liverpool grew worse. Typically she ignored advice to see a doctor, but one night she brought up a spittle of blood. Simply concentrating on being well was clearly not enough. The physician could no longer be warded off. He took X-rays – then, to Vivien's alarm, he asked where Olivier could be contacted. She had an active tubercular infection in her right lung.

In July 1945 Olivier was in Paris. The year before, he had signed a five-year contract as a director of the revived Old Vic Company, now occupying the New Theatre in lieu of its old Waterloo Road home, which had been blitzed. This was to be the start of his ascent to theatrical greatness. It began with a mere ten-minute appearance as the Button Moulder in *Peer Gynt*, continued with the role of Sergius in *Arms and the Man*, and then, in *Richard III*, by marrying technical bravura to a blackly comic psychodrama, he achieved that union between actor and audience that was the most intoxicating power his art had to offer. With this threefold hop, skip and jump in the 1944–5 season, Olivier scaled the summit of his own craft. And the energies that success released in him helped him promote Vivien's own triumph when he directed her in *The Skin of Our Teeth*. 'My joy ... reached its zenith,' he was to recall.

Now he was on the last leg of an Old Vic tour of Allied camps and bases in France. Before Vivien's doctor could contact him, Alfred Lunt and Lynn Fontanne arrived from London with the news that Vivien had tuberculosis.

Korda was still trying to get her to agree to do his postponed production of *Lottie Dundass*, but Vivien's illness quashed this for good. Two physicians, Dr A. P. Cawadias, of St John's Clinic and Institute of Physical Medicine, and Dr W. Irving Pierce, signed an affidavit testifying that it would be 'dangerous for

Miss Leigh to undertake any film work'. Then, asked Korda, very reasonably, why is she still in the stage show? Even in her weakened state, Vivien put up a fight to avoid dropping out of the play. She simply couldn't face inactivity, she said. Her doctor reluctantly let her continue until the end of July 1945. Then she went into University College Hospital for treatment, and was there for six weeks before the patch could be declared safely arrested.

Vivien was a model patient – the sort of sociable convalescent whose own consideration actually made her nurses feel better for her presence. Only once did she show alarm – when she was advised to go into a sanatorium. *'Never!'* But only for six months.... *'Never!'* This seemed sheer wilfulness, and up to a point it was, but behind Vivien's obstinacy lay apprehension. She was far more worried about her mental state than her bodily ailment. Her bouts of alternating elation and depression couldn't be traced to any physical malfunction. If they recurred when she was under long-term supervision there was no telling where she might be put for 'observation'. If she was going to suffer any more attacks, it was better to suffer them at home than in an institution. 'I have everything I want at Notley,' she said, 'including Larry.'

When the doctors told her she would have to rest for nine months, a smile appeared on her face. She had kept herself exquisitely made-up in hospital, as if preparing for the theatre call-boy and not the mid-morning round of nurses and doctors. 'Nine months?' she said. 'Just time to have a baby.' The specialists were shocked, uncertain whether she was serious or joking. She would have to lie in bed for three months at least; after that, she could get up, but there must be no smoking, drinking and only a friend or two at any one time.

Her convalescence began as autumn came to Notley and didn't end until the spring of 1946. But the bonus to winning back her health was the love of Notley that grew out of her enforced rest. In those months, she became its mistress as well as its patient.

She had the rough meadowland shorn with scythes, drainage channels unblocked, new avenues of trees planted, creepers trained up the grey stone walls. Refurbishment expanded from her own L-shaped bedroom through the rest of the house. Sybil Colefax or her partner, John Fowler, brought their decorating skills to bear on lightening the high-ceilinged but rather dark rooms; except for the garden doors, Notley's windows were small and excluded the soft English light which Vivien loved. They conjured up swatches of fabric and scraps of wallpaper patterns as these scarce items filtered back into postwar supply. Leigh Holman visited her and made his own suggestions. Holman's place at Zeals in the West Country, though no abbey, was also cavernous. He advised Vivien to 'go for bigness' in furnishing the rooms. So Notley became a mixture of the professional and the personal, Sybil Colefax's Regency stripes going with the overlarge sofas, refectory tables and floor-to-ceiling pictures purchased to fit the barn-like proportions of the rooms.

In these months, Leigh Holman became a kind of family friend to the Oliviers. There was no bitterness in him at all. 'He was more like a cousin to mother than an ex-husband,' Vivien's daughter Suzanne recalls. 'He gave her good advice on all matters – and always backed his advice with affection.' He brought her books, too, and Vivien read and read and read. She got through the whole of Trollope, and then lighted on the *Life of Buddha* and was captivated by its mix of the mystical and practical – such as how to achieve serenity in easy stages followed by instruction on how to use a boat to weigh an elephant. Emlyn Williams came to see her and discovered the breadth of her reading.

'She was up and about, though taking things quietly. It was sweet to see her, but sad, too. She was all alone. Larry was away in London doing his marvellous season with the Old Vic.'

Williams was already planning his famous appearance as Charles Dickens reading his own works. He thought he'd been through everything the novelist had written. Then Vivien said, 'Have you read *The Battle of Life*?'

'No ... it's a novella, isn't it, about two sisters living in a village? The reason nobody knows it, surely, is because it's not very good.'

'Ah, but have you looked at the first chapter?'

Williams looked it up as soon as he could lay hold of a copy. 'Vivien was so right,' he says. 'The two sisters lived in a village like Evesham or Marston Moor – a great battle had been fought on their doorstep and Dickens's pen had run away with him in his brilliant description of the battle and how the village recovered from it. A marvellous bit of anti-war propaganda! I adopted it for the show – but it was Vivien's intelligence that had spotted its potential.'

As spring began and she was allowed out for short spells, she began to get the garden back into order. The rose garden was cleared of its brambly entanglement and planted with the white floribundas that decorated the rooms in summers to come.

Olivier's brother Richard had moved into the cottage as estate manager and he set about putting the farm and market gardens on a paying footing, buying pigs and a herd of pedigree cows, which Vivien christened after the parts she had played. The meadows soon had their lowing herd of Ophelia, Juliet, Titania, Emma, Cleopatra and Sabina – but never a Scarlett. She had made that role her own: there could be only one Scarlett! The local doctor visited her regularly; a London specialist came down every fortnight. The cook-housekeeper from Fulmer took over the large domain of the stone-flagged kitchen, though often all that Vivien would eat was 'something eggy on a tray'. Notley's great days of entertaining had not yet begun.

At first Olivier commuted daily in his Austin to and from the New Theatre. Then he stayed overnight at Durham Cottage on weekdays. He was beginning to feel drained by the exceptional exertions of the last year or so – yet he was already planning the next Old Vic season, which was to be 'the most concentrated labour' he had ever attempted. He was to pack the parts of Hotspur, Justice Shallow, Sophocles's Oedipus and Sheridan's Mr Puff into four unbelievably crowded weeks of rehearsal.

Though Olivier's 1945–6 season was probably his most sensational in terms of virtuosity, it was also the most punishing in terms of the challenge he set himself. He loved risk-taking. It was as if he functioned at the height of his powers when walking a knife-edge. Star-acting had the effect on Olivier of an aphrodisiac. He revelled in creating a performance. Tyrone Guthrie had told him at the time he was playing the humourless Sergius in *Arms and the Man* that he needed to love the character in order to possess it. This set Olivier off down paths of self-exploration. What he wouldn't have dared do on an analyst's couch, he now achieved through the sheer love of creation. The result was fulfilment of the kind he had never known before – 'an overwhelming feeling, a head-reeling feeling', he called it, when the theatre audience validated his artistry with huge applause, or when the crowd which nightly blocked his stage-door exit acclaimed his celebrity in more alarming ways by trying to touch him, slap him on the back, shake his hand, even tear token buttons off his overcoat.

Of course Olivier had experienced something like it in New York when *Wuthering Heights* made him into a star; but in London, in the heady aftermath of victory, such adulation had turned to a mass hysteria which, as Felix Barker noted, was unique in the history of the theatre. 'Delirious fans, among whom were hundreds of young girls, sent up a wild chant of "We want Larry!" Nothing would move them....'

Olivier's showmanship found appropriate expression in *Oedipus Rex* and *The Critic* in the same nightly double bill. A more cautious man would have given performances on alternate nights. But for Olivier, a great part of the thrill was risking all, *there and then*, on the antithesis the two roles supplied and the virtuosity they required. Such a tragi-comic coupling was intended to leave the audience wondering if anything was beyond his reach – and concluding that nothing was.

All this time, Vivien lay convalescing at Notley, not inactive, but certainly remote and excluded from her husband's triumphs. It was during these months that Olivier's artistry immeasurably outgrew hers. She had neither the talent nor the stamina to keep pace with him. Later on, talking wonderingly to friends about his ability, Olivier would refer to those whom 'God had touched on the shoulder' — after technique had been explained away, what remained was a mystery even to him.

Vivien had come up to London on several occasions to see him on stage and for the first time she glimpsed the heights to which greatness was taking him. At times, he seemed a stranger to her. It wasn't merely that he had outgrown her — Vivien was a realist whenever their respective talents were compared — but he appeared to have grown away from her. There was another love affair going on, one which she couldn't challenge because the rival was that intangible process of self-fulfilment Olivier was experiencing. Vivien was still the centre of one world, but a parallel universe was growing up in which he himself was the centre. Their love for each other from now on had to be reconciled with the passion Olivier manifested for every role he undertook. As Olivier's ambition and power grew, so the substance and satisfaction Vivien found in her marriage to this remarkable man were bound to shrink.

# 15

## 'Walking corpses'

When the Old Vic season finished in May 1946, the company went off to New York almost immediately, hungry for dollars as much as for acclaim. During their six-weeks' season they played *Henry IV, Uncle Vanya, Oedipus* and *The Critic*. Nearly 90,000 people saw them and a third as many again had to be turned away.

Vivien was now well enough to accompany Olivier. She wanted to see old friends and let herself be seen. She wanted to show that her illness had not been incapacitating. Above all, she wanted to be beside her husband again; his consort, if not his co-star.

After that, it was a long summer holiday at Notley for both of them. It was the first chance they'd had since Vivien's illness to invite friends in any numbers to see their estate. They soon established the habit of the long weekend party, supper at midnight on arrival from the West End, a late breakfast, garden work for all willing hands, tennis and croquet for the lazybones, picnics on the river, cocktails in the conservatory, and ever longer evenings of fun and games following dinner with the men in black ties, the women in evening gowns. It was a self-consciously country lifestyle rather like the smart, flirtatious world of the well-made plays of the years just before and after the war. No wonder everyone felt so comfortable. Many of the Oliviers' guests had appeared in such plays; some had even written them.

Vivien's daughter Suzanne, now fifteen and back in England at boarding school after spending the war in Canada with Gertrude, occasionally came down to Notley, though usually when Olivier was away in London. 'Mama had created an atmosphere that was regulated to the last degree, and yet very relaxing,' she recalls. 'Everything had its place, its order of precedence and appearance — yet no one felt put upon. People lay about, the meals arrived unbidden and at just the right moment — all due to Mama's meticulous planning. Nothing went unsupervised.'

It seemed as if Vivien were running Notley Abbey by the tenets of her old convent school, though no one now heard the bells tinkling their summons to devotions, nor the 'clackers' clicking to enforce the day's rota on the cloistered community. Here there were no duties, except the duty to be oneself – which, given the guest list, usually meant to be clever and amusing. Alexander Korda and Merle Oberon; Ralph and Mu Richardson; Michael Redgrave and his wife, Rachel Kempson; David and Primula Niven; Noël Coward; Anthony Quayle and his wife, Dorothy Hyson; Binkie Beaumont; Bobby Helpmann – these were the regulars. Even David Selznick was *persona grata* enough to be invited, once.

In these early years, the Oliviers employed a cook-housekeeper, two Portuguese servants, a local gardener and his wife, and girls who came in from neighbouring villages if extra hands were needed. Despite the luxury, Suzanne Holman confessed that she never felt entirely at ease. 'Mama had a medieval home, which somehow didn't look quite right in Regency stripes.' Others compared it to a film set. But all agreed that Vivien animated it with her presence and tireless hospitality. The library became her favourite room. It was rather lighter in atmosphere than the lofty drawing-room and she would corral the guests there for after-dinner games – especially the mime called simply 'The Game', which television was later to make famous under the title *What's My Line?* Vivien herself preferred paper-and-pencil games; books were always being pulled off the shelves to validate a claim and score a point. Since she did *The Times* crossword every day, it was frequently a dead heat between her and Noël Coward. The canasta craze hadn't yet struck Britain and bridge wasn't smart enough for Vivien's liking. 'If Trivial Pursuit had been invented then,' says Suzanne Holman, 'she'd have taken to it in a big way – but probably spoiled it for herself by memorizing all the answers on the cards.'

Olivier joined in the drawing-room games at Vivien's command, but he couldn't conceal his preference for the outdoors. As money began to replenish their bank accounts, he and Vivien took to landscaping the gardens at Notley. He quickly assumed the role of a gentleman farmer and was soon able to talk plausibly about milk yields and fatstock prices.

Flowers filled the house and gardens. Vivien, who had planted many of them during her convalescence, saw their profusion as a sign of confidence in her own recovery.

She opened again in *The Skin of Our Teeth* at the Piccadilly Theatre in mid-September 1946 to warm notices. That same month, Olivier played King Lear with the Old Vic Company in a short season of only forty-six performances. This time, the critics had reservations. Some found he had insufficient pathos; but the swelling tributary of humour which he fed into the downfall of the king was judged the discovery of the season and James Agate delivered the most frequently repeated of all lapidary verdicts on Olivier – that he was 'a comedian by instinct and a tragedian by art'.

Vivien basked in the reflection of what *The Times* called 'the plenitude of his powers'. Yet she was increasingly aware of how Olivier's acting prowess was outstripping her own. She had accompanied him to New York for the Old Vic season on Broadway earlier that year; how long, she found herself wondering, would it be before she had to accept a supporting role when they played on stage together?

An offer arrived from Hollywood at the end of the summer for them both to appear in a film version of *Cyrano de Bergerac*. Vivien longed to act with her husband again. What a splendid opportunity this would be, she thought. But Olivier was already caught up in his plans for filming *Hamlet*. And her disappointment at having to turn down the Hollywood offer was compounded when it became clear that there was going to be no part for her in the *Hamlet* film. Although Olivier was historically too old to play Hamlet – he was forty – his 'age' on screen fitted the way he conceived the character. Vivien, on the other hand, was visibly too old for Ophelia, and she was temperamentally disinclined to accept the only notable female role that did suit her – Hamlet's mother. She could imagine the winks and nudges this casting would provoke amongst theatre people, and she felt the double standard all the more cruelly when Olivier picked eighteen-year-old Jean Simmons to be his Ophelia.

Vivien sensed her husband's increasing relish for the managerial power that cinema and theatre conferred on him – the power that great talents like his could exert to make things happen (or cause other things not to happen). The springs of creativity lay coiled in the politics of management. In this mood, at full creative stretch, Notley was more precious than ever to him. He saw it literally as a blessed sanctuary. Once within its walls, he told himself, the world would fall away – the pressures of London life would be relieved or at least reduced to the scale of the beloved toy theatre in his study. Yet, as time passed, it became plain that things were not working out this way – work was becoming the refuge from Notley.

For as Vivien's attachment to the place increased, it became a second home to the friends who had crowded their engagement book in London. And at times Olivier worried at the way Vivien drove herself to be the perfect hostess. She was indefatigable: the last to bed (making sure the biscuits and mineral water were at each guest's bedside) and the first to rise (cutting a fresh flower for every breakfast tray). If the strain showed, it was not slowing her down – quite the reverse. It was hard to tell if she had had a little too much to drink or was just a bit overexcited by her own success in keeping the party going at full blast, but whatever it was usually brought out her ribald sense of humour. This made it all the more enjoyable: some friends felt that Vivien on her best behaviour could be, as Anthony Quayle put it, 'a little bit of a Goody Two Shoes'. They liked it better when she held her own in scatological sing-songs with Jock Dent at the piano or zestfully pointed up an anecdote with a precise expletive.

On New Year's Day 1947 Olivier learned that the financing for *Hamlet* had finally been secured and he could begin filming in early summer. In February, he and Vivien took off for Santa Margherita Ligure on the Gulf of Rapallo. With scarce foreign currency wangled out of the British Treasury by the film's wily producer, Filippo Del Giudice, they stayed ten days at the Hotel Miramar – the bill for their party came to £7,000 – while Olivier and his collaborators wrote the screenplay and Vivien soaked up the sunshine on the terrace under the jasmine. The question of what she was to do next had been happily decided for her by one of those cyclical rows in the film industry.

Having made the deal with MGM to exchange Vivien's services for Deborah Kerr's, Korda had fallen out with the American studio over the number of pictures he was entitled to make with Kerr. Meanwhile, he had a pay or play agreement with Duvivier, contracted when he thought Vivien would make *Lottie Dundass*. To resolve both impasses, he cabled Bennie Thau at MGM on 4 February 1947, offering to take back Vivien, even at the risk of her not wanting to appear in any films he proposed. 'I do not hope', he said, 'that Vivien will make two pictures with me ... but I think I can squeeze out at least one of three films now.' The American studio quickly agreed to this, though Thau privately doubted that Korda would succeed with Vivien – after all, she had turned down every film proposed by MGM, including *Young Bess* because she would be playing the more mature Queen Catherine and not the young title role. (Ironically, the film was made six years later with Deborah Kerr as Catherine and Jean Simmons, Olivier's Ophelia, as Bess.)

However, Korda knew that Vivien wanted more than anything to get back to work. The one film he proposed was *Anna Karenina* – and Vivien agreed at once. She felt she could bring to the story of a woman who left home, husband and child something of the truth of her own first marriage. According to Kieron Moore, then twenty-two and the most promising young actor in British films, who played Vronsky, 'She wanted to show the hard, driving nature of Anna's obsession ... the carnal appetite the lovers had for each other ... and the physical nature of love.' Unfortunately, this turned out to be not at all what Julien Duvivier had in mind. As the director sat on his high stool wearing a hat which he occasionally threw on the floor in exasperation and danced around (but never on), he looked to Moore like a man who didn't believe in any kind of love and certainly not the obsessive, destructive kind, but would be prepared to push the claims of romantic love in the interest of commercial success. This was anathema to Vivien and so a battle royal began before the film even started, for Duvivier was a man who liked to have things cut and dried early on. He even asked Ralph Richardson, playing Karenin, to write out how he saw his role. (The canny Richardson didn't oblige him by showing his hand in advance and ultimately walked off with the notices.)

As Korda was often away in the United States during shooting, Vivien's strong will clashed with Duvivier's – and no one was there to arbitrate, still less dictate. The whole production was marred by incompatibility. Vivien's performance was beautiful to look at, but vacuum-packed, betraying her own antipathy to the romantic way Duvivier wanted her to play. Feeling his leading lady there in the flesh, but miles away in spirit and sympathy, poor Kieron Moore cursed himself for not obeying his instinct, which had told him to go to Korda inside the first two weeks' shooting and demand to be replaced. 'Vivien felt it absolute anathema to be forced to play the happy side of Anna – you can see how the film improves as tragedy brings it into line with what she was feeling about the part.' But the man on the high chair insisted on doing it his way and – most frustrating to her – 'never lost his cool' with Vivien, according to Moore, though he once invited the latter to punch him on the jaw.

What probably no one on the set knew was that, throughout the picture, Vivien was undergoing one of her depressive attacks. One sign of this was the presence of her mother, who occupied the chair marked 'Vivien Leigh', while her daughter took direction from Duvivier as a secretary would take dictation. Her mental state simply exacerbated the feeling she and Moore shared – though neither had the rapport off-screen to be frank with each other about it – that their freedom as players had been taken away from them. In later years, Moore wondered how much freedom Vivien would have allowed herself, in any case, for he suspected that she had not one, but *two* directors. Olivier, he thought, was rehearsing her at home; and Duvivier was then remodelling her performance at the studio. It occurred to him that if Vivien had trusted herself and her instincts more, she could have shaken off Olivier and overcome Duvivier.

Ironically, Vivien had never looked so lovely in a film. The setting in Russia before the Revolution allowed Cecil Beaton to design a superb series of costumes for a lady of quality. The clothes were made in Paris, since Korda's other production, *An Ideal Husband*, which was shooting simultaneously on the adjacent set also with costumes by Beaton, had swamped the capacity of the London workshops. Vivien and Beaton went over to Paris for the fittings, staying with Lady Diana and Duff Cooper at the British Embassy. There was a *froideur* between Vivien and Beaton which their hosts remarked on. It was to endure, in greater or lesser degree, for years. It had begun with a commonplace incident. Vivien had called at Beaton's Pelham Place house to view his selection of fabrics for the film. While he was absent from the room, she picked up a framed photograph he'd taken of Greta Garbo and was trying to make out what Garbo had written on it when he abruptly entered, snatched it from her hand and slapped it face down on the side table.

Beaton's diaries at the time record the mutual nagging that haunted their relationship on the *Anna Karenina* set. She suspected he was devoting more attention to the costumes he'd designed for *An Ideal Husband*, which was being shot in colour. This was unjust, but in Vivien's dark mood, everything was suspect, even the size of her gloves, which she accused him of making a mite too small. 'No, it isn't that the gloves are too small but that your hands are too big,' he cried in exasperation. More black looks. He attributed Vivien's dislike of the photographs he took of her to her fear of not looking as young as she believed she should. She ordered the ones she hated to be destroyed. What may really have been at the back of this was the fear that the photographs had caught something of her manic-depressive mood. A gallery portrait (not by Beaton) which she later presented to John Gielgud revealed, in retrospect, her disturbed condition too clearly for comfort.

According to Beaton, she was deft at hiding her true feelings, but there was one occasion when they blazed forth and shocked even him.

It was the day of the King's Birthday Honours, which included a knighthood for Olivier. Beaton breezed into her dressing-room crying, 'Oh, I'm so happy for you about the great news!' He later recorded: 'A face of fury was reflected in the mirror.'

Olivier and Vivien had been in two minds about the honour ever since he had telephoned her on receiving the first tentative communication that he might be singled out for distinction. She was in Paris, vetting the *Anna Karenina* costumes. 'Of course you're not going to accept,' she said. This has sometimes been passed off as a joke. The truth is, while he had envied Ralph Richardson's knighthood earlier in the year, Olivier was nothing if not a stickler for theatrical convention. Did actors, *should* actors accept honours, he had asked Noël Coward. (Undoubtedly, he would have asked Richardson, his customary guru, except that he knew Richardson's answer already.) Coward, who wasn't knighted until later, when he was virtually on his deathbed, thought it was in order. Vivien's reaction indicated the contrary, but it was scarcely a rational response.

In her present mood, her husband's honour acted on her like a depressant. Later on she was to wear the title 'Lady Olivier' with poise and pride. But just then, she regarded it as a courtesy title, extended to her when she was in no fit state to deserve it. She didn't even want to attend the investiture on 8 July 1947. 'She only did so', Beaton recalled, 'when Alex Korda closed production on *Anna Karenina* for the day. But she wasn't enjoying any of it. She acted as though she was holding a grudge against Larry.'

She accompanied Olivier to Buckingham Palace dressed severely, even starkly, in a black outfit unrelieved by a single piece of jewellery. Her hat was trimmed with black as well. Far from celebrating, she looked as though she were in mourning.

Mourning would have better become the première of *Anna Karenina* in January 1948. A huge array of celebrities attended from stage and cinema, society, politics and the diplomatic corps, including five members of the Labour Cabinet, all the Commonwealth High Commissioners and eleven ambassadors, the Soviet Union's envoy among them.

'When I set out for the première,' says Kieron Moore, 'I knew I was going to my own hanging.' He was right. His rise to stardom was almost terminally checked. The force of the abuse he had to bear suggests that the critics' disappointment with Vivien was being displaced on to his performance. Admittedly he was inadequate, but then so was everyone else in the film except the balefully mesmerizing Richardson. For once in her life, Vivien left the party afterwards well before it ended.

Five months later, the whole Royal Family including Princess Elizabeth and her new husband, Prince Philip, turned out for the première of Olivier's *Hamlet*. It was deemed just as extraordinary an achievement as *Anna Karenina* had been a woefully unsatisfactory one. Vivien's film had sadly diminished her; Olivier's film won universal praise and awards, including an Oscar for him and three others for the film. The Oliviers were the new 'royals' of the performing arts, but events were making Vivien more cruelly aware of her consort status.

By the time of *Hamlet*'s West End première, the Oliviers were leading the Old Vic Company on a nine-month tour of Australia and New Zealand, which enhanced their status as public figures and intensified the stress they were undergoing as a married couple.

Vivien's condition was naturally worrying Olivier and he believed that the best tonic for her was work. After all, his own labours renewed him. So he accepted the British Council's sponsorship of a tour to express Britain's gratitude for the Antipodean war-effort. Including Vivien on the tour would restore her self-confidence; playing with him on stage would narrow the gap between their respective achievements. He therefore chose plays in which Vivien could take a leading role or had already acted, namely *The Skin of Our Teeth, The School for Scandal* (as Lady Teazle) and *Richard III* (as Lady Anne). Thus the traditional concept of the Old Vic as a repertory company was turned inside out and it became an actor-manager company — with the manager's wife elevated above the rest of the players.

To allow Vivien to recoup health and strength before the tour, they went down to the Côte d'Azur in November 1947, and spent a month in a villa owned by Leigh Holman's brother. Tarquin Olivier and Suzanne Holman joined them. Olivier was all too conscious of the fact that he had 'upped and gallantly left' Tarquin when he was a mere ten months old. Vivien did her best to bring them together and met with some success. Not surprisingly, perhaps, she found it easier to relate to the child of someone else's broken marriage than to her own. Suzanne told her mother she wanted to study acting. Vivien wasn't happy about her daughter's choice, but she didn't oppose it. Perhaps, as Leigh Holman had done when *she* took up acting, Vivien thought Suzanne would grow out of it.

In the New Year, after a medical check-up, Vivien was given a clean bill of health. On 14 February 1948, after a rowdy all-night party for over fifty of their film and theatre friends at Durham Cottage, they motored to Liverpool Street Station – and realized it was no ordinary expedition they were to lead. There to greet them were all the appurtenances of a royal departure: red carpet, station master in top hat, Commonwealth High Commissioners, television and radio, crowds of well-wishers.... The ceremonial farewell heralded a trip that was more like a vice-regal visit. Indeed, as the King and Queen were scheduled to visit Australia in 1949, the Oliviers' tour took on the character of a rehearsal for the real thing, with civic receptions, honorary degree ceremonies, official speeches and even, on Anzac Day in Canberra, a march past them at which Olivier took the salute. With Vivien at his side, he gave a consummately regal performance. The two of them were the most distinguished Britons to have visited Australia since the war – and the crowds from the Old Country welcomed them like a surrogate king and queen.

Almost from the time their liner left Liverpool, however, Olivier was concerned for Vivien's up-and-down state of mind. His diary records that on their second night out, Vivien turned to him as they sat at the captain's table and 'suddenly with an alarmingly wild look ... said, "Tonight I should like to play dominoes." '

As the tour began in soaring heatwave temperatures at Perth, they had intimations of how exhausting it was all going to be. Unwisely, they kept Notley hours after the show – and shouting matches startled the neighbours. By morning they were on their best behaviour for the next step on the endless treadmill of the social round, but inevitably exhaustion was setting in. At one reception, Vivien took a look at the arranged rows of chairs and simply barged through them. She wasn't sleeping much, and her irrepressible wakefulness made life difficult at times. They took the midnight flight to Adelaide and her shriek of delight at the first peep of sunrise woke everyone with an anxious jolt.

In Adelaide they presented *Richard III* and Vivien joined her husband in the play which had made his reputation as the pre-eminent actor of his generation. Now she viewed his performance in close-up, as it were, as part of the company on stage. It has been a matter for speculation – in particular by Garry O'Connor, the Oliviers' chronicler on this tour – whether playing with Olivier for the first time since 1940 was more disquieting to Vivien than fulfilling. For the first time she experienced how his power and success had nourished him independently of her own love and need of him. The characters he was playing imposed themselves on him like guests being welcomed by a host who was gratified, but continually astonished, that so many had come when invited. Vivien at times felt squeezed to one side by the prior claim they had on their creator's affections.

Cecil Tennant flew out to them in June with a print of *Hamlet*, which had its Australian première in Melbourne, and took stock of the situation. He saw an Olivier who looked at times desperately tired – and a Vivien who was beginning to feel homesick and be subject to fluctuations of temperament.

The previous year, Olivier had set up his own company, Laurence Olivier Productions Ltd, which Tennant was eventually to manage. Its purpose was to invest in plays and ultimately to produce them. Olivier's energetic concentration on planning the future seemed to his agent to be an escape from the entanglements of the present.

The Oliviers had paid impeccable attention to the well-being of everyone in their company. As if to cement their own relationship all the more strongly, they became inordinately attached to their 'family', every one of whom was sent a piece of affectionate doggerel: 'Members of the Co,' it went, 'Please to let us know/ When your birthdays are,/ Be they near or far,/ So that we may wish you/ All that fate can dish you./ A lonely birthday is no joko,/ And we "Parentis" are "in loco."' In spite of this unity of the group, the Australian tour made Olivier feel the loneliness of power – and not only that, but how unexpectedly power could be lost. For when they arrived in Sydney, a letter from the Old Vic's governors informed him that he and his fellow directors, Ralph Richardson and John Burrell, were not to have their contracts renewed. Presumably, their 'star power' was regarded as a liability, granting them greater independence than was deemed wise for full-time directors. 'Off with his head!', Richard III's order, had now been applied to Olivier – on the very day he had *two* shows of the play. 'Laughter was a reflex action,' he wrote, aware perhaps that this was how the audience reacted, too, to just such a sinister conjunction of circumstances on stage. At about this time he had another stroke of bad luck – he tore a cartilage in his knee, an injury provoked by the limp he had assumed for Richard. When times are bad, he noted with some irony, the body climbs aboard the bandwagon, too. His dismissal made it increasingly imperative for him to look to his own safety, his own future.

In whichever Australian city they found themselves, the Oliviers soon got round to asking, 'Who are your own good actors?' Even before they reached Sydney, they had heard reports of a thirty-one-year-old player called Peter Finch.

Australians admired Finch as much on the radio as on the stage, for he was a versatile mimic – he could take off many accents. Probably this was what first made Olivier curious; he, too, set great store by getting the voice right first. Moreover, Finch was playing exactly the kind of role Olivier loved – the comic, cunning hero of Molière's *Le Malade imaginaire*. And when he met Finch, giving a highly condensed version of the play to workers in their lunch hour, he discovered a man who was in many ways a mirror image of his own younger self. Finch had intense physical presence, was buoyant, funny, devil-may-care – and even giggled the way Olivier had been wont to do before Coward cured him of it. He loved carousing as well and took the Oliviers out on the town. In short, he seemed everything Olivier had been when he was at the starting block of his own artistic marathon. Olivier was impressed by the fact that Finch took the theatre to the people – to their workplace. It was a mission that harked back to the very origins of the journeyman-actor and appealed powerfully to Olivier's sense of history.

Olivier knew that his plan to have a London company of his own would soon have to become reality – sooner now than he'd thought before his contract was dropped by the Old Vic. He started recruiting for it there and then. 'If you ever come to London, look me up,' he said to Finch. When he came to England with Tamara, his ballet-dancer wife, two months after the Oliviers had sailed back, Finch was put under contract to Laurence Olivier Productions.

Olivier appreciated that his own expanding management ambitions might limit his future stage appearances – and the scuppering of his hopes of turning the Old Vic Company into the nucleus of a National Theatre only concentrated his mind on establishing his independence. With Finch available, Vivien need not lack a leading man endowed with the magnetic appeal and promise of a younger Olivier. He already knew enough about Vivien's tastes to realize that Finch had the buccaneering handsomeness she found attractive – the sort shared by Buckmaster and Merivale. Whether it also crossed his mind that his wife and this bold, passionate actor, in many ways an *alter ego* of himself, would become lovers is a matter of speculation.

A symptom of Vivien's recurring trauma was an increase in her sexual drive. At the time, there was little understanding of manic-depression and even less of antidepressant drugs – sedation was the usual treatment. In a sense, Vivien had developed her own antidepressant in the form of enhanced sexual activity – which was effective, but could become compulsive.

She had grown increasingly demanding at a time when her husband was exhausted by a strenuous tour coming on top of the marvellous creative achievement at the Old Vic. 'Walking corpses' is how Olivier described himself and Vivien in an unguarded aside to a New Zealand reporter.

To most men the arrival on the scene of a sexually attractive younger man would signal an immediate danger. But Olivier was aware of nothing more than presenting his wife with a diversion – 'Oh, quite innocently, at first,' his conscience compelled him to record in his memoirs – which might relieve the pressure without disrupting the partnership. Their partnership had to be preserved, it would be preserved – both of them had sacrificed so much to achieve it.

Perhaps the most apt comment on Olivier at this time is the oblique one made by his own stage conception of a play that deals with an ageing husband's concern for his wilfully flirtatious wife. His direction of himself and Vivien as Sir Peter and Lady Teazle in *The School for Scandal* reflected the shift taking place in their own married relationship. They first performed the play in Australia, where it was noticed that Olivier had made Sir Peter into a much older-looking and careworn husband than was the custom with this play. When the same production opened in London, in January 1949, Harold Conway wrote in the *Evening Standard*:

> Olivier, it would seem, has psychoanalysed Sir Peter. In that disillusioned, sorely tried ex-bachelor, he has found, not a figure of fun, but a creature of infinite (and inhibited) melancholy.... 'How all occasions do inform against me!' this Sir Peter all but exclaims; and his wounded love, pride and hopes become the dominant focus of the play. It is a performance of masterly sensitiveness by Olivier; and it is matched by Vivien Leigh's Lady Teazle – exquisite to behold, beautifully modulating devilment into contrition by the merest flicker of her eyes, the subtlest inflection of her voice. But Sir Laurence really cannot have it both ways. His chosen way is to glimpse the tears behind Sheridan; and the structure trembles before his success.

When they sailed for home from Wellington on 17 October 1948, Olivier was in physical pain as well as exhausted: he had had an operation for a knee injury and been hoisted aboard ship on a dockside crane. He lay in his cabin for the first two weeks. It was Vivien who dominated social life in ways he might by now have recognized as an early warning of a manic phase. She organized hectic charades, kept everyone in stitches, appeared at dinner in strikingly revealing gowns and danced the night away with the young bachelors of the company. Once, Olivier had to rebuke her for 'humiliating' him by making up to one bold young man a bit too publicly.

To help her release her tensions more productively, he began rehearsals as soon as he was able for the play they planned to alternate with *The School for Scandal* in the New Year: Anouilh's modern-dress version of *Antigone*. Olivier had not at first thought that Vivien was suited to this parable of Occupied France, in which she personified the nation's tragic destiny as well as playing a woman singled out for destruction by the gods. But on his instructions, she lowered her voice dramatically, suppressing any piping lilt and manifesting a deep-toned, sullen resignation which resonated disturbingly through the part. Olivier cast himself as Chorus, commenting on and analysing the action, and so side-stepped the play's confrontation by leaving the role of Creon to George Relph.

But even as she was rehearsing *Antigone* aboard ship, Vivien was reading and re-reading the text of a play about another woman whom the gods made mad before destroying. By the time they reached home, she was as determined to play Blanche DuBois in *A Streetcar Named Desire* as she once had been to play Scarlett O'Hara. Blanche was the other branch of the O'Hara line: the Southern belle whose will had been sundered, not strengthened, by the irruption of brutal reality. Scarlett was the great survivor who seized her opportunity without thought of consequences, who never looked back and put off looking forward until tomorrow. Blanche was immured in the past and ineffectually and piteously trying to find Elysian enchantment in the brutal present.

It was Binkie Beaumont who, once again, laid the stepping-stones to the role by gaining the confidence of Irene Mayer Selznick, who had produced the play in New York in 1947 under the direction of Elia Kazan. Irene's marriage to David Selznick had just been dissolved. Beaumont formed a joint managerial partnership with Olivier to present the play in London. Olivier was to direct it, and so the role was secured for Vivien.

Vivien felt she had matched herself honourably against Olivier's recent *Oedipus Rex* with her performance in another Sophoclean tragedy, even though it was one reworked by Anouilh: she had tapped a potential that even she had not suspected. Now she had within her grasp a role she could define as authoritatively as Olivier had done with Richard III. Blanche DuBois was the part that might turn her into a great actress.

# 16

## 'I don't love you any more'

*I*n retrospect, Olivier maintained that he had 'lost' Vivien on the Australian tour in 1948, but the extent of his loss was not brought home to him until one day in early spring 1949. Thunderbolts have a way of striking at banal moments. Thus it was not at the climax of any stormy argument, but after an uneventful lunch, sitting in the conservatory of Durham Cottage, that Vivien said, 'I don't love you any more.'

Olivier could hardly believe his ears. He recalls sitting there frozen. There was no other man, she assured him. There didn't need to be. Her husband had become 'another man' to her. She loved him still, she said, but more as a *brother*, though he later noted, with sad irony, a number of occasions when 'incest' took place between them.

But could they go on together, he asked. Oh, yes, Vivien said, they would carry on as if nothing had changed – except that they would no longer be partners in anything but their work. Another man might have exploded in anger and animosity at the cruel way the news was broken and the cool manner in which the compromise was proposed. But Olivier characteristically decided to accept it out of guilt as a form of penance for his pride. Their love had been like a religion to him; loss of love was a fall from grace and must be endured with fortitude.

A few weeks earlier, on 22 March 1949, Peter Finch and Edith Evans had opened in Olivier's presentation of *Daphne Laureola*. It was a sensational West End debut for Finch. He received notices which recalled the ones Vivien had got in *The Mask of Virtue*. He was written about and spoken of as 'another Olivier'.

Friends believe that Vivien and Peter Finch had not immediately become lovers, even though fate had arranged for him to be in the theatre literally next door to the one where she was playing in *Antigone*. However, the arrival of such a comet may well have made her own domestic horizon pale.

So the Oliviers began work on *A Streetcar Named Desire* in a troubled and nervous mood. In fact, Olivier was not terribly keen on the play, according to Irene Selznick, and consented to direct it only because Vivien talked him into it. 'Talked' is an understatement: she worried him into it.

His objections were not simply textual, though he thought parts of it boring and repetitive, and proposed cutting them – much to Mrs Selznick's agony. In Olivier's still essentially middle-class view of public life, respectability counted for much. The play's sensational nature offended that respectability. News of its incestuous rape, insanity and nymphomania had appeared in the English papers the minute he'd announced its London production – and with the Lord Chamberlain still censoring the stage's morals, it might be bad timing for an actor-manager just starting out to be put down as an *agent provocateur*. Then for the Oliviers, the 'stage royals', to dirty their hands with such dubious ingredients! He felt they had to tread as prudently as the real royals. Also, the Church might come out against it. For Olivier, a clergyman's son and a prey to guilt, the prospect of fulmination from the pulpit had to be taken seriously.

It is hard at this remove from English middle-class society of 1949 to realize how deeply these considerations mattered. In fact, the play was to be condemned as 'low and repugnant' in the House of Commons and as 'lewd and salacious' by the Public Morality Council. Staging it posed an additional and less obvious risk to Vivien. Her sexuality, aggravated by her recurrent illness, left her elated yet unfulfilled and alarmed by what, in retrospect, it revealed to her about herself. Now her already unsteady psychological balance was being further tested by a play that realistically explored emotions usually portrayed only in safely stylized classical theatre. If there was poetry in Blanche's despair, there was also the risk of contagion in her madness.

Possibly Olivier didn't realize how it would affect Vivien's mental balance in later months. He himself was never possessed by any role he played to the extent of finding it difficult to shake it off once the show had closed. Much later, in a reference to Ronald Colman's film *A Double Life*, about an actor playing Othello who confuses himself with the part and takes his work home with fatal results, Olivier would mention, in parenthesis, that, 'Alas, this was one of Vivien's abiding problems.' Her friend Alan Dent, a theatre critic whose own sensibility made him aware of the risks to Vivien, begged her not to do the part. 'Impossible,' she responded.

The part allowed Vivien to take a stand against the two epithets she hated most when applied to herself – 'pretty' and even 'beautiful'. Both of them she thought too limiting – they trimmed the flame of the dramatic illumination she sought to spread. She even dressed down for the rehearsals, the better to meet the challenge which playing Blanche represented. Bernard Braden, cast as Mitch in the play, recalled her arriving on the first day of the run-through wearing a simple black jersey dress. Renee Asherson, playing Blanche's sister, remarked (none too tactfully perhaps, given Vivien's abhorrence of such terms): 'That's a pretty dress.' Vivien took the compliment – though she may have winced – and replied in sombre tones to match her costume: 'I'm glad you like it, because you're going to see a lot of it.' She wore it every day until they opened. Braden also believed that she plastered make-up heavily on to her face so as to destroy its basic beauty. She went for 'truth' and knew it was more than skin-deep.

Vivien recognized that she had the stage role of the decade and her determination to do it full justice was revealed in a small but important element in her approach. Hitherto, she had always refused, when asked, to dye her hair for a stage or film role. She was very self-conscious about her hair. 'She had crinkly hair, generally not very good hair,' says the London wig-maker and theatrical entrepreneur Stanley Hall. 'She disliked it and it required a lot of attention. But as she was determined this should be a brilliant performance, she did everything she could to help herself get into character and this included bleaching her own hair. I made her a dark wig to wear during the day. A little later, when she came to do the film, I made her bleached wigs, because the idea was that Blanche should have ragged-looking hair, like someone who had gone through life neglecting herself. She used to send the wigs back from Hollywood, by air mail, to be cleaned and redressed by me – didn't trust the American hairdressers.'

Olivier's conception of Blanche was more realistic than Elia Kazan's in New York. He was annoyed to have had to accept so much of Kazan's blueprint, but at least this Blanche would be his own. His Blanche was no longer the New York production's 'pale moth' fluttering briefly into nervous life, only to be broken and discarded. Though Vivien had had her hair dyed blonde to strain the colour even further out of Blanche's faded looks, to London audiences of the time dyed blonde hair denoted a 'tart'. And Blanche's despairing cry to her sister, 'I've run for protection, Stella, from under one leaky roof to another leaky roof,' likewise suffered a downgrading: 'protection' was assumed to be a euphemism for 'prostitution' at a time when the latter word wasn't permitted in the sanitized columns of family newspapers. For Lady Olivier to accept a role like this was scandalous to some people – but even the most self-righteous critics, those who used words like 'cesspit' and 'garbage' about the play, couldn't deny Vivien's courage or withhold their praise for her performance.

Perhaps she succeeded too well. She played Blanche for over eight months at a time of recurring emotional stress. She had mentally left Olivier and was experiencing something akin to Blanche's loneliness. She would talk to friends of 'quicksands' in her life – this was Blanche's trauma too. She seems to have begun her affair with Peter Finch at about this time, though it still had to be covert and sporadic. Towards the end of the run, her behaviour began to endanger her safety. She would dismiss her driver and walk home through the West End's red light district, stopping to chat to the street-girls plying their trade. She said she felt an affinity between their flamboyant appeal and Blanche's more pathetic promiscuity. To Bonar Colleano, the play's Stanley Kowalski, she would later repeat the girls' cutting witticisms and laugh over them. She found many of them were fans of hers and had been to the play with their clients. It is worth remembering that Marlene Dietrich, being escorted back to her London hotel one evening, received a similar salutation from the girls who had enjoyed her worldly *femme fatale* on the screen. Vivien, though, could not dismiss the role as Dietrich did when it had served its purpose.

Alan Dent finally got round to attending the play he loathed – he'd deliberately left town so as not to have to review the actress he loved. Ten days after it opened, he went backstage and his fears were confirmed. 'It was only a few seconds after [Vivien] had taken her last curtain, and she was still [mentally] on the stage. She was still in the mood of the terrifying last scene when Blanche is taken off to the mental hospital. She was shaking like an autumn leaf, and her lips were trembling. She clutched me and put her hand on my shoulder, and said in no more than a whisper: "Was I all *right*? Am I mad to be doing it?"'

Sometimes the lines she had to say sounded to her inward ear like maliciously apposite comments on her current problems or state of mind. She had the feeling of being viewed askance, of being judged. She had to repeat the part nightly for the length of the play's run and repetition dinned the lines into her like an autoconfession written by her accusers. When her mind was at peace, she could refer dispassionately to these 'other voices' that were speaking through her tongue, criticizing and chastising her. It was as if she were being forced to externalize her own guilt, heartbreak or, what she had come to fear most, insanity.

The damage this play did to Vivien's already disturbed psyche was to be severe. Years later, she recognized that herself. 'Blanche is a woman with everything stripped away,' she said. 'She is a tragic figure and I understand her. But playing her tipped me into madness.'

Meanwhile Olivier's ventures into management were suffering severe reverses with plays like *Fading Mansions* and *The Damascus Blade* opening and closing in weeks; and although Christopher Fry's *Venus Observed* gave him a breathing space in November 1949, while he rehearsed Finch in *Captain Carvallo*, it was clear that Laurence Olivier Productions could do with a fresh infusion of cash. The company took all his earnings and Vivien's too, then paid them yearly salaries. But the postwar Labour Government imposed swingeing taxes on high earners and they concluded that, however much they disliked the place, there was nowhere like Hollywood for raking in delectable lump sums to build up capital.

So, in June 1950, he and Vivien announced they were off to make two films. He would star in William Wyler's production of *Carrie*; she in the screen version of *A Streetcar Named Desire*, which Elia Kazan would produce and direct.

The film's effect on Vivien was to be even more traumatic than the stage play's.

Despite her London success, she was by no means an automatic choice for the screen Blanche, nor the only one. A cable from Jack Warner to Kazan, dated 22 November 1950, records that Charles Feldman, the film's executive producer, persisted in wanting Vivien for the role while Kazan preferred other stars. Kazan today admits to having favoured his own stage Blanche, Jessica Tandy; and as late as mid-March 1950, according to Feldman, he was 'high' on Olivia de Havilland. It has been said that he edged away from Vivien because she had worked under Olivier and he admits, 'I did have a "feeling" about that.' He claims not to have seen her in the British stage production and didn't really know how she would work out as an actress for this kind of film. 'I couldn't tell anything from watching *Gone With the Wind*. So much there depends on the way she was positioned and photographed. But in *Waterloo Bridge* she was very good.'

In the end, though, Vivien landed the part. Her fee was $100,000, making her the highest paid English screen actress of the day. Marlon Brando received $75,000.

Kazan's doubts also centred on Vivien's health and strength. Knowing nothing of her manic-depressive state, but aware she had had TB, he spared her the rigours of Hollywood as much as possible and sent Lucinda Ballard, who had done the stage costumes and was to do the film, over to England to obtain Vivien's approval. He'd seen photos of Olivier's costumes for Vivien and was horrified: 'In one word, they were "English". I mean stuffy, dull, ultra-conservative.'

Lucinda Ballard, in his opinion, was 'the best'. For Vivien, she also became 'the dearest'. The two women took to each other the moment Ballard stepped out of the Oliviers' Rolls-Royce at Notley to be greeted by Vivien 'like a child who's hung about the window waiting for her best friend'. They had already met during the Old Vic's spring season in New York just after the war.

She was sitting on an outsize chair with Danny Kaye at a party Ivor Novello gave. She had on a vivid red dress. Her beauty was dazzling. Yet something about her hinted at how she could transform herself into something less of a lady and more of a ... well, entertainer, a comedienne of the kind who plays the resort hotels. I decided she had absorbed Danny Kaye's comic allure by some natural osmosis and tipped into it her own bawdy sense of humour, which only a woman with her looks could get away with. As I got to know Vivien, I saw this chameleon side to her – she could assume a look very easily.

Lucinda Ballard, besides giving Brando his torn T-shirt look, inspired by road-workers whose sweaty garments outlined their physique and gave them a powerful animality, had commanded Tennessee Williams's confidence when she used the phrase 'a terrible daintiness' to describe how she felt Blanche should be dressed. Now she said to Vivien: 'I see her with blondish hair, clothes heavily dated, soft-flowing and in pale tones – absolutely *no* white suit or red satin wrapper like the English production. A prostitute she is not!' Vivien embraced her. That was how she wanted to see Blanche too.

Olivier seemed perfectly friendly when he arrived at Notley, but, pointedly perhaps, did not join in their talks.

'With looks as radiant as Vivien's, and with her dainty frame, it was necessary to conceal and simplify,' the designer recalls.

The first costume I later made for her had a collar of starched chiffon – several collars were cut and changed during the shooting, for they always had to look fresh and give Vivien's face a look of fragility. Vivien was very anxious about how she would look when madness had overwhelmed Blanche. I'd figured out a way of making the strait-jacket out of soft material that would wrap around Blanche, but not imprison her. Vivien thought it essential to let Blanche look peaceful. She was relieved to hear this. It seemed to me Vivien was desperately seeking some kind of personal reassurance. I told her that, in my opinion, Blanche never had sex for money – only for love and, later on, to assuage her loneliness. I said the key to Blanche was her always feeling guilty about what had happened to her husband – his suicide. She was always cleansing herself mentally and physically, always fearful of dirt settling on her.

Lucinda Ballard stayed two nights at Notley, appreciating how Vivien ran a household in the austerity era – the good garden-grown food, the fish mousses, the hothouse fruits. Vivien kept a note-pad to hand to jot down any thoughts, any bit of interesting information. Later, Vivien showed Lucinda over the house and her guest noted the plethora of Olivier mementoes, dozens of photos of him, even the affectionate notes he and Vivien had exchanged on some notable occasion now displayed under the glass top of her dressing-table. But among this treasured bric-à-brac she noticed a large pale pink silk square edged with handmade lace. Under this, Vivien told her, she put her soiled linen when she undressed for the night. It was the old convent-school habit. It also, Lucinda decided, showed how deeply Vivien was imbued with some of the very traits she had been assigning to Blanche.

Nothing of the strain on the Oliviers' marriage was apparent to their guest. Only when she left Notley did Lucinda reflect on Vivien's near veneration of her husband every time his name was mentioned. Could passion be *this* intense, she wondered.

Vivien preceded Olivier to America and went straight from New York to join Elia Kazan in his country home at Newtown, Connecticut. They went over the play in the peace and quiet of the August days. 'She was an instinctual actress,' Kazan recalls, 'and didn't consciously work out the part, except when Larry worked it out with her. It's very hard after that *not* to standardize your performance night after night.'

They went to the West Coast the long way, by train, and were met by Olivier and Suzanne Holman. It was the first time Suzanne had stayed under the same roof with Olivier and Vivien, and she wasn't finding her mother easy to get on with, but blamed it partly on herself:

There were lots of things then in my mother's temperament I didn't take to – don't forget that in looks and personality, she had it *all*. I was gawky and spotty and 'impossible' in the way girls of seventeen are, unless they happen to be Vivien Leigh. She had made up for having relatively few friends when she was younger and now had dozens, and was passionately possessive of them. She never wanted to risk letting people go ... slip out of mind. Love was the most important thing to her. It was my first real experience of them together – and very uncomfortable it was too. What I remember most about my stay in Hollywood was the fights that went on between them – real theatrically pitched arguments behind closed doors. I knew Vivien was naturally high-tempered. I can now see that the film was putting her under a great strain. But in spite of the shouting matches, it never occurred to me their marriage was breaking up. It was just too precious to Vivien. I put it down to two overwrought people at the end of a long day's work on their separate movies.

Hollywood's curiosity in the Oliviers was intense. It was the first time two titled players, each a star in a big-budget, highly publicized production, had lived and worked together in the film capital. Vivien attracted far more attention than Olivier – everyone wanted to know what her Blanche was like. Naturally, rumours circulated that Olivier was coaching her at home. Lucinda Ballard discounts that. 'I suspected Vivien was being made to feel guilty at "betraying" Larry's London production by the way she was adapting herself to Kazan's interpretation. "Larry doesn't like my dressses," she'd say to me, or, *apropos* Blanche's shoes and stockings, "Larry thinks they make my legs look too fat."' Jealousy may have been induced, too, by the enormous media coverage Vivien's film was receiving. 'Nobody in Hollywood gave a damn about Larry in *Carrie* – everyone was agog to find out what was going on on the closed set between Vivien and Brando.'

At first they were very wary of each other. Although Brando's first film, *The Men*, was finished, it hadn't opened; but insiders were claiming that his Method style was the most revolutionary new technique to hit Hollywood since the talkies. Vivien had already seen him on the stage, so she knew her competition; by coincidence he had been cast as the Messenger in Anouilh's *Antigone*, the play in which she had starred on the London stage.

They met for a formal lunch – formal enough for Brando, anyhow, who put on an untorn T-shirt and brown slacks – in Jack L. Warner's private dining-room. It was some days before he got round to ribbing Vivien.

'Why do you always wear scent?' he asked abruptly.

'Because I like to smell nice – don't you?'

'Me? I just wash. In fact, I don't even get in the tub. I just throw a gob of spit in the air and run under it.'

Vivien, unshocked, emitted a deep, appreciative chuckle, which turned into malicious delight as Brando then went on to do a cruelly accurate imitation of Olivier's Agincourt speech, which had obviously been polished on the New York party circuit.

At the press conference held before the shooting started, Brando was upstaged by Vivien, who coolly told the overdeferential reporters that 'her ladyship is fucking bored with formality'. She then dealt crisply with the anticipated innuendoes:

'Do you read your lines to Sir Laurence?'

'No. I always know my lines.'

'Does Sir Laurence read his lines to you?'

'Yes. It's wonderful, really, because he puts me to sleep.'

Then came a query that, in retrospect, elicited a sadly apposite answer: 'What do you think happened to Scarlett O'Hara after Rhett Butler walked out on her?'

Vivien paused a second, then said: 'I think she probably became a better woman. But I don't think she ever stopped loving him.'

Filming was slow at first as Vivien relaxed her hold on her stage Blanche, and a film character far more varied in tone and texture began to take over. 'Some people say she seems to get a grip on the character as the film progresses,' observes Kazan. 'It might be nearer the truth to say that I got a grip on her.'

It was a Vivien Leigh that no stage or screen had ever seen before. She had to vary her effects in the takes and retakes Kazan demanded. No chance here to standardize on a 'safe' reading of the text the way she had done on the London stage. She was not a Method player, but every other member of the cast was, including her director. And the obligation on Vivien to reach into herself and make the connection between 'role and soul', as Lee Strasberg's classes at the Actors' Studio put it, devolved on Vivien too. The strain this imposed on her was unrelenting – and when Brando began shooting scenes with her, near the end of the second week, they became, in Kazan's words, 'two highly charged people exploding off each other'. Vivien had nothing but her own talent to protect her, and she fed into it, like a resourceful tributary, the instinctual feelings of her own trauma.

Her scenes with Brando form a pattern of seduction and repulsion leading to rape. The pattern is modulated by Blanche's alternate piteousness – her trembling removal of the posy pinned to her shoulder like a nosegay on a coffin, her teetering little scurry past the brute that lurks inside Stanley, her tendril-like appeal to her sister's sturdier nature – and her precarious seductiveness in which she is, if anything, more effective and disturbing. She brushes against Stanley, hoping to coax him into a semblance of courtesy. She fishes for compliments. She thrills to the feel of Stanley's rough fingers awkwardly doing up her dress at the back. She sarcastically tries to shame him and his poker-playing friends into paying a lady some dues of politeness. Finally she utters a naked cry of horror and disgust as his beer bottle is crudely ejaculated over her dress.

For Vivien, the most brutal moment came when Karl Malden snaps on the light to expose Blanche to 'reality' – and she ducks, terrified, as if he has made to hit her. 'I don't want the light – I want magic.'

The psychic wear and tear she suffered did not show on the screen: it was to erupt later in notes of delirium and despair which echoed the very text of the madness she had embodied so brilliantly. Many considered the movie a finer work than the stage production.

# 17

## 'Why not Peter Finch?'

*A*fter finishing *A Streetcar Named Desire* and *Carrie* at the end of 1950, the Oliviers returned home by slow freighter via the Panama Canal. No transatlantic liner had been available and Vivien couldn't face a long air journey. It was a melancholy trip. 'We were not exactly a honeymoon couple,' Olivier wrote later. Forced to put up with each other's company for nearly five weeks, they had the reality of what had happened to their marriage brought home to them. Olivier confessed that 'for the first time, the idea of suicide had its attractions'.

To a very few of his Hollywood friends – among them Spencer Tracy – he had confided his fears for Vivien. Tracy scoffed at Olivier's anxiety about her mental balance and put it down to drinking too much, his own affliction. Olivier took comfort in that. A long voyage without parties might not be a bad idea after all.

They tried holding boredom at bay by reading playscripts. What they were seeking was a worthy production to mark the Festival of Britain, the festival of arts and crafts scheduled for 1951, which was intended to be a tonic to the nation and signify Britain's official return to greatness in the world's esteem. Not only was patriotism in the Oliviers' thoughts: so was possible insolvency, as their London ventures had been doing badly and Olivier's fee for *Carrie* was already committed. After disembarking, they continued the search by the somewhat easier process of seeking inspiration over good food and drink on weekend visits to Paris, a habit which occasionally put Olivier in bed for a day or so, while Vivien emerged in fine fettle. It was on one such binge that Noël Coward, observing her marching sturdily down the platform to catch the Golden Arrow ahead of the hungover squad of her husband and friends, remarked: 'She has a body like swansdown and the constitution of a GI on leave.'

Early on, Roger Furse had suggested Shaw's *Caesar and Cleopatra* for the Festival – after they'd rejected *Othello* and Barrie's *Mary Rose*. He followed it up with '... and then give *Antony and Cleopatra* the next night.' It was just the sort of stunt to appeal to Olivier: bold, taxing, sure to be talked about. Actually, the two plays sat uneasily back to back, but at least the switch from comic-ironic to tragic-majestic on successive nights would ensure a return trip by a large part of the audience. Within a week of the announcement, the twenty-six-week season was sold out.

Vivien took an unexpectedly firm stand against any tampering with Shaw's text, such as intimating that the middle-aged Roman general and the teenage Queen might have had an affair off-stage. Perhaps Shaw's schoolmasterly fondness for her when they had met ten years before made her defend the spirit as well as the letter of the text. Fortunately, Shakespeare presented no such difficulty. Antony and Cleopatra were certainly *physical* lovers, glorying in each other's flesh and in their combined destinies. The trouble was, as Olivier set it down thirty-five years later, he saw Antony as 'an absolute twerp' whom Cleopatra had 'firmly by the balls'. Thus they devised a double bill of which half was a play about a tutorial relationship only and the other was one in which the hero was held in fatal thrall by his beloved and would do anything to please her. It offered an ironic, if unconscious, reflection on the state of their own relationship.

Vivien took pains to differentiate the two Cleopatras separated by a historical gap of twenty-one years. As young Cleopatra, she wore a light lipstick and rouge in a girlish blush high up on her cheeks; as the older woman, she painted her jawline to emphasize the self-will and shadowed her cheeks to a concave leanness – 'like Marlene Dietrich', she joked. After the first rehearsal of the Shakespeare play, Olivier counselled her to lower her voice and use the same vocal technique that had made her Antigone so riveting. By altering one element, he advised, the whole concept could be changed. She thus acquired a vocal grandeur that hit the public's ear with novel force amidst the anticipated richness of the verse. 'Cool Miss Leigh may be as she exhibits the wiles of a courtesan of genius,' commented *The Times*'s anonymous critic, 'but she exhibits them with a beautifully exact expressiveness and she grows in momentousness to meet her doom.'

The newsworthiness of the husband-and-wife pairing was commented on as often as the coupling of two plays with a common heroine. Yet it is from this date that a baleful theme began to be reiterated in the reviews of plays starring both the Oliviers. The feeling was that Olivier was giving less than he was capable of in order not to outshine Vivien. The person who first opened this wound was the most talented critic of his generation, Kenneth Tynan, not long down from Oxford, and already feared for reviews that were as callous as they were self-confident. Unusually among English critics, he wrote from a highly personal viewpoint. He said of Vivien: 'She picks at the part with the daintiness of a débutante called upon to dismember a stag,' and asserted that her 'limitations have wider repercussions than those of most actresses. Sir Laurence with that curious chivalry which sometimes blights the progress of every great actor ... climbs down and Cleopatra pats him on the head. A cat in fact can do more than look at a king: she can hypnotize him.'

Tynan, it must be said, had given the Oliviers trumpet warnings in advance of his arrival with the publication the year before of his collected pieces in *He That Plays the King*, which he claimed was 'written by an *aficionado*, out of an almost limitless capacity for admiration'. Vivien — alas! — was a major cause of this qualification 'almost'. 'As Lady Anne,' Tynan wrote of the 1949 revival of *Richard III*, she 'quavered through the lines in a sort of rapt oriental chant.' As Sabina in *The Skin of Our Teeth*, she rated only a sustained backhanded compliment: 'At last this pale featherweight beauty has found her own pretty level ... [her] brand of frail, unfelt *coquetterie* fits the part like an elbow-length glove.' As for *A Streetcar Named Desire*: 'The play should have been retitled "A Vehicle Named Vivien".' His constant refrain was to be that Olivier was sacrificing his genius on the altar of his wife's paltry talent. While many thought it tasteless, this judgment was invariably delivered with the abrasiveness typical of the gossipy trades of acting and journalism.

Vivien came to fear Tynan's notices more than any black-edged letter that might arrive for her in the mail. Her reaction wasn't merely wounded vanity; by charging that Olivier's championing of her was belittling *him*, Tynan struck at more than their stage reputations. They knew their passion for each other was cooling; what preserved them was their partnership in the theatre. And here, Vivien thought, was a critic who was trying to dismember even this. Anything that detracted from the heroic stature of the sort of acting Tynan worshipped had to be torn off like constricting ivy before it choked the host trunk: it was quite clear that Tynan saw Vivien as a parasite of the species. His words went right to the heart of the personal problem between Vivien and Olivier, which is why they hurt so much.

Olivier found 'little joy in getting a good review when your other half is getting a bad one'. The effect on Vivien wasn't slow in showing itself. Cast members noticed she and Olivier had sudden flare-ups, even while waiting in the wings to go on. Neither now bothered to hide them.

For a short time, fortunately, both were distracted from this burgeoning discontent by an illustrious playgoer who had engaged three seats, one for himself, one for his daughter-companion and one for his hat, coat and cane. Winston Churchill was obviously smitten by Vivien; he invited both of them to Sunday lunch at Chartwell, and presented her with a rare present: a tiny picture he had painted of opening rosebuds. It was one of her most prized possessions. She never risked taking it with her on her trips abroad, the way she did with her Renoir or sometimes the Degas and the Marie Laurencin she had now added to the Boudin she'd bought instead of a refrigerator. Churchill's little oil belonged to England and hung always opposite her bedhead, so that, when it was the first thing she saw on opening her eyes in the morning, she knew she was at home.

Whatever rifts were opening in their private and professional lives, the Oliviers in public were still a celebrity couple. They did gala shows for charity. They opened Government exhibitions. They were included in the royal entourage when Queen Elizabeth laid the National Theatre's foundation stone in June 1951. They were treated like uncrowned royalty. Olivier grew bored easily – Vivien never did. People were often nervous of her fashion-plate perfection. 'I think', says Stanley Hall, 'that women felt they couldn't stand up to her mentally or physically. She could do it all. I've seen her enter a room wearing a Balmain dress, the two rows of pearls, beautiful town pumps, and you'd have thought Princess Margaret was coming. A buzz preceded her, everyone separated in front of her, and she'd walk on exchanging smiles and bestowing compliments.' Even her old school friend Patsy Quinn felt the aura. 'I was at a private view at the Lefevre Gallery,' she recalled with wry amusement, 'and Vivien came in and I found myself being led up to her to be "presented" ... a very strange feeling.'

'I think there was another reason why some people were shy of Vivien,' Stanley Hall says. 'She had a man's mind. You could never say to her, "That's a most beautiful dress, Vivien," for she'd cut you immediately. She couldn't take compliments – she reacted like a man. Obviously, she'd still be polite, but she'd simply say, "Thank you," and walk away, never, "Darling, do you think so?" Binkie Beaumont got on so well with her because he knew her mind. "You must always think of her like a man," he'd say.'

Olivier's venture into management had made him Binkie Beaumont's rival; the two men got on together when they had to, but there was no affection between them. Beaumont made it clear he was *Vivien's* friend. Early on in his career, he had developed the practice of investing modest sums in other impresarios' productions, chiefly so that he could glean accurate information about their success or otherwise. He encouraged Vivien to emulate him, and she discovered she had an intuition for new talent or, more importantly, for changing taste, which was often sharper than Olivier's. In her time she was to invest in the new playwrights like Orton and Pinter, even though the plays they wrote were not 'her sort' and had no parts for her.

The Oliviers took the two *Cleopatra* plays to New York at the end of 1951. The very unloading of twenty-seven tons of scenery from the liner *Mauretania* made their landfall look like a Roman triumph before the critics hailed the plays as such. Cleopatra's barge was followed by her pet Sphinx and the machinery that made the stage revolve to create what Walter Kerr called 'the busy hippodrome of excitement'. Some critics had seen them in London and thought Broadway had got the better deal. Vivien's Shavian queen had 'grown in subtlety' since then, said Richard Watts Jr. And indeed she dominated the notices for this play – there was no Tynan on the aisle at the Ziegfeld Theater. Olivier, it was felt, overdid the world-weariness; but instead of simply 'stooping', the better to let Vivien conquer, this was seen to be 'anticipating in his own debility the fall of the Roman empire'.

Even *Time* magazine's anonymous jibe that she was 'an *enfant terrible* auditioning to be a *femme fatale*' seemed like a tap on the shoulder compared with all the slaps on the back.

It was John Gielgud's opinion in later days that her Shakespearian Cleopatra was 'absolutely outstanding ... because there was so much of Vivien in it'. Walter Kerr wrote on this Broadway occasion: 'Behind the petulance and devious feminity ... she has a hard, controlled spine: she can manage with equal authority the shrewish guile of the scene in which she enquires about Antony's new wife and the cold desperation of her decision to die.'

At the Academy Awards ceremony in March 1952, Vivien won her second Oscar – for Blanche in *A Streetcar Named Desire*. Greer Garson accepted it on her behalf, for the Oliviers were on the Broadway stage that night.

Only one occurrence dimmed the brilliance of the season – the death in February 1952 of King George VI. Monarchists by instinct as well as in their chosen roles, the Oliviers felt their sovereign's death even more sharply for being in a foreign country at the time it happened. Yet grief didn't blind Vivien to some urgent practicalities. Together with Olivier, she went over the entire text of both plays, expunging for the performances given in the immediate aftermath of the King's death any references to monarchy that might have been embarrassing.

She also telephoned Emlyn Williams, who was appearing as Charles Dickens in his one-man show at an adjacent theatre – and on receiving Vivien's warning, he did a quick scan of his own text. 'My God,' he told her, 'there are references to George III and George IV and even lines like "I feel like a king." But for you, Vivien, I'd have been biting my tongue off all through tonight's performance.'

Before the Oliviers' season ended, Vivien's mental condition had deteriorated so badly that Olivier was at last forced to acknowledge the gravity of her disorder. He found the pain she was suffering too much to face. Gertrude Lawrence had lent them her New York apartment – a chilling place, to Olivier's way of thinking, decorated in inhospitable tones of grey, which made it feel like living in a brain-cell. On returning one night, he heard sobbing. Passing from one 'cell' to another, he reached the bedroom to find Vivien hunched and desolate, perched on the corner of the bed, 'wringing her hands' and weeping inconsolably.

Their visits to a recommended psychiatrist proved fruitless. Vivien displayed terror lest a lurking photographer catch her entering the discreet door of the analyst's East Side rooms, and her defences wouldn't permit her to yield to his professional probing. Olivier could only sympathize with this.

As he was now nervous about her behaviour, he sent out an sos to Noël Coward. At the end of the run, on 13 April 1952, he and Vivien arrived to stay with Coward at Montego Bay, Jamaica. To Noël, the father-confessor, he unburdened himself of his fear for Vivien's sanity.

Instead of offering sympathetic counsel, Coward rebuked him severely. 'Nonsense ... if anyone's having a nervous breakdown, you are.'

Olivier realized Vivien had got to Coward by the sly back door that the schizoid personality quickly learns to use. It was his first intimation that she could plot against him. They returned to Notley towards the end of April and she entered a fresh depressive spell in which she would sometimes weep copiously, at other times sit and stare at him, and on occasions leave the house and not return overnight. Even when her spirits were high and they entertained, the party atmosphere made him apprehensive – and exhausted. Too many guests were invited even for that commodious residence to hold comfortably.

Olivier had begun preparing his first singing role, as Macheath in the film version of *The Beggar's Opera*. It was to have been a challenge: increasingly, with Vivien in the state she was in, he found it becoming a refuge. In desperation, he sanctioned a project for Vivien that he recognized in retrospect he never should have entertained. But he told himself that it was better for her to deploy her surplus energy in work. She was being offered a film, *Elephant Walk*, to be shot partly in Ceylon. It would take her back to the Asian world of her birth and childhood – perhaps that would be tranquillizing. The question of who should play opposite her was discussed. Vivien appeared to give this some thought and then said, as if a good idea had suddenly struck her, 'Why not Peter Finch?'

Alexander Korda, who was present when she made the suggestion, later said to Olivier that this disingenuous revelation was 'the only truly bad performance' he had ever seen her give.

# 18

## *'I thought you were my friend'*

*E*arly in January 1953, Peter Finch and his wife Tamara were awakened after midnight by a continuous, insistent ringing of their doorbell. Outside stood Vivien, a mink coat inadequately covering a thin silk evening dress that indicated she had come from some function.

According to Finch's wife and to his biographer Elaine Dundy, she was in a state of high excitement. She came immediately to the point. Finch must be ready to leave within a fortnight, she said, to co-star in *Elephant Walk* with her.

Whether Vivien planned to recruit him in this way or not, she certainly judged her man well. Finch belonged to the breed of hellraisers coming into rowdy prominence in postwar theatre and movies: he loved the unexpected, the unconventional, the gamble that scorned the safe bet for the exhilarating hazard of high odds. He agreed within the hour. Vivien didn't leave until first light appeared in the sky: she seemed oblivious of time and place.

The deal he had struck still seemed good to Finch after he'd repaired his interrupted night's rest. At the end of the first week of February 1953, he and Vivien were seen off at Heathrow by Olivier. 'Take care of her,' he called to Finch as Vivien blew him a wistful kiss. As Olivier said later, the penny had dropped. His situation was now rather like Leigh Holman's had been nearly twenty years earlier, as he stood by in a state of numbed perplexity while his wife, whom he loved dearly, scarcely bothered to conceal even in his presence her passion for the youthful 'Larry Olivier'.

Vivien looked small and frail in the falling London snow, though her illness had cost her none of her beauty. Her fee for the film was $150,000 (about £53,000), a very large sum then and a welcome refresher for Laurence Olivier Productions, which was losing money on the St James's Theatre, now under Olivier's management, where even Peter Finch's presence in a slight piece called *The Happy Time* hadn't worked. Finch's fee from *Elephant's Walk*, about a third of Vivien's, would also help defray costs.

No sooner had Ceylon's moist, sensuous heat begun seeping through Vivien's thin tropical dress and, so it seemed to her, into her very bones, than her latent manic-depression showed itself. At first, it was thought that she was exhibiting the normal tourist's elation at the profusion of tropical scenery. Then a hysterical edge appeared as each wave of brown Sinhalese faces broke on her vision. Their eyes frightened her, she said. The exotic location, fringed by deep jungle, acted on Vivien's nervous system like a stimulant. The presence of Finch only heightened her condition. He was playing her screen husband, an English planter, while Dana Andrews, as the plantation manager, played her lover. She insisted on staying up all night, lying out on the hillside with Finch, but she paid for it in the morning when close-up camera shots became impossible. Her behaviour could no longer be ignored, as it was starting to cost the film company money. She began striking mock-erotic postures, 'vamping' the director William Dieterle and – very unusually for her – fluffing her lines. Finch was appealed to by the producer Irving Asher; but even he was unsettled when Vivien started calling him 'Larry'.

Asher sensed the coming breakdown and shot round Vivien, to give her a chance to rest. But when they didn't send for her to come to the set, she grew suspicious, then resentful. A telex was sent to Olivier via Cecil Tennant. Arriving at Colombo on 17 February 1953, Olivier was assailed by a sudden sense of hopelessness. He couldn't even work up any indignation with which to reproach Finch, who, he heard, had been sleeping with Vivien on the hillside at night. His sheer exhaustion probably dispelled his hostility. Olivier's dispassionate view of things surprised even himself: but by now resentment wasn't in his nature. He felt only pity for Vivien and a sort of paternal understanding for Finch – and perhaps a thankfulness that someone else was now sharing the strain. He left inside four days, grimly wishing everyone good luck.

With his going, Vivien relapsed into mania, berating Finch in ribald language. Asher couldn't face the thought of filming the scene with her and a giant (though de-fanged) anaconda, and he called a retreat to Hollywood on 27 March. As the aircraft took off for the extremely long flight, a disturbed Vivien was seen battering at the windows to be let out.

The most sensible thing would have been to have her sedated and put into hospital; but no one was able (or willing) to take charge and suffer the buffets of the sensational publicity that would ensue. On reaching Los Angeles, Vivien was allowed to move into the rented mansion where Finch's wife and small daughter were expected imminently.

Tamara and the child were met on arrival by Vivien – Finch was filming at the studios – and her first words were, 'You've got to get yourself into a sari immediately . . . at 7.30 p.m., seventy people are coming. I'm giving a party for you.'

At Paramount, a replacement for Vivien was being sought desperately. Meanwhile, oblivious of everything, Vivien treated Tamara Finch sometimes like a houseguest, sometimes like a rival in love, alternately having heart-to-heart chats about Finch and then closing herself away in her room to peer darkly at the bewildered woman and child trying to relax at the pool. Eventually Tamara and her daughter moved into another house. Vivien attempted to return to work and gave what seemed a level-headed interview to Louella Parsons. But Finch had been deputed to break the news gently to her that she was being replaced. She sat in her dressing-room and listened, not showing any sign of understanding. He faltered. In a moment, her face contorted, her teeth clenched, she flew at him and in the Mississippi accent she had mastered for Blanche DuBois she snarled the terrifying lines from *A Streetcar Named Desire*: 'Get out of here quick before I start screaming fire.'

Olivier was summoned. He had settled himself into the protective company of the composer William Walton and his wife in Ischia and now had to make a weary journey in stages to Los Angeles, interrupted by a stop-over in New York with the Danny Kayes. It was there that David Niven called him from Hollywood with a story which might have come straight out of a Tennessee Williams play.

It isn't clear whether Olivier had already called on the support of staunch chums like Niven, or whether Niven acted on his own initiative, but Niven had telephoned Stewart Granger, then living in the Hollywood hills with his wife Jean Simmons.

'Viv is very sick,' Niven had said. It was 2.00 a.m., but Granger was immediately ready to do anything to help. Actually, Vivien was not the only sick one. John Buckmaster, Gladys Cooper's son and Vivien's old flame, had turned up out of the blue and moved into the house with her – it was as if two people riven with traumas had heard each other's call signs and answered like vessels in mutual distress. The year before, Buckmaster had been briefly incarcerated in a New York mental hospital after a policeman who had tried to apprehend him for carrying a couple of carving knives on Second Avenue had been accidentally cut by flying glass – he had been bailed out by Noël Coward, who had promised to keep an eye on him. But Coward's eye was thousands of miles away by the time Niven and Granger arrived at Vivien's home.

Each of them has independently given an account of what then ensued – and it would have been a highly comic scene if Vivien's sanity hadn't been so visibly and cruelly impaired. In his second volume of memoirs, *Bring on the Empty Horses*, published in 1975, Niven concealed Vivien's identity under the pseudonym 'Missee'. Granger was more direct when he wrote *Sparks Fly Upward* in

1981: he set the facts down without literary embellishment and they are heartbreaking.

As the two film stars marched together into the house, their first sight was of Buckmaster, naked except for a towel, defending Vivien's bedroom door like a High Priest making his last stand before the infidels come to ravish his earthly goddess. Declaring that he represented a higher power – and probably flexing his muscles to indicate its source – Granger ordered him to 'get the hell out'. To their relief, he did so and was driven back to his bungalow at the Garden of Allah, from where Granger called a doctor.

The plan was to slip Vivien a sedative to render her more amenable when the ambulance arrived. But on returning, Granger found her clad only in a bath robe and sitting in front of a TV screen as blank as her own mind. He prepared coffee and scrambled eggs, both heavily doped, which she then, with inconvenient wiliness, insisted on feeding first to Niven – with the result that he dropped off within minutes. She then stripped off and went out to sit by the pool, into which she tossed or spat the remaining sedatives Granger pressed on her. With the arrival of the paramedics, the scene turned ugly. One nurse sought to soothe her by talking to her in the way a parent talks to a belligerent child. 'I know who you are. You're Scarlett O'Hara, aren't you?' Vivien, according to Granger, screamed, 'I'm not Scarlett O'Hara. I'm Blanche DuBois.'

For her, the scene then mercifully faded out as she was injected with a heavy narcotic, but not before she had uttered a reproach that Granger could never forget: 'Oh ... how could you? I thought you were my friend.'

Olivier arrived a day or so later and summed up the scene as if he were directing it on the stage – perhaps only thus was the tragedy bearable for him. It was like a grim re-enactment of *Romeo and Juliet* twenty-five years on, for Vivien was waiting on an upstairs balcony, staring into space, and speaking 'in the tone of halting, dream-like amazement that people in the theatre use for mad scenes when they can't think of anything better'. The thought of theatre characteristically induced a religious note into his recollection. Vivien confessed 'with the wonderment of a first communion' that she was in love. 'Who with?' he asked with the calm of a priest lending an ear to a supplicant for absolution, rather than the indignation of a betrayed husband. 'Peter Finch,' she answered.

Olivier found himself wondering where the hell Finch was – like an actor-manager reproaching a leading player for being late on cue.

Vivien was transported home to England, her painful journey interrupted by scenes of coaxing, sedation, constraint, appeals and threats, all under the scrutiny of the media. At the airports Vivien struggled alternately with Olivier, Danny Kaye and Cecil Tennant, or pathetically murmured a timid, 'Hello, folks,' at the posses of newspaper and television people.

On arrival at Heathrow, she went straight into Netherne Hospital at Coulsdon, Surrey, a centre for treating psychiatric disorders, and was kept under deep sedation for four days, packed in icebags to bring down her fever and fed on liquid proteins. On the sixth day she was allowed up for a gentle walk – then horror rushed back and overwhelmed her. Rachel Kempson, the actress wife of Michael Redgrave, whose acquaintance Vivien had first made in 1943, recalls, 'She said to me, "I'll never forget Netherne. All those other patients walking around – I thought I was in an asylum." ' From this moment, her resolution *never* to go into hospital lest it turn out to be an asylum became total and unshakeable.

Olivier had returned to Ischia, exhausted, and wasn't at Vivien's bedside in time for her awakening. But she found flowers, chocolates and cosmetics from Noël Coward – along with his 'get well' note that she kept in her purse for the rest of her life, like an amulet.

On 12 April 1953, Coward's diary records that 'I had a mysterious message from a Miss Hartley. I called back and it was poor, darling Vivien.' She had been moved to University College Hospital. 'She started in floods of tears and then made a gallant effort to be gay and ordinary, but the strain showed through and she didn't make sense every now and then.'

It appears that Vivien had her first experience of electro-convulsive therapy (ECT) at this time, while being helped to recuperate. As stabilizing drugs like lithium had not yet become available, ECT was still the usual method of inducing calm in the mentally disturbed. About five shocks were delivered over a few days, with the patient anaesthetized by curare while the electrodes were applied to the temples. Vivien said later to Rachel Kempson, 'It leaves my mind totally numbed and when I come out of it I don't know where I am or what I've been doing. In fact, it's worse than before.' But the treatment was backed by medical authority and Olivier was advised that Vivien must be given ECT at any further sign of instability. When she returned to him at Notley, she looked rested and calm. In some way her husband could not define, she seemed a changed woman.

Had he also become a changed man? He admitted to himself, with surprise as much as sadness, that he now loved much less the woman who had come back to him. Vivien's shock treatment had made her more of a stranger than he could ever have imagined.

Because of this, he found himself viewing her increasingly distantly and dispassionately – as an observer rather than a husband. Vivien, in her altered state, was not the Vivien he had loved and married, and theirs was now a marriage in name alone. Only the proprieties had to be preserved; only the myth had to be protected. If the Fleet Street journalists suspected that all was

Vivien visits Olivier, playing a French-Canadian trapper, on the set of *49th Parallel*; the cup of tea was strictly English.

*Below left*) Olivier's favourite picture of Vivien: as Jennifer Dubedat in *The Doctor's Dilemma*, 1942.
*Below right*) As Sabina in *The Skin of Our Teeth*, 1945.

Whipping her slave in the film of *Caesar and Cleopatra* with Claude Rains looking on; a few minutes later she had the fall which caused her miscarriage.

Vivien's favourite pastime was shopping; it was Lady Teazle's too in *The School for Scandal*.

Two unhappy players: with Kieron Moore in *Anna Karenina*.

(*Below*) Sharing some good news with Alexander Korda during a break in shooting *Anna Karenina*, summer 1947. The film was to be the bad news.

(*Below left*) With Bonar Colleano in the London stage production of *A Streetcar Named Desire*, 1949, and (*above*) showing her temper to Marlon Brando in the Hollywood film two years later. (*Below right*) Peter Finch with Vivien during *Elephant Walk* in Ceylon; their love affair had begun.

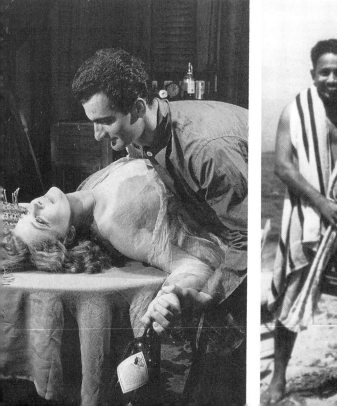

(*Above left*) Olivier and Vivien in *Antony and Cleopatra,* London, 1951, and (*right*) in *Titus Andronicus,* Stratford-upon-Avon, 1955.

Welcoming Marilyn Monroe and Arthur Miller to London for the film *The Prince and the Showgirl,* 1956; Vivien had just announced that she was pregnant.

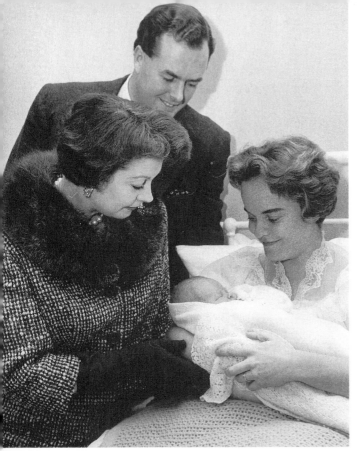

Admiring her daughter Suzanne Farrington's son.

It was overexerting herself in this Royal Variety Performance with Olivier and John Mills that brought on another miscarriage.

After the divorce from Olivier, a new home: Tickerage Mill in Sussex; and (*below left*) a new companion in her life, Jack Merivale, her co-star in *La Dame aux camélias* on the Australian tour 1961. (*Below right*) Back on Broadway and in her first musical, *Tovarich* — a tragic venture.

Vivien as the middle-aged widow in *The Roman Spring of Mrs Stone*, made in 1960, with Warren Beatty as her gigolo lover. Off the set, there was more distance between them.

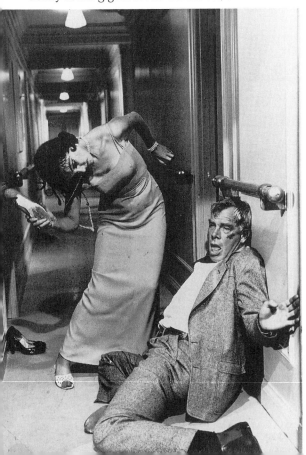

A national tribute in 1985: Vivien on one of the postage stamps issued to mark British Film Year.

Taking it out on Lee Marvin in *Ship of Fools*; the blows were all too real.

not well with the Oliviers' marriage, they were not yet prepared to spoil their readers' illusion.

Terence Rattigan had written a play called *The Sleeping Prince* with the Oliviers in mind as a 'courtier's offering' to Queen Elizabeth II in her Coronation year. It was a comedy about the infatuation of a stiff-necked Continental Prince Regent, in London for George V's crowning in 1911, with a seductive but deceptively innocent-looking American chorus girl. A fairy-tale, he called it. The news that the Oliviers would appear in it – Sir Laurence directing as well – was made the occasion to announce Vivien's return to normal life after her convalescence. Binkie Beaumont, who was co-presenting the play with Olivier, threw a press party at his Westminster home, where Vivien put on a convincingly 'normal' performance in very much the same wide-eyed way that she was to play the role – she embodied the duplicity of innocence.

The role of Mary Morgan, the chorus girl, was exactly the right size and weight for Vivien to cope with easily in her post-convalescent condition. She endowed the character with a nicely parodied innocence and a 'cute' Deep South accent, so that Olivier's predatory Old World roué could believe he had an easy job on his hands until he actually tried trapping this butterfly in the net of his seduction.

The play had its provincial try-out at Manchester in September 1953. Vivien's dressing-room was packed with flowers, including her dressing-table, where, beside the silver-framed photo of Olivier which travelled everywhere with her, there was a posy of red and white roses, 'From Larry'. It lay there like a peace offering.

The London opening was on 5 November 1953, Vivien's fortieth birthday. The general view was reflected by Cecil Wilson who declared: 'Miss Leigh is the most disarming little demon ever to upset a royal applecart.' But some critics felt she was a shade too old for the *ingénue* and Olivier a mite too dull for the Don Juan. It should have been obvious that playing a dull dog entertainingly takes more skill than many a serious characterization. It was certainly a surprise to the critics to find the leading players of the classical theatre adorning this frivolous comedy. Here again they forgot that serious players need to make money, too – and sometimes have fun as well. To the other strains on their relationship was now added the accusation of abandoning the classics to do the 'commercials'.

Money was in the forefront of the Oliviers' minds at this time. Though Vivien had not had to pay back the one-third fee she had received in advance for the film of *Elephant Walk*, in which she had been replaced by Elizabeth Taylor, Olivier had been forced to defer £20,000 of his £50,000 for the film of *The Beggar's Opera*, since it was judged a high-risk enterprise and had an innovative but unproven director in Peter Brook. It received very mixed notices and did no business to speak of. So as well as losing his deferred fee, Olivier became associated with his first undisguised commercial failure for many years and one his artistry couldn't override. Criticism generally, though unfairly, centred on his singing voice; for while professional singers had dubbed his co-stars, he was left to sing Macheath in his own light tenor, agreeable enough but not up to the competition.

Formidable compensation was at hand, however, for he began location shooting on his *Richard III* in Spain in September 1954, and wound it up inside thirteen weeks at Shepperton Studios. He 'adored every moment' of it.

For Vivien, though, it was a disappointment, as she was not to re-create her Lady Anne on the screen. More than her age was against her. *Richard III*, an expensive film co-produced by Korda's and Olivier's companies, needed every built-in reinsurance it could muster. Claire Bloom had been made into a star by Chaplin's *Limelight* in 1952 and, cruel though it might be to Vivien, it was considered that casting her as Lady Anne would bring 'box-office' to the film *and* endow the role with genuine youthfulness – she was just twenty-three – to point up Richard's malevolence as he woos her over her husband's coffin. There was good sense in this. But in her anxious state, Vivien suspected that her husband was attracted to the younger woman by the very qualities that she herself no longer possessed.

As Olivier was putting the finishing touches to his film, she was not fifty yards away on another Shepperton stage shooting *The Deep Blue Sea*.

The film told the story of a woman going through middle age who leaves her husband for another man in the hope he will revive her sexuality, but instead finds herself self-destructively at odds with the world. 'It was a rescue vehicle for Vivien,' Terence Rattigan admitted in later years.

> Korda had wanted Dietrich for the film version of my play. When he couldn't get her, he offered Vivien a role that he said to me was 'too near the truth'. The trouble was that Vivien either wouldn't or couldn't bring herself to expose menopausal reality in a way that made the character into a plausible marriage 'castaway'. Vivien would only have had to look out of the window and men would have been queueing up outside the door of her flat in the film.

There were other reasons why the film lacked harmony of intention and result. Vivien did not hit it off with Kenneth More, who played her lover. More had played the role on stage with, in turn, Peggy Ashcroft, Celia Johnson and Googie Withers – and he wanted Peggy Ashcroft for the film. With ebullient but misjudged loyalty to her, he pressed Korda to have Vivien replaced. But loyalty of this kind needs muscle behind it. More was not yet the box-office star that this film – and his next, *Reach for the Sky* – would make him. Korda took off his spectacles and his eyes narrowed – always a bad sign – and made More aware that he was out of his depth in this part of the sea. But the rebuff rankled with him so deeply that, unusually for a man of his generous and tolerant disposition, he was to deliver a harsh posthumous judgment on Vivien: 'I thought that she was petulant, spoilt, overpraised and overloved.' He plainly never saw the frightened Vivien – she was too good an actress to reveal that.

Despite working in close proximity to each other, the Oliviers met only at lunch – a light meal served them out of a portable refrigerator in Olivier's office. Over the lunch-hour, they discussed their next projects – it seemed that they dared not pause for a moment, lest inactivity bring them face to face with what each feared to confront – the increasing hollowness of the marriage in which they were trapped. They had already decided on a Stratford-upon-Avon season – *Twelfth Night, Macbeth, Titus Andronicus* – though it would mean a huge financial sacrifice for them both. Vivien was getting £50,000 for her role in *The Deep Blue Sea*, Olivier no less (though again with deferrals) for *Richard III*. Top pay for them at Stratford would be £60 a week.

But Olivier was impatient to reclaim his throne in the classical theatre and, for Vivien, not to have played at Stratford would have made her feel like a Catholic who had never seen Rome. Acting again with Olivier, she may have thought, would not only bring her back to his side in the great theatrical tradition, it would also be like having a second chance to regain his love.

She used to return to the set of *The Deep Blue Sea* in a tranquil frame of mind, prompting some of the cast to wonder if sedatives or more basic satisfactions lay behind her change of mood. Perhaps it was just that she saw hope in the future. 'While we were doing *The Deep Blue Sea*,' says Emlyn Williams, who played her husband in it, 'she was already rehearsing in her mind for Stratford. I was preparing my one-man Dylan Thomas show. She would hear my monologue, I would listen to her Lady Macbeth. But she had an odd, funny-peculiar turn of mind. We had one location scene, just the two of us in a car, driving past the camera, turning a corner. ... We did a couple of takes, then a third – there's *always* a third! As we got back into the car again, Vivien said, almost as if she wished it could happen, "Wouldn't it be funny if we drove off now, and nobody ever saw us again." '

# 19

'But, darling, the godparents have been chosen'

Vivien's affair with Peter Finch had flared up again like a recurrent fever. She had made the acquaintance of his mother and would settle down for long chats about him, as if she were already her daughter-in-law. She and Finch hardly bothered to conceal their relationship. When they were in Paris, Vivien would telephone home and talk with her husband in a casual, friendly way – not like a wife so much as an affectionate friend who was within striking distance of a visit and might wish to look him up.

Why did Olivier tolerate this semi-detached relationship with Vivien? There is no single answer, but pity, responsibility and self-interest all influenced him. Vivien was by now a burden on him – a guilty burden. He still loved her, despite the disaffection she had expressed for him: he remembered how much each of them had sacrificed for the other and, even more important to him, how much his own career in earlier years owed to her passionate support of him, the way Vivien had expanded his world so that it was wider than just a theatre stage. The public's image of them was largely Vivien's creation, formed out of the elements of her own romanticism. But Olivier had long outgrown these satisfactions: they became increasingly irksome to a man who had no real public self-assurance outside his theatrical persona. His talent had raced ahead into areas of art and creativity he had once only dimly imagined and never dreamed of possessing. It was obvious to him that Vivien could never hope even to pace him in the great race he was running in the classical theatre. This now absorbed all his energies – or would have done, had Vivien allowed it.

But her mental instability had become more than a source of concern: it was a threat. He had been slow to recognize it for what it was. Anthony Quayle asserts that Olivier told him he had recognized Vivien was mentally ill only when they had taken the two *Cleopatras* to America and she had suffered her incapacitating breakdown. He did not know how to deal with it. He could scarcely bear the pain of seeing his lovely wife close up like a flower in a chill room when stricken by her inexplicable illness. Her obstinacy made it hard for him to bring her help, even had he believed in the usefulness of analysis. Only the constant reassurance of his love for her seemed to bring Vivien peace of mind. The trouble was that she expected Olivier to express this love sexually, in ways that drained him of the vitality necessary for his own greater love affair with acting. He was not, in any case, the most active of partners: as he was wont to remark with rueful realism some years later, 'You can't be more than one athlete at a time.' Vivien's feverish demands had become incompatible with the demands he made on himself, and he was selfish enough to know that the stuff of which great acting is made would not be found in sexual therapy. This situation had created an unendurable tension between his own gifts and Vivien's needs.

In this mood, compounded of guilt, pained despair and self-preservation, he saw Peter Finch as a safety valve. Finch was a formidable actor, but not yet a great one and certainly not a driven one like Olivier. He had sexual energy enough and to spare. He could satisfy Vivien's demanding nature in ways that put her in a much calmer frame of mind — for a time, anyhow. Olivier hasn't ever expressed a jealousy of Finch's superior powers. He was fond of him as a person and, as has been noted, admired him as an actor. He had additional cause for gratitude if the man also relieved him of the demands Vivien made on him. One wonders if he ever entertained the idea that Finch might eventually relieve him permanently of responsibility for her. At any rate, so long as there was no scandal, or none that couldn't be safely contained within his own circle of friends and fellow actors, Olivier seems to have been prepared, at the very least, to accept a situation in which Peter Finch became Vivien's lover.

Why Finch was prepared to indulge and encourage Vivien is an even more intriguing question. He knew her to be dangerously unstable: did he think the *Elephant Walk* crisis wouldn't recur? Elaine Dundy has speculated on good evidence that Finch identified with the casualties of life as a result of the hard time he had gone through in his youth. He felt pity for what he considered to be Vivien's 'victim status', which subjected her to constant emotional crisis. In addition he was physically attracted to her. By reciprocating her evident need for him, he could convince himself he was assuaging her pain and fulfilling the sexual desire of them both. As for Olivier's tolerance, to say that he was glad to have Vivien taken off his hands might be a callous way of putting it, but the two of them were now leading separate existences of the heart. Only work brought them together, and even then it was a torturous togetherness.

The Stratford season of 1955 was ominous from the start. It asked much of Vivien, who was new to all three plays, whereas Olivier had been in two of them already.

John Gielgud was directing *Twelfth Night*. The combined force of two players in imperfect sympathy with each other broke against him, repeatedly demolishing his efforts to structure the comedy. Olivier, in an anti-romantic mood, played Malvolio as a below-stairs outcast bent on crawling upstairs to join his social betters. Gielgud felt powerless to influence this interpretation, shaded as it was with all the realistic human detail Olivier's film work had taught him. Vivien was divided in her loyalties. 'Part of her sympathized with what I was trying to do,' Gielgud says, 'part of her with what Olivier clearly thought she should be doing.' Her Viola was probably nearer Gielgud's interpretation – trim of form, boyish in stride, as ready to cheek her court circle as offer her cheek to her lover's kiss.

By temperament as well as technique, Vivien was closer to Gielgud than to Olivier. She enjoyed Gielgud's intellectual playfulness, his pouncing on an apt word, his love of poetry, his wide reading, his knowledge of his theatrical forebears, to some of the most eminent of whom he was related by blood. Both of them were sprinters on the middle track, unshaped for the gruelling marathons in which Olivier entered himself. They both had a quizzical, well-mannered, amused social assuredness – polishing the apples on the applecart, not upsetting it.

Olivier's eccentric Malvolio stole the show and the notices: Vivien was, in the consensus opinion, simply 'lovely to look at'. The distance by which her husband's unflagging creativity had outstripped her capacity even to pace him was made cruelly apparent.

Talk of Vivien's obsession with Finch and Olivier's grim despair was current but, so far, covert – confined to backstage rather than the front page. But an article published in the *Daily Express* under the name of the paper's theatre critic, John Barber, on the eve of the *Macbeth* production went off like a bomb in Stratford and elsewhere. It was unusually savage in tone for a piece on the Oliviers. Beginning by recalling the glorious post war stirrings of theatrical renewal at the Old Vic, the author's nostalgic lament suddenly changed into a merciless polemic. 'I hate that phrase "the Oliviers",' he wrote.

It kow-tows to the most fashionable couple in show business. The titled lions of Mayfair salons. The pair royally known as 'Larry-and-Viv'. Now look beyond the gloss. Olivier was a great actor. But since his gleaming, viperish Richard III, his fiery Hamlet, he has lost his way. Now, at 48, he is an ageing matinée idol, desperately fighting to win back his old reputation. To young people, his is a name that is attached to no outstanding achievement. She is a great beauty – still, at 42. As an actress, excellent in a dainty, waspish way that seldom touches the heart. It is time we saw them both as they really are.

Though hurt, Olivier took no action over this or over the presence of Peter Finch in Stratford, resuming his affair with Vivien in a rented room. He was totally absorbed in preparing his Macbeth – unaware, even, that Finch was now secretly coaching Vivien in between Glen Byam Shaw's rehearsing her as Lady Macbeth.

*Macbeth* was a play that put the daggers, so to speak, in Vivien's hands. Macbeth begins the tragedy on the heroic scale, but is then diminished by enfeebled will and cornered indecisiveness – and all the while his wife grows in blind audacity. The role appealed strongly to that part of Vivien's nature which disregarded consequences. As Macbeth is paralysed by guilt, his Lady is galvanized by opportunity: something of the Oliviers' natures was already contained in these roles and the way they played them. This *Macbeth* wasn't a *folie à deux*: it was the usurpation of one partner's conscience by the other's willpower – the partner who has been exhausted morally and physically is taken over by the one who is tireless and even walks in her sleep.

The views of the Oliviers' intimate friends tend to run, almost invariably, counter to the press notices they received for the play. For most of their friends, a certain truth was being displayed which the critics would not see so clearly and this explained why they withheld their choicest epithets from the more deserving partner. 'With Vivien, one felt it was something in the relationship with Larry that came out in her performance,' Emlyn Williams recalls. And Anthony Quayle says: 'Like the Macbeths, Larry and Vivien were prodigiously ambitious: they fed each other. Macbeth was the active partner in the production, but his wife was feeding her own mania into the tragedy in the making. She was mesmerizing.'

The Oliviers (with Peter Finch) awaited the Sunday critics' verdicts at Notley Abbey. Tynan's review was ripped untimely from the pages and passed from hand to hand. As Vivien had feared, it was ugly – for her. 'Sir Laurence shook hands with greatness ...' and then '... Vivien Leigh's Lady Macbeth is more niminy-piminy than thundery-blundery, more viper than anaconda, but still quite competent in its small way.'

Fifteen years later, Tynan radically revised this opinion. To the critic John Russell Taylor he revealed that: 'It was one of the worst errors of judgment he had ever made. In retrospect, the combination of Olivier and Vivien, with its emphasis on the way Macbeth is held in sexual thrall by his lady and so will do anything to please her, made more sense of the play than any other reading he had seen.'

It also made sense of Vivien's marriage, too, as Tynan, who later became Olivier's literary manager at the National Theatre, had had the opportunity to discover.

But in 1955, his review triggered off another manic episode that Noël Coward witnessed at the Notley supper table a few weeks after he'd seen Vivien in the play. Coward found her 'quite remarkable ... [with] a sort of viperish determination and physical seductiveness which clearly explained her hold over Macbeth'. Yet here she was, talking wildly at supper, obsessed by the Press's 'persecution', her voice high, shrill and accusatory, her eyes strange. A distraught Olivier later confided in him that life had again become impossible.

There they were, Coward wrote in his diary, 'eminent, successful, envied and adored, and most wretchedly unhappy'.

With Vivien again unstable, Olivier now had to undertake *Titus Andronicus*, a tale (long deemed unactable), of maiming, rape, slaughter and insanity. Vivien had little to say for the first fifth of the play, then absolutely nothing to say once her tongue had been cut out – scarlet ribbons fluttering from her lips imaginatively suggesting the terrible butchery involved. Yet under Peter Brook's direction, she mimed her distress most movingly and, advancing on Olivier as her father with her amputated arm stumps concealed by her cloak, she resembled a maimed and mute Cordelia come to comfort a devastated Lear. Again Tynan's notice appeared to them to have been fashioned like a wedge rather than a hammer – to drive them apart, not just flatten one of them. 'Sir Laurence's Titus ... is a performance which ushers us into the presence of one who is pound for pound the greatest actor alive.... As Lavinia, Vivien Leigh received the news that she is about to be ravished on her husband's corpse with little more than the mild annoyance of one who would have preferred foam rubber.'

Back at Notley, Vivien's exacerbated frustration was visited on her husband. Her relentless party-giving deprived him of sleep and he was relieved when she began staying overnight in Stratford. There she used to go out on the town with Finch after curtain down or stage midnight punting parties on the Avon and dawn picnics in the meadows. The younger members of the company joined in; the wiser ones and the old friends hung back. 'They had separated in all but the act,' says Anthony Quayle, 'and the whole season was nightmarish.' A member of the cast recalls:

> Larry said to me when I was doing *Titus* with him, 'I've never shed a tear on the stage – never been moved at all.' Certainly not on that stage he hadn't. ... I've been on it with Vivien when she would swear under her breath, 'You shit, you shit' ... and Larry would continue to spout the most marvellous poetry and then at the end of it whisper, 'Fuck you, fuck you.' I was tremendously saddened and tried, I'm afraid, to keep well away from them both. I remember Vivien appearing with a swollen eye one day, saying she'd been bitten by a mosquito. Someone had hit her, I thought.'

Yet Vivien, even in this state, manifested the utmost kindness to friends and acquaintances whom she held dear. Rosemary Geddes was then in the box-office at Stratford – she became Vivien's secretary a few years later – and recalls how 'Vivien and Sir Laurence laid on coaches to take the entire theatre, usherettes, cleaners, caterers, everyone, down to Notley one Sunday for a party that went on well into the night and must have cost £2,000 – a huge sum then.' Quayle recalls Vivien pressing a tiny, gift-wrapped object into the palm of his hand on the first night of *Titus Andronicus*. Inside was a nineteenth-century letter-seal made of cornelian, which had been used by William Wilberforce's anti-slavery supporters to impress their abolitionist message on the hot wax that sealed their communications. 'Am I Not Also a Man and a Brother?' was the motto encircling a kneeling Negro. The gift, he reflected, might have been a plea for help from Vivien.

For friends of both of them, parties at Notley were very uneasy affairs now. 'I could feel the awful tensions beneath the gaiety,' Quayle recalls, 'like being in a play with undertones running completely counter to the dialogue. When something happened, it almost came as a relief. I remember Lady Diana Cooper wandering in after dinner in a full suit of chain mail she'd found somewhere in the house – and being rather hurt that we stage people didn't think *that* very odd. Actually we were all on edge at what our host and hostess might get up to next.'

In November-December 1955, apparently in radiant health, Vivien made two attempts to run away with Peter Finch. The first time, the lovers got as far as Le Lavandou in France, but after a few days she was coaxed back to London. The second elopement did not, literally, get off the ground. She and Finch had determined to fly to New York, but they got no farther than the VIP lounge at Heathrow Airport. Fog delayed their take-off, and the waiting period was apparently enough to convince Vivien of what she stood to lose. The greater the physical distance between her and Olivier, the more unthinkable it was to surrender all that he represented to her – it meant forfeiting such a large part of what she was too. The aborted *avventura* had a curious sequel five years later. Vivien had confided in the playwright Terence Rattigan, who was never one to discard the dramatic opportunities that his friends' marriage troubles sometimes presented; he used the incident in his screenplay for *The VIPs*. In the film, directed by Vivien's former *bête noire*, Anthony Asquith, her role was taken by Elizabeth Taylor, as the glamorous but brittle wife of a millionaire industrialist, played by Taylor's then husband Richard Burton, a man who can give her only 'cheque-book affection'. Louis Jourdan was the handsome lover with a fatal weakness of character. This wife also returns, Candida-like, to the man who needs her most.

'Vivien saw through the ruse,' Rattigan confided to a critic who had questioned the unreality of the film, 'but if Larry did, too, he didn't say anything.'

Rattigan, however, was denied the privilege of witnessing the extraordinary scene which reportedly took place at Notley in the wake of Vivien's escapades, a scene which testified to the marvellously defensive way in which acting can keep reality at bay.

Finch confronted Olivier, but instead of two jealous men having it out with each other — a Vronsky come to receive judgment from a mortified Karenin — they got straight down to the drinks and thence into a series of improvisations in which Olivier assumed the paternal posture of an old retainer and Finch the attitude of the young master who is a bit of a scamp. Maybe it was a therapeutic transfer of guilt that was taking place; but any solemn underpinnings to the make-believe were sent flying when Vivien burst in to ask, 'Which one of you is coming to bed with me?' — and all three collapsed in laughter. Vivien told this story in later years.

The night's entertainment ended with all the parties recognizing that irrespective of whoever ended up in bed with Vivien, she would still choose to spend the rest of her days with her husband. The 'spell of Larry Boy', as she used to call it, was just too strong. Finch knew when the curtain had to come down — and he took his leave. Elaine Dundy has concluded that he acknowledged Olivier had 'stolen the show'. Vivien left a few days later to spend Christmas with her first husband Leigh Holman at his house in Devon, a refuge she now sought whenever she needed to calm herself and recover her emotional balance.

The New Year began badly for the Oliviers with the death of Alexander Korda from a massive coronary — followed by the collapse of their plans to make a film of *Macbeth*.

But then both were suddenly in work again. Noël Coward, who had been hesitating over Vivien's condition, decided she was up to playing the lead in his comedy *South Sea Bubble*; and Olivier was asked to direct Marilyn Monroe in the film version of *The Sleeping Prince*, as well as to co-star in it. If he had not repossessed his crown at Stratford as the greatest classical actor of his generation, he might have had more inhibitions about being associated with the woman who was then Hollywood's most potent sex symbol. Then again, with the 'quaking emptiness' of his domestic life, perhaps he might not....

It was Vivien who had suggested Monroe for the role 'if the play's ever filmed' after she'd seen how funny and sexy she could be in the film *How to Marry a Millionaire*. She had no hard feelings about Monroe taking over her role in the play, now retitled *The Prince and the Showgirl*. Marilyn was no challenge to her. Privately, Vivien considered the Hollywood star rather vulgar and not a little obtuse. She enjoyed repeating the tale she had been told of

Marilyn going to Arthur Miller's family home, where she had matzo balls served up so often at the meal table that she finally asked innocently, 'Isn't there any other part of the matzo we can eat?'

*South Sea Bubble* opened at the Lyric Theatre, London, in late April 1956. Critics treated it as the lightweight confection it was. Because it wasn't considered worthy of sharper barbs, it survived unpricked for 276 performances. 'A capacity hit,' Coward called it. But Vivien was not to be in it for the whole of the run. A few weeks after the opening, she announced she was expecting a baby. She was forty-two years old. On hearing the news, Coward was furious. It meant she would have to drop out of the show in due course. He also thought it 'fairly foolish' of her to conceive again at that age. At the press conference on 12 July Vivien sat on a Victorian love-seat, as impeccably dressed as ever, while Olivier stood behind her with an expression that said, 'Why, I just adore babies.' They had already engaged a nanny, Vivien revealed, *and* chosen a name – 'Katherine'. No, they hadn't even considered a boy's name – 'We want a girl.' Someone asked if they were going to ask Marilyn Monroe to be a godmother. 'That's an interesting idea,' Olivier said carefully. 'But, darling,' said Vivien quickly, 'the godparents have been chosen already.' So Marilyn was not destined to be a member of the family by proxy.

Two days later, on 14 July, both of them welcomed Monroe and Arthur Miller at a chaotic London airport press conference.

Vivien sat quietly, glowing with the confident motherhood that had upstaged her more glamorous rival, but she consented to plant a kiss on one of Monroe's cheeks while Olivier occupied himself with the other and the goddess herself looked ecstatic in this osculatory sandwich.

Kisses ran out quickly as filming began and Monroe's chronic unpunctuality and total insecurity turned Olivier's work of directing and acting with her into a nightmare.

But far more disconcerting was a discovery Olivier made about Monroe and her husband. If he had been a little in love with her at the start of the enterprise, it was as nothing compared to the awe he continued to feel for her husband Arthur Miller. Miller was then America's foremost living playwright and he and Olivier used to talk late and long about their love of theatre, acting, playmaking and the rest. Miller was an unresponsive and indeed awkward man on the surface: it took time to get to know him. But his feelings ran even deeper than Olivier's and, over the weeks of shooting, mutual exchanges of admiration and then sympathy led Olivier to believe that Miller's marriage to Monroe was interfering with his creative abilities.

Every hour of his day, and much of his nights, too, was devoted to Monroe. Miller's peculiar tragedy, to Olivier's way of thinking, was that he was a great creative talent who simply couldn't function any longer. In short, he was what Olivier feared he himself might become. Work was still Olivier's angel of mercy. But even work had stopped for Miller. Caring for Monroe's unstable nature, trying to gain a rational purchase on her intangible psyche, left him no time or energy to be visited by any more inspiring angel. He was in the dry season of his art.

Though Miller's fate showed what might happen to Olivier if he remained with Vivien, the American playwright also indicated where salvation might lie.

Olivier at fifty had reached an age when the younger generation in the theatre should have been challenging him for supremacy in the classical tradition he exemplified. However, the business of the generation of 1956 was not to emulate, but to overthrow − and the tidal flow of the times had taken it into rough seas that made Olivier's theatre begin to look like a backwater.

In the play *Look Back in Anger* and in its author John Osborne the younger generation had found a mouthpiece for all it thought wrong with the England that Olivier had once been told, and still believed, he personified.

Olivier had been to the Royal Court Theatre to see *Look Back in Anger* and had detested it. It was Arthur Miller who heard in it the authentic rumble of a revolution and sent him back to see it again. Olivier's conversion followed with the immediacy of St Paul's on the Damascus highroad.

One of those who witnessed the change in Olivier was Peter Hiley, a British Council official in Australia who had co-ordinated part of the Old Vic tour so well that Olivier had offered him an administrative job under Cecil Tennant at LOP.

Larry came back saying, 'This is the new theatre.' He genuinely wanted a part of it. He saw people taking their ties off, wearing T-shirts, going off with young women, talking politics that *were* politics, not just backstage gossip and he thought, This is wonderful − I can be young again! Vivien was not so impressed. She could see through a lot of the phoniness in it. She disliked the raffishness − it offended her fastidiousness.

Above all, Vivien saw in the new theatre no roles for herself to play, whereas for Olivier it was just the reverse. Here were roles that were articulate, composed of rhythms and words − even four-letter words − he had never tried out in the West End theatre. Now he, too, hankered for revolution and the barricades.

As Olivier's new view of himself and his future took shape, he can hardly have failed to see that Vivien's place in it was bound to be diminished. 'For the first time in their theatre experience there was a parting of the ways,' says Hiley. It was the start of the end of that fashionable coupling of power, beauty and talents. For although there was certainly a role for Olivier to play at the Royal Court, there was none for 'the Oliviers'.

Had Vivien's baby been safely born that December or the following January, things might even then have been different. The role of the family man might have found Olivier before he found the generation that offered him a wide choice of adoptive children of protest. But barely had Vivien left the cast of the Coward play on 11 August 1956 and settled into Notley to await her baby, than she suffered a miscarriage. She was five months pregnant: the child would have been a boy.

'We are bitterly disappointed and terribly upset,' said Olivier. Coward was furious. 'Disorganized silliness,' he snorted, and placed the blame on Vivien. She had behaved foolishly.

Says Virginia Fairweather, an acquaintance of the Oliviers and later press representative at the National Theatre:

> Bea Lillie was performing [at the Café de Paris] and later came back to my flat for a party. At about 2.00 a.m., there was a crash at the door. Outside were Rex Harrison, Danny Kaye, Larry and Vivien and Bobby Helpmann – so we started the party all over again. Danny was talking about 'Triplets', the famous cabaret sketch by Dietz and Schwartz, and Bea and I said, 'We'll do it' – because we'd both done it before. Danny said, 'I'll do it with you.' We had a marvellous audience, of course, and Vivien was so taken by it she wanted to try her hand at it the first chance she got. That chance came at one of those beastly Night of the Stars charity shows – when she was about four months pregnant.

Not only that, but Vivien climbed into white tie, top hat and tails to do a song-and-dance act with Olivier and John Mills that involved hours of practice. The miscarriage followed.

Though disappointed that they had lost the baby – he described it later as an attempt at 'fucking his marriage back to life' – Olivier's immediate concern was for Vivien's sanity. Her unstable spells were becoming more frequent. There was an additional apprehension – intrusive publicity.

The media's attitude towards celebrities was changing in the late 1950s. Hitherto, they had tended to collude with them in preserving an image or reputation whch might or might not be valid, but at least made good copy. With the advent of the 'new' novelists and the 'angry' playwrights, interviews became more candid, comment more scathing, reputations more vulnerable. On the new Independent TV network, and even in the BBC, mutually understood limits were being exceeded. Amongst the once sacred institutions that would come increasingly under scrutiny or fire were 'the Oliviers'.

Dr Arthur Conachy, a physician who had treated Vivien with immense patience, kindness and insight since 1949, understood the hazards her condition exposed her to – especially when she was in a manic phase. He warned her and Olivier specifically of the undesirable publicity that could come from a marked and unconcealed increase in, say, Vivien's sexual drive. Above all, she must try to cut down on drinking, which he believed triggered the manic phase. Parties, therefore, became occasions of some nervousness for Olivier. Was Vivien's gaiety normal or did it signal a manic attack? The constant watchfulness he felt necessary gave him an even keener appreciation of being a helpless observer. Everything, in short, compelled him to seek for himself an antidote to the state of his marriage – and that was to create an alternative 'marriage'. The Royal Court was that alternative.

His acceptance of the Archie Rice role in *The Entertainer* was a sort of consummation for him. It extended his love affair with a whole new range of characters cut from the cloth of contemporary life instead of from historical chronicles. And the role wasn't without its pleasurable sense of self-abasement – for Archie the music-hall comic 'died' nightly in front of the hostile house.

The problem was, the play had no role for Vivien. She was too old to play Archie's daughter, too beautiful to be his wife. It was even suggested she should wear a rubber mask to make her look drab and blowsy, though the proposal didn't stand scrutiny any longer than such a mask would have done.

Vivien saw it all as a kind of defection. She saw Olivier being directed by people hardly known to her; the other players didn't even come from the companies that the Oliviers had put together at the St James's or Stratford. She didn't see herself standing *in loco parentis* to this mob. What Olivier found rejuvenating simply made Vivien feel her age. She came to a few early rehearsals of *The Entertainer*, but she made Olivier nervous and he asked her to stay away.

Olivier had been looking for someone to play Archie Rice's daughter and his eye lit on a young actress from Scunthorpe, in Lincolnshire, with a name as homely as her birthplace – Joan Plowright. He felt her proletarian naturalism represented the new generation. Joan Plowright was then twenty-six, and Vivien was soon to realize the risk she represented to her marriage – but she probably never appreciated a richer irony.

Joan Plowright had been anxious, like all talented players in the provinces, to break into the West End; and two years earlier she had written to one highly recommended London agent asking him to represent her. The man accounted himself a very shrewd judge of talent. In his time, which went back to before the war, he had discovered a whole roster of such 'unknowns' and fostered their careers until, to his increasing bitterness, they had been snapped up by more financially powerful or politically resourceful managements. He was, of course, John Gliddon – Vivien's first agent.

He took Joan Plowright to tea at a Regent Street café, warned her of the hard and usually thankless business that acting was, then sent her home after extracting a promise from her to reflect on his cautionary tale and let him know. Unshaken by his homily, she said she'd take the risk and he agreed to represent her. But then Gliddon's own resolve evaporated. He decided he'd had enough of the ungrateful business himself and wrote to Joan Plowright, while she was on a tour of South Africa, to give her his blessing and to advise her to look elsewhere. Thirty years later, Gliddon could still savour the irony in signing up the first Lady Olivier and the actress who was to become the second one.

Joan Plowright's persistence took her to the same stage on which Vivien's husband was about to achieve his great breakthrough to a new style of theatre and, as it turned out, a new style of life.

# 20

## 'Eva Perón was lucky ... she died at thirty-three'

Despite her troubles, Vivien's daily life was kept on course by the strength of her upbringing. Her nature was resilient: she bounced back after each attack. Always her first thought, her first action was to dash off an apologetic note in her large, hasty writing to anyone she thought she'd offended while the attack was on her. 'I always thought it greatly to her credit', says Peter Hiley, 'that the people who worked for her never said, "I can't stand this any longer, I'm off." She was always appreciative of people – never took anyone for granted – and those who helped her were often helped in return. Vivien was a star in private life and a very good actress; Olivier was a superstar on the stage, but otherwise a man like the rest of us.'

Hiley's duties with Olivier's management company had expanded: he had become a sort of comptroller for their households, overseeing Notley and paying bills. 'It was easy to think of Vivien as being extravagant. In fact, she never spent without purpose and always got top value.' She now had her own company, Vivien Leigh Productions Ltd, which contracted out her services and received her fees; it had been set up some years earlier as a tax-shelter. When it came to spending, Olivier was the grumbler, whilst Vivien lived as freely as she thought. It wasn't a case of there being no tomorrow. There *would* be a tomorrow, she knew: but let things take care of themselves till then.

Shopping was among her greatest pleasures, but the purchases were less important than the people for whom they were intended. They were 'friendship trips' as much as shopping expeditions. Sometimes her liberality outran her logic, if not her purse. 'I remember we went to a picture gallery,' Rachel Kempson says, 'and were looking at a Venetian painting. She was considering buying it: it was an awful price. I said to her, "Vivien, dear, I honestly think you shouldn't – I don't think it's authentic." She said, "Oh, don't you?" – and didn't. When we got back home, she said to Larry, "Larry, I've saved you thousands this afternoon, so now I can spend a great deal more."'

Vivien's friends the actresses Rachel Kempson, Coral Browne, Margaret

Leighton, the costume designer Beatrix ('Bumble') Dawson, who'd been to Vivien's old school, and the columnist Radie Harris were all tightly protective of her. At weekends in the country, if Vivien wasn't herself, she'd ring the nearby weekend cottage where Rachel Kempson and her husband Michael Redgrave would be staying. 'Can you come over?' They knew what that portended.

'I'd get over to Notley,' says Rachel Kempson, 'and a distracted Larry would meet me and say, "Oh, you can't help me — she's tried to shut the cook in the cupboard," or something else. I'd say, "Let me sit with her and talk to her." And I'd do that, and we'd walk around the gardens, and she'd get things under control and she'd say, "You know, I'm not really as bad as all that." Her troubles left her so puzzled and apologetic.'

The Oliviers had put Durham Cottage up for sale when Vivien thought her baby was imminent and had taken a short lease on a Chelsea house owned by the composer William Walton. But Vivien found a large flat at 54 Eaton Square; and in spite of the anxieties she harboured about her marriage, she threw herself wholeheartedly into furnishing it. It soon acquired a look that reflected a shared theatrical background and also suggested a happily married and mutually dependent couple. But then illusion was the backcloth of their professional lives too.

Olivier's study had blackberry-purple wallpaper contrasting with an acid-green carpet, heavily pleated yellow curtains — almost stage ones — a purple-and-white *toile de Jouy* sofa and a John Piper painting of Notley. The dining-room — really a deep, pillared alcove opening off the hall, was in Regency stripes. An Aubusson rug in amethyst, ivy and beige dominated the living-room. Vivien's collection of pictures was displayed with a homely casualness, including the Degas painting of the woman washing — Vivien used to say Roger Furse had almost spoiled it for her by bestowing on it the flippant title 'Making a Clean Breast of It'. In the corner of the room, set firmly on a heavy base was a thick post about two feet high covered in scarlet velvet — a scratching post for Vivien's cats. Her most sentimental objects were kept in her bedroom — which reflected her love of flowers wherever one looked. The walls were hung with white chintz strewn with large cabbage roses, the carpet lime green like a spring lawn. Here she kept an unfinished sketch Augustus John had made of her — unfinished because the painter had developed a habit of nipping into the next room to get inspiration from the whisky decanter, leaving Vivien feeling abandoned and chilly, so she upped and grabbed the canvas and walked away with it.... Here, too, she kept her tiny Winston Churchill painting of the rosebuds and her Cellini drawing. The bed was a four-poster, quilted and canopied with roses in bud, sprig and full-blown. If the bed looked faintly familiar to visitors, this was not surprising: it was a reproduction of the one at Tara in *Gone With the Wind*.

It was in this apartment that Vivien lived when in town during the last ten years of her life: it was in this bedroom that she would take leave of life itself.

Rosemary Geddes came to the flat almost daily when Vivien was in England. After working in the Stratford theatre, and later as an office assistant for Peter Hiley, she was now Vivien's secretary. 'Actually, she taught me everything I know,' she recalls. A typical day began at 10.00 a.m., Vivien in the four-poster, eating breakfast off a wickerwork bed-table: Melba toast and honey, orange juice, coffee – she didn't like tea much, and when she drank it preferred China to Indian despite her Darjeeling origins. She would already have done all or most of *The Times* crossword and now she'd dictate business letters – 'never altered afterwards' – and then dress while Rosemary dealt with fan mail, sent off photos, prepared cheques for signature. Her living-in maid, a German called Trudi Flockert, prepared her day-wear.

Clothes for her were part of the job of looking good. She wasn't obsessive about them, but she *was* well organized. Apart from couture dresses, she used a dressmaker, a Mrs Wannamaker, very near by. She never wore slacks, except in the country. She preferred suits for town-wear. Sometimes she'd send me to Harrods to bring back half-a-dozen summer dresses – she was very fond of bluish-mauve colours – and she'd keep one or two she liked. She had loads of scarves and always wore them: seldom a hat. She had about a dozen pairs of gloves, short and long, white and beige, but not the five dozen some writers have said she owned! She wore fairly plain court shoes, from Rayne's mostly, but had her evening shoes dyed to match her gowns, her handbags, too. She changed her handbags every year. She remained faithful to her favourite scent, Joy by Patou, but, when she gave scent as a present to other people, it was Dior. She thought her hair too curly for her liking and would go to have it straightened fairly often – to Phyllis Earle or Elizabeth Arden. Later, she wore wigs, or Phivos would come and do her hair at home while she used the time under the dryer for more dictation.

She smoked a lot. Too much. But this was before smoking was known to be such a killer.

Every so often she'd say, 'Rosemary, I think it's time to give the wardrobe a turning-out,' and then I'd take the clothes she'd tired of round to a high-quality second-hand shop near Sloane Street.

Everyone used to send her flowers and they'd arrive all through the day. One girl in Spain was a fan and a bouquet of red roses would come from her punctually every month. Vivien used Constance Spry, if she needed anything special. She'd spend a good hour or so in the kitchen arranging the flowers and spread them around the flat. I once tried my hand at it. 'Oh, Rosemary, dear,' she said, 'arranging flowers is *not* your forte.'

After she was dressed, Vivien would sign the letters Rosemary Geddes had typed, perhaps adding personal notes on blue writing-paper or white cards with 'Vivien Leigh' in red at the top. She never had mid-morning coffee. Very occasionally she would eat lunch in, preferring salmon mayonnaise and salad. Wine was served, but generally for other people. Vivien stayed faithful to gin and tonic. Most often she'd go out to lunch with women friends, chauffeured by Bernard in the Rolls-Royce with the registration plate 'LOP 1'. The Caprice under Mario and Prunier's were her favourite places to eat.

She would return from lunch by mid-afternoon, do more letters, change if people were coming for cocktails, and invite Rosemary to join her guests before she left at around 6.30 p.m. For evening wear, she generally chose something by one of her favourite couturiers – Balmain, Molyneux, Norman Hartnell or Victor Stiebel – and invariably a mink coat in winter. She had three full-length minks at this period, and a mink stole. But morning or evening, Rosemary Geddes noted, she spent very little time on make-up. Stage training made her fast: her mirror didn't need to cater to vanity – she knew herself too well to need its flattery. 'Appearance was simply part of the job of being Lady Olivier,' says Rosemary Geddes.

Thus, as the 1950s drew to a close, did Vivien preserve the equilibrium of her daily life while events she was powerless to control kept crowding in on her career – and her reason.

Olivier played a packed, but deliberately limited season in *The Entertainer* at the Royal Court: his triumph was total. Then after he and Vivien had both withdrawn from the planned film of *Separate Tables*, after disagreements over the script, they took *Titus Andronicus* on a tour of Europe. Though at first all went well, it turned into a terrifying experience.

They began by playing the Théâtre Sarah Bernhardt in Paris to huge applause. Vivien was made a Chevalier of the Legion of Honour. (Olivier was already a *Commandeur*). She followed that up with a shopping spree at Balmain's, where a plastic dummy of her was kept, so that entire wardrobes could be fitted in her absence. With special Bank of England approval – for foreign currency was still severely rationed – she purchased suits, silk-print dresses and short evening gowns that were easy to pack. Olivier had decided the company would travel by train.

This prelude to the tour provided them with a brief holiday, motoring through Touraine with Jean-Pierre Aumont and his wife Marisa. Vivien had been there before with Olivier, and Aumont noted how she popped into small establishments *en route*, asking after some hotelier or shopkeeper and his family 'like a monarch visiting her vassals'.

It was when the company embarked on the train for Vienna in unseasonably hot May weather that Vivien began to exhibit manic signs, and by the time they arrived she was so seriously out of control that Cecil Tennant and Binkie Beaumont had to fly out to meet them. Vivien looked at their worried faces and said perkily, 'I know a psychiatrist here who'll help me.' They combed the Vienna directory and cross-checked with analysts before she acknowledged she had pulled the name out of the air. It was Binkie Beaumont who snapped her out of this mood of mischievous mania by threatening to send on her understudy that night and every other night till she recovered. 'That night', says David Lewin, the *Daily Express* writer covering the tour, 'she gave a perfect performance.'

But on reaching Belgrade, conduct that had been erratic became alarming. She disappeared for a whole afternoon. The company fanned out in search of her in art galleries, museums, wherever she was likely to have gone, and found her sitting alone on a park bench crying. The next day, in a rush of euphoria, she threw off her clothes in a public garden. It was passed off by the company as a piece of light-headed make-believe after a good lunch. Vivien benefited from the kindness of intimates as well as strangers.

Madness manifested itself again in the worst possible place, on the long train ride to Warsaw in boiling summer heat. Angry and reproachful, Vivien flew at Olivier. He shut himself in his compartment, while she hammered at the glass. Maxine Audley next caught the force of her displeasure and had to retreat into the lavatory and bolt the door. There was no arguing with Vivien, and no one tried. If she hadn't fallen into the sleep of a fractious child who has tired herself out, the tour might have been abandoned there and then. Yet on stage, where she felt safest, she was again perfection.

For Olivier, this trip was the turning point. It brought the awful public exposure he had dreaded; and to those closest to him, like Coward, he confessed he simply could not go on. He loved Vivien still – but he couldn't cope.

Throughout his life, Olivier had made a point of asking Coward, his earliest mentor, for 'permission' to do things – go to Hollywood, accept a title, etc. Now he seemed to be asking for sanction to make the break with Vivien at long last. Coward demurred, not really sure of the truth of the situation. Olivier, though, had reached the sticking point.

The Oliviers looked a curious couple to Larry Adler, the composer and harmonica player who had co-starred with Vivien in *St Martin's Lane*, when he walked into the Caprice for lunch in the first week of July 1957. They sat together on a banquette just past the little podium where Mario, the *maître d'hôtel*, kept his 'bible' of reservations. Vivien looked flushed and excited; Olivier, hunched and grim.

'Larry ... Larry,' she called out to Adler, 'come and join my march.'

Her tone was so penetrating and imperious that the gossip in the fashionable restaurant was hushed; the audience listened expectantly. 'Larry,' Vivien said agitatedly, 'we're going to march on Parliament to save the St James's Theatre from being knocked down by that awful property developer. You *must* join us.'

The 122-year-old theatre, the citadel of Olivier's actor-management endeavours, was going to be torn down to make way for an office block. Privately, Olivier acknowledged he could never make the St James's pay: it was sad, but there it was. Vivien had other views.

'I'm an American ... I can't march on Parliament,' Adler protested. Vivien raised her voice to sergeant-major level. 'How dare you contradict me.... You *must* join me.'

Adler then recalls that Olivier gave him a look 'which said to me, "Larry, get the hell out of here" – which I did.'

A few days later, on 10 July, escorted by a sheepish Alan Dent and not many others, Vivien led her 'march' along the Strand swinging a hand-bell. Two days after that, she interrupted a House of Lords debate – and was escorted from the precincts of Westminster by the gentleman usher known as Black Rod. Even a £500 donation from Churchill and a letter from him admiring her courage, but disapproving, 'as a Parliamentarian', of her disorderly method, did not win the day for Vivien – or the St James's.

She left for a summer holiday in Greece with Leigh Holman and Suzanne; Olivier went to Scotland with Tarquin.

Separate holidays may have been good therapy: but they had most unlooked for consequences.

The national press, seeing the Oliviers taking their holidays apart, began to wonder if their marriage was coming apart too. The couple set their faces resolutely and publicly against any admission of what was indeed the truth. 'My first husband and I are still good friends,' said Vivien. 'Larry and I are very much in love.' Olivier added: 'I have no comment to make on anything which does not exist.'

The hounds were now off the leash. Soon they were being encouraged by one of those moral guardians who pop up so frequently in public life. Mrs Jenny Mann, Labour Member of Parliament for Coatbridge and Airdrie, and a strict Sabbatarian, described Vivien's decision to go off with her first husband as 'a terrible example for people who occupy high places in life to set before young children'. In a BBC television interview, she added: 'It indicates to me that divorce has become too easy. If a woman can find her ex-husband so congenial, she should not have thrown in the towel so quickly when they got married.' Leigh Holman sent a wire to *The Times*, which was the ultimate weapon in a gentleman's arsenal in those days: 'CRITICISM ILL-CONSIDERED AND UNMANNERLY. PRESENCE OUR DAUGHTER GIVES EXPLANATION TO ANY REASONABLE PERSON.'

Back in London, they continued to occupy 54 Eaton Square, but Olivier established a bolt-hole for himself in a nearby square. There was still no formal separation; neither party could face the publicity, nor the shattering of the Olivier legend. Noël Coward had suggested they live an 'open marriage' and now believed they were doing so, by intention or not.

Vivien has related how she was in Olivier's dressing-room at the Palace Theatre, where *The Entertainer* had been revived in September 1957. Olivier was removing his make-up. As he pulled off the bushy eyebrows he wore as Archie Rice, he looked at her reflection in his mirror, and, without turning round, remarked in what was almost a throwaway line: 'I suppose you should know I am in love with Joan Plowright.'

It was at this period that Vivien became 'hysterical', as it was diplomatically put by George Devine, artistic director of the English Stage Company, which had originally presented the play at the Royal Court. Devine was a very understanding friend of Olivier's. He tactfully let Olivier have the key to a furnished room he had rented in Walton Street. For everyone it was a situation that cowed the spirits and compelled a heart-wrenching furtiveness.

When *The Entertainer* transferred to New York, and Olivier and Joan Plowright left for Broadway, Vivien's loneliness was crushing. She imagined them tasting all the pleasures that she and Olivier had known in the springtime of their own affair. A reminder that it was no longer spring for her had come with her daughter Suzanne's marriage to Robin Farrington, an insurance broker. How long would it be before she had grandchildren to care for?

Typically, she braced herself: if no husband was to hand, at least a play was. Binkie Beaumont offered her the role of Paola in *Duel of Angels*, which Christopher Fry had translated from Giraudoux's play *Pour Lucrèce*. Oddly enough, like her first great success, *The Mask of Virtue*, it was about deceit and destroying people in order to gratify others. Vivien was the beautiful, heartless, capricious and promiscuous wife of a well-off French provincial bourgeois. She takes revenge on the community's model wife, an angel of rectitude played by Claire Bloom, by making her believe she has slept with a libertine while drugged. Jean-Louis Barrault was brought from Paris to direct.

Barrault was surprised at the fierce passion Vivien brought to the part. Sharpness, he'd expected: but this was 'a panther'. It was not surprising that in her present mood she should have excelled in the story of one woman's revenge on another. When the play opened in April 1958, the notices were some of the best she ever received.

But a warning was uttered amid the applause. For once again, the role held Vivien tenaciously in its power and even vacationing at Notley that summer there occurred embarrassing evidence of how 'possessed' she was by this other self she displayed on stage.

Jeanne Moreau, the French actress, was a guest at Notley; there was some talk of her appearing in a play with Olivier. The atmosphere round the lunch table became tense as the mood of *Duel of Angels* closed round Vivien. She spoke in the voice she used in the play, scrupulously polite in her words, mercilessly cutting in her intonation. 'Oh, you speak English well enough, do you, to play with Larry? And you think you look young enough to play the part, do you?'

'It was quite awful,' recalls Anthony Quayle, who was present. 'Vivien insulted Moreau all through lunch. Fortunately, Moreau realized she had something wrong with her, and didn't let herself be baited. She really was an angel.'

Vivien and her husband had supper together on her forty-fifth birthday in November 1958. Olivier was preparing to leave for Hollywood, where he was to appear in *Spartacus* with Kirk Douglas under Stanley Kubrick's direction. His impending absence had a calming effect on Vivien, and they were at least able to speak reasonably, if not candidly, for he still could not face up to telling Vivien that he wanted a divorce in order to marry Joan Plowright. His troubled conscience may have been reflected in the extravagant birthday present he gave her: a new royal blue Rolls-Royce, which she had recently seen at the Motor Show.

A few nights later they both threw a large party for over 150 guests at the Mirabel restaurant in honour of Lauren Bacall. They received their guests standing close together, Olivier in black tie, Vivien in an ultramarine evening gown matching her eyes. He presented every woman with a small red rose; she gave every man a scarlet carnation. One would not have imagined they had ever had a moment's difference of opinion in their lives. Many of the people whose names were on the guest-list knew the truth to be otherwise, though the Oliviers managed to look so happy that some of their friends imagined they had patched things up. That, in part, was the intention of the evening: appearances were still desperately important to them. In fact it was almost the last time that Vivien Leigh and Laurence Olivier would play hosts in the world they had done so much to create. Instead of marking a fresh start, it was a joint farewell to their life together.

Early in December 1958, Suzanne had her first child, a boy. 'Scarlett O'Hara Now Granny', ran the headlines. She was offered a play about Eva Perón. 'She died at thirty-three,' said Vivien, 'I'm forty-five. Eva Perón was lucky.' She gave an interview shortly before Suzanne's baby was born, speaking as a 'grandmother-to-be' but sounding like a widow – for once, Olivier's name went unmentioned.

Olivier spent a great deal of time in America in 1959 and, while he was there, corresponded with Joan Plowright. However, both of them were constrained by their apprehension of what Vivien might do to herself if the nature of their relationship were to be made public. Patience was enforced on them, and what Olivier later called 'romantic starvation' had to replace the food of love. Meanwhile, back in London, Vivien was appearing in Feydeau's farce *Occupe-toi d'Amélie*, which Noël Coward had partly transposed into his own style and anglicized as *Look After Lulu*.

Critics thought she did the Feydeau parts better than the Coward interpolations. The truth was that Coward's reputation was dipping into the hollow of critical disdain. Terence Rattigan's was soon to follow it. Olivier had already made his break from the prison of the 'well-made play', but the critics' about-face lost Vivien two of the playwrights best attuned to her range and talents. Her options were dwindling fast.

Though Olivier had told her at the end of 1958 that he intended leaving her, she could not believe in the possibility of it. He came back from America to go to Stratford and play a brilliant Coriolanus.

Godfrey Winn felt the strain Vivien was under that summer when she picked him up one early June evening, alone in the Rolls-Royce and driving it herself, to take him to Notley for the weekend. Vivien had frequently sought refuge and relaxation at Winn's small country house at Falmer in Sussex. He was one of the few men, apart from Coward, in whom she confided, pouring out her anxieties and hopes over cups of tea and honey sandwiches under the mulberry tree.

She was still rehearsing *Look After Lulu* and had Winn hear her lines from Act Two as they drove north. It seemed to him as if she were forcing herself to repeat the part, parrot-fashion, in order to stop some deeper anxiety overpowering her thoughts.

After dinner they walked in the garden, past the massed banks of pinks, tobacco flowers and evening primroses that glowed palely in the twilight. Vivien said: 'We must stay near the house, as Larry has promised to telephone us as soon as the curtain is down at Stratford.'

They continued their walk, but holding to the perimeter of the old abbey, the way a ship hugs the coast's friendly lights when a storm warning is out. Her guest saw that Vivien was hardly paying him any attention.

Anxious to distract her, when they returned to the library, Winn began telling her the plot of a Compton Mackenzie novel he thought had a good part for her if it could be dramatized. He spun it out until after midnight. He prayed for the merciful interruption which she clearly expected. But although she broke in every now and then, commenting on the story he was dismally committed to, Vivien's thoughts were miles away. '[She] sat ... frozen into immobility, with all the beautiful things, which she had collected across the years with love and delicate taste, seeming objects in a cold, impersonal museum as she went on waiting, with dying hope, for the telephone to ring that night.'

PART THREE

# *Jack*

# 21

## *'I love you every day of the year'*

In July 1959 Vivien was shattered to hear that Olivier had decided to sell Notley Abbey. It had ceased to be home to the Oliviers. Moreover, Olivier's brother had died suddenly, and there was simply no way of replacing him with another farm manager on the same family footing. Everything seemed to be closing down round Vivien, falling apart.

Olivier was tortured by the same melancholy and felt much more guilty about it. 'It was like being on a life raft that can only hold so many,' he said about the approaching end of his marriage. 'You cast away the hand grasping it. You do not take it on board, otherwise it's the end for you both. Two instead of one. If I went on, sooner or later it would go too far. I knew I had to get out. I knew I had to cut the hand away from the life raft.'

His fears were not exaggerated. He had already been frightened by his violent reaction to one particularly manic and vindictive mood of Vivien's. She had refused to allow him to get his night's rest and had followed him from room to room, nagging and provoking him. In a reflex of anger, he threw her off him. She stumbled across the room and, to his horror, hit her head sharply against the bedpost – the result was a sizeable wound. Apprehensive at what more he might be provoked into doing, Olivier quit the house.

But still the public separation was delayed. When *Look After Lulu* transferred from the Royal Court to the West End in September 1959, Virginia Fairweather persuaded them to pose affectionately together in Vivien's dressing-room in order to throw the reporters off the scent of a break-up.

And then in December a devastating article appeared in a German magazine with a wide British circulation. It erred in detail, but was substantially correct in asserting that the Oliviers were no longer living together as man and wife. The British newspaper lawyers still urged caution on their editors, but the harm was done and the story was out. Still more crushing to Vivien's spirits was her father's death a week before Christmas at the age of seventy-five.

As he had so often done when grief or illness overwhelmed her, Noël Coward showed his practical sympathy. She must spend Christmas with him in his new chalet in Switzerland. 'Bring plenty of perfume,' he telegraphed. 'The decorators have just moved out and I am terrified of catching painter's colic.' Vivien could not help laughing through her tears as she comforted her mother.

After Ernest's funeral, Gertrude stayed on in London. However, on Christmas Day, Vivien found herself ensconced 3,000 feet up in the Swiss Alps in Coward's pink stucco house, which was positively reeking with the bath-salts he had laid down to cover the smell of fresh paint.

This temporary respite from her troubles would have been abruptly shattered had she known what was passing through Olivier's mind at the time. He spent Christmas 1959 on Stewart Granger's ranch in California. Like Vivien, he too wanted to be alone and yet among friends. During the day, he rode on horseback over the hills, analysing his sentiments and trying to face up to the once unthinkable prospect of getting a divorce from Vivien. During the evenings he agonized aloud to Granger and his wife, Jean Simmons. He didn't know that his hosts' marriage was also in a badly strained state at the time. Considerately, they had decided to keep the truth hidden from their perplexed and hesitant guest. 'Can you really be happy, Larry, knowing that you're making someone you love utterly miserable?' asked Granger. Olivier replied, 'My God, Jimmy, why do you think I'm hesitating?'* As Granger was later to recall events, however, Jean Simmons was simultaneously urging Olivier not to sacrifice his own chance of happiness in order to protect the feelings of someone he'd ceased to love.

The day before he was due to leave, Olivier announced he had reached a decision. He could not face the future with Vivien: he was going to ask her for a divorce. Granger recalled: 'He then said something I'll never forget. "It was really seeing you two together, how much you loved each other, that made me decide I wanted that kind of happiness too."' The truth, of course, was quite the opposite. But Olivier had not perceived that. Ironically, Vivien's fate was sealed by a false impression of someone else's connubial happiness. It was some months, though, before she was to learn of this decision. Even with his mind made up, Olivier still hesitated to act.

Vivien's friends thought it essential not to let her spend too much time by herself in England, but to get her away from familiar places that now, as she said, held 'only memories without a heart'. Fortunately, plans were well advanced to take *Duel of Angels* to New York with a new director, Bobby Helpmann, and a new co-star, Mary Ure. 'But who will we get to play my husband?' she asked Cecil Tennant. American Equity wouldn't permit any more players to be

---

* Stewart Granger was actually born James Stewart and, though he had changed his name to avoid confusion with the Hollywood star, friends continued to call him Jimmy.

imported from England. She couldn't stand a strange American, she added. Tennant had a happy thought: 'Why not Jack Merivale?' By virtue of his Canadian birth, Jack was exempt from Equity's constraints on foreign talent.

When Jack flew over to New York in February along with Peter Wyngarde, who was repeating his starring London role, he found Vivien installed at Hampshire House, and 'in a very low state'. It had begun to sink in that Olivier was probably not going to come back to her. After the shock of separation came the gnawing feeling of humiliation. She was resentful of Olivier's resurgence of energy and embittered further by the resources of youth and talent possessed by his mistress. She was very lonely. Yet Jack Merivale hesitated to occupy the gap in her life. 'To tell the truth,' he says, 'I was shy. It was obvious things had gone terribly wrong, yet Vivien still seemed obsessively attached to Larry. She had photos of him all around her. And once, at rehearsal, when I was wearing a plaid suit, she reached out and fondled it and said wistfully, "Larry's got a suit just like that. Oh God, I wish he were here." That was enough to put any thought of something closer than friendship out of my head.'

Yet the old attachment he had felt for her on that fatal *Romeo and Juliet* tour in 1940 kept returning. Vivien clearly liked him — and why not? He was handsome, dashingly but not heedlessly impulsive, well-read, candid but not unkind in saying what he thought of people, and he had a practical attitude to those in trouble. Vivien liked that kind of sparky companionship. Before they met in New York, he had told her over the phone, 'Wait till you see the beard I'm growing for you.' He hit a responsive chord and she laughed — as if by growing a beard for his part, and not gumming one on nightly, he was testifying to the sincerity of his affection for her. Yet Jack Merivale obeyed one self-imposed rule. His own marriage had gone adrift because of someone else coming between him and his wife. 'As a consequence,' he says, 'it was one of my principles never to interfere in anyone else's married life.'

They became companions before they became lovers. He found himself thinking more and more expectantly of the drinks that Bobby Helpmann and he used to have with Vivien in her suite after rehearsals. And then they grew closer when they moved to New Haven for the out-of-town opening of *Duel of Angels* in March. On the walks they took round the Yale campus and on the shopping expeditions Vivien headed, trawling the stores for a harvest of first-night gifts, Jack's last inhibitions vanished and eventually Vivien asked, 'When are we going to make love properly?' 'Properly', he reflected later, with amusement, 'was her favourite word for what she really approved of.'

So they accepted each other's love, not in any desperate way, but there was a growing dependence on Vivien's part that turned into mutual trust.

Vivien had another suitor on this pre-Broadway tour. It indicates Jack's growing strength of affection that he began to feel annoyance at the intrusion of young 'Jonesy' Harris, the good-looking son of Ruth Gordon and Jed Harris – the same Jed Harris who had been Olivier's persecutor when he directed him in *The Green Bay Tree* on Broadway in 1933. (Olivier got his revenge by basing his Richard III on Harris.) Jonesy Harris showed his devotion to Vivien with small but costly gifts, well beyond Jack's power to match – like the Tiffany swizzle stick in gold with a diamond point on each of the little branches and a ruby in the centre. At the end was a tag with 'Jonesy' and 'Vivien' on it. Jack reflected, with some satisfaction, that Jonesy obviously didn't know Vivien's taste in drinks rarely ran to champagne.

The young rival gallantly retired when he saw how close Jack and Vivien had become. 'Jack will be dead in five years,' he was reported to have said to someone, 'Vivien will wear him out.' But Jack and Vivien were tender as well as passionate lovers. 'For the rest of her life,' he says, 'except for a few months, I was with Vivien all the hours of the day I could be – and in my thoughts I was with her all the rest of the time.'

Vivien's obstinacy, though, still startled him on occasion. At the dress rehearsal of *Duel of Angels* in New York, she declared, 'The front row is far too close and I want it taken out.'

'You can't!' everyone shrieked.

'Then I don't appear,' she said decisively. And out came the front row.

The Broadway opening was scheduled for 19 April 1960, and as Vivien went round the Fifth Avenue stores completing her shopping for first-night presents, Jack grew worried. He dreaded to think what lavish gift she had in mind for him. He was not only an independent man: he was a sensible one – he didn't like to see money squandered. 'Now, Vivien, remember: nothing more than ten dollars tops – understood?' he said. But then he had to think what he would give her. Cartier's did a little medallion of St Genesius, the patron saint of players, for around twenty dollars. That wasn't really extravagant, he thought. But when Vivien saw Cartier's name on the box, she said severely, 'I think I've been double-crossed.' Then she saw the medallion and was thrilled. On the back Jack had made them inscribe: 'Vivien!' The exclamation mark was a joke between them. 'At that time I didn't want to write, "Darling" or "For My Dearest", as we were still fairly discreet, or hoped we were. The joke was that Bobby Helpmann in directing our play tended to begin every instruction to her with a cry of "Vivien!" – much mimicked by the company.'

Before the curtain went up, Trudi Flockert, Vivien's maid who doubled as her dresser, pinned the medallion safely inside her Dior costume. It was next to her heart when she made her entrance on Jack's arm. He felt her trembling. Then he felt a wave of applause beating out 'quite tangibly' from the packed house.

'I disengaged myself from her grip, stepped back and half turned away, leaving her to acknowledge the ovation alone.'

Never one to be outdone in the gift department, Vivien bought a matching St Genesius medallion for Jack and dated it for the first night of their tour with *Duel of Angels* when they got to Los Angeles a couple of months later. With it came a note. 'My Darling – Why I have written May 15 on this little present I don't know – but as I love you every day of the year, it matters not. I hope very much that you will like it – use it – and not lose it. It is to thank you for all your kindness and goodness to me and it is to tell you that I love you – My beloved. Vivien.'

Vivien's performance in the New York production was even more highly acclaimed than it had been in London. The character's cool calculation suited her range and she had learned to slow down her delivery to suit the deeper proscenium stages on Broadway, where dialogue took longer to register with the audience. Every one of her lines counted – and Vivien, with surgical precision, made sure they cut too.

Jack noticed that Vivien was unusually volatile afterwards, but this he attributed to the night's excitement. He knew her to be impulsive. He recalled one night when they'd been making love in her Hampshire House suite when Vivien, all of a sudden, leaped out of bed, ran to the telephone and placed a person-to-person call to Olivier in London. As Jack impatiently awaited her return to him, she settled down for a long confab with her husband about their separation. Then she came back to seek sympathy at her lover's side.

The truth was that, although Jack knew Vivien had had a breakdown, he thought it was simply 'one of those things' that happened to theatre folk now and then. Vivien's closest friends were extremely discreet – more like guardians, where she was concerned – and didn't make even amorous newcomers privy to all the painful facts in the case. Thus at this stage of their affair Jack Merivale had no inkling of Vivien's lengthy history of recurring manic-depression. Ironically, the story of Olivier's awakening was about to repeat itself.

It happened quite soon after the play opened. Like the other plays on Broadway, *Duel of Angels* was affected by an actors' strike which closed the theatres for the first time in forty years. To Jack's bewilderment, Vivien began involving herself in the politics of the dispute. Her own restlessness found an outlet in the worsening relationship between players and management. Eventually, the theatre owners decided on a lock-out, with the result that the performers, from the stars to the humblest chorus girl, stood outside the stage door an hour or so before curtain-up, indicating their willingness to go on stage. When the show's deadline passed, they would all stream off to the bars and taverns, then regroup later on for an Equity meeting. Vivien followed the flow of talent into the bars — then showed up at the meetings. The drinking simply exacerbated the unstable mood she was already in.

'To my horror,' says Jack, 'she'd get on her hind legs and start to hector her American colleagues on the unfairness of milking the British players working on Broadway for five per cent of their salaries to support the strike. I'd try to pull her down and shut her up — she was becoming very unpopular.' She got some of her facts wrong, too, but apologized on the spot and, to Jack's relief, was applauded for frankness at least.

Vivien had moved from Hampshire House into a rented house on 63rd Street belonging to the actress Edith Meiser. As Vivien's close friend Radie Harris noted pointedly, it was 'within walking distance of Bloomingdale's' — in other words, convenient for shopping. Radie Harris recalls an amusing insight into the childlike way Vivien's mind sometimes worked. Coming down the escalator at Bloomingdale's, where she'd gone shopping during the Equity strike, she stumbled — and Jack Merivale caught her in the nick of time. If she'd fallen and hurt herself, she said, she'd have sued Equity. 'How could you do that?' asked Jack. 'Because if Equity hadn't caused the strike,' Vivien snapped, 'I wouldn't have been shopping at Bloomingdale's.'

It was about this time that Jack received a call from Olivier. Vivien had written him a twenty-two-page letter, telling him she'd fallen in love. Olivier, according to Jack, expressed his delight. Then he said, 'Is there any chance of a union, dear boy?'

Jack would have liked to say yes: but the truth was, he was perplexed by Vivien's behaviour, worried about her drinking, and genuinely confused about her state of health, which he still attributed to physical and not mental causes. He replied: 'As things stand at present, Larry, I don't honestly think so.'

Across the line from 3,000 miles away came what sounded like a long deep sigh.

News from Olivier of the state Vivien was in reached Bobby Helpmann, who was not a man given to mincing words and, in any case, he knew how violent Vivien could become. Olivier contacted Irene Selznick in New York. Mrs Selznick got in touch with Jack. And so for the first time he heard the full history of Vivien's condition.

Jack Merivale's reaction to the story Irene Selznick told him was simple. He had made his commitment to Vivien through love; he was not going to desert her now out of concern for his own future. Irene Selznick invited both of them to come over to her country place the following Sunday. She wanted to talk to Vivien — she was urgently in need of medical advice and had to be convinced of it. The three of them had a long, heart-wrenching discussion, and the upshot was that Vivien agreed to electro-convulsive therapy.

On the Monday, Jack and Irene took her to the Manhattan office of a qualified physician who examined her and then prepared for the first EC T session. Waiting in the anteroom, thoughts of *A Streetcar Named Desire* probably weren't far from their minds as they watched Vivien, pale but determined, enter the doctor's treatment room. For what seemed a long time, there was silence – then Jack heard a short, high-pitched shriek and leaped to his feet. But it wasn't Vivien, just the scream of a baby in the street outside. He fell back in his chair with relief.

What did shock him was Vivien's numbness when she finally emerged. A few hours later, he could still see the marks of burns where the electrodes had been applied to her temples. She had to play in *Duel of Angels* that evening wearing heavier make-up than usual – but her performance was word-perfect. 'It was harrowing – her courage made me cry.'

Olivier telephoned to know what was going on. Jack told him about Vivien's ECT burns. 'Oh, the bastard,' Olivier groaned. Her London physician, Dr Conachy, was consulted and, to everyone's exhausted relief, he decided against continuing the ECT treatment in New York. Medication would be the best compromise, until she could see him. Vivien was most relieved – but her gratitude to Jack for standing by her, perhaps protecting her from things she feared more than the shock treatment, increased to the point of passionate dependence. She was forever expressing it in little notes, sometimes writing to him while seated beside him in a car or aircraft, thanking him for patience, for understanding – in short, for simply *being there*.

The nineteenth of May 1960 was a day she never forgot. For on that date the letter she had been dreading arrived in New York. Olivier had written many pages filled with tender affection and taken much of the blame for what had happened on himself, but clearly, quite clearly, he was a man who had now reached the limits of endurance. He explained that he wanted Vivien to release him from a relationship that had broken down irretrievably so that he would be free to marry Joan Plowright.

Even though she had expected this, to see it set down in Olivier's small precise handwriting stunned Vivien. As Jack happened to be out of town, she impulsively telephoned her nearest and dearest friend in New York, Lucinda Ballard.

'She said to me to come round as quickly as I could. I found her sitting in her car outside the house she was renting on the East Side, ready to go off to her doctor's. She wasn't hysterical, but she was dreadfully distressed. She explained that Larry wanted a divorce. I said to her, "Vivien, what are you going to do?" "I'm going to do what he wants, of course," she said.'

Vivien visited her physician, who prescribed some tranquillizers: then she went on to lunch with Robert Helpmann. Perhaps it was the effect of the martinis on top of the Valium she'd taken, but she listened to bad advice from a man who disliked Olivier and called him 'Old Sourpuss' behind his back. At the very least, Helpmann's advice was heedless of Vivien's long-term interests. At worst, it was malicious, deliberately intended to cause the maximum embarrassment to Olivier, who was appearing with Joan Plowright in Ionesco's *Rhinoceros* at the Royal Court Theatre back in London. Vivien was in no fit state to appreciate the distressing consequences of her next move.

Lucinda Ballard was watching television that afternoon when it was announced that Vivien Leigh, Lady Olivier, was preparing a statement about her marriage to Sir Laurence. Then, late in the evening, Vivien herself appeared on the screen, pale-faced and lonely-looking, speaking in a low voice like that of a shy child. She didn't sound angry, just hurt and numbed. What she said was brief and to the point. The press statement was equally terse: 'Lady Olivier wishes to say that Sir Laurence has asked her for a divorce in order to marry Miss Joan Plowright. She will naturally do whatever he wishes.'

The next day, 21 May, the news was splashed all over the London morning papers. It was the eve of Olivier's birthday. According to Virginia Fairweather, 'All hell broke loose.' She woke Olivier up with a telephone call at 9.00 a.m. and read him Vivien's statement. Looking grey and drawn, Olivier rushed over to the home of George Devine, the Royal Court's artistic director, to confer with him on how to weather the publicity and protect Joan Plowright. She dropped out of *Rhinoceros* that same evening, being replaced by her understudy, and went to an undisclosed address in the country to stay there until the storm blew itself out, as they hoped it would.

Olivier had naturally been shocked to have his private request to Vivien disclosed to the world without warning. But her rashness had also put him at some legal risk. Before the reform of the British laws on divorce, *prima facie* evidence of alleged collusion between the parties to a divorce was sifted by an individual called the Queen's Proctor and, if found proven, the penalties could be severe – quite apart from the delay that might ensue in granting the divorce.

Jack Merivale was appalled, too. But his fears were more for the effect of events on Vivien's state of mind. Though she said she would consent to the divorce, her actions showed what a contradictory and divided view of the future she held. On 29 May 1960, she gave an interview to the New York *Daily Mirror* about her present feelings and future plans. Notley Abbey had been sold and this, she said, left a deeper wound than her husband's infidelity. 'It was the only home I ever had.... We had [sic] a flat in London, but it is rented out so often that it has never been a home.' She spoke of keeping busy – a film about Eva Perón, perhaps another on the life of Abraham Lincoln's wife, Mary Todd

Lincoln, a project that was also attracting Bette Davis's interest at the time. Then she added: 'More than anything else, I'd like to film *Macbeth* with Larry.'

Yet as if desperate not to jeopardize relations with the one person on whom she now depended so much, she kept reassuring Jack of her devotion. 'My Darling,' she wrote two days after the interview, '[This] is to put in writing that I love you I love you and I absolutely love you. So there.'

Despite the fact that the actors' strike had been settled, it was decided not to re-open *Duel of Angels* in New York but to transfer it to the coast for a July opening in Los Angeles and San Francisco, then take it on tour. This would give Vivien a month of free time – a blessing! She could fly to London to consult Dr Conachy and – she hoped – see Olivier. Then she and Jack would take a holiday before Los Angeles. They spent her last day in New York at the dolphinarium. The water and the playful mammals seemed to calm her. Then Jack saw Vivien off to London on 10 June. She intended to stay only three or four days, so he didn't accompany her. Instead, she stayed a fortnight – a restless, troubled, unstable fortnight during which the reality of Olivier's desertion really and truly sank in amid the places that had once seen their happiest years together.

Wearing a beige suit, fox fur and dark glasses, Vivien looked nervous, refused to answer press questions at Heathrow and was whisked off in a chauffeured blue Cadillac to Eaton Square pursued by photographers. Olivier had already packed and moved to a temporary address. Vivien discovered some of her dearest possessions from Notley – *objets*, books, porcelain and other tiny mementoes of a life and celebrity she had shared – stacked disconsolately in cardboard boxes waiting for her to unpack them. Notley itself had already been sold to a Canadian writer named Swanson. Her mother came over – 'looking a good sixteen', Vivien noted with mock envy in a letter to Jack. Bumble Dawson was already at Eaton Square. Together the two women took it in turns to watch over Vivien throughout the night while reporters kept a sleepless vigil in the square outside the elegant terrace.

She had hoped to see Olivier there and then, but his solicitors warned him not to strengthen the suspicion of collusion. He declined a meeting and went on stage for *Rhinoceros* to give a technically impeccable performance – although the critics had had their doubts whether playing a 'little man' suited him.

Although Vivien was publicly saying and doing all the things expected of a wife who has obediently yielded to her husband's request for a divorce, in private it was a different story. She had no sooner arrived than she began frenziedly mustering her women friends in order to make an eleventh-hour appeal to Olivier to change his mind. One of these friends was Rachel Kempson. She went to see Olivier and relayed Vivien's heartfelt pleas as persuasively as she could. Without avail. 'He told me, "I shall never love anybody as much as Vivien, but it isn't possible to live with her and do my work – I just can't keep it up. She's too exhausting for me."'

'Larry', says Rachel Kempson, 'felt that Vivien was draining his creative energy into her own personality and drive.'

It wasn't simply Olivier as a living human being that Vivien missed, however: it was what he still stood for. They had been known as 'the Oliviers' – and now Vivien found it impossible to see herself apart from him. She was undergoing an identity crisis as well as a marital one. Olivier was vulnerable to the same sense of loss. The decision to separate was having effects on his personality. One of his fellow actors had to look twice in the coming months when Olivier entered a restaurant, just to assure himself it really was he. It was as if he were already adopting a much more ordinary image to assume the role of husband to a talented but much more ordinary woman than Vivien. Vivien had made him into a social animal and when she was no longer there to parade him and exhibit him the social glamour faded quickly and physically out of his looks. The West End to him meant the stage: otherwise, he was quite happy to relax back into privacy. But Vivien could never visualize him other than as part of the great romantic myth she had so determinedly pursued. For her, he was most of what she had known, loved and achieved – she still didn't really believe it would come to a divorce. To Elspeth March, an old friend and the former wife of Stewart Granger, she later confided, 'Larry was an angel, in spite of everything. I know we've both suffered, Elspeth, but you could never say your husband was an angel, could you?'

It was unbearably painful for Olivier to have to withstand this sentimental siege. As Virginia Fairweather put it, 'Like any man labelled "the guilty party", he was conscience-stricken at the idea of ending a marriage that had meant so much even though it had now gone sour.'

Bobby Helpmann's presence in London, Virginia Fairweather believes, was additionally unsettling. 'What Bobby couldn't appreciate was that the last thing Vivien wanted was to be divorced from Larry. He was like Iago. If he hadn't inspired her public communiqué assenting to the divorce, Vivien would have slept on Bobby's so-called bright idea and in the morning it wouldn't have happened.' Maybe it wouldn't have happened the way it was happening now: but one has to conclude that the end would have been the same.

Vivien spent 12 June resting in her apartment and receiving treatment from Dr Conachy, who had been called overnight to give her sedatives. The next day, as if intent on torturing herself so as to feel it all more deeply, she motored down to Notley with John Mills's wife Mary Hayley Bell. Like most sentimental journeys back into a happy past, it was disastrous. 'They have made it so awful,'

Vivien wrote to Jack. She had afternoon tea in the estate cottage with the gardener and his wife, Mr and Mrs Cook, but it was more an occasion for mourning than for reminiscing. When she toured the house with its new owner, she noticed that the room she had once intended to be the nursery for her expected baby was now part of the butler's flat.

Notley was not Tara: returning did not heal the wound, but only opened it wider.

That evening, escorted by Bobby Helpmann and the director Michael Benthall, she went to the theatre — but not to *Rhinoceros*, where a large crowd of newsmen had waited every evening since she arrived. She went to see Alec Guinness in *Ross*, Terence Rattigan's play about Lawrence of Arabia, but she was too distraught to concentrate 'and it is not a play one can just sit at,' she wrote to Jack. In fact, she dozed off, affected perhaps by Dr Conachy's tranquillizers, then awoke and left before the end. Scrupulous as ever, she sent a note round to Guinness the very next morning apologizing for her early departure and promising to come and see the play again before she left for America — a trip now postponed in the hope of still somehow being able to see Olivier.

Her restlessness grew. She cancelled visits to other plays on the spur of the moment — there was really only one she wanted to see and it was the one she simply could not face. She began showing the symptoms of an incipient manic attack. Noël Coward came to see her alone, as he had thought, and found 'a flat full of people ... Vivien almost inarticulate with drink'. The next day she woke him up at 8.30 a.m., begging him to come over. He refused. He didn't want to speak to her again, he said, 'so long as she continued behaving like that, whereupon she said, "Oh God!" and hung up and that's the end of that.'

In public, she managed to retain her dignity and wit. She gave one interview only, to John Freeman (who was later British envoy in Washington), and deflected his inevitable question about Olivier: 'Men are hell between forty-five and seventy. Marie Tempest used to say you could live with them again after seventy.'

Finally, on 18 June, Olivier came to see her, slipping into their apartment block through a rear door. She pleaded once again with him not to take the step that, in different ways, both of them were dreading. Was there even then no chance of reconciliation? He was racked with pain, but adamant. There was not.

Two days later, Jack Merivale in New York received a surprise call from Kenneth More.

'Vivien — is she all right?' he blurted out as soon as he heard who was calling.

'Absolutely ... she's coming back to you, old boy.'

Vivien didn't wait to embrace Jack before pouring out her gratitude for his loyalty and devotion, which her visit to London had only strengthened. On the PanAm airliner *en route* to New York she set down her feelings in a letter that she handed Jack on landing:

My Darling Love,

I am on my way to you with a beating heart – and the only point of this little scribble is that it makes me feel nearer. I wonder every minute if you are awake. I was at 5.00 this morning.... This has been a most extraordinary week. I think the most extraordinary of my life. Alone and yet so infinitely close to you. Sweet dear love, I ache and long to see you.

Jack went out to Idlewild Airport, a little apprehensive nonetheless about the state Vivien might be in.

'I was absolutely knocked out with surprise and delight when I saw this graceful little thing coming down the aircraft steps as if she couldn't wait to see me. It was like an "All clear" again. It was at that moment that I fell *wholly* in love with her and had *no doubts at all* that we would spend the rest of our lives together.'

# 22

# 'Warren, shall we dance?'

Cautiously but firmly, Jack Merivale now began to take Vivien in hand. First, she must cut down on her drinking. From now on, no hard liquor – out went her favourite gin and tonics. Only wine was allowed when he was around.

They had a fortnight before *Duel of Angels* opened in Los Angeles and spent it as lazily and happily as they could ever have hoped in a beach house at Quogue on Long Island. To Jack's relief, Vivien took to running this smaller world of hers with the same painstaking enthusiasm she had once lavished on managing the grander 'court' of Notley. She barbecued lobsters and white fish, made mayonnaise with finicky concern ('Good, but not quite thick enough'), only faltered when she couldn't recall how long freshly picked garden peas needed boiling ('Is it eight minutes, or twenty?'). She lazed around in white Italian slacks, a yellow headscarf and yellow beach shoes; she swam strongly in the little bay beyond the sand dunes.

David Lewin, the *Daily Express* journalist who was to accompany her and Jack to Los Angeles, asked: 'If you had your life over again, would you want it any differently?'

'No. I would want to be an actress and marry Larry. I would want everything again, except the last few months.'

When the time came to take the train from Pennsylvania Station to Chicago, she had lost the plumpness of face drinking had given her, making her look almost matronly at times, and regained her trim girlish figure. Trudi Flockert had preceded them with eight suitcases, but what Vivien had still to take with her was far from light. Her travelling items were eclectic as well as numerous: twenty-two items of luggage, a Renoir, a Picasso (for giving the homely touch to hotel suites), a carpet-bag that was a publicity souvenir of Mike Todd's film *Around the World in 80 Days*, books, her cat Poo Jones, a portable cat-house and a collapsible scratch-box.... There was also an amateurish painting of cherry trees in flower by one F. Olson, who clearly belonged to the Central Park school of painting. Vivien and Jack had lingered behind the old fellow and watched how raptly he had painted the trees (one of them upside down) on his canvas. For twenty dollars, it was theirs – Jack's present. She treasured it as much as Renoir's anemones.

As they settled into their 'drawing-room' compartment, a handsome young black attendant asked if they wished for anything to drink.

'Will you be with us all of the trip?' Vivien asked him.

'Yes, ma'am.'

'Then do tell me your name.'

'Name, ma'am? Larry, ma'am.'

Vivien and Jack smiled: they could not escape that name.

In Chicago they had to change trains. During the nine-hour wait they lunched at the Pump Room, where the waiters in red coats and silk breeches reminded Vivien of a superior English hunt. She chose the wines, Jack noted, as if tracking down a rarity, but drank very sparingly herself – his words were being heeded. After lunch, they visited the Chicago Museum of Art. Lewin noted: 'Paintings seem to please and soothe her.' On the night before they arrived in Los Angeles Vivien dipped into her carpet-bag, took out the dog-eared *Duel of Angels* script and had Jack hear her lines.

Their stay at the Château Marmont was restful. They had George Cukor's pool for private relaxation – Vivien wearing an old costume of Constance Collier's several sizes too large, but so confident of her pose and figure that she clowned happily around in it. They had the feeling that their Hollywood friends didn't quite know what Giraudoux was driving at in the play. But snobbery was everything in that town – *Duel of Angels* was the thing to be seen at.

Just before they opened, Cukor threw a supper party at Don the Beachcomber's for Vivien and Jack, Ava Gardner, John and Mary Mills and their fourteen-year-old daughter Hayley, who had just finished *Pollyanna* and been signed up by Walt Disney. After the initial stiffness, talk turned to *Duel of Angels*.

'I know you and John are coming for the first night,' said Vivien. 'Are you bringing Hayley?'

Mary Mills demurred: it wouldn't really be suitable, she intimated, in spite of obstinate noises from Hayley indicating that it would.

'Children should be allowed to go to that sort thing and sort it out for themselves,' said Vivien very firmly. 'I'll send you an extra ticket.'

Jack now recalls:

The day after we opened, the *Los Angeles Times* had a mention of Hayley Mills being at the play – wasn't she a bit young? At once the mischievous little Vivien fired off a half-dozen cables to Mary purporting to come from shocked mothers' groups protesting at Hayley Mills, a Walt Disney contract star, seeing 'Leigh's sex drama'. To Vivien's rapturous delight, the phone rang and it was Mary saying, in a death-bed voice, 'We're in terrible trouble.' One of our cables had been signed 'Up the Mothers' Club', but the word 'Up' had been put separately on the line above, so that it looked as if it came from 'The Mothers' Club'. Mary must have been so alarmed she didn't look at where the rest of the cables came from. Eventually, after killing herself laughing, Vivien sent an explanatory cable and signed it, 'Up the Fathers' Club'. At moments like that, she was a very happy child.

Jack, too, had cause to feel contented. At the very start of the tour, he had set down his love for Vivien in a long letter to Olivier. It appealed to Jack's sense of honour to let even her estranged husband know how devoted he had become to her.

Jack discovered that Olivier had been deeply moved, to the point of shedding tears of relief and gratitude. His happiness for Vivien, Jack and – he candidly admitted – himself transcended any feeling of bitterness he might have remotely entertained. Even if, in the past, he had felt bitterness, it had always evaporated – leaving a sense of desolation in his life. It was an intense relief to him that all of them could be happy again, although he warned Jack to be on the watch for any little signs of Vivien's impending attacks, such as an unwonted lack of consideration in her attitude to people. In short, it now seemed as if a prayer had been answered, one that might bring peace of mind and happiness to Vivien as well as himself. If another man could bring these things, then he gave both of them his blessing.

Before Jack had got to know Vivien's nature, he had made a few innocent mistakes that turned out to be costly – but for her, not him. He had admired the striking design of a black and white Thunderbird back in New York. Now one turned up at the Château Marmont, followed by a cable from Cecil Tennant, who'd been sent the bill, saying, 'For God's sake, be careful,' or words to that effect – but his warning was ignored. Vivien at once sent a cable back defending her right to spend her money as she chose and signing it defiantly: 'Squanderbug'.

They drove the car overnight to San Francisco at the romantic urging of Vivien, who liked the idea of the coast road in the moonlight. It meant starting out after curtain-fall at 11.30 p.m. The cat Poo Jones rather spoiled things by yowling shrilly. 'If you'd been popped into a car at nearly midnight and driven off you knew not where, you'd yowl, wouldn't you?' said Vivien. Jack wearily admitted the truth of that.

But well before they got to their destination, the brand-new Thunderbird began clanking ominously. They abandoned it at a garage and hired a bright red Impala (not Vivien's favourite colour) which meant transferring all their luggage, all twenty-eight of Vivien's cases, Jack's more modest allowance, Poo Jones, the Picasso and the Renoir – 'perched atop the pile like any old photos of your Uncle Harry' – so that they hit San Francisco at dawn like travelling gypsies.

The city's cosmopolitan feeling agreed with Vivien. She was high-spirited without being over the top. They went sailing on the bay with a friend of Tarquin Olivier's, caught Bob Newhart at the Button Down nightclub, went up to Lake Tahoe, where *Gone With the Wind* was showing at the little local cinema. Outside was the famous poster of Gable wrapping his arms round Vivien and looking ready to eat her. Jack pushed himself in front of it, took Vivien likewise in his arms and had a photo taken of them.

In Chicago, their next stop, they wrote out a postcard to one big happy American family eating an early supper at a table near theirs and had it delivered after they left to do the play. They had all looked so devoted to each other, it must be a good omen.

They closed the play in Washington, D.C., returned to New York and then decided on a whim to go back to England by boat, just as they'd made a snap decision to cross America by train. But before leaving, Vivien insisted on surprising Olivier, who was also in New York, with a backstage visit to the St James Theater, where he and Anthony Quinn were playing *Becket*. (Joan Plowright was playing in *A Taste of Honey* at the Lyceum next door.) Jack was relieved to see that Olivier was as embarrassed as himself: but he covered it up with small talk about Jack's beard – 'You ought to run an electric shaver over it, Jacko.' Jack was relieved that Vivien's happy disposition wasn't harmed by the encounter. They took a Cunarder the next day.

At first Jack was miffed to find that Peter Wyngarde was also travelling with them – but as it turned out, they hardly met after the first night in the Verandah Grill. An understanding purser cast a look at the connecting door between Jack's cabin and Vivien's stateroom and said, 'I expect you'd like this open, sir.' And the No. 2 purser who had tried to expel Poo Jones to the ship's kennels was driven back when he opened the bathroom door to vet the cat's sleeping arrangements by a wave of scent – Floris Stephanotis – that Vivien had just poured in the tub. Coughing, he neglected to ask if this was for m'lady or the cat.

At Cherbourg, Jack experienced for the first time the bruising intrusiveness of the British Press who boarded the ship *en masse* to interrogate Vivien's handsome travelling companion. In self-defence, he fell back on the old 'just good friends' cliché. 'How am I doing?' he asked in a sweat. 'Fine, just fine,' Vivien purred, with a cat-like smile.

Though the French let cats into the country, they tried to impound her Renoir on the grounds that it belonged to France. On the quay was Vivien's chauffeur, Bernard Gillman, in his smart grey uniform – and alongside him a spanking new Rolls-Royce, also grey. In fact, its paintwork was barely dry. When Cecil Tennant had called Vivien in New York and told her that the new Rolls-Royce would meet her, he'd mentioned it was sable coloured. Vivien nearly screamed. She hated that particular colour. Kenneth More owned a coffee-and-chocolate Rolls-Royce that she referred to tartly as 'two tones of shit'. Let her Rolls-Royce be resprayed, she commanded – grey. And it was, though, to her annoyance, the upholstery was still beige. No matter: off to Paris they drove, Vivien in the back with Jack, navigating from one eating place to the next in the *Guide Michelin* – the book she often said she wanted to take to heaven.

In Paris they stayed at the Hotel Raphael, which was heaven in a sense, though Jack found the prices a bit celestial – he was paying for himself, while Vivien's bill was paid by Warner Bros., for whom she was to make her new film *The Roman Spring of Mrs Stone*.

When she received Gavin Lambert's script, she had agreed at once to star as Tennessee Williams's middle-aged American widow who goes to Rome to pick up her life – and is instead picked up by a handsome young gigolo, to be played by Warren Beatty. It was a brave film for Vivien to undertake. Age, abandonment, loneliness, all her current anxieties, had to be implied or exposed in the part, the performance and her looks. But she didn't hesitate. Perhaps enacting Mrs Stone's cruel fate helped deflect the reality of change in her own life. Perhaps Jack's presence made her feel infinitely luckier than Mrs Stone. Perhaps, like Olivier, she simply found work was the best hiding place.

She had demanded that Balmain do her wardrobe; and this was why she had come to Paris. Filming was scheduled to begin in a month's time in Rome. Meanwhile she approved the first sixteen out of thirty changes of costume that Balmain's *atelier* planned to cut and fit on the dummy they kept of her, then she and Jack took off for a short vacation, after which they would return to Paris for final fittings.

She enjoyed motoring out into the French countryside. Once they went to the thatched cottage where Marguerite Gautier, the original *dame aux camélias*, had lived for a time. It was not quite big enough for Vivien's taste. Another time they went to visit the Duff Coopers in their Empire-style mansion at Chantilly – this *was* big enough for Vivien.

Towards the end of October they set off with a friend, Willy Peploe, on a motoring tour of France in the Rolls-Royce. November arrived and so did Vivien's forty-seventh birthday. With her usual instinct, she located an enchanting small hotel called La Cardinale at Baix, on the bank of the Rhone, and there she held her birthday supper, with Bernard the chauffeur making four at table. In the morning, Jack took a picture of Vivien looking out of her high bedroom window at distant poplars.

That evening they arrived at Noël Coward's home near Gstaad, Switzerland, where they were received by the Master in his 'Las Vegas outfit' of red blazer, red socks and red monogrammed slippers. Vivien was not outshone, though: she wore a beautiful Oriental jacket with the latest Mao collar that flattered her long neck. Coward later recorded in his diary: 'Vivien in splendid form, out-wardly at least, inwardly still hankering after Larry ... but she seems very fond of Jack, who is constantly fulfilling a long-felt wish.'

Coward himself drove them to Geneva for pre-Christmas shopping, while Bernard took the Rolls-Royce back to Paris. When they reached Paris they learnt that the authorities back in Rome, still reeling under the impact of Fellini's *La Dolce Vita*, had withdrawn co-operation on any subsequent film that depicted the city's immorality – so *The Roman Spring of Mrs Stone* would have to be shot at Elstree Studios, in England.

Vivien was disappointed to be denied her Roman 'spring', even though it would have had to be a wintry masquerade at that time of year. But there was one good reason why a return to England was welcome: she wanted to see the new country home she had bought the year before in order to fill the void created by the sale of her beloved Notley.

Dirk Bogarde had suggested a property near the village of Blackboys, Sussex, called Tickerage Mill, an elegant, five-bedroomed Queen Anne house that scarcely suggested the hard grind of milling. It had about ninety acres of land, including woods, a river, a barn on the skyline which had been listed in the Domesday Book of 1086 and the all-important lake – for Vivien still believed that the presence of water was a good omen, and was not to be daunted by the association between damp and tuberculosis. The drive dipped to reveal the house set in a fold of land – Vivien saw it in spring, surrounded by daffodils, and immediately declared it was for her. Jack was a little alarmed: yet he was mistaken in believing its purchase would strain her financially. Vivien maintained four different bank accounts with sums that (for this period) were quite large in each one. She paid £18–20,000 for Tickerage, purchasing it from Kenneth Letts, a member of the diary publishing company; today, it would fetch near the £1 million mark.

The professional decorators had taken it over while Vivien and Jack had been away, and now Vivien's ideas and colours stamped every room as unmistakably hers. Her two Oscars were in evidence: one was now used as a doorstop, while the other held down tissues in the lavatory.

Vivien was grateful to have a home that was entirely of her own making: for before 1960 ended she saw the formal dissolution of the life that she and Olivier had made together. On 2 December, dressed in a close-fitting red-and-black check suit and black knitted hat, nervously screwing her black leather gloves into a ball between her hands, she sat in the London Divorce Court. Only she and Roger Gage, Joan Plowright's actor husband, were present: the other parties were in America. Vivien's counsel introduced into court a declaration in which she admitted two cases of adultery, one in London, the other in Ceylon, not naming the man (or men) in either instance. As Olivier and she had resumed their marital relationship after these infidelities, her lawyer contended her husband had condoned them. Gage's counsel then named Olivier as co-respondent in his petition and an enquiry agent gave the usual routine evidence of finding him and Joan Plowright in their night attire in a London flat in June 1959. This was the commonplace 'discovery' required by the law before the divorce proceedings were reformed some years later.

Vivien than gave evidence. What she said in court does not quite tally with what was well known to both parties at an early date − for instance she said that he confessed his infidelity to her after the German magazine article had been published. 'He admitted he had been in love with Miss Plowright for three months,' said Vivien. But this inconsistency may be attributed to her state of mind at the time of the divorce.

A few minutes later, dabbing at her eyes with a white handkerchief, then weeping openly with her head in her hands, Vivien heard the judge exercise his discretion in her favour and award costs against Olivier in both cases. The twenty-year marriage of the Oliviers had been dissolved in just twenty-eight minutes.

After the hearing, seated in the back of her silver-grey Rolls-Royce, dark glasses inadequately masking her small, pale face, and a car rug over her lap, Vivien was driven back to Eaton Square. Jack was waiting for her. She fell into his arms and wept. Her mother and Bumble Dawson looked on, for once at a loss for words of comfort.

'I lived a long time in a very flattering, very artificial, very insincere kind of world − the world of an actress.' Vivien spoke the words just a few days after her divorce. They were those of Karen Stone, the Mrs Stone of Tennessee Williams's story, but they might have been a commentary on her own life. She was being directed by José Quintero, a New York stage director making his first film. Both of them, for different reasons, were very nervous. Vivien's nerves had shown the minute she entered Elstree Studios and, with uncharacteristic sharpness, demanded her dressing-room curtains be changed − they were stiff with dirt, she said. 'But Vivien had a lifestyle she lived up to,' says Jack Merivale, 'and expected other people to respect it. It wasn't a case of star tantrums.'

Vivien was not the first choice for Mrs Stone: other actresses had been considered and rejected before Tennessee Williams said suddenly and firmly, 'Vivien must play it.'

When first approached, says Gavin Lambert, who wrote the screenplay, she refused. Lambert felt that maybe she had been alarmed by the cruelty of the way Mrs Stone was described in the *novella*. But once she had received the film script, she changed her mind. Lambert has recalled a meeting at Eaton Square – 'the only sign of edginess was the number of cigarette packs scattered around the room, a new brand called Olivier'.

Vivien asked for only one change in the script. To emphasize how age was creeping up on Mrs Stone in the film's prologue, Lambert had shown her standing disconsolately in the wings of a theatre where she was playing Viola in *Twelfth Night*. She was disguised as her twin brother Sebastian. The actor playing Sebastian, wearing an identical costume, approached her and the camera moved in to show how much older Vivien looked than her 'twin'. She thought this made the point too bluntly. After all, she said, she intended playing Viola in *Twelfth Night* after the movie, 'and why give the critics free ammunition?'

Two weeks before shooting began, according to Lambert, Vivien told him and the director José Quintero, that she felt 'dry' and was going for electric shock treatment. She did this 'with no more fuss than someone with a headache asking for an aspirin. Her lack of self-pity was touching and elegant,' Lambert concluded. Knowing Vivien's fear of the treatment, one has to add that this impression must have been well rehearsed.

Warren Beatty concealed any nerves he felt – he had not been the first choice for the part of her gigolo lover – with appropriate cock-sureness. Vivien had at first taken to Beatty. Charles Castle, who was Quintero's personal assistant, says: 'She felt she needed a light flirtatious relationship with him in order to make their love scenes work in the film.' But she cooled when she met Beatty's current girlfriend; Joan Collins was not to Vivien's liking at all.

Lotte Lenya, giving one of her most gloating manifestations of meddlesome evil, played the procuress who supplied boys to the lonelyheart expatriates of Rome, both male and female. And *she* didn't like Jill St John, cast as the rich girl who is Beatty's next prey after he has robbed Mrs Stone of her money and love. 'Altogether', says Peter Yates, the film's assistant director and later the maker of *Bullitt* and other successes, 'it was a tense production.'

'However,' he adds, 'Vivien was a perfectionist. The only time she showed her temper was at someone whom she considered not to be one. Once Beatty had to stride into her apartment in the film, wearing a custom-made suit that

Mrs Stone has paid for, and shove Vivien roughly aside the better to preen himself in the mirror. He felt this action might cost his character sympathy and had trouble getting it right. "If he doesn't do it next fucking time, I'm going home," said Vivien.'

Stanley Hall had made Vivien a blonde wig for the film, reminiscent of Garbo's page-boy bob. 'I was amused at how she'd wear it off the set – she disliked her own hair – even after shooting, snatching it off like a wool beret whenever she was indoors, sticking it on again when she went outside.' It may have saved her from disfiguring injury, or worse. For in one sequence Karen Stone is out riding and comes to a crossroads in the woods, signifying the uncertainty that her life as an exile has reached in Italy. Vivien's horse was – incredibly enough – the same one that Olivier had ridden in his film of *Richard III* and was used to breaking into a martial gallop at the sound of a clapperboard. It did so this time. Fortunately, Vivien ducked down low on its neck as it galloped under the low-hanging branches. Even so, some hit her. Her wig and her own hair cushioned the blow and she insisted on repeating the scene within minutes.

She showed her stubbornness in another sphere when the producers decided to show the rushes of the previous day's shots in black-and-white only, although the movie was being photographed in colour. Vivien threatened a walk-out unless this false economy was dropped: which it was.

Christmas 1960 developed into a chain-reaction of party-giving, perhaps to relax everyone's nerves. First Emlyn Williams and his wife threw a party at their Pelham Crescent home; then the next night Terry Rattigan played host in his Eaton Square apartment next to Vivien's; after that, it was her turn. The fun often became feverish. 'Here we are, a group of "greats" in London theatre,' said Jack, surveying their guests, 'and we're acting like children.' The revellers instantly decided to form a club called 'The Group'. Vivien was elected treasurer (because she got rid of money faster than anyone else); Margaret Leighton was secretary; Rex Harrison was chairman. The fun lasted over four or five days – and had a sequel. 'Soon afterwards,' says Jack Merivale, 'I received a Turnbull and Asser package with a specially made-up tie inside it – dark blue with a pink alligator on it. Terry Rattigan had got each one of us a club tie like that. I wore mine until I ran into him one day, some months later. "Why have you got that thing still on?" he asked. "It's our club tie, isn't it?" "Not any longer. It's been withdrawn. Maggie Leighton and I were at lunch the other day and saw some bounder wearing it who wasn't one of us."'

*The Roman Spring of Mrs Stone* was slow-going. Watching a scene being shot on Mrs Stone's penthouse terrace, Lotte Lenya darkly observed: 'All Vivien does is listen, all Warren does is talk.' But Sam Spiegel, who happened to be visiting, said, 'Why worry about Warren. It doesn't matter. He's going to be a star, anyhow.'

The imperfect sympathy between Vivien and her leading man hurt the picture in the end. His gigolo came over a fatal bit short of the requisite charm and Vivien's vulnerable matron a mite harder than she should have been. Neither really liked the other off set: the camera showed it, so the movie had a colder heart than even Tennessee Williams's novella.

In order that no taint of moral turpitude should blemish Vivien's divorce proceedings, she and Jack Merivale were living in separate, though nearby, dwellings: Vivien in Eaton Square, Jack in a small flat that Peter Hiley had found for him on the Belgravia/Victoria border. She often sent him a letter through the post that could have been taken round by hand inside five minutes; but then, as she said, writing a letter was an act of love, delivering it just a job. On St Valentine's Day 1961, he sent her a huge bouquet of lilac and she wrote in reply: 'Thank you, dear dear one. You have made what is nearly a year now a time of happiness that I never thought possible.'

But always in her thoughts was the last, tenuous link legally binding her to Olivier. The decree *nisi* was due to expire in early March 1961. The minute it did, Olivier would be free to remarry. By coincidence – or was it an omen? – she received an invitation from MGM to come to America the second week in March. It was the centennial year of the American Civil War and *Gone With the Wind* was going to be shown at a gala in Atlanta, Georgia. Vivien and Olivia de Havilland were now the only stars of the film still living. Her mind jumped back to 1938 – when she had impulsively gone to America to be with Olivier and stayed on to play Scarlett O'Hara. What if she were to go again this year and end up regaining the man who represented the world she had lost? She recalled Scarlett's determination, against all odds and reason itself, to pursue Ashley Wilkes even though his engagement to Melanie was imminent. How had Margaret Mitchell put it? 'He wouldn't marry her if he knew I loved him! How could he?' Scarlett had told herself. 'There's no reason why things won't come out the way I want them – if he loves me. And I know he does!'

Vivien used the MGM invitation to re-arrange her shooting schedule so that she had four or five days in the United States. She left on 8 March 1961, and stretched her time off to ten days.

But her meeting with Olivier was hardly held in the romantic circumstances that Scarlett would have envisaged. It was in a smart but crowded restaurant, with Joan Plowright present for at least part of the time. Vivien's relationship with Joan Plowright paralleled her feelings for Jill Esmond more than twenty years before: she simply couldn't see either woman as wife to the man *she* loved. At times she felt quite benignly disposed to a woman who could make Olivier happy and sometimes wrote her friendly notes; at other times (and they were more numerous), she became very despondent.

Joan Plowright, unlike Jill Esmond, was aware of Vivien's instability and how it affected her actions. It is to be assumed that she and Olivier were prudent in discouraging Vivien from any hope of a reunion. The cocktail-hour hubbub of the New York restaurant, in which Anne Edwards in her biography of Vivien asserts that the meeting took place, had nothing in common with the heat-heavy siesta hour at Twelve Oaks, where a kindly but firm Ashley Wilkes had told Scarlett: 'Can't I make you see that a marriage can't go on in any sort of peace unless the two people are alike?' But the message of rejection Vivien received was the same.

The next day she flew to Atlanta accompanied by Radie Harris. A young reporter quizzed her before take-off: 'What part did you play in *Gone With the Wind*?'

Had he seen the film? she asked. No, he hadn't. 'Then, sir,' said Vivien, with a touch of Scarlett's dismissiveness, 'we have nothing to say to each other on this or any other subject.' Unabashed, the newsman asked what film she was currently making. '*The Roman Spring of Mrs Stone* – and I'm *not* playing the Roman Spring,' was Vivien's parting shot.

Atlanta was a triumph. Radie Harris admired the way she had anticipated and overcome the problem of competing, at the age of forty-seven, with the image of the girl on the screen who had been twenty-six at the time. 'She had a ballgown designed to look like the one Scarlett might have worn. It was of beautiful white satin, appliquéd with blue flowers over a wide full skirt over a wide petticoat. The off-the-shoulder line revealed just enough of her bosoms ... her hair she wore off her face, parted in the middle and piled high and held back with two diamond *barettes*. Her favourite three-strand pearl necklace with the diamond drop pin, matching earrings and her long white gloves completed the ensemble.'

'Scarlett, we love you!' burst on her ears as the limousine inched its way down Peachtree Street, where, over twenty years earlier, she had turned to Olivier and exclaimed that it was like a coronation. Many among the thousands cheering her now had been youngsters in 1939. 'Now they were mothers and fathers,' noted Radie Harris, 'bringing their children and grandchildren for a close-up of Vivien Leigh.'

On 17 March 1961, the very day that Vivien boarded the airliner at New York to return to London, Olivier and Joan Plowright were married by civil licence at Wilton, Connecticut – and were playing on their respective stages on Broadway that same evening.

Charles Castle witnessed Vivien's arrival back on the set of her film. 'She had obviously been crying her eyes out. She looked awful – woebegone and bloated. She was in the middle of doing her big love scene with Warren Beatty, too, where she had to act tenderly and affectionately. José Quintero had to handle her very carefully. Until her dying day, I don't think Vivien believed Olivier was beyond recall.'

The 'wrap party' at the end of shooting was held on the night-club set where Mrs Stone catches sight of the young rich girl flirting with her gigolo lover. The same orchestra played for the artists and crew. The tables were now spread with real food and drinks. Everyone dressed up in black tie and evening gowns. According to Castle:

> She had been on a buying spree to get us all end-of-shooting presents – from Asprey's, no less. She must have got through £1,000 – my own gift was a lizard-skin wallet initialled in gold. Everyone's gift had their initials on it.
>
> This one and that one got up and said a few words. The usual pleasantries. Then Warren took the microphone and said something on the lines of, 'I want you all to know how much I've enjoyed being in England, even if the film turns out to be a bomb.'
>
> There was a hush at these words. Everyone felt they had given their blood. Now it seemed to some of them that their efforts were being discounted even before they were judged.... Then Lotte Lenya rose from where she sat. And going up to Warren, she seemed to goose him none too gently. Resentment that had been gathering dissolved into mere embarrassment.
>
> Then Vivien Leigh got up from where she was sitting with Jack Merivale, walked gracefully over to her rather forlorn-looking co-star and said sweetly, 'Warren, shall we dance?' The band started up. And away they danced like royalty. The situation was saved.

# 'What time is it in London?'

A fter the film finished shooting, Vivien proposed a holiday: 'Let's go to Tobago.' Jack protested: 'That would be frightfully expensive.' But Vivien's eyes gleamed mischievously. 'Alex Korda gave me about $3,000 after *Lady Hamilton* and I put it in the Bank of Montreal. It's still there. We can go on that.' Then a sudden thought struck her. 'But perhaps I should see Dr Conachy before we go – I wouldn't want to spoil it for you.'

Jack took her in his arms and told her that he was sure she would never be ill again.

They spent 'three of the most perfectly happy weeks' they'd ever had together: they played cards and swam and Vivien learned to snorkel. She also put on weight and went to an exercise clinic on returning home to lose twenty pounds – for she wanted to look and feel her best. In June, she was to lead an Old Vic company on a tour of Australia and New Zealand.

The tour had been conceived while she was doing *Duel of Angels* in America. 'I think it's being unfaithful to *Duel* not to put it on again, if I get a chance,' she'd said. Bobby Helpmann put the idea to Michael Benthall at the Old Vic, who said yes – provided they did two more plays. Vivien then said, 'I'd love to play *La Dame aux camélias* if I could find a good English adaptation.' It wasn't that her own tubercular illness made her especially sympathetic to Dumas's heroine dying of consumption in her lover's arms. She had always glossed over her TB, except on one fraught occasion when she'd cried, 'Why can't I have some clean kind of illness like cancer?' Dying held no morbid fascination for Vivien, but a good dramatic role with a dying fall to it did.

Arnold Weissberger, her New York lawyer, had found an acceptable text in English. Jack was cast as her lover Armand. The third play was *Twelfth Night*; as she was familiar with it, the strain would be less.

It was typical of Vivien, with her strong desire for security and friendship, that she had a special tie designed for the men in the company and a scarf for the women. The colour was clear azure with a laurel wreath promising a victorious tour. Inside the wreath were three embroidered emblems: a tiny white flower (*La Dame aux camélias*), a pair of angel's wings (*Duel of Angels*) and crossed swords (*Twelfth Night*). Everyone had his or her initials threaded into the pattern. It was exactly the sort of talisman Vivien set great store by.

Bobby Helpmann had proposed going on to South Africa. Jack put his foot down hard: 'Not only on racial grounds, but because I knew that someone like Vivien would be provoked into condemning apartheid so publicly it would cause a scandal – and twenty-five years ago, that wouldn't have served anyone's cause. She was absolutely without prejudices, racial or religious, but also without politics. She once told me she voted Liberal. "Why, angel?" "Because everyone else I know is voting Tory or Labour." *That* was Vivien's politics.'

Instead of going to South Africa, they decided to tour the plays in seven South American countries. All told, they would be away a year. Bernard and the Rolls-Royce were sent ahead to Australia on a freighter. Vivien and Jack, looking so absorbed in each other that rumours of marriage began appearing in the press, took off from the London airport via the polar route to Los Angeles – to see their Hollywood friends – and thence to Australia. Four days beforehand, Olivier and his new wife had embarked on the *Queen Elizabeth* from New York to London. Years of great professional achievement lay ahead of Olivier: but now he was settling down into a contented marriage with the relief of someone who, after being told to sit up straight and pay attention, slumps into the easy chair of new-found normality. His first child by Joan Plowright was born that December; and none of the worldly honours he had gained, he remarked, exceeded the private joy of seeing the baby held up to him at the window each morning as he left their big terraced house in Brighton to catch the commuter train up to London, his spectacles, his breakfast kippers and *The Times* or the *Daily Mail* blending him reassuringly into the indistinguishable rush-hour of ordinary mortals who hadn't been 'touched by God'.

Vivien and Jack were due to open in Melbourne on 12 July 1962, with *Duel of Angels*. The tour began on a sour note. Even coming in from the airport there was a bad omen. Vivien spied a poster with her name below instead of above the title. 'I must ring up Uncle Cecil,' she said – her way of referring to Cecil Tennant. 'What time is it in London?'

Fortunately, by the time they reached the city centre, they'd realized the posters for the play were composed in three strips and it just happened to be the first one she saw that had got them in the wrong order. But 'What time is it in London?' became a catchphrase that Jack and Bobby Helpmann exchanged if they spied clouds on the horizon.

And there were indeed a few clouds. It proved a big mistake to open with *Duel of Angels*, a difficult, allusive work for Melbourne audiences unused to

Giraudoux's schematic meditation on vice and virtue. And as the first night clashed with the Lord Mayor's ball, smart Melbourne used the play as a curtain-raiser to the social event, to judge by the constant coming and going. It was a fiasco. Vivien was furious and spoke her mind on a TV show. In vain, Bobby Helpmann reminded her this was the city where Olivier had been told on the 1948 tour that there were three Australians who could play Richard III as well as, or better than, he could.

Jack had had what he thought was a good idea before leaving England. He'd arranged for *Gone With the Wind* to be shown in Melbourne before they arrived to 'beat the drum' for Vivien and the play. It didn't work out. They loved the film, hated the play. *Twelfth Night* was a set book for school exams that year and had been done by three other companies before they arrived. As for *La Dame aux camélias*, it was a success for Vivien. But Robert Taylor's Armand in the Garbo film was clearly preferred to Jack's less romanticized version, even though his was nearer to Dumas's original conception.

They played six weeks in Melbourne – too long. 'They were bored with us,' Jack recalls. But at least Vivien's vitality held up. Jack noted how she shared Katharine Hepburn's tendency to 'raid the territory' – to seek out all the excitement and curiosities a place held. Like an impatient greyhound she dragged him and an ashen-faced Bobby Helpmann off in the small hours to Sherbrooke Forest to catch a lyre bird performing its fantastic range of vocal mimicry at dawn on its stick-and-mud 'stage' as if parodying the human actors watching. 'That kind of determination to see all of life was typical of Vivien,' says Jack.

Then it was on to Brisbane, where he gently dissuaded her from buying replicas of the lacy wrought-iron balconies that had taken her fancy on their hotel. 'Let the blacksmith down the road at Tickerage have a try first, darling.' Again he saw Vivien's impulsive-imperious side in action. Her Rolls-Royce had gone ahead to wait for her in Sydney, so Bernard rented a Ford convertible. 'A marvellous car, m'lady, perfect for this heat ... a good red colour.'

'Take it away,' Vivien commanded, 'paint it white.'

A chastened Bernard did so, regretting the vanishing firecracker red that Vivien found so unacceptable.

While in Brisbane, they drove out to the remarkable gardens called the Oasis, notable for their wild birds and azaleas, and were reluctantly admitted, as the place was due to close in twenty minutes. Jack found himself gazing at a cockateel on its perch, a white bird with a saffron comb, which was making a loud, unfriendly noise. 'Out of temper like the bird because of the rudeness of the gate people, I stood in front of it repeating, "Fuck the Oasis.... Fuck the Oasis," hoping it would pick up the refrain. Before I knew it, Vivien had returned from viewing the azaleas and joined in. We went home well pleased, imagining the day some Australian tourists would be told, "This is a fine example of a cockateel," and the bird would cry, "Fuck the oasis!" in the voice of Vivien Leigh.'

The Brisbane heat was appalling, and wearing crinolines for *La Dame aux camélias* made Vivien feel as though she were in a Turkish bath. They gave a beach barbecue for the company and rented a cabin for themselves on Orpheus Island on the Great Barrier Reef — then moved on to spend three months in Sydney.

Cecil Tennant visited them there with dispiriting news. The tour was losing money. Jack knew why. 'People looked at the come-hither label "The Old Vic" and said to themselves, Oh yes, Vivien Leigh — but who else? She was the only "name" on the bill. They soon rumbled our explanation that the Old Vic was a *tradition* as much as a repertory company.'

Their stay was marked by Vivien sinking into deep but mercifully short periods of dejection. But she perked up on her forty-eighth birthday. Jack had told her he'd discovered a marvellous little out-of-the-way restaurant. They drove across Sydney Bridge in the gathering dusk, parked outside what looked like a dark old house out of a horror movie, and followed an ancient retainer upstairs to the attic. By now Vivien was wondering if she had come to a wake or a feast. The door creaked open. Total darkness. Then the lights were suddenly snapped on and the whole hidden company burst into 'Happy Birthday'. A figure identifiable as Basil Henson with his *Twelfth Night* wig on back to front danced forward with a huge book. 'Vivien Leigh,' he announced, 'this is your life.'

'When she heard that,' says Jack, 'she nearly turned and fled. It was a bad moment. However, once they started on the script that Frank Middlemas had written, she was soon laughing at how she'd been born in a slum ... become a child acrobat ... been sold into white slavery in South America ... seduced an African prince ... etc., etc.' The characters of her fictitious life were impersonated by members of the company in eccentric disguise, including drag.

North Island, New Zealand, which was their last stop, produced another surprise — an eighty-nine-year-old admirer of Vivien's in the shape of a phil-anthropic brewing millionaire called Sir Ernest Davis. He was an eccentric and obsessive fan of theatrical talent, especially when combined with beauty. 'He actually proposed marriage to her,' says Jack, 'saying they needn't worry about "all that physical stuff".'

Vivien was amused by this crusty, rather deaf old boy who affected a sharp trilby hat that made him look like a race-track bookie. He lent her his yacht, actually a converted naval cruiser, and took her racing where her usual luck, and some nudging from Sir Ernest, netted her a useful windfall. In turn, she gave him a ninetieth birthday party, making sure his yacht and his champion racehorse Bali-hai were represented on the icing of the cake, the bill for which came to a staggering £40. 'It was the only time I ever saw her jib at paying for something,' Jack recalls. A large number of candles adorned the cake – she helped Sir Ernest use a pair of fire-bellows to blow them out. When he died later that year, everyone (not least his family) was surprised to discover he had left Vivien shares in his brewery worth £17,500 'in consideration of the love and affection shown me and the great happiness brought to me'. Said Vivien tactfully: 'Sir Ernest was kind to all the company.'

One morning, while they were in Wellington, Vivien slipped away to do something she had sworn she would never do – audition for a role.

Abel Farbman, a New York impresario, was offering her the lead of the Grand Duchess Tatiana Petrovna in a musical version of the 1933 comedy *Tovarich*, about a former Imperial Russian couple taking a job as butler and chambermaid in a bourgeois French household. The play had already been staged in English with Cedric Hardwicke and Eugenie Leontovich, and been filmed with Charles Boyer and Claudette Colbert. And Vivien's old flame John Buckmaster had scored his first notable stage success when he appeared in a supporting role in the London production in 1935.

Vivien was apprehensive, yet intrigued. She had sung on stage before, but had never considered playing the lead in a musical, which would require her to dance, too. So she and Farbman met in the cavernous Wellington opera house to hear how she came across. With piano accompaniment she sang the number 'I'll be loving you – always'. She sounded low and husky and seductive and Farbman was enthusiastic. But she asked for time; and he promised to visit her again with a record of the music and lyrics when she reached South America.

The company was well received in South America, where their tour began in Mexico City on 29 March 1962. The language barrier mattered less than the prestige of the Old Vic and the presence of 'Scarlett O'Hara'. Their memory of the continent was of going from one vast opera-house theatre to the next, their voices tumbling into the crevasse usually filled by the orchestra, while the theatre backstage resembled a populous, restless village, so many people worked there.

In one capital, Jack was amused to see, Vivien was up-staged. The very rich South Americans went over to Paris twice a year to replenish their wardrobes with the latest fashions. Vivien had been on tour for the better part of a year and nowhere near any couturier. She wore her best Balmain to one party – and heard an elegant Latin woman say with a sniff, 'Huh, last year's!'

On 8 April, while staying at the Tamanaco, Caracas, Jack had a packet delivered to him. Inside was a beautiful ring. 'My Darling,' said the note, 'Before you become upset (quite unnecessarily) by this present, remember I chose it long long in advance – in remembrance of a day that changed my whole life.' Vivien had always named 8 April as the day they fell really in love. She concluded: 'You have taught me more than you imagine, Dear Love – Happy Anniversary! Your very own Angelica.' Jack remembered that she used to say Leigh Holman had taught her about being a wife and Olivier about being an actress – but he had taught her about living.

Her spirits stayed high and she laughed as loudly as everyone else at one stop-over, where the sight of a capsized ship in the bay prompted Bobby Helpmann to say, 'It must have been carrying Vivien's luggage.'

But when they reached Santiago de Chile, around mid-April, things began to go wrong. Vivien gave a 'rather expansive party' at the Prince of Wales country club and seemed to Jack to be in suspiciously high spirits. At the next stop, Buenos Aires, things turned dangerous. She took off with several gentlemen who had declared themselves 'seduced by her beauty' – and for the first time she didn't include Jack in the invitation. He followed the group, just to make sure she wasn't misbehaving. When she returned, 'All hell broke loose.'

Vivien picked up a brass eight-day travelling clock and threw it through the (fortunately) open window of their forty-fourth-floor suite. It had been her first anniversary present to Jack. Next morning, he went down to the street, fearing to find a body – he couldn't even find the clock. 'That's the worst thing you've ever done,' he told her sternly. In general, his firmness worked with her: he kept her off the heavy drinking, off the medicinal drugs she had mixed with it. At the parties they attended her eyes often met his in silent enquiry as she took a drink from a passing tray. If Jack frowned, Vivien put the glass back.

She listened to the *Tovarich* recording when it arrived and decided to do the show in New York. 'I've always had a secret ambition to do a full-scale musical,' she said. 'Everyone always looks as if they're having such fun.' For Vivien, though, the fun was to turn into humiliation and terror.

But she finished the South American tour in good shape in May, and although Jack tried coaxing her to fly back home directly, she successfully pleaded to take up the open invitation they had to stay with Lucinda Ballard and her husband Howard Dietz, the former MGM publicist turned composer and lyricist, at their Sands Point home on Long Island. It was a good 'staging post'.

With Lucinda, she felt herself at home. She would get up at the crack of dawn and roam around the garden and go swimming. She took to the Dietzes' grandchildren and would read them *Winnie the Pooh* while they all had nursery tea with cinnamon toast.

By June 1962, she and Jack were back in her own garden at Tickerage. Vivien had been collecting seeds from the vast array of exotic plants she'd seen on tour – coral trees and the snowball-covered viburnums were her favourites. Now these took their chance in the earth of Sussex, and some she gave to Leigh Holman for planting on his West Country estate. 'Perfect happiness for Vivien', says Jack, 'was making lists from gardening catalogues.' She had wooed her former gardener, Mr Cook, and his wife away from Notley to work for her, and now her staff was supplemented by a redoubtable Scottish lady known as Mrs Mac, a former golf champion who, according to Vivien, used to hold the plates at table with one knee bent in a golfing stance. She liked her share of the wine that was going and it slowed her down, so meal times tended to be more approximate than the punctual Vivien could have wished. 'Once,' says Jack, 'Vivien deputed me to go into the kitchen and read her a lecture. I'd done myself quite well with the drink while we were waiting and felt rather guilty lecturing this penitent lady while Vivien hovered behind me with her Cheshire-Cat smile.'

'Ay, it doesn't suit me, does it?' Mrs Mac used to plead in mitigation: it became a catchphrase of Vivien's.

Suzanne felt her mother had become 'wiser, gentler, more resigned and more considerate of other people's feelings – altogether easier to get on with.' Vivien's grandchildren gave her a sense of continuity and a feeling of family life she herself had never enjoyed. 'Her personality definitely began changing,' Peter Hiley confirms. 'She became more aware of the value of friends, especially the ones who had taken her side after the break-up. She became less other-worldly and began to show some sense of consequence.'

Vivien and Jack drove over to Chichester, where Olivier had become director of the Theatre Festival in 1961, and was appearing in all three productions for the first 1962 season. They saw him as Astrov in *Uncle Vanya* and went round to his dressing-room afterwards. He told Jack that it would have been a good part for his father. On such occasions Olivier was always tongue-tied. 'Vivien and I saw his Othello in 1964,' says Jack. 'She told him what a marvel it was and he simply said, "Oh, it's the moustache that makes it." Not exactly a throwaway line, but technically a very acute point. The moustache gave Larry's rather thin lip a negroid fullness. Vivien said to me afterwards, "Larry's approach to make-up was always to get the mouth right first."'

Friends now filled the house almost every weekend. Among them was Tarquin Olivier. He had formed a lasting affection for his step-mother and used to seek her advice. The gardening year, established on Notley's grander scale, was now adapted to the cosier acreage of Tickerage. Once Jack and Vivien got into a punt and poled along the stream flowing through the grounds into the River Uck, snipping and cutting their way through tangled overhead foliage as if venturing into a tributary of the Amazon. On fine weekends, a trestle table was erected on the stone-flagged terrace above the lake and guests would help themselves in the easy-going English way. On the lake below was a swan, several moorhens and a large randy drake that, as Vivien said, 'kept on duckling'. At night, as moonlight fell on the waters, there'd be paper-and-pencil games by the firelight indoors, where Poo Jones, liberated from quarantine, occupied the hearthrug. A young cat called Nichols and Vivien's poodle Sebastian (a replacement for a corgi that would keep clamping its jaws round the cat's head) were regarded no less affectionately by their mistress.

Vivien, it seemed to many, had at long last achieved a certain stability.

# 24

## 'Does Larry know?'

*T*he male lead in *Tovarich* had been offered to Jean-Pierre Aumont. Like Vivien, he was intrigued but apprehensive. At fifty-three, he was a popular film and stage actor in France and America, but had never done a stage musical. 'So what?' she said, when he telephoned her. 'We'll have fun.' That was all the encouragement he needed.

Aumont admired Vivien's spirit and thought the English critics carping in their attitude to a woman who was, as he wrote in his memoirs, 'too refined, too elegant, too insolently seductive'. He came to Tickerage in September and they put their heads together over the *Tovarich* script and listened to a recording of the music, tentatively singing the lyrics to the backing. Her confidence was greater than his. After all, she told him, it was the trend just now for straight players to sing. Look at Rex's success as Professor Higgins; Paul Scofield and Laurence Harvey in *Espresso Bongo*; even Sybil Thorndike, at eighty, doing a musical of *Vanity Fair*. Aumont left feeling stimulated by the visit – and by Vivien.

A week after her forty-ninth birthday, Vivien took off for New York, leaving Jack behind, to appear in a John Huston film called *The List of Adrian Messenger*. As soon as he could, he would join her in New York – he had asked his agent Laurie Evans to find him a play to do there. After all, she was not opening on Broadway until March 1963. He would miss her terribly, he thought.

Her suite in Dorset House had fifteen vases of flowers in it when she arrived, and a 'Welcome' cable Jack had dispatched from London. She turned in early – and awoke next morning in a muted panic. Now she was there – and far from Jack – she realized the scale of the task she had accepted. Her first letter to Jack, written on 13 November, at the end of the working day, expressed the dawning of misgivings that were soon to overwhelm her.

Abel [Farbman] arrived at noon and we talked over the script – Delbert Mann [the director] at 2.30 p.m. I had a session with him. Then to the office with the lot of them to hear the new songs! the new ideas! Oh dear, one wonders how anything *ever* gets settled. I came *home* (Good heavens!) – back – at 6.30 p.m., quite bewildered as to how I should ever get through it. I feel so alien in this medium.

She didn't yet have Aumont to turn to in mutual bewilderment: he wasn't due to arrive until December. She was beginning to realize that an American musical did not happen like a play – it collected itself together rather than presented itself in a more or less finished form. The text of a play didn't alter much between the first rehearsal and the final performance. With a musical, there was no fixed shape, no assured content, no reliable structure until it was actually on the boards that first night – and even then, everything might be subject to revision or annulment the next day. In a world of this kind, Vivien had limited skill and none of the experience that would have allowed her to say confidently, 'No, it won't work – try it this way.' Now it *had* to work – and it had to work *their* way.

The hard grind started the next day with Delbert Mann. Byron Mitchell, the boy with whom she danced a Charleston in the show, took her to buy dancing pumps in their lunch break. She began work on the songs with composer Lee Pockriss at the piano. Two brand-new lyrics were produced out of nowhere. She was terrified; and then, sustained by courage like a rush of adrenaline, she began to get the hang of it all and ended the day delighted with herself. Having old friends to hand helped, too. The Dietzes took her to see *Who's Afraid of Virginia Woolf?* She had been asked to do it in Paris with Barrault directing her – in English, of course. But now she found it 'a v.v.v. long play . . . I found a great deal to fascinate and interest . . . Nora Hogan effective – but I think a perfect brute of a role and one which I am very thankful I can write and say I do not have the slightest interest in.'

The next night Leueen McGrath and her husband gave a supper party for her. 'After dinner,' she wrote to Jack, 'I was rather firm about re-hanging a Modigliani. Leueen said she was *most* grateful as it was exactly where *she* had always wanted it.'

But then she had to move from the rehearsal room with its kindly piano and forgiving pianist to the awesome void of a theatre where her small voice was swallowed up in the cruel acoustics. 'It is frightening me to death,' she wrote on 28 November. To bolster her self-confidence, a recording was made of her singing. She was agreeably surprised. And so her mood see-sawed up and down in a way which Jack would have recognized as an alarm signal if he had been there. Even Jean-Pierre Aumont sensed all was not well when he joined them in early December. 'Midnight was the precise hour when Vivien . . . began to bloom,' he wrote in his memoirs. 'My going to sleep was out of the question.' He thought her dancing was magical. 'The way she crossed that stage was as great as Margot Fonteyn in *Swan Lake.*' But he noted how her enthusiasm waxed and waned with disturbing rapidity.

She hated doing one part of the show especially: the scene where the Grand Duchess recalls how her jailers raped her just before she managed to flee from Russia. Aumont remembers Vivien stumbling again and again over this passage and trying repeatedly to persuade Delbert Mann and Abel Farbman to drop it. Perhaps she feared the phantoms of Blanche DuBois might return to haunt her – as indeed they eventually did.

On Christmas Eve, something like hysteria struck her and she informed them all that she simply couldn't go on with it. She *hated* the show! Aumont wondered whether she specifically hated the twenty-five minutes of it in which she didn't appear – or Tania Elg, who was playing a secondary role but whose songs were first class. 'These rehearsals', she wrote to Jack, 'are so unlike anything one has ever known it is difficult to get an overall picture.'

They moved to Philadelphia for the opening of the try-out in January and for the first time had a full orchestra. 'Thirty against two, it's not fair,' she said to Aumont. Yet the audience gave them a warm reception – and herself an ovation when she broke into a spirited Charleston. She was in high spirits until Noël Coward, who had been out front, came round to see her. He thought the show 'shit', but believed her name and Aumont's would make a success of it. At the same time, he told her severely, it was beneath her dignity and beyond her talents. She couldn't sing, she couldn't dance, the story was stupid, the production ludicrous *and*, he added, wagging his finger, it was her own conceited fault for not listening to his advice. 'She flew at me then,' he entered in his diary. 'Poor darling. She is a bad judge.' He 'forbade' her to appear on Broadway in it.

Now everyone's nerve snapped. Though the audience appeared to like it, the Philadelphia critics deemed it *passé*. Delbert Mann was replaced by Peter Glenville. Vivien wrote despairingly, 'My voice is not up to it. The notices are quite right about that – neither, may I say, is J-P's – indeed Noël says his is very much worse!' Her mania grew apace with the spate of rewrites and additions. Aumont recalls her looking at the queue at the box-office and saying sorrowfully, 'Poor people! They're buying tickets to see one play without suspecting that they're going to see another.'

Back in London, Jack realized the situation was fraught with terrifying possibilities and called Dr Conachy, who in turn called Vivien. No question of electric shock treatment without the comforting presence of Jack: but he air-mailed her some pills. It wasn't medication that Vivien needed. She had lost all perspective. Even Boston's warm reception was a depressant. She had never felt so mentally ill. She needed her throat painted for the New York previews and wrote: 'I keep hearing myself groan and wonder whether the mikes are picking it up.' In such a mood she was intolerant of even her partner in martyrdom. 'It is nightmarish acting with dear old J-P.'

The greatest good luck the show had when it opened in New York was a newspaper strike, which delayed many of the notices until well after it had become a popular hit with audiences. Word of mouth blessed it: and even the reviews, when they finally appeared, were not all that damning – for Vivien, anyhow. 'There's no doubt that singing for her is a late and cautious acquisition,' Howard Taubman wrote in the *New York Times*. 'Her voice is low and colorless, but she manages to keep the rhythm and keep the melody.... What she connotes above all is a sense of style. In a simple black dress and organdie apron, she is the smartest servant in Paris.' Even the dreaded Kenneth Tynan, who was in New York covering the shows on Broadway for his newspaper, turned in a more humane report than usual. 'Miss Leigh ... looking imperiously pretty and compensating for a drawling sub-Dietrich voice with a nippiness in her pins that rivals the young Jessie Matthews.' That spring she won the Tony Award for her role.

Jean-Pierre Aumont's view of his co-star is shrewd and interesting. He thought her a sublime screen actress, but much less of a free spirit on stage. She was lively, pert and quick with her own lines, he recorded, but seemed at a loss when someone else was speaking theirs. 'She had either to speak or walk for her magic to function,' his memoirs relate. 'As soon as she finished a line or a passage she appeared to lose interest in the situation and would contemplate her partner with an impatience which soon became annoyance. That another actor should have something to say seemed like a case of *lèse majesté*.'

Jack finally arrived in New York to play a role in *The Importance of Being Ernest*, and saw how dangerous her condition was. She grew increasingly fractious and by the summer was missing performances. It was decided to let her take a week off and return to England for treatment from her doctor.

Aumont has recalled in his memoirs that he invited her up to the country house he was renting at Mamaroneck the night before closure. They were looking at home movies showing his two small sons when she started groaning. Perhaps the children reminded her of the family she and Olivier had never had. The next day at the matinée he found her in her dressing-room, hugging to herself a photograph of Suzanne's family while a phonograph played the waltz from *Gone With the Wind*.

What then followed was harrowing and horrifying. It was thanks only to Aumont's skilfulness and compassion that most of the audience didn't suspect

Vivien was having a breakdown on stage. She sang her first number three times faster than usual – the conductor simply couldn't keep up with her. She turned her back on Aumont during their duet. In the second act, she had to confess to to having been raped – and this was the detonator. Suddenly she began clawing at her co-star and kicking his shins – all of which he had to pretend was part of the scene they were playing. Then she stopped quite abruptly and stood totally silent. Aumont relates how he tried coaxing the lines out of her. 'Answer me,' he prompted. Vivien advanced to the footlights, ignoring him, and said to the audience, 'An actress needs time to think before answering.' Then she walked off. No one would take the responsibility of distraining her. But at the finale she resisted being drawn into the general on-stage waltzing. She stood to one side, sad and tearful and staring numbly into nothingness.

She was driven home to a house she was renting from Edward Molyneux, the English couturier, and there threw a tantrum because her maid was occupying the garden room with the best view. She insisted on returning to the theatre for the evening show. Jack went with her, but he knew when to call quits. 'Put the understudy out,' he ordered.

'Then I had to hold Vivien up physically against the wall and stare at this wild little face insisting *she* was going to go on, while I, just as stubbornly, said, "You're *not!*" '

When Jack left for his own play, she remained in the locked dressing-room, reciting all her lines with only her maid and the two doctors who had been called for an audience.

Aumont needed all his control to get through his performance that night, for when he had entered his own dressing-room, all the pictures of his family that he'd put up round the mirror had been ripped off and screwed up or torn into pieces. It was the darkest chasm Vivien had yet fallen into.

According to Jack Merivale, a scene like a replay from the aftermath of *Elephant Walk* now ensued to get Vivien back to England. Jack Merivale says, 'I always remember her telling me that when they'd been sedating her in Hollywood at the time of *Elephant Walk*, she thought she'd heard Larry saying, "Give her some more" – for the sedative wasn't taking – and she never forgot that. This time I had to hold her down while she was being injected. It was agony.'

Vivien had originally asked Jack to fly back to London with her when her show was closing for the week. He demurred ... the expense ... his own play ... she'd be back in five days. 'Oh, Jack,' she had pleaded, 'do come. We'll be married at Tickerage on Thursday.'

Jack had still said no; not that he hadn't been touched and very much tempted, but he had told himself that she wasn't really responsible for what she said while in that state. 'I only hoped she'd say it again in happier circumstances.'

Now, as he struggled with her, he found himself thinking, She's going to hate me forever.

And then, quite suddenly, as the tranquillizer took over, all the sweetness came back into her face and she relaxed. She started to murmur something and Jack bent down to catch her words. 'Does Larry know?' she asked.

Jack later reproached himself for not returning to England with Vivien. But he had injured his back and was in need of urgent treatment; and he had been assured by Arnold Weissberger and Kay Brown, Selznick's former assistant and now an executive in Vivien's agency, that the BOAC staff would watch over her every minute of the flight home. But she awoke unexpectedly early from sedation and had to be restrained. They arrived at Heathrow early on the morning of 30 September. Vivien was carried off on a stretcher, a white veil over her face. Laurie Evans had brought her furs to shield her from the early wintry weather. An ambulance took her directly to Eaton Square, then to a St John's Wood nursing home where she had ECT. By 2 October, she was well enough to call Noël Coward at Martha's Vineyard, sounding to him 'odd but calm'. She telephoned Jack daily, two or three times, which again lulled him into a false security – until the phone rang and a distraught Bumble Dawson told him to get over right away as, 'There's no one looking after Vivien.'

In pain with his strained back, he arrived at Tickerage, fearing the worst, only to discover a full household of servants, a secretary – and Bumble Dawson. He was furious at having been misled. Vivien was oddly cold towards him. He discovered Bumble had given her the impression that she had had to winkle him out of New York – and this confirmed him in his suspicion that Bumble resented Vivien's having found a man to replace Olivier.

Vivien went through the longest period of depression Jack could recall. The shock therapy hadn't worked. The curtain over her face didn't lift for months. During this time she neglected her usually immaculate appearance, used foul language and, although not talking gibberish, said such outlandish things it was hard to follow her line of thought. Gertrude was caring for her and Jack watched Vivien turn into a little girl again as her mother nursemaided her up the stairs to bed for the few hours she would consent to sleep. At times she set out to goad him. Once he was washing glasses in the little scullery she had turned into a flower-room. She came in spoiling for a fight, for no reason he could see. 'That's right, hit me . . . hit me. Go for my eyes like that other bastard.' Jack was using a little rubber dishmop impregnated with soapy water and he lightly smacked her forehead with it. The soap splattered all over her face. It was totally unexpected – and so surprising and silly, just like slapstick, that she stopped shouting and just as suddenly started laughing.

But the weeks lengthened and still she didn't snap out of it the way she used to.

One day all three of them were in the drawing-room.

Gertrude was sitting on a sofa and Vivien hanging around the fireplace with those large, hard, dull eyes that she had when she was in such a state, with a troubled face and a pursed-up mouth, moving ornaments about for no reason at all. We'd learnt she'd been to a chemist's and bought a preparation supposed to do wonders for one's nerves – 'Calm-a-Girl', or something like that. She hadn't been taking it for much more than a day or so. Suddenly as I was looking at her the 'curtain' was lifted. Her eyes became astonishingly clear. Her mouth relaxed. I saw my Vivien come out and look at me again. I looked directly at her and said hello. Then I said, 'I'm going to church on Sunday.' Gertrude looked up from what she was doing and said, 'Why?'

'Haven't you seen?' I said. 'Vivien's come back to us.'

She passed her fiftieth birthday with her first husband at his West Country manor house and then she and Jack met up with the Dietzes and holidayed in Tobago in the first months of 1964. Sad news awaited their return. She had always trusted Dr Conachy to come to her rescue – now he had died. Fortunately, his successor, Dr Michael Linnett, well acquainted with her troubles, prescribed new drugs and wrote a covering letter of advice to any physician Vivien might need to call on in an emergency.

Though she was much better, she was still reluctant to accept work. A film offer had come from the producer Stanley Kramer, who was planning to shoot *Ship of Fools* that summer. It was based on Katherine Anne Porter's portentous allegory of prewar Europe's self-deluding attitude to fascism. Vivien had tried to struggle through the book, but gave up and settled for the screenplay. She had first thought she was wanted for the role of the Countess, a left-wing aristocrat who travels first-class, loves the people and has an affair with a handsome ship's doctor. But this role went, appropriately, to Simone Signoret. Vivien was to play Mary Treadwell, an American divorcee, menopausally waspish, fond of the bottle – a sort of Karen Stone at sea, except that in what proved to be a deadweight production she wasn't 'drifting', but 'becalmed'.

Vivien felt the part was a secondary one – and not very well developed. She may also have heard that Katharine Hepburn had already turned it down. But Laurie Evans pointed out Kramer was paying her £50,000 (and expenses) spread over a number of years, thus easing her heavy British income tax. That was a plus. Signoret would get top billing in all non-English countries, Vivien in the rest. That was an honourable draw. She had no excuses left.

She flew to Los Angeles alone, where Hepburn and George Cukor had rented a house for her high in the Hollywood Hills, overlooking the jewelled spider's web of night-time Los Angeles. They had hung the walls with Impressionist paintings belonging to themselves and to friends to make her feel at home. The pool was heated and she could swim in the nippy night air in magical clouds of steam. When Jack arrived and they stood on the terrace, it all looked like wonderland and Vivien said, 'Let's take out citizenship papers.' So much for her reluctance to go to America, Jack thought.

As often happens with professionals, the two stars who were expected to clash became good if not close friends. (They were of course being paid the same.) Signoret knew of Vivien's illness, but would probably have detected it anyhow. 'From one minute to another, she was scintillating or desperate,' she recalled in her memoirs. She also noted how Vivien preserved the graciousness of her days as Lady Olivier. She employed a *cordon bleu* chef to cook for her during the production and asked guests to dress for dinner. Often she ended the night with the waltz theme from *Gone With the Wind* on the phonograph, inducing a mood of wistful nostalgia.

Nostalgia lay heavily over the cocktail party that Kramer gave for the Press on 18 June prior to shooting. It took place on the set of the ship's dining-room at Columbia Studios. Vivien had had a behind-the-scenes spat over her name being misspelled 'Vivian' on the invitation cards, but none of this showed as she entered. One reporter wrote: 'Tennessee Williams once said of her, "When she takes the stage she commands it as if she had first arrived there suspended from the bill of a stork." And the tribute stood up here.'

Shooting began in July and her first scene was calculated to inspire all her dread. She had to enter the ship's dining-room, where almost all the rest of the stars were already seated and eating – among them Lee Marvin, José Ferrer, Elizabeth Ashley, George Segal, Oskar Werner and Lilia Skala. In front of this awesome gallery of spectators she had to speak her first line in her Mississippi accent: 'Ah asked foah a table alone,' addressed to the waiter who is seating her with Marvin. As if this wasn't off-putting enough, one more star was present on the set. A rather ailing star, it was true, but still radiating a daunting authority as he sat in a special armchair with his name on it: 'SPENCER TRACY'. Tracy had been invited by his friend Kramer to 'kibitz' on the start of the film.

Vivian advanced into the dining-room in a smart brown and beige check suit and matching scarf that she had approved from among the designs submitted to her, uttered her line and followed it up with a withering glance at the hulking Marvin who had to remain seated – 'Please doan botha gettin' up.' Kramer called, 'Cut.' From the peripheral gloom of the set, Vivien heard Tracy's hoarse voice saying in a loud whisper to Kramer: 'Nice to see a professional.'

This was an auspicious beginning and things went well at first. Kramer encouraged her to make suggestions. He once had a set rebuilt back to front because that was how she said she had visualized the scene – it worked, too. And she was credited with having the tipsy Mary Treadwell suddenly break out into a frenetic, spiky Charleston all alone in the ship's companionway – a wild outburst of faded youth. It was, of course, a carry-over of the Charleston she'd used to stop the show nightly when she did *Tovarich*. Much of Vivien's role in *Ship of Fools* looked like a recycling of bits from earlier films: Mrs Stone's menopausal panic, Blanche DuBois' sexual fear … but there was a cruel, self-lacerating feel to the role and her playing. Alone in her cabin, and in torment, she grabs a make-up pencil and wildly draws a cosmetic caricature of herself on her face – a self-inflicted purgatory that suggests growing old better than any lines of dialogue.

As the tone of her role darkened, what Jack had feared began to happen. Vivien's behaviour grew erratic. She insulted other stars. Some, like Signoret, understood and didn't take it to heart. But one younger actress, to whom Jack apologized, wasn't so forgiving. 'I'm not going to be spoken to like that!' Lee Marvin, who proved the best of friends, received the most painful of knocks. He had one scene in which his character barges into Vivien's cabin while drunk and forcibly kisses her in mistake for someone else. It was Vivien's rape phobia all over again. She had to hit Marvin with the spiked heel of her shoe – and she did it for real, and so hard, that his face was badly marked. She began keeping people waiting and one morning, when she was overdue by more than two hours, Kramer went to her dressing-room – and there saw a scene that might have come straight out of the film.

In front of her dressing-table, looking like the ageing Mary Treadwell, sat Vivien, trying to make up her face and being forced to start over and over again. 'Stanley,' she said on seeing him, 'I can't make it today.'

After she'd got up and sung what Jack called 'a very filthy song indeed' at Rosalind Russell's party, it was plain that ECT was urgently needed. But who to turn to? Cukor called Katharine Hepburn and this kind and resourceful woman located a discreet Los Angeles doctor qualified to give the treatment. Hepburn hadn't really got to know Vivien well, despite being at her impromptu marriage, and indeed recalled that the only bit of advice she had hitherto given her – 'Don't smoke' – had been followed by Vivien smiling sweetly and immediately lighting a cigarette. But this time she was able to help and she and Jack coaxed Vivien into the car. Hepburn lay full-length along the back seat so that her easily recognizable features wouldn't draw attention to them as they drove downtown. She kept up an encouraging stream of small talk from this prone position as Jack drove and Vivien sat tense and grim beside him. It was the doctor's vacation period and Jack asked why he was willing to come in and treat Vivien. 'Because I like her,' was the simple reply. Jack held Vivien's hand while a pentathol injection was administered and he felt her relax. The ECT took only a minute or two, but several more sessions followed, again with Hepburn lending her support.

The aftermath was as painful as ever. Vivien felt terribly ashamed of herself. 'Everyone must know I'm as mad as a hatter,' she said.

Jack held her tightly. 'You're *not*! You're *not* mad!' he rapped out. 'You have a mental condition and that's entirely different. *That* can be coped with.'

# 25

## 'My love will be keeping you company'

Vivien now spent more and more of her time at Tickerage. She had guests to stay and entertained friends almost every weekend. One day in mid-October 1964, two somewhat special guests caused her unusual anxiety. Princess Margaret and her husband Lord Snowdon, who were staying with friends near by, had said they would call in for drinks before lunch. That morning, Jack was amused to see, Vivien got up extra early. Was the garden all in order? Of course: Mr and Mrs Cook knew the drill by now. Well then, the house? Again not a cushion with a dent in it, not an ashtray unemptied. She settled down, with relief, to await the distinguished visitors. Jack himself came downstairs quite late, after a good lie-in, and felt slightly mischievous as he took in the pristine state of things. Being in charge of drinks, he surveyed the tray and said, 'My God, Vivien, what have you been thinking of? There's no champagne. Royalty always drink champagne.' He spoke with such knowing authority that Vivien was startled by her gaffe. 'I'll put some on ice right away. God, I hope it'll be chilled enough — they'll be here in twenty minutes.'

'So they were,' Jack recalls, 'and when all the bobs and bows and introductions had been made, I said to the Princess, "And what can we offer you, Ma'am?" Fast as light, she said, "A good big gin and tonic."' Vivien's eye met Jack's, crookedly, across the room. But when the Princess and her husband had gone off to lunch elsewhere, they made things up over the champagne. 'It was one of the few occasions I saw Vivien flustered,' says Jack.

She spent her fifty-first birthday at Leigh Holman's home, as was her annual practice now. In any case, Jack had to pack and be off to California the next day, 6 November. Bryan Forbes, who was directing *King Rat* for Columbia there, had cast him as one of the British prisoners of war in the notorious Changi concentration camp. The job had been arranged while Vivien was making *Ship of Fools*. Vivien had made plans of her own to occupy her in Jack's absence.

For the first time since she had left India in 1920, as a child not quite seven years old, she was going to return to the land of her birth. Two friends who lived in India had enticed her to make the trip. As residents, they could plan it for her in detail. She was travelling with her old friend Lady Alexandra ('Baba') Metcalfe, daughter of Lord Curzon, the last viceroy of India, so that diplomatic privileges were likely to be extended to the party and ease their travel arrangements. Hamish Hamilton, the publisher whose friendship with Vivien went back to the days of her courtship by Leigh Holman, and his wife Yvonne were also in the party. So Jack felt she was in safe hands; but to make doubly sure she carried a covering letter from Dr Linnett addressed to any physician whom she might need to consult.

Vivien's left arm was 'nearly paralysed', as she put it, from all the vaccination shots pumped into it: but her handwriting flowed as passionately as ever across a postcard she sent Jack on 10 November: it showed a view of New Haven Green, where they had first fallen in love during the *Duel of Angels* tour: 'My Dearest Angel, My love will be keeping you company all of the time in the air and on the land and *everywhere.*'

The party left on 19 November. Three days later, she sent off her first dispatch to Jack. 'Arrived in Delhi in glorious sunshine, welcomed by absolutely charming Americans and given a delicious breakfast. Now we are in the air in a tiny plane seating about 10, flying towards Katmandu. The sun is shining and the air very clear. Oh, the sight of these extraordinary mountains – Oh dear, how I wish that you were seeing them with me.'

Vivien was now approaching the great range of the Himalayas. It was more than a holiday: in the deepest sense, it was a homecoming. As the little aircraft flew on, heading for Nepal, Vivien looked down on the very mountains on which Gertrude Hartley, fifty-one years before, had turned her eyes almost daily, breathing in their beauty in the hope that it would be passed on to the baby waiting to be born.

'November 23,' Vivien wrote, 'And I must tell you the first sight of the Himalayas is unforgettable – peaks of blue-white that you think *must* be clouds. Quite indescribable.'

They stayed in the British Embassy in Nepal.

Lots of rooms – but simple – mine has two beds, lovely views, but no bath – so have to use the Hamiltons' who are downstairs ... Temples everywhere – little markets ... *beautiful* faces – all dust roads, every colour of cattle and dogs. Everywhere people lying down in their tiny shops, just pondering. After lunch we drove to the funeral city. All along the river are alcoves where the dead are burnt and rowed [sic] into the river. Above are lines of small temples, heavily carved grilled windows and, in the centre, the worshipped penis sometimes surrounded by flowers and little offerings.

The Nepalese who brought her breakfast had a name for the mystical impact that the place made on her. 'It translates as "Moon God". Not bad, is it?'

But the tone of her letters to Jack didn't reflect the emotional vicissitudes of the tour, the fears she sometimes fell prey to and the quarrels that her manic state made her sometimes pick with her companions – all of whom were models of forbearance. She also cut a very odd appearance. Perhaps because she feared the glaring look that came into her eyes when she was in one of her states, she adopted a most peculiar sun-hat with dark goggles actually built into a brim that came right down on to her face, making it look as if she were wearing a bandit's mask. She wore it indoors, too, and even at dinner parties.

They had the King of Nepal's private aircraft at their command and, 'One day we flew to a place called Pokra – a very funny day. On arriving at the airport we asked for horses to take us to the lake. No horses. Mules? No mules. So I said, "There are two bullocks. Please attach them to a cart and we shall get in." A most peaceful way of travelling. The lake water was the colour of pale jade and very warm.' The king's plane also took them along the ridge of the Himalayas, as close as it could get to Everest. To Vivien, it was thrilling. Fate had brought her, as she neared the end of her stay on earth, to the very peak that dominated her birthplace.

She left India bound for Athens, where she stayed with Baba Metcalfe for a few days, then set off for Corfu where she had arranged to meet Jack and spend Christmas with the Furses, who had a villa there. But for once her well-made plans came to grief, for the rather mundane reason that Jack lacked the means to join her. Instead of his part in *King Rat* stretching over several days' filming, he found it being wrapped up in a day. After paying union dues, withholding tax and his agent's fee, he had barely enough left from his earnings to get him back to London. There he decided to wait for Vivien's arrival at the end of December.

One person who saw her on Corfu was Emlyn Williams, who had a villa next door to the Furses. 'She was in, shall we say, *extremely* good spirits,' he recalled, 'poised impudently on a tightrope, but very amusing and looking exquisite.' They were both asked to 'a tremendously grand evening party at a villa in the hills that was more like a *palazzo*, the house of a fearfully distinguished Greek dowager, a mixture of Lady Bracknell and one of Proust's blue-blooded ladies. One knew that Vivien would be on show, the centre of attraction for a hundred invisible lorgnettes.'

The night was very hot and stuffy – and the guests even stuffier. There were endless presentations. Vivien was patient at first – but in a lull she looked around the score of magnificently arranged dinner-tables at which they would shortly be seated and said to Williams, 'It's going to be a long, long haul and I *know* I'm going to fall asleep in the middle of it – Come with me.'

The two of them retired behind a marble pillar. 'Vivien opened her bag,' Williams recalls, 'and there was an impish gleam in her eye as she took out an eyebrow pencil. "If I do fall asleep, it'll seem so *rude*. Darling, make me up." I was bewildered – then she closed her eyes and held out the pencil. "Draw me some eyes on my eyelids, so that if I close my eyes it'll look as if I'm wide awake and taking everything in." '

Williams was both fascinated and horrified; but after two glasses of ouzo, he was more fascinated than horrified. 'So I gave her new eyes, considerably less beguiling than her own, and the effect was ... macabre. And yet, when she opened her own eyes, *alles in Ordnung*. I thanked my stars I was dining at a different table, with my back to her.'

Vivien returned to London after Christmas and filled Tickerage with friends and family for the New Year, including Suzanne and her children. 'The children', says Rachel Kempson, 'brought out her maternal feelings, yet like any grandmother she would complain about their manners. "Oh, Vivien!" I said at last. 'Do stop! Most young children's manners are not what we would like them to be." And she laughed.'

'Life was simpler now for mother,' says Suzanne. 'She was so much happier at Tickerage.' Peter Hiley agrees. 'Though her attacks recurred, they were monitored much more closely thanks to Jack.' Her fear of the attacks was even worse than the attacks themselves. When she felt a 'high' coming on, she would hold Jack tightly and say, 'You won't let them send me to a madhouse, will you?' And he would reply, 'Over my dead body – absolutely never. You have my solemn word.'

The first weeks of 1965 brought a visit from Tarquin Olivier, accompanied by his eighteen-year-old wife, whom he had married that January. 'Vivien was like a second mother to Tarquin now,' says Rachel Kempson. 'He used to confide in her and ask her advice. She had gone to his wedding, which didn't please Larry a bit. Vivien did nothing she shouldn't, except perhaps talk too much, but I think he wanted it to be Jill Esmond's day.'

Jack had to be especially vigilant over these weekends in case the hospitality that Vivien lavished on her guests got out of hand. Those who knew Vivien's condition became allies. 'I remember we used to go to the pub up the road at Blackboys,' says Rachel Kempson, 'but occasionally someone would say, "Watch it," so then I'd say, "Well, then, *don't* let's go – we don't have to go." It would only torment Vivien and we didn't want worse to follow.'

One guest who himself was drinking heavily and feeling sad and sorry at how things had turned out was Peter Finch. He spent the last day of February with Vivien at Tickerage. He had been divorced and had remarried since their long-running affair: and a petition to dissolve his second marriage had been presented only a few days before his visit. He talked of retirement, going to Italy to live, cultivating a vineyard. Vivien looked at him and said, 'I'll be working until I drop dead.'

Work was provided before very long when the American impresario Leland Heyward brought her a stage play, *La Contessa*, adapted by Paul Osborn from a Maurice Druon novel. She was intrigued. The Contessa had been a real woman, the Marquesa Casati, one of the most extravagant personalities of the 1920s, who had raced automobiles, bred wild animals, taken lovers by the dozen and spent, spent, spent. Her recklessness and her contempt for consequences fascinated Vivien. When she had fallen on hard times, she had taken a taxi all the way from London to Oxford and back to borrow £50 from a friend – the loan had evaporated in the taxi-fare. 'Vivien was much taken by that,' says Jack. She agreed to do the play.

It was financed by a film company, Seven Arts, which hoped a success in the theatre would lead to a movie. Binkie Beaumont presented it for H. M. Tennent, Bobby Helpmann directed it, Bumble Dawson did the costumes: the old team was reunited. Helpmann, however, had little faith in the play – justifiably as it turned out. It opened in Newcastle in April 1965, and closed in Manchester in May without ever reaching London. 'The postmortem', Jack Merivale recalls, 'was severe and depressing.'

Quite apart from the play being unashamedly romantic at a time when audiences were flocking to the 'kitchen sink' plays, it was believed that its failure was due to Vivien's having to play a raddled old woman of seventy-one, whereas people came expecting to see her fabled beauty. 'They hate my appearance, so they don't like the play,' she said. 'If the structure was different and I appeared in a flashback as the beauty the Contessa was supposed to have been, I think we would have had a success.' She added that she had seen the play as 'a bridge to parts where I don't have to be a beautiful woman ... I thought it would make me acceptable as an actress who didn't have to be cast in that way any more.'

But Stanley Hall assigns a less obvious reason for the play's failure. 'The character was a flamboyant figure and Vivien wasn't temperamentally cut out to play that kind of woman. Even as Camille in *La Dame aux camélias*, I thought her too conservative – she was very economical in the resources she employed and her style didn't fit a big "display" part. She had an innate good taste that was visible through the orange "fright" wig and harridan make-up. The Contessa should really have been Bobby Helpmann in drag.'

Vivien's business interest in the stage was still keen. She had gone on investing the occasional sum in plays and playwrights. But even she could overlook a crucial detail. 'She came back from a phone call she'd taken while we were at dinner one evening,' Jack recalls, 'and said, "I've just put £500 in a new play called *Time and Yellow Roses*. Sounded interesting." "Who's in it?" I asked. "Damn, I forgot to ask." And away she went and called Binkie again. Then she came back, didn't say a word, sat down, looked at me wryly and said, "Flora Robson. That's five hundred quid down the drain." She always thought Flora played for sympathy a bit too much – and this play needed a Gladys Cooper of forty years ago.'

Vivien was only too well aware 'how few roles were available for stars of her age,' Radie Harris later recalled. 'Most of the good ones for women were at the National. And the National, of course, was now being run by Olivier.

The solution was provided by Broadway and a production of Chekhov's first play, *Ivanov*, which John Gielgud directed and in which he starred. It had been produced in London the previous year and the American impresario Alexander Cohen was to present it in New York. It wasn't an ideal choice for Vivien. She appeared as the first wife of Ivanov, an unscrupulous fortune hunter, was more off stage than on, and died at the end of Act III around the half-way mark. She was to replace Yvonne Mitchell who had played it in London; Jack was to take over Richard Pasco's role as a doctor, his membership of American Equity again commending him to the production.

Whatever the size of Vivien's role, her agent Laurie Evans made sure she had the comforts and consideration of a star, which meant a limousine on twenty-four-hour call chauffeured by a tough native of Brooklyn called Nathan – whom Gielgud promptly called 'Nathan Detroit'. The car even had one of the new-fangled car phones in the trunk, though as the device was as big as a short-wave radio, Vivien grudged it the space she could have used for her luggage.

It was a happy group, however rancorous the mood of the play. They did a wide tour before opening, taking in New Haven where Jack and Vivien were able to relive their days of falling in love. But much of the time she was irritated at being unable to shake off a cold and a bad cough. She should have been more worried about it than she was, for it was probably an early warning of the recurrence of her latent TB. Indeed, her part had a grim irony that struck everyone in retrospect, for her character's early death in the play is due to tuberculosis. Gielgud, as Ivanov, breaks the news to her first with a brutality that precipitates his own self-loathing: 'Listen! You are dying! The doctor told me so, do you know? You are going to die! Quite soon.'

Vivien never discussed death, according to Radie Harris, except to say that she 'would rather have lived a short life with Larry than face a long one without him'. She had already made her will – but this, says Peter Hiley, was simply part of her general obsession with not leaving any loose ends, rather than the result of any real concern with mortality.

The play received respectful reviews and the cast mixed ones – Vivien included. Richard Watts Jr in the *Post* found her 'nothing short of magnificent', especially when news of her impending death is broken to her and, 'She stands there in silence, slowly realizing the awful import of what she has heard.' But Stanley Kaufmann in the *Times* said of her that, 'What is written as light chatter is played as light chatter, without the Chekhovian undertone,' so that the confrontation seems 'a cut-and-dried quarrel scene, not the bursting of an inner dam'. Gielgud says, 'One of the troubles we felt was the American audience's difficulty in accepting an English cast playing Russians.' Business slumped and salary cuts were taken by the principals to keep the play open.

It was with relief that Vivien, Jack, Gielgud and a friend of theirs all slipped off after the close of the production to tiny Young Island, in the Caribbean off St Vincent.

'It was lucky we weren't near any Cartier store,' Jack recalls, since Vivien started a shopping spree – always a sign of coming trouble – and took to slipping over to St Vincent on the boat like a truant schoolgirl and coming back laden with purchases. One day she brought back a huge parakeet and announced she was taking it home to Tickerage. 'But, dearest, do you think a bird and a cat in a cottage in England are going to get on together?' Jack asked. Vivien relented when he persuaded her that the bird wouldn't be able to stand the English winter, but she still didn't want to abandon it and everyone was made to tape a message that the parrot could be taught by repetition. 'You first, Jack,' she said. 'I want you to whistle Sibelius's First Violin Concerto.' Jack managed a few phrases. Then it was Gielgud's turn. Picking up the microphone and eyeing the huge bird that was perched peacefully near them, the most glorious speaking voice on the English stage said: 'Shit and sugar', several times, very precisely, for the parrot to learn and repeat.

To Jack's consternation, Vivien's misbehaviour increased on their return to New York. On their last night, she dragged him off to a disco run by Sybil Burton, then on to the Persian Room of the Plaza, where Jean-Pierre Aumont and his wife Marisa Pavan were performing. He spotted them and introduced Vivien to the audience, who were delighted with this bonus to the evening. Before Jack could restrain her, Vivien had jumped up on stage with Aumont. 'Let's do a duet from *Tovarich*,' she cried. 'God only knows what memories that must have brought back to him,' Jack says. Undeterred by having no music, she started to sing, lost the words and then attempted to break into the Charleston. As usual Aumont behaved like a perfect gentleman. They didn't get back to the house on 72nd Street they were renting from Joan Fontaine until 5.00 a.m.

Radie Harris was waiting for Vivien three hours later at Kennedy Airport and saw her turn up to catch the 9.00 a.m. plane 'with a haggard Jack Merivale and Trudi, ready to face photographers and in great high spirits'. Once back in London, she submitted to a course of ECT treatment in the Eaton Square flat.

She spent the rest of that year in England, gardening at Tickerage and motoring to lunch at friends' homes. One visitor to Tickerage had special memories for her. He was John Gliddon. There was no bitterness between them: it was a recap of old times. But the former agent was wryly amused to note Vivien's impatience at the non-arrival of lunch at the set hour – it was one of the cook's 'off' days. When life didn't co-operate with her, she still became terribly tetchy, he thought on departing.

Vivien's next offer of a role came from an unexpected source – Russia. Would she play Mme von Meck, Tchaikovsky's mistress, in a film biography of the composer's life that was to start shooting in Moscow in January? *Lady Hamilton* and *Waterloo Bridge* had been shown in public cinemas in the Soviet Union, though *Gone With the Wind*, a more 'imperialist' picture (as well as a more expensive one to buy and distribute) had not been seen there. She was – and has remained – one of the best known English actresses in that country. She was strongly tempted, until the offer of a new play arrived.

Towards the end of 1966, she was asked to be in the London production of Edward Albee's *A Delicate Balance*, with Michael Redgrave as her co-star, and accepted eagerly. It was due to open late in the summer of 1967: there would be a provincial tour first.

'I think she was as baffled by the play as I was,' says Jack Merivale. 'It was the first time I can recall seeing her actually get down to work on a text, trying to figure it out. Albee came to the flat, in tennis shoes, which didn't much enthuse her, and wriggled out of any explanation of what his play was about.'

Rehearsals were due to begin in June. 'It will be a great relief to be working again,' she wrote to Cindy Ballard.

Jack was going into *The Last of Mrs Cheyney* at the Yvonne Arnaud Theatre in Guildford and couldn't spend as much time with her as he wanted, for his rehearsals had already begun.

She returned to Eaton Square from Tickerage on the last day of May and almost as soon as she stepped into the hallway with its silver-grey wallpaper and Chinese Chippendale mirror, she felt faint and decided to go to bed. She had been coughing, despite the summer warmth. Now she began to bring up blood. The doctor was sent for. 'That hurts,' she said, when he pressed her side. Dr Linnett took an X-ray in her bedroom since she maintained her refusal to go into hospital. He later told Jack that things looked serious. 'He said there was a great black hole in her lung.' Her TB had flared up violently.

Vivien's reaction was to make a face at the medication prescribed her – 'Tastes perfectly awful,' she said. She was quite confident. She'd got over TB before and she'd get over it again. In the face of her refusal to go into a clinic, the only possible treatment was a lengthy rest at home in bed. She would have to lie down for at least three months. 'Shorter than last time,' she said. There were to be very, very few visitors, for a few minutes only, no excitement and no alcohol or cigarettes. Vivien accepted this discipline reluctantly.

*A Delicate Balance* was postponed. 'At least it'll give me time to try and understand it,' she said to Jack.

Jack's own play was proving a success and looked set for a transfer to the West End, which pleased him as he would be nearer Vivien. He had a telephone in his dressing-room at Guildford and used to call her every evening after the show to tell her he was on his way home.

As news of her illness got out, her bedroom, which she said was 'like a chemist's shop', began to resemble a florist's too. Trudi Flockert had left her services some months earlier and now she had a new young maid, a willing girl who found it hard to resist Vivien's demands for pills. Michael Redgrave called often and the Albee script grew dog-eared as they heard each other's lines. Soon the stream of visitors increased from a well-regulated trickle to something like a cocktail party, especially after Jack had left for Guildford. Emlyn Williams looked in and found her smoking. 'I was worried,' he recalls. But most people were not – or not much, anyhow.

Vivien was far more worried for Olivier than for herself when it was announced at the end of June that he was suffering from cancer of the prostate. Joan Plowright telephoned her the news before it was made public. It was in an early stage, she said, so there was good hope. But the thought of 'Larry Boy', as Vivien called him, being bedridden like herself and – so she thought – in much greater danger, distressed her even more than her own condition. She begged every visitor for news of him; he was across town, lying in St Thomas's hospital.

Noël Coward, doing what he called his 'district visiting', looked in on both of them on 2 July. 'Vivien was sitting up in bed looking pale but lovely, and smoking, which she shouldn't have been doing. She was gay and enchanting as she always is.' Then he went on to find Olivier 'writhing' on a bed at St Thomas's.

She perked up as better news about Olivier reached her. She seemed to imitate his recovery, for Jack found her out of bed, watering the pot plants. 'I'm allowed out for an hour a day,' she said, a shade guiltily he thought. She seemed unsteady on her feet: but this might have been because she'd been lying down so long.

Stanley Hall called often. She wanted to talk about her wigs for the Albee play. He was creating them with grey streaks at her request. She did not want to conceal her age.

He arrived on the evening of 6 July with a 16 mm movie projector and a copy of a film she wanted to see – the James Ivory–Ismail Merchant production *Shakespeare Wallah*, about a nomadic troupe of Anglo-Indian players bringing Shakespeare to the hill towns. To fill in the programme he added a short about Rembrandt's paintings. Vivien enjoyed *Shakespeare Wallah*. It was a sad but uncannily apposite choice for the last entertainment she would set eyes on. Through the picaresque wanderings of the repertory players, she saw again the landscape of her own Indian childhood; through their performances, often more impromptu than inspired, but always springing from a deep love of their art, she relived the first stirrings of her own passion for acting and the world of the stage. At the very end of her life she was indeed returning to her beginnings.

The next day, 7 July, was the men's finals at Wimbledon and she and Jack watched them on television before he left for his evening performance – the finals in those days were still played on a Friday. The good sportsmanship the players showed was refreshing. '"Quite charming," I said to her,' Jack recalls. '"Not bad," she replied. Those were the last words we exchanged face to face.'

When he rang her later from his dressing-room her voice sounded feeble. 'Are you all right?' – 'Yes.' – 'Have you got Poo Jones with you?' – 'Yes.'

Reassured, he drove back, reached London unexpectedly early and dropped in at a pub for a drink before he let himself into the Eaton Square flat shortly after 11.00 p.m. There was silence. He eased open Vivien's bedroom door. She was sleeping with Poo Jones beside her on the bed. Everything looked in its customary place. She had even signed the letters that Rosemary Geddes had typed out earlier that day. Rosemary had stayed on despite Vivien's illness. The letters were neatly stacked and ready for posting. A tumbler half-filled with water suggested she'd taken her sedatives. No point in disturbing her.

Jack went to the kitchen and made himself a cup of soup. It was about 11.30 p.m. when he next opened the bedroom door quietly to take a last look at her.

To his horror, Vivien was lying sprawled on the floor, as if she had stumbled crossing to the bathroom. The water carafe was beside her. Her body was still warm from the bedclothes – but she wasn't breathing. Jack immediately tried applying the kiss of life. No response. He lifted her on to the bed. Then he desperately dialled her doctor's number. It was the start of the weekend: an assistant answered. In great distress, scarcely believing his own words, Jack said urgently, 'It's Lady Olivier. Something's happened. I think she may be dead.'

He then telephoned Bumble Dawson, who came right away – and eventually stayed the night. Another call was made to Alan Webb, an actor friend who lived near by. He, too, rushed over. Gertrude was on holiday in Scotland: Jack at that moment had no notion where to contact her.

The doctor's preliminary examination confirmed his worst fear: Vivien was dead.

Jack was in such a state of shock that he didn't think of telephoning Peter Hiley at his home in Hampshire until 3.00 a.m., 'but the minute he heard my voice, he told me later, he knew what had happened.' Hiley was round at Eaton Square by 9.00 a.m., and quickly helped Jack take charge of things. An hour earlier Jack had braced himself to telephone St Thomas's to speak to Olivier personally. From the unexpectedly early hour of his call, Olivier guessed the worst before he was told. Although still in pain, he immediately discharged himself from hospital and was driven to Eaton Square. Unconfirmed reports of Vivien's death had begun reaching Fleet Street during the early hours of the morning – too late for the papers to carry them – and Olivier had to slip into the terrace of apartments by the same back entrance he'd last used when he and Vivien met at the time their marriage was breaking up.

Jack was waiting for him. Each knew the anguish in the other's mind. And pausing only for a mutual murmur of sympathy, Jack led Olivier to the bedroom, opened the door to admit him and then, softly and respectfully, closed it and left him alone with Vivien.

In his memoirs, Olivier confessed: 'I stood and prayed for forgiveness for all the evils that had sprung up between us.'

# Epilogue

## *Tickerage*

Jack succeeded in reaching Vivien's mother in Scotland later that Saturday morning. At first she was totally incredulous. 'But she *can't* be dead ... she *can't* be dead,' Gertrude kept repeating. And when Vivien was in due course taken from Eaton Square, Gertrude Hartley insisted on going to see for herself that her daughter's life had indeed been extinguished – she still could not take it in.

To die at the age of only fifty-three, in one's own home and from tuberculosis – a disease that had been virtually eradicated in the twentieth century! The first reaction everywhere was one of disbelief – even among the millions who knew Vivien only by name and through the roles she had played. When the news agencies began relaying the loss round the world, one headline was used again and again in newspapers and magazines in every language: 'Scarlett O'Hara is Dead'.

But how could myths die? The answer in Vivien's case was tragically simple. Her lungs had become filled with fluid and, like someone trapped under water, Vivien had suffocated.

Because it was summer, many of those who were closest and dearest to her were out of town or out of the country, so that the news reached them by radio or newspaper and their grief was intensified by the helplessness that distance induces.

Thus, on the Sunday morning after Viven's death Baba Metcalfe was in the arena at Pamplona awaiting the arrival of the bulls when she glimpsed a local newspaper with her friend's picture on the front page. 'Keep the paper,' she said to her companion, not paying it much attention as it was in Spanish. She meant to send the article to Vivien. When her friend told her the news, Baba sobbed for an hour while all round the crowds were singing and screaming.

Rex Harrison was filming at the Studios de Boulogne in Paris. He immediately thought of the several visits Vivien had paid to see him in T. S. Eliot's *The Cocktail Party*. She had been deeply attracted to the theme of the play, about people in anguish finding a guardian to help them through bad times. 'You have at least a tiny compensation,' Harrison later wrote to Jack Merivale. 'Yours was a guardianship of great worth in the Eliot sense.'

Arnold Weissberger and Milton Goldman, Vivien's New York lawyer and agent respectively, were aboard the *Queen Elizabeth*. Incredulously, they read the report on the front page of the ship's newspaper which was pushed under their stateroom doors. Noël Coward was in London and was awakened by his secretary-companion Cole Lesley coming into his suite 'suffused with tears' to break the news. 'She was a lovely, generous and darling friend,' Coward recorded, all past tiffs forgotten, 'and I shall miss her always.' Binkie Beaumont wrote from the Hotel Cipriani in Venice; Bobby Helpmann from the Gran Hotel Bolivar, in Lima, Peru; John and Mary Mills from the Continental Plaza, Chicago — 'I had received a letter from her written on an odd collection of postcards that very morning,' said Mary Mills. Again and again the letters and cables spoke of the devotion Vivien had enjoyed in the last decade of her life from Jack Merivale. 'DEAR JACK — OUR HEARTS GO OUT TO YOU,' cabled Katharine Hepburn, and George Cukor, 'YOU'VE BEEN WONDERFUL.' Cukor said he was arranging to hold a small memorial service for Vivien in the garden of his Hollywood home where she'd often come to relax and recuperate from those gruelling days on *Gone With the Wind*.

Most touching, perhaps, of the hundreds of letters from Vivien's friends was one from Lucinda Ballard, who'd been with her husband Howard at their Sands Point home on Long Island when she heard the news:

> I was lucky that Cathleen Nesbitt was staying with me. I rushed into the room I always feel is Vivien's and had Cathleen's loving arms to cry myself sick in.... Then I did a strange thing. I dragged Cathleen out and bought lots of things I didn't need. Masses of geraniums, pink and red, to plant by the pool, and garden furniture and I don't know what all. And Cathleen said to me when we returned exhausted, 'Lucinda, do you realize that you have done what Vivien would do? Worn yourself out shopping.'

Many other letters dwelt on the roles Vivien had played, and even *not* played. Peter Wyngarde, her fellow actor in *Duel of Angels*, reflected that when next he heard of someone else being given a role suitable for Vivien, he would wonder why she had turned it down. Lady Diana Cooper wrote that of all the demanding roles she did play, 'I think the most difficult was her own life's part.'

At ten o'clock on the Saturday evening that her death was made public, every theatre in central London extinguished its front-of-house lights. And for an hour the West End went into mourning for Vivien Leigh.

Jack Merivale found himself paying professional tribute to Vivien in his own way, too. Although she had always tended to side with Noël Coward's view that nothing was sacrosanct – 'Why *must* the show go on?' as Coward had wittily put it in a lyric – Vivien had always turned to the discipline of work when the balance of her mind was threatened. Now Jack in his own distress went through with the matinée and evening performances he was due to give at Guildford that same Saturday – to do otherwise and let the company down would have been unthinkable to him and, he felt sure, to Vivien. Peter Hiley and Bumble Dawson dealt with all the calls – and in one case a caller from the Press masquerading as a distant relative of Vivien's – that kept the Eaton Square flat under siege for a time.

Vivien's obituaries began appearing in the Sunday papers and by Monday they occupied entire columns. In an odd way, she had anticipated what many of them had to say, for Vivien had learnt the hard way, from her first-night notices, that in England at least her greatest natural asset was sometimes judged a disadvantage. 'In Britain, an attractive woman is somehow suspect,' she said in an interview barely two years before her death. 'If there is talent as well, it is overshadowed. Beauty and brains just can't be entertained: someone has been too extravagant.' Now the *Observer's* drama critic J. C. Trewin reflected that, 'She had the misfortune to be one of the most physically beautiful actresses of her period.' It blurred, he felt, any true assessment of her acting. 'She was an undervalued intellectual artist, a personality of endearing grace, loyalty and humour. We can be certain that stage historians will remember Vivien Leigh for more than her "fatal gift of beauty".' Harold Hobson in the *Sunday Times* also spoke ominously of her 'invincible attractiveness', which 'threatened to become a handicap ... its significance relegated into that typical English prejudice that pretty women have nothing but their faces to commend them and hide under their looks a plentiful lack of talent.'

And *The Times*, in a thirty-inch double-column obituary, spoke of her as 'one of those actresses who, always themselves, are always different, always learning, always turning their looks and personality to new, scrupulously prepared dramatic account'.

Other tributes appeared in less august places, and were not so scrupulously prepared. On one of the pillars in the doorway of Vivien's apartment at 54 Eaton Square, an unknown fan wrote up in pencil, but with somewhat more literacy than graffiti artists usually muster and with far, far more feeling: 'A great actress for ever and ever.... We vote you The Young at Heart and a True Beauty.'

Vivien's will was lengthy and detailed. She'd left nothing to chance. She had bequeathed her eyes to medical science to be used in corneal grafting. (Unfortunately this gift couldn't be accepted by the authorities in view of

Vivien's medical history.) Then came a request that carried a grievous shock for Gertrude when it was relayed to her. Vivien directed that she should be cremated, not interred. As cremation was against the tenets of Roman Catholic orthodoxy, it looked like her ultimate rejection of the Church to which her mother had handed her over as a child of not quite seven. Its guidance and discipline had toughened Vivien's will and confirmed her faith in her own worldly ambitions, but in matters spiritual, its effect had been to encourage revolt. 'Vivien, have you any religion?' the playwright Dodie Smith had asked her some years before her death, when Vivien had been strenuously, but unavailingly wooed to take the leading role in one of her plays. Dodie Smith had felt she was a troubled woman and that perhaps religion might be of help to her. 'No, and I sometimes think I ought to get one,' Vivien replied. 'Something new to acquire, no doubt,' Dodie Smith thought to herself rather tartly, since it struck her that Vivien's talents were acquisitive rather than creative. Whatever the truth of that, religion wasn't added to her collection of arts and skills: her faith in herself remained truer than any Faith that was urged on her by her mother.

Gertrude's protests were in vain. She had to be content with a Requiem Mass being said at St Mary's, Cadogan Street, on 12 July, attended by about a dozen of Vivien's family and closest friends. They then went on to Golders Green where, early in the afternoon, Vivien Leigh was cremated.

Cecil Tennant, 'Uncle Cecil' to the Oliviers, was among the mourners. After the cremation he got into an almost brand-new saloon car to drive home to his country house near Chertsey and then pick up his children from a party they'd been attending in the neighbourhood. When they were late arriving, his wife walked up the hill near their home – and from there she saw the car crashed against a tree. The children were injured; her husband was dead. The accident was never satisfactorily explained. 'I was delegated to break the news to Larry,' says Peter Hiley. 'It was almost a worse shock than Vivien's death, coming totally out of the blue. And then Cecil had been such a prop to them both.' The world of 'the Oliviers' was indeed being cruelly dismantled.

When all had been counted up, Vivien's estate amounted to a considerable sum – much more than people had thought she was worth. But then she had been an astute investor and a high earner to the end. In money and property, her estate totalled £252,681 gross – an equivalent sum by mid-1980s values would be around £2.5 million. Death duty claimed £41,429, reducing the estate to £152,573 net. But she had taken out a policy on her life that paid for the death duty, since tax wasn't levied on life insurance. Vivien left her life as she had lived it – well ordered.

There was a very lengthy list of bequests to family, friends and servants, including sums of money, totalling in all £12,000 and many of her paintings. 'This demonstrated both her love for people and her awareness of their personal interests and needs,' says Peter Hiley. As the letters of condolence from Vivien's intimates were succeeded by hundreds of letters from people all over the world, who had at some time caught a glimpse of her, met her or been touched by her performance on stage or screen, Jack Merivale found himself not only penning answers to them, but scraping together where he could some small item, a scarf, a headband, even a sheet of writing paper, to satisfy the request for a keepsake. The great anonymity of 'the fans' broke down into a reiterated sense of personal loss. It was months before he'd finished – months before he realized he had been in a state of extended shock ever since her death.

A service of thanksgiving was held at the Trafalgar Square church of St Martin-in-the-Fields on 15 August 1967. Twenty minutes before it began, the church was filled to capacity. Crowds massed on the steps, many crying softly into handkerchiefs, and eventually in the interests of safety the police halted the traffic along the whole of the square's east side. Inside it was like a roll-call of Vivien's two worlds of theatre and cinema.

Olivier was accompanied by Ginette Spanier from Balmain. Leigh Holman sat with his daughter; sunk in his thoughts, Jack Merivale sat apart from the other two men who, along with him, had shared Vivien's life. In the congregation of the famous were names like Attenborough, Guinness and Rattigan; Cicely Courtneidge, Anna Neagle, Peggy Ashcroft, Gladys Cooper, Irene Worth, Rachel Kempson, Kay Hammond and Googie Withers; Binkie Beaumont, Peter Brook, Michael Benthall, Herbert Wilcox and many, many more.

Coward had been asked to read the lesson, but had begged to be let off, saying he would be too distraught – and he was among the absentees. John Clements read from Revelations; Rachel Kempson, standing before the altar, recited the Prayer of St Francis, which Vivien had kept at her bedside; and Emlyn Williams read a conflation of lines from John Donne:

Look upward; that's toward her, whose happy state
We now lament not, but congratulate....
She, to whom all this world was but a stage,
Where all sat hark'ning how her youthful age
Should be employ'd, because in all she did
Some Figure of the Golden times was hid.
Who could not lack, whate'er this world could give,
Because she was the form, that made it live.

John Gielgud gave the address and spoke of Vivien's restless drive and astonishing resilience; how she had 'often suffered from ill health and fits of great depression [but] made light of the fact and never admitted to it or talked about it to other people'. Then choosing his words with care, he hailed her as 'a great beauty, a natural star, a consummate screen actress and a versatile and powerful personality in the theatre'.

Some months after the service, on the morning of 8 October, Vivien's immediate family consisting of her mother, Leigh Holman and Suzanne Farrington, as well as a very few of her intimates headed by Bumble Dawson, gathered at Tickerage. 'My mother's perfume was everywhere at Tickerage,' said Vivien's daughter to Peter Hiley. To Jack, she was an all but tangible presence, too. Tickerage was the home she had made for herself – unlike Notley, which had belonged to the grander reign of herself and her husband. She had found contentment there and her coming to terms with life. It would have to be sold, of course, for Jack hadn't the money to buy it and Suzanne would eventually inherit her father's manor house in Devon. Jack took many a last walk through the woods they had planted with wild anemones, aconites and bluebells – it was one of Vivien's favourite parts of the estate – and knew he wouldn't be there to see them usher in her favourite season of the year. But there was one last thing he had to do – to make sure the wish she had expressed in her will was carried out.

He led them all down to the old mill pond – 'the lake', as Vivien used to call it. And there, as she had directed, he scattered her ashes on the water and she was made one with the element that she had always believed to be a benign influence on her life. Gertrude had wanted to have a priest at hand. Jack resisted the idea. She could have a priest bless the spot later, he told her, but it had not been Vivien's wish. To his way of thinking, the love that accompanied the dispersal of her ashes was sufficient and required no formal blessing from the Church.

Tickerage was put on the market soon afterwards and sold almost immediately for £40,000.

By contrast, Hollywood's celebration of Vivien's life and art seemed almost rowdy. It took place on 17 March 1968, on the campus of the University of Southern California, Los Angeles. The sponsors were the Friends of the Libraries, who had previously honoured Aldous Huxley, Somerset Maugham and Cole Porter; Vivien was their first actress. Among the famous who paid spoken tribute were Greer Garson, Gladys Cooper, Judith Anderson, Wilfrid Hyde-White, George Cukor, Claire Bloom, Joseph Cotten and Stanley Kramer. It was an anecdotal evening and quite convivial – Cukor at one point fell off his chair and Garson was asked if she could get to the stage to introduce a clip from *Waterloo Bridge* without falling over him. The mutual ribbing was reminiscent of a show-business 'roast' rather than a theatrical tribute. Two critics were among the most persuasive and eloquent speakers. Charles Champlin, arts and entertainment editor of the *Los Angeles Times*, spoke not only of Vivien's achievements, but of 'her very great bravery and persistence in the face of what was surely a disproportionate share of trials and afflictions'. And then came Gavin Lambert, critic and screenwriter of *The Roman Spring of Mrs Stone*. His words added a necessary gravity to the evening's levity.

> Vivien had a duality in her nature, as marked as the break in the body of a rock.... Much has been rightly written about her beauty, her elegance, her unflinching personal loyalties. Too much, in a sense, because it implies that was all there was to her. The rest, I think, is what made her deeply beautiful. On one side was a cool intelligence – 'I understand hatred, but I don't harbor it, because I think it's frightfully ageing' – and, on the other, a disturbing throwaway like, 'I've never slept much, ever. Since I was born, I haven't slept much.' As an actress, her comic gift was an example of how the sharpest comic sense has, behind it, something desperate.... Similarly, her flair for clothes and houses, and impeccable food, wine and flowers when she entertained, were not just 'taste'. They reflected the need for outward order because inwardly there was chaos.

London and Hollywood: they remembered Vivien in their characteristic ways. Each assessed her strength according to its craft and fashion. To the hundreds of theatre people assembled to give thanks for her life and friendship in St Martin-in-the-Fields, Vivien was first and foremost a stage actress. Not a pre-eminent one – not by any means. There were others who were finer players, better judges of their own powers and limitations. But Vivien represented theatre, not as a profession, but as a way of life. Though the breadth of her ambitions was rarely matched by the peak of achievement, she seized the unexpected challenge or created the testing opportunity with a passion that only cooled off once it was run into the mould of a nightly performance.

Acting for Vivien represented a need – love, order, conquest, security – that had to be satisfied before her powers could transfigure the role she was playing. When the role fitted the needs, then there was real success. Gielgud considered her Lady Macbeth to be among the finest he'd ever watched; other discerning critics nominated her Shakespearian Cleopatra as the one they preferred. In both parts there was a measure of desperation, an impulse to test the limits that afforded no chance of withdrawal, which had its source in Vivien as much as in the text. The duality that Gavin Lambert had perceived in her was personal as well as acted.

Several theatre critics remarked on the paradox that the Oliviers 'were never both at their best when acting together. They never achieved their ambition to

become a great acting team.' It is certain that Vivien felt the disparity cruelly –
and Olivier, on occasions, guiltily. But she never could have raised herself to
his eminence. The spirit in her drove her engine as powerfully as his was driven:
but it was a smaller engine. Olivier felt his great locomotive of talent drawing
away from her and the more he put into fuelling it, the less energy he had left
over for creating a partnership with Vivien. Ultimately, even their marriage
ceased to be a partnership.

But the aura of 'The Oliviers', at its post-war brightest, shed an illumination
that extended far beyond the footlights. They didn't *need* to be on stage together
for the world to think of them as a unique pair. Their public possessed them in
a way that the Lunts were possessed in America or the Barraults in France. Their
marriage gave them a lustre; their alliance of talent, looks and beauty, a power;
and their prominence in the immediate postwar years, when the British needed
emblems of greatness to compensate for a dulled sense of destiny, gave Laurence
Olivier and Vivien Leigh an almost hallowed status.

All this found its place, by reference or implication, in the way the stage
remembered Vivien.

But Hollywood's tribute, more raucous than ritualized, was in many ways a
truer estimate of Vivien's gifts as an actress – and a star. For Vivien played
parts that were not only honoured there and then by her Hollywood peers, but
that have successfully challenged time and changing trends. View it as beginner's
luck or well-planned stratagem, it remains remarkable that a next-to-unknown
English girl could seize the part of Scarlett O'Hara, the most marvellous role
that the times had to offer, and endow it so vividly with her own characteristics.
It remained hers, and hers alone, while she lived, and by outliving her, it has
won her a measure of immortality.

As Blanche DuBois, Vivien assumed another of the great figures of popular
American mythology and made it hers. Her reputation will never be simply an
echo of critics' compliments, the way it so often has to be for stage players: we
can see in these two performances where Vivien Leigh's soul and talent survive.

But whether she was acting on the stage or screen, the cost to Vivien in
emotional terms was high – higher sometimes than the success she earned and
more lasting in terms of the damage done; for her mind, in the words of the
baffling play she was studying at the time of her death, was always in delicate
balance.

In 1969, on what would have been her fifty-sixth birthday, the name of
Vivien Leigh was added to the plaques of theatrical figures such as Ellen Terry
and Ivor Novello at St Paul's, Covent Garden – the actors' church. And in 1985
her face, features sharply angled in 1930s style by Angus McBean, appeared
on one of five postage stamps, along with those of Hitchcock, Chaplin, Peter

Sellers and David Niven, issued to commemorate British Film Year. These were formal tributes compared with the warmth and regard that her memory held for those who knew her nature and her performances.

Leigh Holman died in the 1970s without having remarried. He had always remained close to Suzanne and his grandchildren. Jill Esmond still keeps her silence on the events of fifty years ago. Laurence Olivier, created a Life Peer in 1970, with a son and two daughters by his marriage to Joan Plowright, celebrated his eightieth birthday in 1987. Jack Merivale married the actress Dinah Sheridan in 1986.

As for Gertrude Hartley, she lived into her mid-eighties, cherishing the memory of her brilliant, wayward child. She religiously updated the scrapbooks in which she had pasted thousands of cuttings about Vivien, always cutting away even slightly uncomplimentary references to her. Deprived of a gravestone to honour her memory, she arranged for a bench to be placed in the private gardens of Eaton Square, opposite Vivien's old apartment. On it, she caused a plaque to be placed with lines from *Antony and Cleopatra*: 'Now boast thee, Death, in thy possession lies / A lass unparallel'd.' Sometimes Gertrude would be asked about Vivien's childhood and her committal to the grey flint convent at Roehampton thousands of miles from the sensuous country of her birth and an immeasurable distance in spirit from family and home. Hadn't she ever felt that such a little girl would miss her mother? Gertrude's abiding certainties always allowed her to answer with complete conviction: 'Miss me? Of course not! I was always with her in spirit. Why, Vivien told me that she used to put my picture under the blanket at nights, to keep me warm.'

# Chronology

1913  5 November: born at Darjeeling, India.
1920  March: taken to England for schooling at Convent of the Sacred Heart,
       Roehampton.
       September: schooling begins, two months before seventh birthday.
1921  30 November: confirmed, just after eighth birthday.
1927  7 July: leaves Roehampton to begin round of convent schools on the
       Continent.
1931  Easter: schooling completed, returns to England to live with parents in
       London.
1932  February: enrolled at RADA, has to wait until May to begin drama courses.
       February–March: meets Leigh Holman at South Devon Hunt Ball,
       Torquay.
       20 December: marries Holman at St James's, Spanish Place.
1933  3 June: presented at Buckingham Palace.
       12 October: gives birth to daughter Suzanne.
1934  August: filming *Things Are Looking Up* (London opening *circa* February
       1935).
       29 November: signs contract with John Gliddon to represent her.
       November–December: filming *The Village Squire* and *Gentlemen's
       Agreement* (London openings April and June 1935, respectively).
1935  25 February: opens in *The Green Sash*.
       April: filming *Look Up and Laugh* (London opening August 1935).
       15 May: becomes overnight sensation in *The Mask of Virtue*; is offered
       film contract by Korda.
       14 August: signs long-term contract with Korda.
1936  17 February: opens in *Richard II* at Oxford University Dramatic Society.
       3 April: opens in *The Happy Hypocrite*.
       April (*circa*): becomes romantically involved with Olivier.
       22 June: opens in *Henry VIII*.

July–August: filming with Olivier for the first time in *Fire Over England* (London opening 25 February 1937; New York opening 4 March 1937).

21 August: son (Tarquin) born to Olivier and Jill Esmond.

August–September: filming *Dark Journey* (London opening 28 March 1937; New York opening 22 August 1937).

25 October–5 November: vacations in Sicily with Oswald Frewen and secretly arranges to meet Olivier (with Jill Esmond) at Capri.

December–January 1937: filming *Storm in a Teacup* (London opening 6 June 1937; New York opening 21 March 1938).

1937 5 February: opens in *Because We Must*.

11 March: opens in *Bats in the Belfry*.

May–June: filming with Olivier in *Twenty-One Days* (London opening 7 January 1940; New York opening as *Twenty-One Days Together*, 22 May 1940).

3–9 June: opens with Olivier in *Hamlet* at Elsinore.

Mid-June (*circa*): breaks up with Leigh Holman and moves into Durham Cottage with Olivier.

July: holidays with Olivier in Venice.

September–October: filming *A Yank at Oxford* (New York opening 24 February 1938; London opening 1 April 1938).

27 December: opens in *A Midsummer Night's Dream*.

1938 March–April: filming *St Martin's Lane* (London opening 18 October 1938; New York opening, as *Sidewalks of London*, 14 February 1940).

July: holidays with Olivier in South of France: he is offered *Wuthering Heights* role.

13 September: opens in *Serena Blandish*.

5 November: sees Olivier off to America to film *Wuthering Heights*.

29 (?) November: follows Olivier to Hollywood, hoping for Scarlett O'Hara role.

10 December: is presented to David O. Selznick during burning of Atlanta sequence.

20 December: signs contract with Myron Selznick agency to represent her.

21 December: tests for Scarlett O'Hara role.

25 December: is told by Cukor that she has got the part.

1939 16 January: signs long-term contract with Selznick International Pictures.

26 January: begins filming *Gone With the Wind*.

13 February: protests (with Olivia de Havilland) at firing of George Cukor.

27 June: finishes role in *Gone With the Wind* and tests, on same day, for part in *Rebecca*.

3 July: catches Olivier's closing night performance in *No Time for Comedy* in New York.

11 July: sails for England with Olivier.

17 August: sails back to America with Olivier (and mother) and receives news *en voyage* of rejection for *Rebecca* role.

3 September: hears declaration of war while aboard Colman's yacht with Olivier *et al.*

15 December: attends *première* of *Gone With the Wind* in Atlanta.

December–January 1940: filming *Waterloo Bridge* (New York opening 16 May 1940; London opening 28 November 1940).

1940 5 January: receives news of Leigh Holman's divorce petition (naming Olivier as co-respondent).

29 January: is named co-respondent in Jill Esmond's petition for divorce from Olivier.

29 February: wins Best Actress Oscar for Scarlett O'Hara in *Gone With the Wind*.

9 May: opens with Olivier in *Romeo and Juliet* in New York. Play closes within two weeks.

July: gets offer to star with Olivier in Korda's film *Lady Hamilton*.

31 August: marries Olivier in civil ceremony at Santa Barbara, California, attended by Katharine Hepburn and Garson Kanin.

October–November: filming with Olivier in *Lady Hamilton* (New York opening, as *That Hamilton Woman*, 3 April 1941; London opening 2 August 1941).

27 December: sails with Olivier for Lisbon and thence by air to Bristol.

1942 4 March: opens in *The Doctor's Dilemma*.

1943 Spring: embarks on three-month concert-party tour of North Africa to entertain Allied troops.

Winter: Oliviers acquire Notley Abbey as country home and begin renovating it.

1944 June: begins filming *Caesar and Cleopatra*.

Mid-July: has accident on set of film and suffers subsequent miscarriage.

September: suffers period of depression necessitating temporary withdrawal from filming.

1945 January: finishes filming *Caesar and Cleopatra* (London opening 11 December 1945; New York opening 5 September 1946).

22 February: is subject of legal action by David O. Selznick to stop appearance in *The Skin of Our Teeth*. Action fails.

18 May: opens in *The Skin of Our Teeth*.

August: TB compels withdrawal from play and nine-month convalescence at Notley Abbey.

1946 11 September: re-opens in *The Skin of Our Teeth*.

1947 February: vacations in Italy with Olivier while he prepares *Hamlet* film. May–August: filming *Anna Karenina* (London opening 22 January 1948; New York opening 27 April 1948).

8 July: accompanies Olivier to Buckingham Palace for his knighthood.

1948 February–November: accompanies Olivier and Old Vic Company on tour of Australia and New Zealand. Plays in *Richard III, The School for Scandal, The Skin of Our Teeth*. Meets Peter Finch in Sydney.

1949 21 January: opens in *The School for Scandal* in Old Vic repertory season.

26 January: opens in *Richard III*.

6 February: opens in *Antigone*.

Spring: tells Olivier she no longer loves him.

11 October: opens in *A Streetcar Named Desire*.

1950 1 August: arrives in New York *en route* to Hollywood to film *A Streetcar Named Desire*. Spends weekend at director Elia Kazan's Connecticut home.

7 August: arrives on the Coast by train along with Kazan. Is joined by daughter Suzanne and Olivier (who is there to film *Carrie*).

August–September: filming *A Streetcar Named Desire* (New York opening 29 September 1951; London opening 2 March 1952).

December: returns with Olivier to England by slow freighter. Marriage very strained.

1951 10 May: opens with Olivier in *Caesar and Cleopatra*.

11 May: opens with Olivier in *Antony and Cleopatra*.

19 December: opens in *Caesar and Cleopatra* in New York.

20 December: opens in *Antony and Cleopatra* in New York.

1952 20 March: wins Best Actress Oscar for Blanche DuBois role in *A Streetcar Named Desire*.

April: recuperates from New York run and mental disturbance with Noël Coward in Jamaica.

23 April: returns to Notley with Olivier to rest through summer and autumn. Is offered role in *Elephant Walk* opposite Peter Finch.

1953 February: leaves with Finch for Ceylon to begin filming *Elephant Walk*. Suffers mental breakdown accompanied by bouts of mania.

17–21 February: is visited by Olivier in Ceylon.

17 March: is flown to Hollywood in mentally disturbed state.

24 March: is visited in Hollywood by Olivier, who flies home with her.

Is put under observation at Netherne Hospital, later transferred to University College Hospital and given electro-convulsive therapy.

Summer: recuperates at Notley, joins Korda on yacht cruise.

5 November: opens with Olivier in *The Sleeping Prince*.

1954 September–October: filming *The Deep Blue Sea* (London opening 24 August 1955; New York opening 12 October 1955).

1955 12 April: opens with Olivier in *Twelfth Night* at Stratford.

7 June: opens with Olivier in *Macbeth* at Stratford.

16 August: opens with Olivier in *Titus Andronicus* at Stratford.

November–December: makes two abortive attempts to run off with Peter Finch.

1956 25 April: opens in *South Sea Bubble*.

12 July: announces she is going to have baby.

12 August: suffers miscarriage.

Autumn: moves with Olivier from Durham Cottage to 54 Eaton Square.

1957 April–May: tours European countries with Olivier in *Titus Andronicus*. Suffers severe manic-depressive spell.

10 July: marches down the Strand, London, in protest against proposed destruction of St James's Theatre.

12 July: interrupts House of Lords sitting with vocal protest.

July: draws criticism from MP for going on Continental holiday with ex-husband Leigh Holman.

6 December: attends daughter Suzanne's marriage.

1958 24 April: opens in *Duel of Angels*.

8 November: Oliviers give star-studded party for Lauren Bacall – last appearance in their old glamour.

5 December: becomes grandmother.

1959 9 July: opens in *Look After Lulu*.

Summer: Notley Abbey put up for sale.

18 December: father dies.

Winter 1959–60: renews friendship with Jack Merivale and falls in love with him.

1960 19 April: opens in *Duel of Angels* in New York.

19/20 May: receives Olivier's plea for divorce and issues press statement in New York agreeing to it.

10 June: flies to London to try and persuade Olivier to change his mind.

20 June: returns to New York and Jack Merivale.

12 August (*circa*): Jack Merivale writes to Olivier declaring he and Vivien are in love.

16 August (*circa*): Olivier replies, giving them his blessing.

October–November: returns to Europe with Jack Merivale and tours France and Switzerland. Moves into new home, Tickerage Mill.

2 December: divorced from Olivier.

December 1960–March 1961: filming *The Roman Spring of Mrs Stone* (New York opening 28 December 1961; London opening 15 February 1962).

1961  8 March: flies to New York in last attempt to regain Olivier and to attend re-release *première* of *Gone With the Wind* in Atlanta.

17 March: returns to London to finish filming. On same date Olivier marries Joan Plowright in civil ceremony in Connecticut.

April: finishes furnishing Tickerage Mill as country home and moves in.

April: holidays with Jack Merivale in Tobago.

July 1961–May 1962: leads Old Vic company on tour of Australia and New Zealand and Latin America in *Twelfth Night*, *Duel of Angels* and *La Dame aux camélias*.

1962  12 November: flies to America to appear in *Tovarich*.

1963  18 March: opens in *Tovarich* in New York.

30 September: has mental breakdown and drops out of *Tovarich*.

1 October: rushed to London for ECT treatment and recuperation.

Autumn 1963–Winter 1964: long depressive bout at Tickerage.

1964  March: restored to health and vacations with Jack Merivale in Tobago.

June–August: filming *Ship of Fools* in Hollywood while undergoing ECT (New York opening 28 July 1965; London opening 20 October 1965).

September: returns to London.

19 November: leaves for tour of India. Spends Christmas in Corfu.

1965  9 January: attends marriage of Olivier's son Tarquin at St Mary's, Chelsea.

6 April: opens in *La Contessa* in Newcastle. Play closes in Manchester in May.

1966  3 February: flies to New York with Jack Merivale to do *Ivanov*.

3 May: opens in *Ivanov* in New York.

July: returns with Jack Merivale to London after manic attack in New York.

1967  May: is taken ill with recurrence of TB and forced to postpone rehearsals for *A Delicate Balance*.

7 July: is found dead in her bedroom at 54 Eaton Square by Jack Merivale.

8 July: West End theatres extinguish front-of-house lights in tribute to Vivien.

12 July: cremated at Golders Green, London.

15 August: Service of Thanksgiving at St Martin-in-the-Fields, London.

8 October: Jack Merivale scatters ashes on the lake at Tickerage.

1968 17 March: Friends of the Libraries, University of Southern California, hold tribute to Vivien attended by many Hollywood celebrities.

1969 5 November: Commemorative plaque unveiled at St Paul's, Covent Garden (the 'actors' church').

1985 May: Included with Chaplin, Sellers, Hitchcock and David Niven in set of stamps marking British Film Year.

*Note: dates for the shooting schedules of Vivien Leigh's films in Britain and America are approximate, as precise records of many productions have been lost or are not available.*

# Bibliography

Aumont, Jean-Pierre, *Sun and Shadow*, Norton, 1977

Barker, Felix, *Laurence Olivier*, Spellmont/Hippocrene, 1984

Barker, Felix, *The Oliviers*, Hamish Hamilton, 1953

Barrault, Jean-Louis, *Memories of Tomorrow*, Thames & Hudson, 1974

Beames, John, *Memoirs of a Bengal Civilian*, Chatto & Windus, 1961

Beaton, Cecil, *The Happy Years: Diaries 1944–48*, Weidenfeld & Nicolson, 1972

Behlmer, Rudy, *Inside Warner Bros. 1935–1951*, Weidenfeld & Nicolson, 1985

Behlmer, Rudy, *A Memo From David O. Selznick*, Macmillan, 1973

Bradley, John (ed.), *Lady Curzon's India*, Weidenfeld & Nicolson, 1985

Bragg, Melvyn, *Laurence Olivier*, Hutchinson, 1984

Brown, Ivor, *Theatre 1954–5*, Max Reinhardt, 1955

Cottrell, John, *Laurence Olivier*, Weidenfeld & Nicolson, 1975

Dean, Basil, *The Mind's Eye*, Hutchinson, 1973

Deans, Marjorie, *Meeting at the Sphinx*, Macdonald, 1947

Dent, Alan, *Vivien Leigh: A Bouquet*, Hamish Hamilton, 1969

Dundy, Elaine, *Finch, Bloody Finch*, Michael Joseph, 1980

Edwards, Anne, *The Road to Tara*, Hodder & Stoughton, 1983

Edwards, Anne, *Vivien Leigh*, W. H. Allen, 1977

Fairweather, Virginia, *Cry God for Larry*, Calder & Boyars, 1969

Findlater, Richard (ed.), *At The Royal Court*, Amber Lane Press, 1981

Flamini, Roland, *Scarlett, Rhett and a Cast of Thousands*, Deutsch, 1976

Friends of the Libraries, *Vivien Leigh: An Appreciation*, 1969

Gielgud, John, *An Actor and His Time*, Sidgwick & Jackson, 1979

Granger, Stewart, *Sparks Fly Upward*, Granada, 1981

Greene, Graham (ed.), *The Old School* ('A Child of the Five Wounds' by Antonia White), Oxford University Press, 1985

Guinness, Alec, *Blessings in Disguise*, Hamish Hamilton, 1985

Harris, Radie, *Radie's World*, W. H. Allen, 1975

Harrison, Rex, *Rex*, Macmillan, 1974

Harwell, Richard (ed.), *Gone With the Wind: The Illustrated Screenplay by Sidney Howard*, Lorrimer.

Kanin, Garson, *Hollywood*, Hart-Davis, MacGibbon, 1975

Kiernan, Thomas, *Olivier*, Sidgwick & Jackson, 1981

Korda, Michael, *Charmed Lives*, Allen Lane, 1980

Kulik, Karol, *Alexander Korda*, W. H. Allen, 1975

Lambert, Gavin, *On Cukor*, W. H. Allen, 1973

Leaming, Barbara, *Orson Welles*, Weidenfeld & Nicolson, 1985

Lejeune, C. A., *Thank You for Having Me*, Hutchinson, 1964

Madsen, Axel, *William Wyler*, W. H. Allen, 1974

Mitchell, Margaret, *Gone With the Wind*, Macmillan, 1936

Morley, Margaret, *Olivier*, LSP Books, 1978

*New York Times Film Reviews*, Arno Press

O'Connor, Garry, *Darlings of the Gods*, Hodder & Stoughton, 1984

Olivier, Laurence, *Confessions of an Actor*, Weidenfeld & Nicholson, 1982

Olivier, Laurence, *On Acting*, Weidenfeld & Nicolson, 1986

Pascal, Valerie, *The Disciple and His Devil*, Michael Joseph, 1971

Payne, Graham, and Morley, Sheridan (eds.), *The Noël Coward Diaries*, Weidenfeld & Nicolson, 1982

Peary, Danny (ed.), *Close-Ups*, Workman Publishing, 1978

Robyns, Gwen, *Vivien Leigh*, Leslie Frewin, 1968

Selznick, Irene Mayer, *A Private View*, Weidenfeld & Nicolson, 1983

Signoret, Simone, *Nostalgia Isn't What It Used To Be*, Weidenfeld & Nicolson, 1978

Smith, Dodie, *Look Back with Gratitude*, Miller, Blond & White, 1985

Tabori, Paul, *Alexander Korda*, Oldbourne, 1959

Taylor, John Russell, *Vivien Leigh*, Elm Tree, 1984

Tynan, Kenneth, *Curtains*, Longmans, Green, 1961

Tynan, Kenneth, *He That Plays the King*, Longmans, Green, 1950

Vickers, Hugo, *Cecil Beaton*, Weidenfeld & Nicolson, 1985

White, Antonia, *Frost in May*, Virago, 1985

Williams, Tennessee, *Memoirs*, W. H. Allen, 1976

Williams, Tennessee, *A Streetcar Named Desire*, Penguin, 1986

Winn, Godfrey, *The Positive Hour*, Michael Joseph, 1970

# Source Notes

## PROLOGUE

Reconstruction of a week-end at Notley draws on various sources, printed and oral, among them Godfrey Winn, Vivien Leigh, Rachel Kempson (Lady Redgrave), Virginia Fairweather, Peter Hiley and Jack Merivale.

Page

9 'Larry's going to ...' Vivien Leigh to author, winter, 1959. Rex Harrison's auto-biography, *Rex*, pp 123–4, also makes reference to V.L.'s fascination with Eliot's 'guardians'.

10 'I gave it to Larry ...' V.L. to author.

11 'When I was ...' V.L. to David Lewin, *Daily Express*, 16 August 1960.

11 'It makes yer laugh ...' Rachel Kempson to author, 12 August 1986.

12 'I've never been so ...' Virginia Fairweather to author, 8 March 1986.

12 'You would make ...' Godfrey Winn to author; Barbara Leaming's biography *Orson Welles*, p 383, makes specific reference and this is version quoted.

12 'That's how my father ...' Godfrey Winn to author.

13 'Would you mind ...' Godfrey Winn in *The Positive Hour*, pp 388–90.

14 'They're a lovely green ...' V.L. to author.

14 'I never forget ...' Conflation of V.L. to David Lewin, *Daily Express*, 18 August 1960, and V.L. to author.

15 'How lovely for you ...' V.L. to Godfrey Winn.

16 'The Song.' Jack Merivale (and others) to author, 11 March 1986.

17 'Thank goodness ...' Godfrey Winn, *op. cit.*, p 390.

18 'I have ten ...' Godfrey Winn, *ibid.*, pp 384–5.

## CHAPTER 1

22 'It's for your birthday ...' V.L. to author (among others).

25 'I won't sing ...' Felix Barker in *The Oliviers*, p 78.

## CHAPTER 2

29 'Catholicism isn't ...' Antonia White, *Frost in May*, p 122.

31 'Like the rest ...' Lady Lambert (Patsy Quinn) to author, 29 September 1986.

31 'When I come ...' V.L. to David Lewin, *Daily Express*, August 1960.

32 'Wouldn't it be ...' Lady Lambert to author.

32 'She had a "foreignness" ...' *ibid.*

34 'Break the will ...' Antonia White, *op. cit.*, p 219.

34 'Mother Brace-Hall ...' V.L. to parents, quoted in Alan Dent's *Vivien Leigh: A Bouquet*, p 44.

36 'The Reverend Mother ...' Felix Barker, *op. cit.*, p 83.

37 'You deserve ...' Godfrey Winn to author.

## CHAPTER 3

38 'They had ...' Lady Lambert to author.

38 'That's Leigh Holman ...' V.L. to author.

39 'She didn't seem ...' Leigh Holman quoted in the *Sunday Telegraph*, 19 June 1965.

41 'Darling, where did you ...' Felix Barker, *op. cit.*, p 86.

41 'Vivian, that's terribly ...' Lady Lambert to author.

43 'Had a baby ...' Felix Barker, *op. cit.*, p 89.

43 'That was a very messy ...' Lady Lambert to author.

46 'I wouldn't accept ...' John Gliddon to author. This quote and others from Gliddon derive, unless otherwise stated, from interviews with the author on 27 March, 30 April and 10 October 1986. To make for a more attractive text, quotes attributed by Gliddon to others have, where appropriate, been rendered in direct speech.

## CHAPTER 4

49 'Far better than ...' Godfrey Winn to author.

49 'A simple comedy ...' *Kinematograph Weekly*, 18 April 1935.

50 'Too heavily steeped ...' *Ibid.*

50 'Moyra Lind ...' *Ibid.*

50 'A sociological ...' *Kinematograph Weekly*, 2 May 1935.

50 'There were the usual ...' John Gliddon to author.

50 'The dramatists have ...' *The Times*, 26 February 1935.

51 'Uncontrollably nervous ...' Basil Dean, *The Mind's Eye*, p 207.

51 'Jeez! It's a swan!' *Ibid.*, p 207.

51 'Well, she ...' John Gliddon to author.

55 'Sydney, put your ...' Felix Barker, *op. cit.*, p 97.

56 'Every day ...' V.L. to David Lewin, *Daily Express*, 17 August 1960.

56 'She had to cry ...' quoted in Dent, *op. cit.*, p 23.

56 'One of the biggest ...' Harold Conway, *Daily Mail*, 16 May 1935.

57 'NEW 19-YEARS-OLD STAR ...' *Ibid.*, 16 May 1935.

57 'A new young British ...' *Ibid.*, 16 May 1935.

58 'My husband does not ...' V.L. to Margaret Lane, *Daily Mail*, 17 May 1935.

58 'I believe ...' *Ibid.*

58 'It was a very arduous ...' *Ibid.*

59 'One of the film critics ...' Paul Tabori, *Alexander Korda*, p 187.

61 'Isn't it amazing?' Seton Margrave, *Daily Mail*, 18 May 1935.


CHAPTER 5

62 'Miss Leigh has incisiveness ...' James Agate, *Sunday Times*, 19 May 1935.

63 'Absolute beginner ...' Sydney Carroll, *Daily Telegraph*, 23 May 1935.

63 'Mr Prentiss ...' Sydney Carroll, *Daily Telegraph*, 30 May 1935.

64 'If you want a label ...' *Vogue*, 28 October 1936.

66 'Apart from her looks ...' Laurence Olivier, *Confessions of an Actor*, p 77.

66 'Only fools ...' Laurence Olivier, quoted by Melvyn Bragg, *Laurence Olivier*, p 35.

67 'I was deeply ...' Laurence Olivier, *op. cit.*, p 37.

67 'A palpable exaggeration ...' *Ibid.*, p 12.

67 'Work is life ...' *Ibid.*, p 25.

67 'Only with the blessing ...' *Ibid.*, p 41.

68 'She was in love ...' *Ibid.*, p 61.

71 'A passionate ...' Peggy Ashcroft, quoted by Melvyn Bragg, *op. cit.*, p 46.

72 'I painted her ...' *Daily Mail*, 2 April 1936.

73 'What a silly ...' V.L. to author.

74 'Miss Vivien Leigh ...' Max Beerbohm, quoted by Felix Barker, *op. cit.*, p 109.

74 'Oh, there's a Devil ...' Clemence Dane, quoted by Alan Dent, *op. cit.*, p 41.

74 'I think I'll have ...' and 'And how's little Tarquin ...' Laurence Olivier, interviewed by Hedda Hopper, H.H. Collection, Margaret Herrick Library, Academy of Motion Picture Arts and Sciences, Beverly Hills.


CHAPTER 6

76 'Where Vivien ...' Vincent Korda to author, 1977.

77 'So much cuddling ...' Graham Greene, *Spectator*, 5 March 1937.

77 'Alex, we must ...' Paul Tabori, *op. cit.*, p 188.

78 'Pumped into ...' Oswald Frewen, quoted in Alan Dent, *op. cit.*, p 23.

78 'Then they'd often go ...' Oswald Frewen, *Daily Telegraph*, 19 June 1955.

78 'It turned into ...' Source to author, 22 June 1986. Source requests anonymity.

79 'Wicked cosmopolitan ...' and 'Pretty, innocent ...' Graham Greene, *Spectator*, 27 March 1937.

79 'Goodness, why ...' John Gliddon to author.

79 'Olivier was the ...' Anthony Quayle to author, 22 June 1986.

80 'She was so natural ...' Oswald Frewen, quoted in Alan Dent, *op. cit.*, p 24.

80 'Apparently he often ...' V.L. to Leigh Holman, quoted in Alan Dent, *op. cit.*, p 29.

80 'Larry, the other ...' Oswald Frewen, *ibid.*, p 25.

82 'I could be a king's ...' John Gliddon to author.

83 'I am an English actress ...' Victor Saville to author, *circa* 1967.

83  'All she wanted ...' Rex Harrison, *op. cit.*, p 52.
83  'To mention Larry ...' Anthony Quayle to author.
83  'Wild hysteria ...' *Ibid.*, p 51.

## CHAPTER 7

84  'High spirits ...' Margaret Mitchell, *Gone With the Wind*, p 61.
84  'Vanity leaped ...' *Ibid.*, p 71.
84  'No pang ...' *Ibid.*, p 428.
84  'Religion had always ...' *Ibid.*, p 498.
84  'A hard self-honesty ...' *Ibid.*, p 170.
84  'Like a child ...' *Ibid.*, p 1007.
84  'Scarlett's mind ...' *Ibid.*, p 526.
85  'The way she knows ...' *Ibid.*, p 183.
85  'Scarlett O'Hara was ...' *Ibid.*, p 5.
85  'The green eyes ...' *Ibid.*, p 5.
85  'While Scarlett wasn't ...' V.L. to Robert Carroll, *Motion Picture*, February 1940.
86  'I have no enthusiasm ...' Rudy Behlmer (ed.), *A Memo from David O. Selznick*, p 140.
87  'You're England ...' Charles Laughton, quoted in Melvyn Bragg, *op. cit.*, p 48.
87  'The Danish authorities ...' Lilian Baylis, quoted in Felix Barker, *op. cit.*, p 126.
87  'I had my doubts ...' Basil Dean, *op. cit.*, p 251.
88  'I have some retakes ...' *Ibid.*, p 252.
89  'I feel part ...' V.L. to author.
89  'Not exciting ...' Laurence Olivier, *op. cit.*, p 78.
90  'The talk inevitably ...' C. A. Lejeune, *Thank You for Having Me*, pp 176–7.
91  'I won't think ...' Margaret Mitchell, *op. cit.*, p 1010.
91  'I believe ...' Anthony Quayle to author.
92  'You, Mr Olivier ...' John Gliddon to author.
94  'A mixture ...' Gavin Lambert, Friends of the Libraries 'Tribute to V.L.', 17 March 1968.

## CHAPTER 8

100  'Rapturous torment ...' Laurence Olivier, *op. cit.*, p 78.
101  'Why are you ...' Angus McBean to author, 24 April 1986.
102  'Reached out ...' Melvyn Bragg, *op. cit.*, p 48.
102  'Which Vivien ...' Anthony Quayle to author.
103  'She didn't like ...' Larry Adler to author, 20 August 1986.
104  'You want to play ...' V.L. to author.
105  'Then I don't ...' Axel Madsen, *William Wyler*, p 185.
105  'Look, Vivien ...' *Ibid.*, p 185.
105  'Bit of fame ...' Felix Barker, *op. cit.*, p 141.
106  'And she was appalling ...' Stewart Granger to author, 25 September 1986.

107 'With an almost demonic ...' Laurence Olivier, *op. cit.*, p 83.

108 'To Heathcliff ... To Scarlett ...' Godfrey Winn to author.

109 'Pure, driving ...' Laurence Olivier, *op. cit.*, p 83.

109 'It was for me ...' and 'It was Wyler ...' John Cottrell, *Laurence Olivier*, p 142.

## CHAPTER 9

110 'Crouched in the back ...' Laurence Olivier, *op. cit.*, p 83.

110 'Why are you coming ...' V.L. to author.

110 'I think we ought ...' Laurence Olivier, *op. cit.*, p 84.

113 'Hey, genius ...' There are quite a few versions of Myron Selznick's historic words. Roland Flamini gives this one in his massively researched book *Scarlett, Rhett and a Cast of Thousands*, p 154, with the exception of the first word, which he renders as 'Here ...'. George Cukor repeated virtually the same line to the author (Chicago, November 1978), with 'Hey ...' as the opening word. The difference has been split (honourably) between the two. Surprisingly, V.L. averred she could not remember what Myron Selznick said in introducing her to David.

113 'Good evening ...' and 'an inspired bit of agentry', George Cukor to author.

113 'I saw her in ...' George Cukor to Max Breen, *Picture-goer*, 9 April 1938.

113 'One of the biggest thrills ...' Rudy Behlmer, *op. cit.*, p 180.

113 'I took one look ...' *Ibid.*, p 180. Behlmer does not name the magazine in which Selznick wrote the article in 1941.

114 'Shhh! ...' *Ibid.*, p 180.

114 'Green eyes ...' Margaret Mitchell, *op. cit.*, p 5.

114 'She was Rabelaisian ...' George Cukor to author.

114 'I don't think ...' *Ibid.*

115 'I am afraid ...' V.L. to Leigh Holman, quoted in Alan Dent, *op. cit.*, p 29.

116 'The part's been cast ... I guess ...' Quoted by Felix Barker (among others), *op. cit.*, p 152.

116 'My heart sank ...' V.L. to author.

117 'The lucky Hungarian ...' Rudy Behlmer, *op. cit.*, p 183.

119 'I will never ...' V.L. to Leigh Holman, quoted in Alan Dent, *op. cit.*, p 30.

119 'I don't want ...' John Gliddon to author.

119 'All their standards ...' *Ibid.*, p 30.

120 'Better an English ...' Referred to by Roland Flamini, *op. cit.*, p 171, and quoted to author in form used in text by George Cukor.

## CHAPTER 10

122 'If you boys ...' *Gone With the Wind: The Illustrated Screenplay by Sidney Howard*, p 55.

122 'Madder than a hornet ...' Clarence Bull interviewed by Hedda Hopper, *op. cit.* AAMPAS library.

124 'If you quit ...' V.L. to author.

124 'Her new *film* contract ...' This contract between V.L. and Selznick International Pictures Inc., signed 15 January 1939, is often referred to in this book and elsewhere. Its details are seldom quoted. In the interests of motion-picture history, they were as follows: For *GWTW*, V.L. was to be paid $1,250 a week (minimum 16 weeks). Her total salary was to be $20,000. Option clauses comprised: First option: to employ V.L. in two pictures to be produced during period of 58 weeks from a date to be determined, but not later than 15 August 1939, at $2,916.66 per week; second option at $3,333.33 per week; third at $3,540.00 per week; fourth at $4,166.66 per week; fifth at $5,208.33 per week; sixth at $6,250.00 per week. For reasons made explicit later in text, this contract proved void because of V.L.'s refusal to honour it. Information made available at MGM/UA Studios, Culver City, California, 24 September 1986.

125 'They treated Gliddon ...' John Gliddon to author.

126 'It's not my practice ...' *Ibid.*

126 'Miss Leigh, you can take ...' Roland Flamini, *op. cit.*, p 263.

126 'Ham it up ...' *Ibid.*, p 262.

127 'They each have a child ...' Ruth Waterbury, *Photoplay*, December 1939.

128 '*Of course* we're living ...' V.L. to author.

128 'As God is my witness ...' *GWTW* screenplay, p 243.

129 'For God's sake ...' Roland Flamini, *op. cit.*, p 292.

129 'She brought me up ...' *Ibid.*, p 293.

129 'Oh Rhett ...' *GWTW* screenplay, p 339.

129 'Ways to Kill Babies ...' Roland Flamini, *op. cit.*, p 293.

130 'I simply didn't ...' Felix Barker, *op. cit.*, p 158.

130 'Oh, David, I'm so grateful ...' Roland Flamini, *op. cit.*, p 294.

131 'She already knew ...' Radie Harris, *Radie's World*, p 164.

131 'They're a little cowed ...' Alan Dent, *op. cit.*, p 32.

132 'Cukor viewed them very seriously ...' Rudy Behlmer, *op. cit.*, p 273.

132 'His broad lowering brow ...' Frank Nugent, *New York Times*, 14 April 1939.

133 'That beautiful 15 years ...' Laurence Olivier interviewed by Hedda Hopper, *op. cit.*, AAMPAS library.

133 'They clung ...' Radie Harris, *op. cit.*, p 166.


CHAPTER 11

134 'Resentful ...' Irene Mayer Selznick, *A Private View*, p 223.

134 'I know it's early ...' V.L. to author.

135 'You are finished ...' Laurence Olivier, *op. cit.*, p 86.

135 'It is difficult ...' Felix Barker, *op. cit.*, p 153.

136 'The lights darkened ...' Irene Mayer Selznick, *op. cit.*, p 219.

137 'She's not going ...' Rudy Behlmer, *op. cit.*, p 234.

137 'Trailer for *Rebecca* ...' *Ibid.*, p 234.

137 'And now I am going ...' Felix Barker, *op. cit.*, p 166.

137 'They're playing ...' Quoted by many sources, including Roland Flamini, *op. cit.*, p 327, with the variation of 'the song', but possibly apocryphal.

137 'Reminds you ...' V.L. to author.

138 'She is *my* Scarlett ...' Anne Edwards, *The Road to Tara*, p 288.

139 'Miss Leigh is not ...' David O. Selznick memo., 17 November 1939, MGM/UA archives.

139 "Miss Leigh shapes ...' Bosley Crowther, *New York Times*, 17 May 1940.

140 'So kind ...' and 'bald and cold ...' Source requests anonymity.

140 'The love-birds ...' Unattributed clipping in Constance McCormick Collection, University of Southern California Film Department.

141 'A bit too luxurious ...' Felix Barker, *op. cit.*, p 169.

141 'Make a fortune ...' V.L. to author.

141 'Nothing will stir ...' Felix Barker, *op. cit.*, p 167.

142 'Good luck ...' Jack Merivale in interviews with the author on 27 February, 6 March, 11 March, 18 March, 25 March, 3 April, 29 April and 4 December 1986. Unless otherwise stated, all subsequent Merivale quotations derive from these sources.

144 'I have wanted ...' Laurence Olivier to Lloyd Lewis, *New York Times*, 4 May 1940.

144 'I have never ...' *Ibid.*

145 'Mannered and affected ...' Brooks Atkinson, *New York Times*, 10 May 1940.

145 'Gulping down ...' John Mason Brown, *New York Post*, 10 May 1940.

145 'His legs ...' Andrew Pollock, Brooklyn *Daily Eagle*, 10 May 1940.

145 'The general romantic ...' John Anderson, *New York Journal American*, 10 May 1940.

145 '[Her] slender ...' Brooks Atkinson, *op. cit.*

145 'She is bright ...' John Anderson, *op. cit.*

145 'Scarlett O'Hara ...' Walter Winchell, *Daily Mirror*, 10 May 1940.

145 'Being celebrated ...' Richard Watts Jr., *New York Herald Tribune*, 10 May 1940.

146 'In view of Shakespeare's ...' John Anderson, *op. cit.*

146 'Send back the wine ...' V.L. to author.

146 'Darlings, how brave ...' Felix Barker, *op. cit.*, p 174.

CHAPTER 12

147 'Larry and I were too greedy ...' Jack Merivale to author.

148 "That terrible house ...' Anthony Quayle to author.

150 'At that time ...' Katharine Hepburn to author, 15 April 1986.

151 'At ten o'clock ...' Ronald Colman to Felix Barker, *op. cit.*, pp 182–3.

151 'For the soul ...' Information from Society of the Sacred Heart, Digby Stuart College, Roehampton Institute (formerly Convent of the Sacred Heart), 18 March 1986.

151 'Because apparently ...' Alan Dent, *op. cit.*, p 36.

152 'This is a love ...' Vincent Korda to author.

153  'Lady Hamilton ...' *Lady Hamilton* screenplay, Walter Reisch & R. C. Sheriff, 1940.
153  'My dear Vivien ...' Baroness Budberg quoted in Alan Dent, *op. cit.*, p 60.
153  'And then what? ...' and 'There is no "then" ...' *Lady Hamilton* screenplay.
153  'What we are doing ...' *Ibid.*
153  'Even if it forces ...' *Ibid.* (Korda addition).
155  'Suddenly changed expression ...' Garson Kanin, *Hollywood*, pp 92–3.
155  'An ominous scraping ...' Laurence Olivier, *op. cit.*, p 93.


## CHAPTER 13

157  'Why are you laughing? ...' V.L. to author.
158  'In the early years ...' Irene Mayer Selznick, *op. cit.*, p 237.
159  'Rather odd ...' V.L. to David Lewin, *Daily Express*, 15 August 1960.
159  'Sole director ...' Valerie Pascal, *The Disciple and His Devil*, p 87.
159  'My red-headed Circe ...' *Ibid.*, p 88.
160  'It is my impression ...' C. A. Lejeune, *Observer*, 3 August 1941.
160  'I am not at all ...' *Ibid.*
161  'Easily the finest ...' Campbell Dixon, *Daily Telegraph*, 1 August 1941.
161  'He's a duck ...' Felix Barker, *op. cit.*, p 194.
161  'This is where ...' Alan Dent, *op. cit.*, p 36.
162  'I could have understudied ...' Richard Attenborough to author, 1 May 1986.
163  'In her twenties ...' Marjorie Deans, *Meeting at the Sphinx*, p 65.
163  'It's a curious ...' *Ibid.*
163  'Too tear-y ...' Valerie Pascal, *op. cit.*, p 103.
163  'Vivien's shyness ...' Valerie Pascal, *op. cit.*, p 104.
163  'You know ...' Felix Barker, *op. cit.*, p 193.
164  'Many of Mrs Campbell's ...' *Ibid.*, p 194.
164  'The compliment ...' V.L. to Alan Dent, *Sunday Times*, 9 July 1961.
164  'Inasmuch as ...' Dan O'Shea to F. L. Hendrickson, 27 September 1943, MGM/UA archives.
165  'Pascal is going ...' *Ibid.*
165  'Oh, no, Vivien ...' John Gielgud to author, 5 November 1986.
165  'I think it was I ...' *Ibid.*
166  'There was a remarkable ...' Felix Barker, *op. cit.*, p 219.
166  'How very inspiring ...' John Gielgud to author.
166  'How peculiar! ...' Felix Barker, *op. cit.*, p 209.
166  'She buttonholed ...' Alec Guinness, *Blessings in Disguise*, p 122.
167  'At a party ...' Information supplied by Felix Barker to author, 23 January 1987.
167  'Well, it was ...' V.L. to Felix Barker, 4 January 1952.
168  'I pity ...' Majorie Deans, *op. cit.*, p 42.
168  'Will you say? Felix Barker, *op. cit.*, p 221.
168  'Rains is not stringy ...' *Ibid.*, p 222.
168  'With Vivien Leigh ...' Valerie Pascal, *op. cit.*, p 104.

168 'There was more ...' C. A. Lejeune, *Observer*, 15 December 1945.

169 'I've had a fine time ...' Alan Dent, *op. cit.*, p 11.

169 'I am a Queen ...' George Bernard Shaw, *Caesar and Cleopatra* screenplay.

169 'There'll be plenty ...' Virginia Fairweather to author, 8 March 1986.

170 'She's not right at all ...' Alan Dent, *op. cit.*, p 39.


CHAPTER 14

173 'Because of her ...' Rudy Behlmer, *op. cit.*, pp 344–5.

173 'We are aware ...' MGM/UA archives.

174 'Whether there is ...' *Daily Mail*, 24 February 1945.

174 'Any appreciable damage ...' *The Times*, 27 February 1945.

175 '*Annus Mirabilis* ...' *Vogue*, January 1945.

176 'Ten days after ...' Felix Barker, *op. cit.*, p 226.

176 'Through it all ...' James Agate, *Sunday Times*, 20 May 1945.

177 'Englishness ...' Melvyn Bragg, *op. cit.*, p 52.

177 'In lovely serenity ...' Laurence Olivier, *op. cit.*, p 15.

178 'My joy ...' Laurence Olivier, *op. cit.*, p 112.

178 'Dangerous for Miss Leigh ...' Affidavit signed Drs Cawardias and Pierce, copy in MGM/UA archives, 15 June 1945.

179 'I have everything ...' and 'Nine months ...' V.L. to David Lewin, *Daily Express*, 18 August 1960.

180 'He was more like ...' Suzanne Farrington (V.L.'s daughter) to author, 23 April 1986.

180 'She was up and about ...' Emlyn Williams to author, 4 August 1986.

181 'Overwhelming ...' *Ibid.*, p 236.

181 'Delirious fans ...' *Ibid.*, p 240.

181 'God had touched ...' Rosemary Geddes to author, 26 August 1986.


CHAPTER 15

183 'Mama had created ...' Suzanne Farrington to author.

184 'If Trivial Pursuit ...' *Ibid.*

184 'Mama had a medieval ...' *Ibid.*

186 'A little bit ...' Anthony Quayle to author.

186 'I do not hope ...' Korda cable, 4 February 1947, MGM/UA archives.

186 'She wanted to show ...' Kieron Moore to author, 3 September 1986.

187 'Vivien felt ...' *Ibid.*

188 'No, it isn't ...' Cecil Beaton, quoted by Hugo Vickers, *Cecil Beaton*, p 309.

188 'Oh, I'm so happy ...' Cecil Beaton, *The Happy Years: Diaries 1944–48*, p 125.

188 'Of course, you're not ...' Godfrey Winn to author. The remark appears, with slight variations, in different accounts of the incident: cf., Felix Barker, *op. cit.*, 'You won't take it, of course', p 260.

188 'She only did so ...' Beaton to Thomas Kiernan, *Olivier*, p 231.

189 'When I set out ...' Kieron Moore to author.

190 'Upped and gallantly ...' Laurence Olivier, *op. cit.*, p 180.

190 'Tonight I should like ...' Felix Barker, *op. cit.*, p 268.

191 'Members of the Co ...' Quoted in Garry O'Connor, *Darlings of the Gods*, p 67.

192 'If you ever come ...' Elaine Dundy, *Finch, Bloody Finch*, p 129.

193 'Walking corpses ...' Garry O'Connor, *op. cit.*, p 146.

193 'Oh, quite innocently ...' Laurence Olivier, *op. cit.*, p 128.

193 'Olivier, it would seem ...' Harold Conway, *Evening Standard*, 21 January 1949.

193 'Humiliating ...' Laurence Olivier, *op. cit.*, p 130.

## CHAPTER 16

195 'Lost ...' Laurence Olivier, *op. cit.*, p 128.

195 'I don't love ...' *Ibid.*, p 131.

195 'Incest ...' *Ibid.*, p 132.

196 'Alas, this was one ...' Laurence Olivier, *On Acting*, p 176.

196 'Impossible ...' Alan Dent, *op. cit.*, p 44.

197 'That's a pretty ...' Gwen Robyns, *Vivien Leigh*, p 132.

197 'She had crinkly hair ...' Stanley Hall to author, 18 June 1986.

197 'I've run for protection ...' Tennessee Williams, *A Streetcar Named Desire*.

198 'It was only a few seconds ...' Alan Dent, *op. cit.*, pp 103–4.

198 'Blanche is a woman ...' V.L. to Alan Dent, *Sunday Telegraph*, 9 July 1961. She had put it only slightly less brutally the year before in saying to David Lewin, 'I think it led to my nervous breakdown later,' *Daily Express*, 15 August 1960.

199 'High ...' Rudy Behlmer (ed.), *Inside Warner Bros.*, p 321.

199 'I did have a "feeling" ...' Elia Kazan to author, 15 April 1986.

199 'I couldn't tell ...' *Ibid.*

199 'In one word ...' Rudy Behlmer, *op. cit.*, p 318.

199 'The best ...' *Ibid.*

199 'The dearest ...' Lucinda Ballard Dietz to author, 16 April 1986.

199 'Like a child ...' *Ibid.*

200 'I see her ...' *Ibid.*

200 'With looks as radiant ...' *Ibid.*

201 'She was an instinctual ...' Elia Kazan to author.

201 'There were lots ...' Suzanne Farrington to author.

201 'It was my first ...' *Ibid.*

201 'I suspected ...' and 'Larry doesn't ...' Lucinda Ballard to author.

202 'Nobody in Hollywood ...' *Ibid.*

202 'Why do you always ...' V.L. to author.

202 'Her ladyship ...' V.L. to author.

202 'Do you read ...' Constance McCormick Collection, Film Department, USC.

202 'Some people say ...' Elia Kazan to author.

203 'Two highly charged ...' *Ibid.*

203 'I don't want ...' Tennessee Williams, screenplay of *Streetcar Named Desire*.

## CHAPTER 17

204 'We were not ...' Laurence Olivier, *Confessions of an Actor*, p 138.

204 'For the first time ...' *Ibid.*, p 138.

205 'An absolute twerp ...' Laurence Olivier, *On Acting*, p 111.

205 'Like Marlene Dietrich ...' Godfrey Winn to author.

205 'Cool Miss Leigh ...' *The Times*, 12 May 1951.

205 'She picks at the part ...' Kenneth Tynan, *Curtains*, p 10.

206 'Written by ...' Kenneth Tynan, *He That Plays the King*, Preface.

206 'As Lady Anne ...' *Ibid.*, p 36.

206 'At last this pale ...' *Ibid.*, p 42.

206 'The play should ...' *Ibid.*, p 143.

207 'I think that women ...' Stanley Hall to author.

207 'I was at a private ...' Lady Lambert to author.

207 'I think there was another ...' Stanley Hall to author.

208 'The busy hippodrome ...' Walter Kerr, New York *Herald Tribune*, 20 December 1951.

208 'Grown in subtlety ...' Richard Watts Jr., *New York Post*, 20 December 1951.

208 'An *enfant terrible* ...' *Time*, 31 December 1951.

208 'Absolutely outstanding ...' John Gielgud to author.

208 'Behind the petulance ...' Walter Kerr, New York *Herald Tribune*, 22 December 1951.

208 'My God, there are ...' Emlyn Williams to author.

209 'Wringing her hands ...' Laurence Olivier, *Confessions of an Actor*, p 141.

209 'Nonsense ... if anyone's ...' *Ibid.*, p 142.

209 'Why not Peter Finch ...' *Ibid.*, p 152.

209 'The only truly bad ...' *Ibid.*, p 152.

## CHAPTER 18

210 'Take care of her ...' Elaine Dundy, *op. cit.*, p 179.

211 'You've got to get ...' *Ibid.*, pp 185–6.

212 'Get out of here ...' Tennessee Williams, *op. cit.*

212 'Viv is very sick ...' Stewart Granger, *Sparks Fly Upward*, p 289.

213 'Get the hell ...' *Ibid.*, p 290.

213 'I know who you ...' *Ibid.*, p 293.

213 'I'm not Scarlett O'Hara ...' *Ibid.*, p 293.

213 'Oh, how could you ...' *Ibid.*, p 293.

213 'In the tone ...' Laurence Olivier, *op. cit.*, p 155.

213 'With the wonderment ...' and 'Who with?' and 'Peter Finch ...' *Ibid.*, p 156.

214 'She said to me ...' Rachel Kempson to author.

214 'I had a mysterious ...' Graham Payn and Sheridan Morley (eds.), *The Noël Coward Diaries*, p 211.

214 'It leaves ...' Rachel Kempson to author.

215 'Miss Leigh is ...' Cecil Wilson, *Daily Mail*, 6 November 1953.

216 'Adored every moment ...' Laurence Olivier, *Confessions of an Actor*, p 162.

216 'It was a rescue vehicle ...' Terence Rattigan to author *circa* 3 October 1963.

217 'I thought that she was ...' Alan Dent, *op. cit.*, p 82.

217 'While we were doing ...' Emlyn Williams to author.

## CHAPTER 19

219 'You can't be more ...' Laurence Olivier, *Confessions of an Actor*, p 229.

219 'Victim status ...' Elaine Dundy, *op. cit.*, p 204.

220 'Part of her ...' John Gielgud, *An Actor and His Time*, p 143.

220 'I hate that phrase ...' John Barber, *Daily Express*, 10 June 1955.

221 'With Vivien ...' Emlyn Williams to author.

221 'Like the Macbeths ...' Anthony Quayle to author.

221 'Sir Laurence shook ...' Kenneth Tynan, *Curtains*, p 99.

221 'It was one ...' John Russell Taylor, *Vivien Leigh*, p 99.

222 'Quite remarkable ...' and 'eminent, successful ...' Graham Payn and Sheridan Morley, *op. cit.*, p 278.

222 'Sir Laurence's Titus ...' Kenneth Tynan, *Curtains*, p 104.

222 'They had separated ...' Anthony Quayle to author.

222 'Larry said to me ...' Source to author. Source requests anonymity.

223 'Vivien and ...' Rosemary Geddes to author.

223 'I could feel ...' Anthony Quayle to author.

223 'Vivien saw ...' Terence Rattigan to author.

224 'Which one of you ...' Elaine Dundy, *op. cit.*, p 207.

224 'Quaking emptiness ...' Laurence Olivier, *op. cit.*, p 167.

225 'Isn't there any ...' V.L. to author.

225 'A capacity hit ...' Graham Payn and Sheridan Morley, *op. cit.*, p 327.

225 'Katherine ...' *Daily Mail*, 13 July 1956.

225 'But far more disconcerting ...' The suggestion that Olivier viewed his own fate in terms of the creative paralysis engendered by Arthur Miller's marriage to Monroe was first advanced by Thomas Kiernan in his biography *Olivier*. He attributed it to remarks made to him in 1979 by Kenneth Tynan. Coincidentally, Tynan made the same suggestion to this author and in 1979, too, at the American première at the Plit Center, Los Angeles, of *A Little Romance*, which was attended by Olivier. (It was the last time the author saw Tynan before his death.) While Olivier's autobiography contains no explicit confirmation of Tynan's view, the circumstantial evidence does tend that way.

226 'Larry came back ...' Peter Hiley to author, 26 August 1986.

226 'For the first time ...' *Ibid*.

227 'We are bitterly ...' *Daily Mail*, 13 August 1956.

227 'Disorganized silliness ...' Graham Payn and Sheridan Morley, *op. cit.*, p 330.

227 'Bea Lillie was ...' Virginia Fairweather to author.

227 'Fucking ...' Laurence Olivier, *op. cit.*, p 181.

## CHAPTER 20

230 'I always thought ...' Peter Hiley to author.
230 'I remember ...' Rachel Kempson to author.
231 'I'd get over ...' *Ibid.*
232 'Actually, she taught ...' Rosemary Geddes to author.
232 'Never altered afterwards ...' *Ibid.*
232 'Clothes for her ...' *Ibid.*
233 'Appearance ...' *Ibid.*
234 'Visiting her vassals ...' Jean-Pierre Aumont, *Sun and Shadow*, p 216.
234 'I know a psychiatrist ...' David Lewin, *Mail on Sunday*, 24 October 1982.
234 'She gave a perfect ...' *Ibid.*
235 'Larry ... Larry ...' Larry Adler to author.
235 'I'm an American ...' *Ibid.*
235 'Which said to me ...' *Ibid.*
235 'As a Parliamentarian ...' *Daily Express*, 24 July 1957.
235 'My first husband ...' *Ibid.*, 18 August 1957.
236 'I suppose ...' V.L. to David Lewin, *Daily Mail*, 5 October 1963.
236 'A panther ...' Jean-Louis Barrault, *Memories of Tomorrow*, p 309.
237 'Oh, you speak ...' Anthony Quayle to author.
238 'She died at 33 ...' Godfrey Winn to author.
238 'We must stay ...' Godfrey Winn, *op. cit.*, p 393.
239 'She sat ... frozen into immobility ...' *Ibid.*, p 394.

## CHAPTER 21

243 'It was like being ...' Laurence Olivier to Curtis Bill Pepper, *New York Times*, 5 March 1979.
244 'Bring plenty ...' Godfrey Winn to author.
244 'Can you really ...' Stewart Granger, *op. cit.*, p 400.
244 'He then said ...' *Ibid.*, p 401.
244 'Only memories ...' V.L. to author.
245 'Why not Jack ...' Jack Merivale to author. For dates of interviews, see previous reference.
247 'My Darling ...' V.L. to Jack Merivale, 15 May (?) 1960.
248 'How could you ...' Radie Harris, *op. cit.*, p 173.
249 'She said to me ...' Lucinda Ballard to author.
250 'Lady Olivier wishes ...' *Daily Mail*, 21 May 1960.
250 'All hell ...' and 'Grey and drawn ...' Virginia Fairweather, *Cry God for Larry*, p 33.
250 'It was the only ...' New York *Daily Mirror*, 29 May 1960.
251 'More than anything ...' *Ibid.*
251 'My Darling ...' V.L. to Jack Merivale, 31 May 1960.
251 'Looking a good sixteen ...' V.L. to Jack Merivale, 11 June 1960.
252 'He told me ...' Rachel Kempson to author.

252 'Larry was an angel ...' Stewart Granger to author, 26 September 1986.

252 'Like any man ...' Virginia Fairweather to author.

252 'What Bobby couldn't ...' *Ibid.*

253 'They have made it ...' V.L. to Jack Merivale, 15 June 1960.

253 'And it is not a play ...' *Ibid.*

253 'Alone ...' Graham Payn and Sheridan Morley, *op. cit.*, p 441.

253 'Men are hell ...' V.L. to John Freeman, *News of the World*, 19 June 1960.

254 'My Darling Love ...' V.L. to Jack Merivale, 25 June 1960.


## CHAPTER 22

255 'Good, but not ...' and 'Is it eight ...' V.L. to David Lewin, *Daily Express*, 15 August 1960.

255 'No. I would want ...' *Ibid.*

256 'Will you be ...' Jack Merivale to author.

256 'Paintings seem ...' David Lewin, *Daily Express*, 15 August 1960.

260 'Vivien is splendid ...' Graham Payn and Sheridan Morley, *op. cit.*, p 452.

261 'He admitted ...' *Daily Herald*, 3 December 1960.

261 'I lived a long time ...' Gavin Lambert, *The Roman Spring of Mrs Stone* screenplay.

262 'Vivien must play it ...' Gavin Lambert, essay on V.L. in *Close-Ups*, p 313.

262 'The only sign ...' *Ibid.*

262 'And why give ...' *Ibid.*

262 'With no more fuss ...' *Ibid.*

262 'She felt she needed ...' Charles Castle to author, 18 June 1986.

262 'Altogether, it was ...' Peter Yates to author, 16 April 1986.

263 'I was amused ...' Stanley Hall to author.

263 'All Warren does ...' Charles Castle to author.

264 'Thank you, dear one ...' V.L. to Jack Merivale, 14 February 1961.

264 'He wouldn't marry ...' Margaret Mitchell, *op. cit.*, p 71.

264 'There's no reason ...' *Ibid.*, p 74.

265 'Can't I make you ...' Margaret Mitchell, *op. cit.*, p 108.

265 'What part did you ...' Radie Harris, *op. cit.*, p 183.

265 'She had a ball gown ...' *Ibid.*, p 183.

265 'Now they were mothers ...' *Ibid.*, p 183.

265 'She had obviously ...' Charles Castle to author.

266 'She had been ...' Charles Castle to author.


## CHAPTER 23

267 'Let's go ...' Jack Merivale to author. For dates of interviews, see previous reference.

271 'In consideration ...' *Daily Mail*, 12 October 1962.

271 'Sir Ernest was kind ...' *Ibid.*

271 'My Darling, before ...' V.L. to Jack Merivale, 8 April 1962.

273 'Wiser, gentler ...' Suzanne Farrington to author.
273 'Her personality ...' Peter Hiley to author.

## CHAPTER 24

275 'So what ...?' Jean-Pierre Aumont to author, 28 March 1986.
275 'Too refined ...' Jean-Pierre Aumont, *op. cit.*, p 215.
275 'Abel [Farbman] arrived ...' V.L. to Jack Merivale, 13 November 1962.
275 'A v.v.v. long ...' *Ibid.* 14 November 1962.
275 'After dinner ...' *Ibid.*, 21 November 1962.
276 'Midnight was ...' Jean-Pierre Aumont, *op. cit.*, p 217.
277 'The way ...' Jean-Pierre Aumont to author.
277 'These rehearsals ...' V.L. to Jack Merivale, 28 December 1962.
277 'Thirty against ...' Jean-Pierre Aumont, *op. cit.*, p 219.
277 'She flew at me ...' Graham Payn and Sheridan Morley, *op. cit.*, p 527.
277 'My voice ...' V.L. to Jack Merivale, 28 January 1963.
277 'Poor people ...' Jean-Pierre Aumont, *op. cit.*, p 223.
277 'I keep hearing ...' V.L. to Jack Merivale, 22 March 1963.
278 'It is nightmarish ...' *Ibid.*
278 'There's no doubt ...' Howard Taubman, *New York Times*, 7 April 1963.
278 'Miss Leigh ...' Kenneth Tynan, *Observer*, 7 April 1963.
278 'She had either to speak ...' Jean-Pierre Aumont, *op. cit.*, p 228.
279 'Answer me ...' *Ibid.*, p 295.
280 'Odd but calm ...' Graham Payn and Sheridan Morley, *op. cit.*, p 547.
282 'From one minute ...' Simone Signoret, *Nostalgia Isn't What It Used To Be*, p 308.
282 'Tennessee Williams once ...' Harold Heffernan, New York *Journal American*, 28 July 1964.
282 'Ah asked foah ...' Abby Mann screenplay for *Ship of Fools*.
282 'Please doan bother ...' *Ibid.*
282 'Nice to see ...' Jack Merivale to author.
283 'Stanley, I can't ...' Stanley Kramer at Friends of the Libraries 'Tribute to V.L.'

## CHAPTER 25

286 'My Dearest Angel ...' V.L. to Jack Merivale, 10 November 1964.
286 'Arrived in Delhi ...' *Ibid.*, 22 November 1964.
286 'November 23 and I ...' *Ibid.*, 23 November 1964.
286 'Lots of rooms ...' *Ibid.*
287 'It translates ...' *Ibid.*
287 'One day we flew ...' *Ibid.*, 28 November 1964.
287 'She was in ...' Emlyn Williams in letter to author, 19 August 1986.
288 'The children ...' Rachel Kempson to author.
288 'Life was simpler ...' Suzanne Farrington to author.
288 'Though her attacks ...' Peter Hiley to author.

288 'Vivien was like ...' Rachel Kempson to author.

288 'I remember ...' *Ibid.*

289 'I'll be working ...' Peter Finch to author, *circa* 1972.

289 'They hate ...' V.L. in interview given to Newcastle (or Liverpool) newspaper, quoted in Gwen Robyns, *op. cit.*

289 'The character was ...' Stanley Hall to author.

290 'How few roles ...' Radie Harris, *op. cit.*, p 188.

290 'Would rather have ...' *Ibid.*, p 189.

290 'Listen! You are dying ...' Anton Chekhov, *Ivanov*, tr. Adriane Nicolaeff.

291 'Nothing short ...' Richard Watts Jr., *New York Post*, 4 May 1966.

291 'What is written ...' Stanley Kaufmann, *New York Times*, 4 May 1966.

291 'One of the troubles ...' John Gielgud to author.

292 'With a haggard ...' Radie Harris, *op. cit.*, p 189.

292 'It will be ...' Lucinda Ballard to author.

293 'Shorter than ...' *Ibid.*

293 'Somewhat prone ...' Stanley Hall to author.

293 'I was worried ...' Emlyn Williams to author.

293 'Vivien was sitting ...' Graham Payn and Sheridan Morley, *op. cit.*, p 651.

295 'I stood ...' Laurence Olivier, *op. cit.*, p 228.

## EPILOGUE

296 'She was having ...' Jack Merivale to author.

297 'You have at least ...' Rex Harrison, letter to Jack Merivale.

297 'Suffused with tears ...' Graham Payn and Sheridan Morley, *op. cit.*, p 652.

297 'I had received ...' Mary Hayley Bell (Mrs John Mills), letter to Jack Merivale.

297 'Dear Jack ...' Katharine Hepburn and George Cukor, letter to Jack Merivale.

297 'I was lucky ...' Lucinda Ballard, letter to Jack Merivale.

297 'I think the most ...' Lady Diana Cooper, letter to Jack Merivale.

298 'In Britain ...' V.L. to Robert Ottaway, *Queen*, 10 March 1965.

298 'She had the misfortune ...' J. C. Trewin, *Observer*, 9 July 1967.

298 'Invincible attractiveness ...' Harold Hobson, *Sunday Times*, 9 July 1967.

298 'One of those actresses ...' *The Times*, 10 July 1967.

299 'No, and I sometimes ...' Dodie Smith, *op. cit.*, p 242.

300 'Look upward ...' This text is taken from that printed by the Friends of the Libraries in their memorial tribute to Vivien; it does not quite correspond to the 'conflation of lines' made by Emlyn Williams and read by him at V.L.'s Thanksgiving Service. In a letter to the author (8 December 1986), who remarked on the discrepancy, Emlyn Williams comments: 'When Jack [Merivale] suggested the poem, I loved it but felt it could only be really apposite if adapted – so I adapted it. I felt Dr Donne would have approved had he known Vivien. Jack certainly made no adverse comment, nor anybody else. What's un-Donne is Un-Donne ... Sorry.'

301 'A great beauty ...' John Gielgud, V.L.'s Service of Thanksgiving, 15 August 1967.
301 'My mother's perfume ...' Peter Hiley to author.
302 'Her very great bravery ...' Charles Champlin, Friends of the Libraries 'Tribute to V.L.', 17 March 1968.
302 '[Vivien] had ...' Gavin Lambert, *Ibid.*
304 'Miss me ...' Referred to by Elaine Dundy in *New York Times* review of Anne Edwards's biography of V.L., 1977.

# Index

Hopkins, Miriam, 117, 130
Horne, David, 50
Howard, Leslie, 39, 49, 70, 116, 119, 137
Huston, John, 275
Hyde-White, Wilfred, 301
Hyson, Dorothy, 83, 184

*Ideal Husband, An* (film), 187, 188
Ionesco, Eugene, 250
Isleworth Film Studios, 52–3
*Ivanov* (Chekhov), 290–1

*Jezebel* (film), 105
*Joan the Maid* (Anderson), 163
John, Augustus, 231
Johns, Glynis, 158
Johnson, Celia, 216
Jones, Dr Ernest, 81, 82, 83
Jorgensen, Robert, 87
Jourdan, Louis, 223

Kanin, Garson, 9, 150, 154–5, 167
Kaufman, George, 65
Kaufmann, Stanley, 291
Kaye, Danny, 199, 212, 213, 227
Kazan, Elia, 194, 197, 199, 201, 202, 203
Kempson, Rachel, 9, 184, 214, 230–1, 251–2, 288, 300
Kerr, Deborah, 163, 174, 186
Kerr, Walter, 208
*Kinematograph Weekly*, 49
*King Lear*, 184
*King Rat* (film), 285
Kipling, Rudyard, 26
Korda, Alexander, 77, 92, 93, 101, 103, 178, 209, 216; early casual attitude to Vivien, 52–3; five-year contract, 59–61, 70, 72; failure to employ Vivien, 69–70, 72, 76; rumoured affair with her, 75–6; first employment of her, 77, 78, 82; and *Fire Over England*, 77, 86; ambitions for Vivien, 87–8; and *Twenty-One Days*, 87, 88, 89; new contract with Vivien and Selznick, 117–18, 124, 125–6, 131, 174; and *Lady Hamilton*, 149–50, 151–2, 153, 160; disposal of remainder of contract, 174, 186; at Notley, 184; and *Anna Karenina*, 186, 188; death, 224

Korda, Vincent, 76, 151
Kramer, Stanley, 281, 282, 283, 301
Kronborg Castle, 87, 88
Kubrick, Stanley, 237

*Lady Hamilton* (film), 15, 149, 151–3, 160, 267, 292
Lambert, Gavin, 94, 259, 302
Lambert, Patricia Quinn, Lady, 31, 32, 37, 38, 41, 43, 55, 207
Lanchester, Elsa, 103, 104
Lane, Margaret, 58
Laughton, Charles, 70, 75, 87, 103–4
Laurence Olivier Productions Ltd, 11, 176, 191, 192, 198, 210
Lawrence, Gertrude, 69, 208
Lee-on-Solent, 158
Leigh, Vivien: as Notley hostess, 6–17, 183, 185, 200, 209, 222–3; birth and early years in India, 21–7; love of gardens, 23, 29, 180, 273; first stage appearance, 25; wilfulness, 25, 173, 179; appearance, 25–6, 28, 42, 66; religious education, 26, 28–35; at school in England, 27, 28–35, 43; determination to become great actress, 32, 33, 38, 48, 71, 102, 119, 133, 194; confirmation, 33; impulsiveness, 33, 34, 37, 65, 66, 247; Grand Tour of Europe, 35–7; enrolled at RADA, 38; meets Leigh Holman, 38–40, 48; at RADA, 40, 42, 44, 57; marriage, 41, 67; presented at Court, 42; birth of Suzanne, 43; lack of interest in bringing up child, 43; early films, 44–8, 49–50, 51, 52–3; obtains agent, 46–8; adoption of stage name, 47; stage début, 50, 52; dwindling interest in husband and child, 52, 54, 59, 64, 99; change of 'Vivian' to 'Vivien', 54; ruthlessness, 55, 66, 67, 91; overnight sensation in *Mask of Virtue*, 55–61; long-term contract with Korda, 59–62, 70, 72; personal appearances and modelling, 63–4; first extra-marital affairs, 64–5, 73, 75; first view of Olivier, 65–6; increasing interest in him, 69, 71, 72–3; lost film opportunities, 69–70, 75; resumes stage career, 71, 72–4, 76, 83; affair with Olivier, 72–3, 74, 76–83, 86, 88, 91, 99, 100; resumes filming, 75, 77,